VIRGINIA WOOLF OUT OF BOUNDS

Selected Papers from the Tenth
Annual Conference on Virginia Woolf

VIRGINIA WOOLF OUT OF BOUNDS

Selected Papers from the Tenth
Annual Conference on Virginia Woolf

University of Maryland Baltimore County
June 7 - 10, 2000

Edited by Jessica Berman and Jane Goldman

New York
Pace University Press
2001

Copyright © 2001 by
Pace University Press
One Pace Plaza
New York NY 10038

All rights reserved
Printed in the United States of America

Library of Congress Cataloging-in-Publication Data Available

ISBN 0-944473-55-5 (pbk. : alk. Paper)

Contents

Archives and Readers

Woolf and Other Writers

Orientalism/Colonialism

32 /40

Abbreviations

AHH	*A Haunted House*
AROO	*A Room of One's Own*
BP	*Books and Portraits*
BTA	*Between the Acts*
CDB	*The Captain's Death Bed and Other Essays*
CE	*Collected Essays* (4 vols.)
CR1	*The Common Reader*
CR2	*The Common Reader, Second Series*
CSF	*The Complete Shorter Fiction*
D	*The Diary of Virginia Woolf* (5 vols.)
DM	*The Death of the Moth and Other Essays*
E	*The Essays of Virginia Woolf* (6 vols.)
F	*Flush*
FR	*Freshwater*
GR	*Granite & Rainbow: Essays*
JR	*Jacob's Room*
L	*The Letters of Virginia Woolf* (6 vols.)
M	*The Moment and Other Essays*
MEL	*Melymbrosia*
MOB	*Moments of Being*
MT	*Monday or Tuesday*
MD	*Mrs. Dalloway*
ND	*Night and Day*
O	*Orlando*
P	*The Pargiters*
PA	*A Passionate Apprentice*
RF	*Roger Fry: A Biography*
TG	*Three Guineas*
TTL	*To the Lighthouse*
TW	*The Waves*
TY	*The Years*
VO	*The Voyage Out*

Introduction

Jessica Berman and Jane Goldman
Virginia Woolf Out of Bounds

Both refused and refusing, Virginia Woolf, in so many ways, has always been out of bounds. She champions the cause of women denied access to the intellectual bastions of patriarchy, insisting on trespassing, but she also celebrates as liberating and exhilarating the collective potential of women's outsider status. The impetus of invasion across lines of privilege that is at work in her writing, places her, unsettlingly, on the threshold of numerous intersecting worlds and disciplines. **The Tenth Annual Conference on Virginia Woolf: Virginia Woolf Out of Bounds** invited scholars, students and independent readers to think about Virginia Woolf as she pushes us to cross regional, temporal, and disciplinary boundaries of all kinds. As the inaugural conference of the millennium **Virginia Woolf Out of Bounds** sought to address the future of Woolf study, especially as an opportunity for new intellectual exchanges and mixtures and for the expansion of Woolf Studies towards new writing, new media, and new academic concerns. In the first plenary session Susan Stanford Friedman and Sonita Sarker brought Woolf into contact with post-colonial studies. Featured Panels ranged from "Woolf's Later Inscriptions of Sexualities," to "the Archive, the Library and the Reader," "Woolf and the Material World," and "Woolf and the City." A major highlight of the conference was a plenary panel with Michèle Barrett and Susan Gubar simply titled, "A Room of One's Own: Cultural Digressions." Conference sessions brought Woolf into contact with such contemporary writers as Martin Amis, Michael Cunningham, Alice Munro, Chitra Banerjee Divakaruni and A.S. Byatt. Other sessions took Woolf into the domains of sound and silence, politics and performance, intimacy and sexuality. A major feature of the conference was a series of sessions focusing on Woolf in the classroom on both the secondary and collegiate level. Much as at the Ninth Annual Conference *Orlando* seemed to set the mood, at the Tenth Annual Conference *The Waves* emerged as the key text, the subject of interpretation on the stage and in art, and the inspiration for several presentations and the annual conference banquet.

Punctuating the conference schedule were several featured art events, including "Painting *The Waves*" by Isota Tucker Epes and Suzanne Bellamy, a major new series of prints on "Conversations With Woolf and Stein" by

1

Suzanne Bellamy, "A Room of Her Own Music Inspired By The Writings of Virginia Woolf" by Joyce Zymeck, and a wonderful stage perfomance of *The Waves* as adapted by Marjorie Lightfoot. Susan Gubar turned her digression on *A Room of One's Own* into a bravura performance which had Woolf's narrator transported to the grounds of a down-at-heels contemporary public university. Those able to remain until the last session were treated to Michael Cunningham, author of *The Hours*, comparing Woolf to Jimi Hendrix (both riff in the same manner), and describing how 'Woolf saved [his] life." The conference truly did venture out of bounds.

Still the selected papers from a conference must differ from the conference itself, where so much vitality appears in the moments between and among papers and panels. We can not present here the very successful workshop on publishing or the discussion of the anonymous readings of quotations from Woolf that were posted on bulletin boards at the conference hub. It is impossible to represent the surprise many felt at seeing so many Woolfian themes emerge during the screening of Satyajit Ray's film "Charulata," or at watching actors perform a fully-emoted *Waves* during the performance directed by Alan Kreizenbeck and performed by a very impressive group of undergraduate students. Finally, we can not transcribe here the sound of Joyce Zymeck's musical responses to Woolf, the text of Michael Cunningham's extemporaneous talk (never written down, he tells us), or, for some, the funniest moment of the conference, the sight of Isota Tucker Epes imitating Gertrude Stein walking into a Bryn Mawr auditorium around 1934 wearing her enormous flapping shoes. These moments must be left to those present who will surely remember them for a long time to come.

While we cannot present these performances within the confines of a book, these selected papers nonetheless push Virginia Woolf out of bounds. From the fairy tale of *Mrs. Dalloway* (as presented by Ann Martin) to the shop windows of *Night and Day* (as presented by Elizabeth Outka), from Woolf and the nature of matter (as presented by Michael Whitworth) to Woolf and the science of sex (as presented by Lisa Carstens), from Woolf and her nineteenth-century predecessors (as presented by Emily Blair, Caroline Webb, David Vallins, and Donald Blume) to Woolf and contemporary writers (as presented by Nancy Knowles, Karin Westman, Debrah Raschke, Kathryn Laing, and Jane Lilienfeld)—all of the papers in this volume push and strain at generic and disciplinary boundaries of all kinds, and invite us to make juxtapositions and comparisons, both salient and audacious.

We are privileged to have been able to publish papers from across several of the featured and plenary panels and from a wide range of the sessions from the conference. In our selection, we have followed, where possible, the recommendations of conference attendants and participants for the inclusion of particular papers; and we have tried to give a fair sampling of the depth and range of presented topics while also maintaining focus on the conference topic: "Virginia Woolf Out of Bounds." We have gathered these papers into new groupings, mingling, for example, papers on pedagogy with other efforts to re-read *A Room of One's Own*. We have sought to include a number of papers on Woolf and other writers, a significant section of the conference, and to represent with a sampling the confluence of work on Woolf through other arts, both in the section by that name and in the papers here printed on Woolf and photography.

Woolf's transgressive energies in the related fields of gender, sexuality, and feminism, not surprisingly, inform the opening section of our selection, constituting as they do the enduring mainspring of Woolf scholarship. *Orlando* continues to inspire sophisticated meditation on theories of the body and performativity (as with so many of our contributors, Lisa Carstens and Jane de Gay are to be congratulated for their refreshing engagement with unfamiliar theoretical terrain in Woolf studies). Patricia Moran's pyrotechnic exploration of the "aesthetics of sexual trauma" in Woolf's later work builds on more recent departures concerning trauma; and Diana Swanson makes us think again about gender and authority in relation to the narrative voice of *Jacob's Room*.

Woolf scholars' ongoing and energetic retrieval of the past in terms of cultural contextualizing and engagement with historical and material documentation is evident in the different forms of archival work presented by Edward Bishop (exploring the status and significance of draft transcription and the critical politics of the "avante-texte") and Melba Cuddy-Keane (mining the B.B.C. archives to contextualize Woolf's writing "within a circulating economy of public debate about high, middle, and low brows"). Such projects not only enrich Woolf studies but also feed into broader critical moves to historicize modernism under the theoretical auspices of new historicism and cultural materialism, and as such are as much concerned with the intertextual, in their differing ways, as they are with the historical. The conference interest in intertextuality is amply represented in the section on "Woolf and Other Writers"—where Nancy Knowles, Karin Westman, Debrah Raschke, Kathryn Laing and Jane Lilienfeld connect Woolf to a variety of texts from throughout the twentieth century—but this intertextuality is notable in other sections too.

The section on Woolf and orientalism/colonialism reflects the increasing body of scholarship to emerge in this field. Chene Heady greatly enriches our understanding of anti-colonial politics in *The Voyage Out*. Woolf's notorious "blackface" performance in the Dreadnought Hoax continues as *locus classicus* and a point of departure for Steven Putzel's controversial look at Woolf and British Orientalism and for Genevieve Abravanel's informative reading of *The Waves*. But her less well documented (and therefore critically underestimated) performance as a "Gauguin girl" may well rival it, and complicate our understanding of Woolf's transgression of race, gender, and aesthetic boundaries, if more information is yielded by archivists.

A Room of One's Own dominates the middle sections of our selection. Michèle Barrett's and Brenda Silver's plenary panel papers offer very different approaches to Woolf's manifesto. Each heads a new section in our selection. Barrett pushes the bounds of feminist theory in reassessing reason and truth in *A Room of One's Own*, whereas Silver takes Woolf's web into a new dimension in her reading of *A Room of One's Own* as hypertext. A series of papers on teaching from Lois Gilmore, Karen Levenback, Katie Marts, and Nancy Shay show that *A Room of One's Own* prompts innovation and boundary crossing not only in scholarly research but also in the classroom and demonstrates the continuing productive importance of that text.

On the other hand, Laura Doyle brings *A Room of One's Own* into important new contact with phenomenology, reading her concern with the body and with politics in light of the work of Maurice Merleau-Ponty. Among the philosophical approaches to Woolf's work, Justine Dymond uses the writings of Merleau-Ponty and Emmanuel Levinas to test the limits of corporeality in *To the Lighthouse*. Levinas also informs Todd Avery's discussion of Woolf's radio broadcasts. Michael Whitworth inspires us to look in other directions, as he reads Woolf within the discourse of contemporary thoeretical physics.

Moving to "Cultural and Material Woolf," we are invited to think of Woolf, not only as broadcaster, but as photographer too in Maggie Humm's paper, and to consider her more carefully as photographic subject in Nicola Luckhurst's fascinating discussion of Gisèle Freund's colour work. Woolf's engagement with the colonial postcard is revealed in Mark Wollaeger's illuminating reading of *The Voyage Out*. Her concern with and anxiety about fashion is taken materially in Jennifer Wicke's analysis of *Moments of Being,* while Elizabeth Outka points us to the importance of linking Woolf's early work to the realms of consumer culture.

"Intertexts and Contexts" explores a variety of further textual, cultural and geographical allusions in Woolf's work, opening with Vanessa Manhire's exploration of Woolf's intertexts with English folk music, and continuing through Caroline Webb, David Vallins, and Donald Blume's rereading of Woolf in the light of her nineteenth-century allusions. We close the volume with Marilyn Schwinn Smith's look at Woolf's Russia and Diane Gillespie's incisive reading of Spanish references in *The Waves*, demonstrating how Woolf moves out of bounds not just in an abstract sense but also in terms of literal questions of geography.

Questions of geography also haunt the editing of this volume as we write this from both sides of the Atlantic, relying on the internet (and a few expensive phone calls) to bring us together. Jessica's experience as conference organizer brought to our dialogue a commanding and detailed overview of the conference themes, participants and papers, and irreplaceable insight into the vitality and intimacy (however sizeable the attendance) of its proceedings. While Jane's last minute absence from the Conference itself was disappointing, her fresh eye on the papers proved invaluable and enlightening. Our collaboration has been not the less exciting for having been largely electronic. The conference was fortunate to have been able to present papers by Woolf scholars from around the world, and we have tried to retain an international mix of contributors in this volume. We are privileged to have been able to present an inclusive range of papers by scholars both beginning and justly-celebrated, which reflects the welcoming community of readers who meet at Woolf conferences. As the conference grows in size and sometimes in formality, we hope this community will remain open and flexible, a place where all questions are welcome and scholars greet each other on a first name basis. We look forward to 2001 when the Eleventh Annual Conference will take place in Britain for the first time, at the University of Wales, Bangor, and this welcoming and increasingly international spirit of collaboration "out of bounds" will surely continue.

The Tenth Annual Conference on Virginia Woolf: Virginia Woolf Out of Bounds would not have been possible without the help and generous financial assistance of many. For their financial contributions to the conference we would like to thank: the Department of English and the Program in Women's Studies at the University of Maryland, Baltimore County (UMBC); the Center for the Humanities, UMBC; the Office of the Dean of Arts and Sciences, UMBC; the Office of Institutional Advancement, UMBC; and the Office of the Provost, UMBC. Several public sessions at the conference were made possible (in part) with funds from the Maryland Humanities Council, through a grant from the National Endowment for the Humanities, whom we thank.

Special thanks also go to the Woolf 2000 conference committee: Judith Allen, Mark Hussey, Karen Levenback, Vara Neverow, and Pierre-Eric Villeneuve and to the Woolf Conference Steering Committee, which is composed of previous organizers. Finally, we wish to acknowledge the long hours and hard work of Josh Glover, Sandy Jones, Tammi Palmer, and especially Christiana Quezado, whithout which this conference would have been impossible.

Gender, Sexuality and Feminism

Patricia Moran
Gunpowder Plots: Sexuality and Censorship in
Woolf's Later Works

When Woolf first conceived of a sequel to *A Room of One's Own* in 1931, she imagined this new work would address "the sexual life of women" (*D3* 6), a subject that struck her as possessing incendiary potential: "I'm quivering and itching to write my—whats it to be called?—'Men are like that?'—no thats too patently feminist: the sequel then, for which I have collected enough powder to blow up St Pauls" (*D4* 77). Yet the various texts that arguably emerged from Woolf's engagement with "the sexual life of women"—"Professions for Women," *The Pargiters* (abandoned and published posthumously), *The Years*, *Three Guineas*—play down or subordinate women's relationship to their corporeality. Instead, in these texts Woolf shifts her focus to the ways in which the middle-class woman's acculturation teaches her to censor her physicality, a censorship that typically results in female silence. These texts are also marked by increasingly negative assessments of maternal and female heterosexuality; and while Woolf at times condemns the cult of chastity in *The Years* and *Three Guineas*, she herself moves toward a valorization of the asexual woman (or the aged woman whom Woolf imagines to have outlived her sexuality) in her essays and fiction. (I'm thinking here of Eleanor in *The Years* and Lucy in *Between the Acts*). The revolutionary plots which were to blow up Saint Pauls did not materialize.

My paper begins, then, with a set of questions: what happened to the revolutionary fervor with which Woolf opened her last decade of writing? Why did Woolf never inscribe the "sexual life of women"? Or, perhaps more accurately, why did her inscriptions take such an attenuated and fragmentary bent? In tracing Woolf's revisions from *The Pargiters* to *The Years*, critics such as Mitchell A. Leaska and Grace Radin have suggested that Woolf's aesthetic principles were forefront in the removal and dilution of didactic or polemical passages on female sexuality. While such deletions would be consistent with Woolf's lifetime conviction that anger and didacticism damaged works of art and betrayed the personal grievances of the author, another set of aesthetic principles might also have governed the surviving traces of Woolf's original plan to examine "the sexual life of women," something we

6

might call the aesthetics of sexual trauma. *The Years* and *Between the Acts* both feature a specific traumatic event which then recurs throughout the text in question (e.g. Rose's traumatic encounter with the exhibitionist; Isa's reading about the gang rape). These scenes of trauma differ from those in earlier novels: while not as traumatic and far-reaching as the war in *Mrs. Dalloway*, for example, these sexual traumas are traumatic enough to damage the characters to whom they occur.[1]

It was, in fact, at the end of this decade that Woolf recovered the memory of her own sexual abuse at the hands of her half-brother, a process of recognition and recovery that arguably emerged from her engagement with "the sexual life of women."[2] In her two extensive discussions of this experience, Woolf connected the trauma associated with sexual abuse to female speech and reticence in ways consistent with the literature of trauma.[3] In one of these accounts, a letter to Ethel Smyth, Woolf writes

> I'm interested that you can't write about masturbation. That I understand. What puzzles me is how this reticence co-habits with your ability to talk openly magnificently, freely about—say H.B. I couldn't do one or the other. But as so much of life is sexual—or so they say—it rather limits autobiography if this is blacked out. It must be, I suspect, for many generations, for women, for its like breaking the hymen—if thats the membrane's name—a painful operation, and I suppose connected with all sorts of subterranean instincts. I still shiver with shame at the memory of my half-brother, standing me on a ledge, aged about 6, and so exploring my private parts. Why should I have felt shame then?
> (*L6* 459-60)

To speak about female sexual experience is to rupture the hymen, to lose one's chastity, as I've discussed elsewhere (Moran). Today I want to draw attention to Woolf's inability to account for the shame she (re)experiences in recalling this memory. She cannot explain her sense of shame; she simply reexperiences it: "I still shiver with shame." Images of censorship and repression thus converge at the site of naming female sexual experience: "as so much of life is sexual—*or so they say*—it rather limits autobiography if this is blacked out" (emphasis added). Even as Woolf comments on a constraint based upon repression/censorship, then, she replays it: an unnamed "they" say life is sexual, whereas Woolf apparently speaks as an asexual woman whose experience has been blacked out.

Woolf was, of course, in the process of writing the autobiographical "A Sketch of the Past," wherein she first describes the scene of abuse (April 1939):

> There was a slab outside the dining room door for standing dishes upon. Once when I was very small Gerald Duckworth lifted me onto this, and as I sat there he began to explore my body. I can remember the feel of his hand going under my clothes; going firmly and steadily lower and

7

> lower. I remember how I hoped that he would stop; how I stiffened and
> wriggled as his hand approached my private parts. But it did not stop.
> His hand explored my private parts too. I remember resenting, disliking
> it—what is the word for so dumb and mixed and feeling? It must have
> been strong, since I still recall it. This seems to show that a feeling about
> certain parts of the body; how they must not be touched; how it is wrong
> to allow them to be touched; must be instinctive. (69)

Woolf tries to account for an emotion that evades description, a single
"word" that somehow could contain so "dumb and mixed a feeling." Her
explanation for this evasive feeling, moreover, turns the blame upon herself:
it was wrong of her to allow herself to be touched, as if she had choice and
control of the matter.

I do not intend to dwell upon the biographical aspects of trauma in
Woolf's life, which have been much discussed (e.g. DeSalvo, McNaron).
Instead, I wish to draw attention to how Woolf's descriptions correspond to
theoretical models of traumatic memory. Traumatic memory differs from
what theorists label "narrative memory": the latter "consists of mental constructs, which people use to make sense out of experience" (160); ordinary
events can typically be integrated into subjective assessment almost auto-
matically, without conscious awareness. Traumatic events, however, cannot:

> frightening or novel experiences may not easily fit into existing cogni-
> tive schemes and either may be remembered with particular vividness or
> may totally resist integration. Under extreme conditions, existing mean-
> ing schemes may be entirely unable to accommodate frightening
> experiences, which causes the memories of these experiences to be
> stored differently and not be available under ordinary conditions: it
> becomes dissociated from conscious awareness and voluntary control.
> (van der Kolk and van der Hart 160)

Traumatic events exist in a kind of time lag: they are not experienced fully
by the victim at the time of the trauma, yet they recur with startling intensity, with a compulsive force over which the victim is powerless. These
memories remain unnarratable: they "lack verbal narrative and context" and
instead "are encoded in the form of vivid sensations and images" (Herman
31). Traumatic events *possess* their victims, moreover, forcing them to relive
their terrorizing moments of self dispossession. Roberta Culbertson has
written that, instead of normal memory, victims experience a series of "body
memories" that accompany the threefold aspects of trauma (numbness at the
time of victimization; the absorbed message of the perpetrator; the reductionism of survival):

> These memories of the body's responses to events are primary, prior to
> any narrative, and they may well surpass the victim's narrative ability
> because they pass beyond his knowledge. Memories of these split bits of
> experience are for this reason intrusive and incomprehensible when they

reappear: there is nothing to be done with them. They obey none of the standard rules of discourse: they are the self's discourse with itself and so occupy that channel between the conscious and the unconscious that speaks a body language. They appear at first when the chatter dies down, then more and more forcefully, as if they will come out, will be eliminated by the body. But they are fragments, not something told. (178)

Indeed, according to Toni McNaron, modernist literary forms function as objective correlatives for traumatic states of mind.

Theorists of trauma stress the necessity for the victim's creating a narrative of the traumatic event, taking "fragmented components of frozen imagery and sensation" and reassembling them into "an organized, detailed, verbal account, oriented in time and historical content" (Herman 177). Analysts stress the need for the victim to recover the *emotional* affect: "the patient must reconstruct not only what happened but also what she felt," Herman writes. "The description of emotional states must be as painstakingly detailed as the description of facts" (177). But the therapeutic narrative of trauma is not what Woolf creates in *The Years* and *Between the Acts*. Here Woolf focuses on "iconic" scenes of sexual trauma, particularized sets of images and bodily representations that crystallize the experience (Herman 38): these scenes intrude upon and rupture the narrative in a way that mimics traumatic experience and that refuses integration. Hence the reader bears witness in only the most limited way: in reading the traumatic event we are forced to experience the traumatic event *as it functions for the character*. The narrative dispossesses us in a sense, abandons us, refuses narrative coherence. (Note: Isa reads about the gang rape in the newspaper; we read the traumatic account with her).

In these last two novels, significantly, Woolf relegates traumatic experience to a modality of memory that contrasts with the models of memory she offers as "normative." The model of memory in *The Years* is two-fold: the first model posits an "I" as a knot at the center of experience, a model Eleanor enacts in "drawing on the blotting-paper, digging little holes from which spokes radiated. Out and out they went; thing followed thing; scene obliterated scene" (*TY* 367). Here the model of memory is additive, broadening out from and glossing a primary sensory self or ego. The second model does not foreground the "knot" but rather examines the interplay between the multiple strata of past memories and the present moment, a model that Woolf typically employs to depict intersubjective relationships. When North meets Sara and Maggie after many years, for example, he finds that "At first he scarcely remembered them. The surface sight was strange on top of his memory of them, as he had seen them years ago" (*TY* 346); later in the same episode, he wonders whether there was "always [. . .] something that came to the surface, inappropriately, unexpectedly, from the depths of people, and made ordinary actions, ordinary words, expressive of the whole being[?]" (*TY* 349). The past lies beneath and glosses the present

9

moment; significantly, the "something" that comes to the surface suggests that "knot" or "center" in the web of Eleanor's drawing, a coherent register of personality.

Rose's traumatic memories, by contrast, exist in the isolated medium of traumatic, "iconic" images that remain solely her own, recalling Culbertson's description of traumatic memory as the "self's discourse with itself" (178). After Rose first sees the man, a sight that Woolf presents imagistically and in the more immediate format of free indirect discourse—"he sucked his lips in and out. He made a mewing noise. But he did not stretch his hands out at her; they were unbuttoning his clothes" (*TY* 29)—Rose experiences a traumatic nightmare, and then finds herself incapable of narrating the experience: "'I saw . . .' Rose began. She made a great effort to tell her the truth; to tell her about the man at the pillar-box. 'I saw . . .' she repeated. But here the door opened and Nurse came in" (*TY* 42). Later in the novel Rose again tries to narrate the trauma and again fails. A chance action recalls her past: suddenly

> she saw Eleanor sitting with her account books; and she saw herself go up to her and say, "Eleanor, I want to go to Lamley's."
>
> Her past seemed to be *rising above* her present. And for some reason she wanted to talk about her past; to tell them something about herself that she had never told anybody, something hidden. She paused, gazing at the flowers in the middle of the table without seeing them. There was a blue knot in the yellow glaze she noticed. (*TY* 167, emphasis added)

In contrast to North's encounter with Sara and Maggie, when he feels the present floating on top of the past, Rose's past "rises above" the present, dominates it, dominates the knot in the center, returning Rose to the perceptual, traumatic experience of her childhood. The knot Rose sees outside herself suggests the splitting and dissociation typical of traumatic memory. No wonder, then, when Martin comments "What awful lives children live!" turning to his sister for affirmation—"Don't they, Rose?"—she answers, "Yes . . . And they can't tell anybody" (*TY* 159).

Rose never does succeed in narrating her traumatic encounter. Significantly, Woolf does point to the therapeutic model of narrative sharing; Eleanor later ponders that "we all talk so much of ill-health . . .because sharing things lessens things [. . .] Give pain, give pleasure an outer body, and by increasing the surface diminish them" (*TY* 352). The surface in *The Years* tends to mean the present, the here and now, narrative life, ordinary time: Rose does not succeed in giving pain an outer surface body and hence deep in the strata of her memory she retains the vivid images of her traumatic experience. By extension, her experience remains unintegrated in the book: because she never "works through" the experience, it remains fixated within the book's multiple strata of the past.

I will close with a few remarks about Isa in *Between the Acts*. As in *The Years*, Woolf embeds a traumatic event early in the novel: Isa reads about a young woman's gang rape by soldiers. This event was based on an actual gang rape of a young girl who subsequently became pregnant; her doctor's trial and acquittal for performing the abortion "began the process of abortion law reform in England" (Wilt 30).[4] Isa is an "abortive" poet, afraid of her husband, and as an Irishwoman the colonized in relation to her husband Giles. By having Isa read about the kind of sexual trauma that routinely draws attention in newspapers, Woolf succeeds, I think, in inscribing the "sexual life of women": not the kind of factual material she initially envisioned, but the more elusive and more fragmentary corporeal shock of sexual trauma, the kinds of experiences that evade language. Instead of trying to explain women's sexual lives, Woolf represents the traumatic events that dispossess women and that curtail female sexual expression. She thereby succeeds in finding words that can describe "so dumb and mixed a feeling."

Notes

[1] Marlene Briggs, Karen DeMeester, Toni McNaron, and Laura Smith have also discussed Woolf's work in relation to trauma theory; Briggs, DeMeester, and Smith focus on war trauma in *Mrs. Dalloway*. McNaron studies more generally the effect of Woolf's traumatic experiences upon her narrative aesthetic.

[2] I refer not to Woolf's experiences with George, which she never repressed, but to the experiences with Gerald, which she does not discuss until 1939.

[3] That language is inadequate in conveying the nature of traumatic experience is a hallmark of trauma literature. For a particularly moving account by a Holocaust survivor, see Elie Wiesel. Many theorists of trauma discuss this aspect at length (e.g. Felman and Laub, Herman, Tal, van der Kolk and van der Hart).

[4] As Wilt points out, the actual newspaper account would have appeared in 1938, not in 1939, Woolf's setting of *Between the Acts*. It is an interesting coincidence that Woolf set Isa's reading of the rape in the year of her own recovery of the memory of Gerald's sexual abuse.

Works Cited

Barrett, Eileen, and Patricia Cramer, eds. *Re: Reading, Re: Writing, Re: Teaching Virginia Woolf: Selected Papers from the Fourth Annual Conference on Virginia Woolf.* NY: Pace U P, 1995.

Briggs, Marlene. "Veterans and Civilians: Traumatic Knowledge and Cultural Appropriation in *Mrs. Dalloway*." McVicker and Davis 43-50.

Caruth, Cathy, ed. *Trauma: Explorations in Memory.* Baltimore and London: The Johns Hopkins UP, 1995.

Culbertson, Roberta. "Embodied Memory, Transcendence, and Telling: Recounting Trauma, Re-establishing the Self." *New Literary History* 26 (1995): 169-195.

DeMeester, Karen. "Trauma and Recovery in Virginia Woolf's *Mrs. Dalloway*." *Modern Fiction Studies* 44, 3 (Fall 1998): 649-673.

DeSalvo, Louise. *Virginia Woolf: The Impact of Childhood Sexual Abuse on Her Life and Work.* Boston: Beacon Press, 1989.

Felman, Shoshana, and Dori Laub, eds. *Testimony: Crises of Witnessing in Literature, Psychoanalysis, and History.* New York: Routledge, 1991.

Herman, Judith Lewis. *Trauma and Recovery.* NY: Basic Books, 1992, 1997.

Leaska, Mitchell. Introduction. *The Pargiters: The Novel-Essay Portion of* The Years. By Virginia Woolf. New York and London: Harcourt Brace Jovanovich, 1977.

Lee, Hermione. *Virginia Woolf.* New York: Knopf, 1997.

McNaron, Toni. "The Uneasy Solace of Art: The Effect of Sexual Abuse on Virginia Woolf's Aesthetic." *Women's Studies: An International Forum.* 15, 2 (1992): 251-266.

McVicker, Jeanette and Laura Davis. *Virginia Woolf and Communities: Selected Papers from the Eighth Annual Conference on Virginia Woolf.* Pace U.P., 1999.

Moran, Patricia. "'The Flaw in the Centre': Writing as Hymenal Rupture in Virginia Woolf's Work." *Tulsa Studies in Women's Literature* (Spring 1998): 101-121.

Radin, Grace. The Years: *The Evolution of a Novel.* Knoxville: U of Tennessee P, 1981.

Smith, Laura A. "Who Do We Think Clarissa Dalloway Is Anyway? Re-search Into Seventy Years of Woolf Criticism." Barrett and Cramer: 215-21.

Tal, Kali. *Worlds of Hurt: Reading the Literatures of Trauma.* Cambridge and New York: Cambridge U P, 1996.

van der Kolk, Otto, and van der Hart, Onno. "The Intrusive Past: The Flexibility of Memory and the Engraving of Trauma." Caruth 158-182.

Wiesel, Elie. "Why I Write." *Confronting the Holocaust: The Impact of Elie Wiesel.* Ed. Rosenfeld and Greenburg. Bloomington: Indiana U P, 1978.

Wilt, Judith. *Abortion, Choice, and Contemporary Fiction: The Armageddon of the Maternal Instinct.* Chicago and London: The U of Chicago P, 1990.

Woolf, Virginia. *Between the Acts.* New York: HBJ, 1941.

——. *The Diary of Virginia Woolf.* Ed. Anne Olivier Bell, assisted by Andrew McNeillie. Vol. 3. New York: HBJ, 1980. Vol. 4. New York: HBJ, 1982.

——. *The Letters of Virginia Woolf.* Ed. Nigel Nicolson and Joanne Trautmann. Vol. 6. New York: HBJ, 1980

——. *Mrs. Dalloway.* New York: HBJ, 1925.

——. "A Sketch of the Past." *Moments of Being: Unpublished Autobiographical Writings.* Ed. Jeanne Schulkind. Second Edition. San Diego: Harvest, 1985. 61-138.

——. *The Years.* New York: HBJ, 1937.

Emily Blair
Prostituting Culture and Enslaving Intellectual Liberty: Virginia Woolf's Disavowed Victorian Predecessor Margaret Oliphant

In this paper, I examine Virginia Woolf's abusive dismissal of the work of Margaret Oliphant in *Three Guineas*. Woolf suggestively places Oliphant in the space of the "three separate dots" (91), the space that makes it difficult for her to ask the "daughters of educated men" who earn their living by reading and writing to help the barrister to prevent war and protect culture and intellectual liberty. My goal is not to garner sympathy for Oliphant, but instead to note both a continuity and a shift in Woolf's comments on lesser women writers as she establishes the outside boundary for a tradition that thinks back through its mothers. In *The Field of Cultural Production*, Pierre Bourdieu usefully explains that those artists who are most freed from external constraints, and Bourdieu includes Woolf here, "are those who have taken most advantage of a historical heritage accumulated through collective labour against external constraints" (63). To be sure, Woolf often narrativizes the history of women's writing in terms of the many phantoms and obstacles in her way. She acknowledges the "many famous women, and many more unknown and forgotten" who have been before her "making the path smooth, and regulating [her] steps" (*DM* 235). She acknowledges how when she came to write "there were very few material obstacles in [her] way" (*DM* 235). I hope to illuminate how Woolf distances herself from both the economic necessity that Oliphant experienced and the reproductive sexuality that she exemplified. Woolf concludes that because Oliphant must "earn her living and educate her children," she must prostitute her culture and she must enslave her intellectual liberty (*TG* 92). I read Woolf's dismissal of Oliphant against her earlier reviews of lesser women writers, her encomium of Aphra Behn, and Oliphant's autobiography to illustrate Woolf's anxiety about the woman writer who makes a deliberate compromise by producing both texts and children.

Woolf's attack on Oliphant recalls and continues her 1924 review of Mrs. Humphry Ward. In this review, titled "The Compromise," Woolf anticipates her abuse of Oliphant more than twenty years later. She pictures an elderly Mrs. Humphry Ward whose imagination was starved by her fatal compromise between the writing of history and the profits to be made from the marketplace "writing at breathless speed" novels which we "must call bad" (*BP* 142). Woolf condemns Ward whose profits from writing buy beautiful dresses, butlers, carriages, luncheon and weekend parties. Mrs. Humphry Ward stands as an early example of the compromised woman writer; the woman writer Woolf does not figure into the history of women's writing that she creates in *A Room of One's Own*.

In *A Room of One's Own,* her praise of Aphra Behn, like her attack on Oliphant in *Three Guineas,* defines a decisive point in her argument for the evolution of women's writing. Woolf's narrative assessment of Behn's career focuses on how she overcomes the external constraints of the private sphere at the same time that it registers what Mary Poovey and others have identified as the dominant fears associated with woman since the seventeenth century—her promiscuity and her lust after money (5). For Woolf, Aphra Behn's writing career "turns a very important corner on the road" to establishing a heritage of mothers for Woolf to think back through in order to create herself (*AROO* 63). Behn brings the great lady writers of the sixteenth century out of the solitary confinement of their parks and into the public marketplace. Woolf images Behn's circulation there as she invites her reader to follow this movement; "We come to town and rub shoulders with ordinary people in the streets" (63). Woolf thus calls attention to the way that Behn leaves the private sphere, extending women's mobility; Behn works hard to succeed in making "enough to live on" (64). This economic independence initiates "the freedom of the mind, or rather the possibility that in the course of time the mind will be free to write what it likes" (64). Woolf suggestively alludes to Behn's sexuality—Behn's "unfortunate adventures" (63), her "sacrifice, perhaps, of certain agreeable qualities" (64), and her shady amorousness (66). With these allusions Woolf records a general uneasiness about Behn's promiscuity by parodying the parents whose response to their daughter's wanting to earn money by their pens is "Death would be better!" than living the life of Aphra Behn (64). Yet Woolf relegates the question of women's chastity as a possible topic of study "if any student at Girton or Newnham cared to go into the matter"(64). Significantly, she maintains her focus on Behn's career as evidence that women's writing ceased to be "merely a sign of folly and a distracted mind, but was of practical importance" (64).

In arguing that "The importance of that fact outweighs anything that she actually wrote," Woolf raises and elides the question of Behn's aesthetic value (64). She closes her discussion with a delight in Aphra Behn's irreverent placement in Westminster Abbey as she exhorts all women together to let flowers fall upon her tomb. Woolf's delight in Behn's entrance into the literary marketplace in *A Room of One's Own* corresponds with her own pride and sense of power and independence as her readership and sales increased after 1926. Hermione Lee notes that "It's a mark of her satisfaction in her earning power that in 1928 she starts to keep an account book, and does so until 1939. The book frequently notes double sums (about twice or three times more in America than in England) paid for the same piece" (551).

Nevertheless, Woolf's pride in the ability of the woman writer to make money and her uneasiness concerning the literary woman in the market place shifts during the 1930s. Woolf does less reviewing and she comes "to resent the traps and compromises" that the market requires (Lee 551). In June of 1937 she records in her diary that she has "put 3 Guineas daily into practice." Woolf writes "No I will not write for the larger paying magazines" (*D5* 96). I want to focus not only on how Woolf's 1938 attack on Oliphant in *Three Guineas* marks a shift in her attitude toward making money by her pen, but also on how her attack implicitly judges the aesthetic value of Oliphant's work as it conflates that value with Oliphant's sexuality. Oliphant represents Woolf's fears of uncontained female production. Here making money from literary production ceases to be "rubbing shoulders with ordinary people" and becomes a form of "prostitution" and "intellectual harlotry" for the woman writer.

Woolf does not extend her praise of Behn's physical entrance into the marketplace to Mrs. Oliphant's established presence there. In contrast to Aphra Behn, who has earned women the right to speak their minds, Mrs. Oliphant, Woolf argues, "sold her brain, her very admirable brain, prostituted her culture and enslaved her intellectual liberty in order that she might earn her living and educate her children" (*TG* 91-92). While Woolf describes Behn as "a middle-class woman with all the plebian virtues of humor, vitality and courage; a woman forced by the death of her husband and some unfortunate adventures of her own to make a living by her wits" (*AROO* 63-64), she denies the same egalitarian praise to Oliphant.

Woolf opens her discussion of Oliphant with "the facts that make it difficult" for her to go on with her argument (*TG* 91). These facts are the "illuminating document" before her, "a most genuine and indeed moving piece of work, the autobiography of Mrs. Oliphant" (*TG* 91). The facts of Mrs. Oliphant's autobiography, Woolf argues, smear the mind and deject the imagination (*TG* 91). Paradoxically, the very same freedom that Aphra Behn has won for women to "come to the rescue of their families" by writing implicates Oliphant's production, which is interested and liable to the early nineteenth-century distinctions between the hack who writes for money and the artist who writes for pleasure. Woolf's attack on Oliphant employs such male-authored literary hierarchies that create aesthetic value by distancing it from economic necessity. To be sure, Bourdieu suggests that such judgements offer "a new mystery of immaculate conception" (*Distinction* 68). Woolf's assessment of Oliphant's visible overproduction suggestively contrasts with Aphra Behn's "shady," semi-transparent legacy to the woman writer.

Oliphant's life offers parallels to Behn's. She too suffers the death of her husband early in marriage and her literary production, like Behn's, becomes the sole support of her family. Oliphant wrote "some ninety-eight novels, fifty or more short stories, more than four hundred articles, numerous travel books, and several biographies" (Jay vii). Some accounts in 1870 in *The Saturday Review* and in 1881 in *The Spectator* ranked her as second woman novelist to George Eliot after Elizabeth Gaskell's death (Rubik 6). Other contemporary reviews resonate with Woolf's review of Mrs. Humphry Ward linking Oliphant's prolific production to her mercenary motives, her taste for silk dresses, and her overindulgence of her sons. In her autobiography, Oliphant resents such criticism as she defends her steady production "working too fast, and producing too much" (Coghill 44). This self-defense both articulates and anticipates many of the same external constraints that Woolf argues in *A Room of One's Own* face the nineteenth-century woman writer. Oliphant laments the fact that she does not have a room of her own to write in: "I had no table even to myself, much less a room to work in, but sat at the corner of the family table with my writing-book, with everything going on as if I had been making a shirt instead of writing a book" (Coghill 23). She elaborates "up to this date, 1888, I have never been shut up in a separate room, or hedged off with any observances" and continues that "I don't think I have ever had two hours undisturbed" (24). Oliphant even comments that she believes that Miss Austen "wrote in the same way, and very much for the same reason" (24). As the sole supporter of her own and her brother's children, Oliphant articulates the pressure of her family as an external constraint on her artistic production. This pressure divides her attentions unlike "men who have no wives, who have given themselves up to their art, [who] have had an almost unfair advantage over us" (5).

Woolf's reading of Oliphant's autobiography does not acknowledge the way that Oliphant's career struggles with and overcomes these external obstacles or indeed the debt that she owes to Oliphant as one of her foremothers. Woolf ignores this subtext in Oliphant's autobiography and focuses on the way that Oliphant subordinates her writing to "Other matters, events even of our uneventful life, [that] took so much more importance in life than these books" (Coghill 23). On the contrary, Woolf seems to read the autobiography as an admission of Oliphant's deliberate artistic compromise marking instead a continuity with her earlier review of Mrs. Humphry Ward. Because Mrs. Oliphant is motivated to enter the marketplace, her writing is aesthetically impure and sexually unchaste, adulterated by the admixture of money, advertisement, and publicity, which demystify its conception.

As Woolf lays out the facts of Mrs. Oliphant's writing career for her gentleman reader, her language belies the way that she marks Oliphant's writing with sexuality and class. Woolf seeks confirmation of Oliphant's intellectual prostitution by asking her gentleman reader to "souse" himself in Oliphant's innumerable contributions to literary papers—"Novels, biographies, histories, handbooks of Florence and Rome, reviews, and newspaper articles" (*TG* 91). Woolf's use of the verb "souse" inadvertently reveals the way that Oliphant's production exceeds the bounds of what Woolf defines as proper for the maintenance of intellectual liberty and the protection of culture. "Souse" is a visceral verb: it images an immersion or plunging into liquid. This immersion often has intoxicating properties. Thus by asking her gentleman reader to "souse" himself in Oliphant's innumerable literary productions, Woolf images both an overwhelming fluidity and an unnatural excitation that impairs the reader of Oliphant's work. Woolf then implicitly questions Oliphant's motives for entrance into the literary marketplace. She juxtaposes her discussion of Oliphant to her argument that asking the daughters of educated men to sign the barrister's manifesto to protect disinterested culture and intellectual liberty would be to ask a publican to sign a manifesto in favor of temperance. This analogy suggests that both the publican and "the daughters of educated men who have to earn their living by reading and writing" might realize the impairing nature of the product they sell, but they continue to sell it to make a living (*TG* 92). It is not in Oliphant's case the culture that compromises the woman writer; in contrast, it is the woman writer who cannot abstain from production who compromises the culture.

Significantly, the suggestion that the gentleman reader "souse" himself in Oliphant's innumerable literary productions evokes a latent meaning of "souse" as an "attack." This latent meaning is supported by Woolf's use of the verb "smear" when she tells her gentleman reader Mrs. Oliphant's work has "smeared [the] mind and dejected [the] imagination" (*TG* 91). "Smear" formulates her attack in terms that imbricate artistic and sexual value with class. "Smear" like "souse" belies a desire to attack, but more interestingly it conceives of this attack in terms of staining someone's reputation. Again Woolf seems to attribute this corrupting agency to Mrs. Oliphant's work; her innumerable literary productions, she suggests, smear the mind, making it dirty and greasy. This soiling suggests class difference and recalls Woolf's earlier statement in *Three Guineas* that "Mrs." "is a contaminated word; an obscene word" (52). Woolf argues "The less said about that word the better. Such is the smell of it, so rank does it stink" (52). Such an association of "Mrs." with odor betrays nineteenth-century metonymies between odor and class.

It implicitly places the married woman in the lower class where economic necessity drives production, making its conception visible. Woolf notes that we have to applaud Mrs. Oliphant's choice and to admire her courage because of the "damage that poverty inflicts upon mind and body, the necessity that is laid upon those who have children to see that they are clothed and fed, nursed and educated" (92). Woolf's one paragraph case against Oliphant marks her motherhood, the visible products of her sexual experience, with four references to her children. Three of these references appear in the text and the fourth is a footnote that quotes the *Dictionary of National Biography* entry on Mrs. Oliphant. The entry notes that Oliphant "lived in perpetual embarrassment owing to her undertaking education and maintenance of her widowed brother's children in addition to her own two sons" (174). Like Oliphant's literary production, the product of her maternity is out of control. Oliphant's troubled sons reverberate with Woolf's characterization of the production of intellectual prostitution, its "anemic, vicious and diseased progeny" who are "let loose upon the world to infect

17

and corrupt and sow the seeds of disease in others" (93). Woolf's attack then suggests how Oliphant circulates both "her very admirable brain" and her children in the public sphere. Both are blemished. Ironically, Woolf's implicit critique that having children prevents Oliphant from using "her very admirable brain" to produce high quality work echoes Oliphant's own fear that a fine novel and fine boys were mutually exclusive (Corbett 105).

Mrs. Oliphant's career has rhetorical value for Woolf: it establishes the limit between what nourishes culture and what indiscriminately corrupts it. Even though Woolf identifies Oliphant as the daughter of an educated man, a woman of her own class, her attack moves Oliphant outside the boundaries of that class and in Bourdieu's terms takes advantage of the obstacles that Oliphant faces to theorize a woman's writing that finds production mixed between the public and private spheres suspect. Woolf works to distance the moment of creation from necessity and thus elevates her own lack of necessity to earn money by her pen. In this way, her portrait of Oliphant reinscribes earlier fears of the woman's lack of containment, the corrupting influence of her desire for money and her sexual productions.

Works Cited

Bell, Anne Olivier, ed. *The Diary of Virginia Woolf.* Vol. 5. San Diego: Harcourt Brace & Company, 1984.

Bourdieu, Pierre. *Distinction: A Social Critique of the Judgement of Taste.* Trans. Richard Nice. Cambridge: Harvard University Press, 1984.

——. *The Field of Cultural Production.* Ed. Randal Johnson. New York: Columbia University Press, 1993.

Coghill, Mrs. Harry, ed. *The Autobiography and Letters of Margaret Oliphant.* 1899. Edinburgh and London: William Blackwood and Sons, 1899.

Corbett, Mary Jean. *Representing Femininity: Middle-Class Subjectivity in Victorian and Edwardian Women's Autobiographies.* New York and Oxford: Oxford University Press, 1992.

Jay, Elisabeth, ed. *The Autobiography of Margaret Oliphant: The Complete Text.* Oxford: Oxford University Press, 1990.

Lee, Hermione. *Virginia Woolf.* New York: Alfred A. Knopf, 1997.

Poovey, Mary. *The Proper Lady and the Woman Writer: Ideology as Style in the Works of Mary Wollstonecraft, Mary Shelley, and Jane Austen.* Chicago and London: The University of Chicago Press, 1984.

Rubik, Margarete. *The Novels of Mrs. Oliphant: A Subversive View of Traditional Themes.* New York: Peter Lang, 1994.

Woolf, Virginia. *A Room of One's Own.* New York: Harcourt Brace Jovanovich, Inc. 1929.

——. *Books and Portraits: Some further selections from the literary and biographical writings of Virginia Woolf.* Ed. Mary Lyon. London: Hogarth Press, 1977.

——. *The Death of the Moth and Other Essays.* New York: Harcourt Brace Jovanovich, Inc. 1942.

——. *Three Guineas.* New York: Harcourt Brace Jovanovich, Inc. 1938.

Jamie Carr
Novel Possibilities: Re-Reading Sexuality and "Madness" in *Mrs. Dalloway*, Beyond the Film

Mid-way through writing *Mrs. Dalloway*, Virginia Woolf sketched in her diary what marks a profound connection between her eponymous character, Clarissa Dalloway, and Clarissa's textual double, Septimus Warren Smith. "I want to give life & death, sanity & insanity," writes Woolf; "I want to criticise the social system, & to show it at work, at its most intense" (*D2* 248). In its active critique of the "social system," *Mrs. Dalloway* problematizes discourse in order to resist those processes through which human beings are categorized, are assigned subject positions. The novel thus assembles and mobilizes ethical "truths"—namely, counterdiscursive and parrhesiastic truths—which unfold around "the restrictions acting upon human life" (Bernauer 7),[1] around, specifically, discursive productions of sexuality and "madness." Clarissa and Septimus are coupled in the novel so as to articulate these ethical truths—truths about the moralizing and normalizing discourses that govern society, that coerce and confine the soul.

The striking and signifying absence of the novel's ethical truths from the 1997 cinematic production of *Mrs. Dalloway* and from various reviews of that film, however, makes even more palpable these truths. A concern of this paper, then, is what happens to the ethics of a novel when it is "made" into a popular cultural production. Specifically, which narratives, which truths, are privileged and constructed and which are lost in and by readings of a text that deny the very pulse that drives that text?

Re-Reading Resistance: Assembling a Counterdiscursive Sexual "Identity" for Clarissa

The film version of *Mrs. Dalloway* sits on the shelf at Blockbuster video, appealing with a four-star rating, a "Two thumbs up!" praise, and a romanticized picture of the young Clarissa and Peter kissing on a sunny English afternoon. It is the story of this picture that draws a particular viewing audience and that movie reviews most closely attend to—the story of young, romantic, love. Rather ironically, it is also the story demanded by what Woolf scathingly refers to in her essay "Modern Fiction" as that "powerful and unscrupulous tyrant who has [the writer] in thrall, to provide a plot, to provide comedy, tragedy, love interest, and an air of probability embalming the whole" (*CE2* 106). Tragedy, love interest, probable, recognizable characters and stories—such are the narratives that proliferate in and define popular culture readings of this novel-turned-film. *Newsweek*, for instance, entices viewers with this elucidation: "the Clarissa of 30 years before rejects the feverish idealism of one suitor, Peter Walsh, for the unexciting security of another, Richard Dalloway" (Kroll 80); another reviewer likewise reduces the story to: "we see the young Peter asking the young Clarissa to marry him and thus break out of her cosseted life, [. . . and] we see her opt instead for the quite conventional young Richard" (Kauffmann 22); and, in one of the most amusing reviews: Clarissa "*dump[s]* a young adventurer named Peter Walsh in favor of the safe Richard Dalloway" (Stuart 55; emphasis added). "The tyrant," Woolf reminds us, "is obeyed" (*CE2* 106).

The epistemological limits of these various film reviews essentialize Clarissa on the basis of her sexuality; they make the claim, explicitly or implicitly, to know her "true self," presenting her unequivocally as a hetero-sexual woman torn between two men. Such realist "readings" of Woolf's novel construct the privileged, because normative, narratives of metaphysi-cal being (the probable) and of heterosexual love (plot, tragedy, love interest), which are antithetical to the ethical practices of the novel. For what is to be made of the Clarissa of the novel, a married woman whose "virgin-ity preserved through childbirth [. . .] clung to her like a sheet" (*MD* 31), a wife who "had failed" her husband "again and again" (31), "this *being Mrs. Richard Dalloway*" (11; emphasis added), who "could not resist sometimes yielding to the charm of a woman," who

> did undoubtedly then feel what men felt. [. . .] It was a sudden revela-tion, a tinge like a blush which one tried to check and then, as it spread, one yielded to its expansion, and rushed to the farthest verge and there quivered and felt the world come closer, swollen with some astonishing significance, some pressure of rapture, which split its thin skin and gushed and poured with an extraordinary alleviation over the cracks and sores! Then, for that moment, she had seen an illumination; a match burning in a crocus; an inner meaning almost expressed (31-32)?

These sexually metaphorical moments of "revelation," as Clarissa ironical-ly refers to them, about her feelings for women (which are not narrated as part of Clarissa's thoughts in the film), create moments of greater ambigui-ty—for they are only *almost* expressed. And, it is Clarissa who "would not say of herself, I am this, I am that" (*MD* 9). The novel, unlike the various readings of it cited above, mobilizes a counterdiscursive identity for Clarissa Dalloway; it refuses to identify her as "this" or "that," refuses to elaborate for her a "true self," a metaphysics, of sexual identity, and so, as Peter remarks, though she is "so transparent in some ways," she is "so inscrutable in others" (77) so that all we have of her is "a mere sketch" (78).

Woolf perceives at the beginning of the century what Judith Butler will contend at its close, that "the notion that there might be a 'truth' of sex, [. . .], is produced precisely through the regulatory practices that generate coherent identities through the matrix of coherent gender norms" (Butler 17). The "truth" Woolf assembles in *Mrs. Dalloway* fails, deliberately, to generate a coherent sexual identity for Clarissa. The film reviews partici-pate, then, not in Woolf's *counter*discursive politics, but rather in the "regulatory practices" Woolf was writing against; they participate in the production of "coherent identities" and "coherent gender norms" from which follows "the heterosexualization of desire" (17). And since, as Butler further explains, "the cultural matrix through which gender identity has become intelligible requires that certain kinds of 'identities' cannot '*exist*'—that is, [. . .] those in which the practices of desire do not 'follow' from either sex or gender" (17; emphasis added), in one of the few explicit references to sexuality in the reviews of the film, the narratives that continue to get privileged are unmistakable: John Simon remarks in the *National Review* that he has "always mistrusted writings about men and women in love, sex, and marriage by authors lacking those experiences" (57).

"But here we have Virginia Woolf," the writer continues, "in her long and totally asexual marriage to Leonard Woolf, whatever the exact nature of her lesbian mopings and gropings with Vita Sackville-West may have been. Something like this surfaces in the novel [. . .], where the young heroine chooses the safe Richard [. . .] over the passionate Peter [. . .], and has a *quasi*-sexual involvement with her best friend, Sally Seton" (Simon 57; emphasis added). The ambiguity of Woolf's sexuality, like that of Clarissa's, (read, perhaps as *im*probable) so disturbs Simon that he needs to identify it; reified as asexual or lesbian, Woolf, then, is not to be trusted (one cannot fail to read the homophobic and essentialist underpinnings of such an assertion). We can, however, Simon concludes, trust our "young heroine" who overcomes something that resembles a heterosexual relationship in favor of a "real" one.

The fear of sexual *ambiguity*, the fear of not being able to "say of any one in the world [. . .] that they were this or were that" (*MD* 8), causes the film and the film critics, and inevitably then, the viewing audience, to resist reading Clarissa as anything other than a heterosexual woman torn between two men, proliferate "the notion that there might be a 'truth'" to sexual identity, sanction normative sexual and gender "behaviors," indeed, reproduce the cultural matrix from which these readings themselves materialize. This cultural matrix, these readings, these film reviews provide "an air of probability embalming the whole" (*CE2* 106) and so assert a particular reading of Woolf's work that effaces the counterdiscursive truths the novel tells; namely, they deny that the "identity" Clarissa inhabits in the novel exists because her "practices of desire do not 'follow' from either [her] sex or gender" (Butler 17). The romantic representation of Clarissa and Peter on the jacket of the video version of *Mrs. Dalloway* is far from ambiguous. It is, quite unmistakably, an intelligible portrait of heterosexualized desire. It is the picture of the *effect* of regulatory practices, of normalizing discourse, of the narratives of metaphysical being and of heterosexual romantic love.

Reconstructing "Truth": Mobilizing Parrhesiastic Truth as a Practice of Freedom—the "Case" of Septimus

Woolf's *Mrs. Dalloway* tells a truth about "the restrictions acting upon human life" (Bernauer 7)—those discourses that seek to identify and to categorize so as to govern; its critique of the "social system" manifests as truth-telling about the coercion and confinement of the soul. Just as the novel assembles a counterdiscursive truth of sexuality for Clarissa, so too does it mobilize an ethical truth around the production of "madness" through Septimus Warren Smith. Septimus inhabits in the novel the role of "truth-teller"; he exposes and critiques the power of discourses to regulate subjectivity, exposes and critiques, specifically, the medical adjudication of "madness."

In her biography of Woolf, Hermione Lee examines Woolf's "madness" through the language of a variety of narratives—letters, prescriptions, Leonard Woolf's diary accounts, and Woolf's own rich memoirs and diary entries—and suggests that "there is a gap between the inner, 'incomprehensible' language of the ill person, and the language of witnesses and retrospect" (Lee 191). This gap marks a battleground, Lee argues, a space to enact resistance to medical terminology and to mobilize a language of personal knowledge. It is a place where Woolf "transforms illness into a language of power and inspiration" (Lee 190), into "a creative language which describes *the value* of illness [that] *competes with, and overcomes*, a clinical or psychoanalytical language for madness" (188; emphases added). To read Woolf's "madness" as a clinical case, to medicalize it, is to deny all that Woolf worked toward, to neglect "what it did to her, and what she did with it" (Lee 194) as evidence of "a life of heroism, not of oppression, a life of writing wrestled from illness, fear, and pain" (195).

It is *this* life of heroism, a life of value, that Woolf gives to Septimus, who, through his "madness," struggles against the medical discourses that seek to *assign* "illness, fear, and pain" in order to become what Michel Foucault calls a parrhesiast, a truth-teller, one who performs "a kind of verbal activity where the speaker has a specific relation to truth through frankness, a certain relationship to his own life through danger, a certain type of relation to himself or other people through criticism, [. . .] and a specific relation to moral law through freedom and duty" (Foucault qtd. in Kebung 13). Septimus struggles to speak ethical truths against the governing effects of medical discourse, against the backdrop of diagnoses, of judgment, of confinement.

In a move that prefigures Foucault, Woolf establishes in *Mrs. Dalloway* a relationship between the medical and the juridical—it is through the story of Septimus that Dr. Holmes and Sir William Bradshaw are exposed as "judges" who, though "different in their verdicts," "yet ruled, yet inflicted" (*MD* 148). Likened to judges, physicians have the power to condemn and confine the "guilty," those like Septimus who feel they have committed and must pay for a crime. Thus it is against the dangers Bradshaw has the power to impose—the danger of being held in seclusion, of being silenced, of being restrained, the danger of the submission and annihilation of his soul and his will that Septimus risks the truths he must tell.

Septimus likens physicians to monsters, to torturers, to vultures, to what he perceives as "human nature": "Human nature," he verbalizes, "was on him—the repulsive brute, with the blood-red nostrils" (*MD* 92); "Once you fall [. . .]. Holmes and Bradshaw are on you. They scour the desert. They fly screaming into the wilderness. The rack and the thumbscrew are applied. Human nature is remorseless" (*MD* 98). Septimus perceives the risks to his own life because "he knew the truth" (MD 140) of the power physicians could effect—through discourse and through physical control. In his role as parrhesiast, he is frank in his criticism of the medical field for its drive to pinion, "to force the soul," to impose their will upon his own: "He was in their power!" (147). As a truth-teller, he demands freedom from such authority as he asks, "'Must,' 'must,' why 'must'? [. . .] 'What right has Bradshaw to say 'must' to me?'" (147). His truth-telling competes with the medicalizing discourse that wants to categorize him in order to place and restrict him.

Thus, to claim as Jay Carr does in his *Boston Globe* review that "Septimus convinces us he has no choices, that he's drowning in his obsessions" (*D6*), as *People Weekly* claims, that Septimus "is losing a battle against despair" (Gliatto 22), indeed as the film portrays him, is to deny reading Septimus as a parrhesiast; it is to deny the truths he tells. Such readings adhere instead to a clinical understanding of Septimus. To read Septimus *this* way is to deny, further, the counterdiscursive narrative the novel mobilizes, that which Clarissa comprehends in the novel (but not in the film) that "Death was defiance. Death was an attempt to communicate" (*MD* 184).

When Clarissa is told of Septimus's suicide in the film, she asks "Why, why did he do it?"; "He's thrown it all away, his life, just like that" (Atkins).[2] The narrative the film puts together of this climactic moment in the novel is at odds with the ethics of the novel. Woolf writes in her diary that she wanted to "adumbrate [. . .] a study of insanity & suicide: the world seen by the sane & the insane side by side" (*D2* 207). But in the film, the world is not allowed to be seen by the "insane," by the one who has suicided. Rather, we see only the sane, the rational, hear only the condemnation of "throwing it all away," are not permitted to "read" the narrative of truth-telling. Rather than "an attempt to communicate" as the novel names it, rather than a use of freedom to tell a "truth," suicide is the effect of a view of life held by the weak, a view of life in which its very beauty *is* the thing "obscured, [. . .] every day in corruption, lies, and chatter" (Atkins), until death makes one realize life's beauty and its ephemeralness. My intent is not to condemn this reading, however moralizing, but rather to point to how it functions as a regulatory practice, a normalizing narrative that does not offer the possibility of a counterdiscursive truth.

For *in the novel*, Clarissa comprehends Septimus's suicide for what it is. "A thing there was that mattered," she exclaims, "a thing, wreathed about with chatter, defaced, obscured in her own life, let drop every day in corruption, lies, chatter. *This* he had preserved. *Death was defiance. Death was an attempt to communicate*" (*MD* 184; emphases added). To read Septimus's suicide as something *other than* a waste is to read it as an act of resistance, an act of freedom in the face of domination, an act of truth-telling in the face of the "corruption, lies, chatter" that "force the soul," that restrict human life.[3] It is to read his suicide, indeed, as evidence of "a life of heroism, not of oppression, a life of [truth-telling] wrestled from illness, fear, and pain" (Lee 195). To read Septimus's suicide in this way is to submit to ambiguity and to fear not unlike the ambiguity and fear provoked by Clarissa's sexuality.

While at times acknowledging the experimental possibilities of film, as indeed there are, Woolf had also presciently recognized at least one of the possible functions of film: to efface any critical possibility of counterdiscursive or parrhesiastic truths. The film version of *Mrs. Dalloway*, as well as its various reviews, have participated in the narratives, the discourses, the cultural matrices that reify, pinion, normalize, have identified with all of those elements Woolf ascribes to plot; they have obeyed the tyrant, have presented "tragedy," "love interest," "an air of probability embalming the whole" to placate and please the audience. That is, the privileged, normative narratives they tell are for the "faces mobbed at the door of a picture palace; apathetic, passive faces," as Peggy Pargiter criticizes in *The Years*; "the faces of people drugged with cheap pleasures; who had not even the courage to be themselves, but must dress up, imitate, pretend" (*TY* 388). And so, the thing that matters, the ethical truths that Woolf's *Mrs. Dalloway* makes palpable, are lost.

Notes

[1] I take this phrase from James Bernauer's critical study of Foucault's later work on ethics. Foucault, like Woolf, sought to counter the discursive production of subjectivities through a critical manipulation and a working beyond of those subject positions to which one has been assigned. This counterdiscursive work is ethical in that it involves and effects practices of freedom.

[2] To avoid confusion, since the film also bears the title *Mrs. Dalloway*, I will refer to the author of the screenplay, Eileen Atkins, when citing the film.

[3] In "The Ethics of the Concern for Self as a Practice of Freedom," Foucault suggests a way in which suiciding can be read as an act of resistance in the face of domination: "Even when the power relation is completely out of balance, when it can truly be claimed that one side has 'total power' over the other, a power can be exercised over the other only insofar as the other still has the option of killing himself, of leaping out the window, or of killing the other person" (292). The ethics of Septimus' truth-telling is enacted in his suicide; though others attempt to have power over his life, he performs an act of resistance.

Works Cited

Bernauer, James W. *Michel Foucault's Force of Flight: Toward an Ethics for Thought.* New Jersey: Humanities International, 1990.

Butler, Judith. *Gender Trouble: Feminism and the Subversion of Identity.* New York: Routledge, 1990.

Carr, Jay. "Redgrave's 'Mrs. Dalloway' Seizes Woolf's June Day." Rev. of *Mrs. Dalloway,* dir. Marleen Gorris. Perf. Vanessa Redgrave, Natasha McElhone, and Rupert Graves. Fox Lorber Films, 1997. *The Boston Globe* 6 March 1998: D6.

Foucault, Michel. "The Ethics of the Concern for Self as a Practice of Freedom." *Ethics: Subjectivity and Truth.* Ed. Paul Rabinow. New York: The New Press, 1997.

Gliatto, Tom. "Virginia Woolf's *Mrs. Dalloway.*" Rev. of *Mrs. Dalloway,* dir. Marleen Gorris. *People Weekly* 2 March 1998: 22.

Kauffmann, Stanley. Rev. of *Mrs. Dalloway,* dir. Marleen Gorris. *The New Republic* 9 March 1998: 28-29.

Kebung, Konrad. "Michel Foucault's Parrhesia and the Question of Ethics." Diss. Boston College, 1994.

Kroll, Jack. Rev. of *Mrs. Dalloway,* dir. Marleen Gorris. *Newsweek* 2 March 1998: 80.

Lee, Hermione. *Virginia Woolf.* New York: Knopf, 1998.

Mrs. Dalloway. Screenplay by Eileen Atkins. Dir. Marleen Gorris. Perf. Vanessa Redgrave, Natasha McElhone, and Rupert Graves. Fox Lorber Films, 1997.

Simon, John. Rev. of *Mrs. Dalloway,* dir. Marleen Gorris. *National Review* 23 March 1998: 57-58.

Stuart, Jan. Rev. of *Mrs. Dalloway,* dir. Marleen Gorris. *The Advocate* 3 March 1998: 55-56.

Woolf, Virginia. "Modern Fiction." *Collected Essays,* Volume 2. London: Hogarth, 1966.

——. *Mrs. Dalloway.* 1925. San Diego: Harcourt, 1981.

——. *The Diary of Virginia Woolf,* Volume Two 1920-1924. Ed. Anne Olivier Bell. New York: Harcourt, 1978.

——. *The Years.* 1937. San Diego: Harcourt, 1965.

Ann Martin

Sleeping Beauty in a Green Dress: *Mrs. Dalloway* and Fairy Tale Configurations of Desire

Alex Zwerdling suggests that Woolf thought of the writer in the glare of publicity as "like a trouser mender in Oxford Street, with a horde of reviewers pressing their noses to the glass and commenting to a curious crowd upon each stitch" (110). For Reginald Abbott, the image of the tailor or artist in the shop window indicates Woolf's "ambivalence toward the modern marketplace" where the writer's work is demoted to the status of a commodity (195). But in terms of *Mrs. Dalloway*, this approach to consumer culture seems rather limited. While Woolf does indeed question the utopian promise of capitalist expenditure, especially through the figure of Doris Kilman, she also emphasizes the possibilities that attend consumerism, which Jennifer Wicke characterizes as the "active, even productive or creative process" of consumption in the space of the modern city (14). In this sense the commodity is a mobile signifier, a kind of intertext that indicates the individual's response to desire. And just as the skywritten ad for toffee in *Mrs. Dalloway* is not only decoded but responded to in a range of different ways, so too are the allusions that inform our understanding of the modernist text. Like the tailor who mends trousers in the window, the writer—Woolf—consumes texts from her culture and sews them together. The resulting product is in turn consumed by the reader. Writing and reading are thus processes based on mediation and on negotiation and as such signal the use of culture on the part of the writer, the viewer, the reader, and the critic.

I want to look at how Woolf's use of the fairy tale known as "Sleeping Beauty" relates to this dynamic process of consumption, where the intertext can be read resistantly and subversively; in this case, can be read according to Clarissa's desire for other women. The starting point for my examination is a passage from *Mrs. Dalloway* that echoes the scene of the tailor in the window in Oxford Street. On the day of her party, Clarissa Dalloway sews a tear in her green dress. As she does so, she is watched and inevitably judged by Peter Walsh. The scene connects to "Sleeping Beauty" in some powerful ways. Beverly Ann Schlack has summarized the main ties between the two texts, which include the needle and scissors that recall the spindle of the spinning wheel that sends the girl into a hundred-year slumber (60). Clarissa's attic room echoes overtly the tower in which the Sleeping Beauty falls asleep, Peter Walsh becomes a version of the Prince who bursts in on the slumbering Princess, and the chaste kisses they exchange provide a counterpoint to the kiss that revives the Sleeping Beauty.

In one possible reading of the allusion, Clarissa, like the fairy tale heroine, becomes the commodity or the object of desire in the window (on the chesterfield, in the bed, on the shelf) that Peter's gaze situates in terms of masculine desire. Certainly, the married identity of Mrs. Dalloway is a commodity in itself as Clarissa is connected metonymically to the goods on display as she walks along Bond Street: "this being Mrs. Dalloway; not even Clarissa anymore; this being Mrs. Richard Dalloway" (14). The system of heterosexual exchange seems to pin down her identity. Like the mend in the dress, where the thread pulls the lips of the cloth together, Clarissa has been sewn into the role of "Mrs. Richard Dalloway." In this sense, the fairy tale becomes a *point de capiton*. The story of "Sleeping Beauty" is sewn into the signifying field of patriarchal relations, and the fairy tale in *Mrs. Dalloway* is seen as a stable archetype of heterosexual love applied interchangeably to Richard and Clarissa, or to Peter and Clarissa. Either way it is a story in which, as Jack Zipes suggests, the heroine is characterized by "docility and self-abandonment" (24) and is a passive recipient of her fate: the prick of the spindle, the prick of the prince, the finality of marriage.

I would like to suggest, though, that Woolf's allusion to "Sleeping Beauty" does not necessarily lead to such a univocal narrative of gender, nor does it indicate such sexual and textual stability. First, as Schlack (60) and Susan Squier (104-105) indicate, Clarissa's reaction to Peter while she sews is hardly positive or passive: she sees him as an enemy rather than as a lover. Second, Peter's reaction to himself in the role of Prince Charming proves problematic. Though his gaze appears to control the scene and Clarissa's place as a passive heroine in it, his Symbolic mastery collapses in an eruption of the Real when he dissolves into tears and flees the room.

How then do we read Woolf's allusion to the fairy tale if references to "Sleeping Beauty" do not stabilize heterosexual relations in *Mrs. Dalloway*? One approach might be to see her invocation of the tale as ironic, where "Sleeping Beauty" and other tales told in the past by rural, working-class women are placed incongruously in the context of a debased twentieth-century consumer culture. But such a reading would have to ignore the historical circulation of fairy tales and the ways in which they have been told, retold, transcribed, written, rewritten, staged, filmed, used in advertising—in short, bought and sold by both men and women—since the day they were shared. Another view might posit the irony as part of Woolf's critique of the fairy tale itself, where the patriarchal archetypes on which "Sleeping Beauty" is based are dramatically out-of-step with the lesbian experiences depicted in the novel (see Emily Jensen, Eileen Barrett, and Gay Wachman). But this would involve a definition of fairy tales as prescriptive texts that interpellate the reader completely, which is clearly not the case. Contemporary writers from Angela Carter (*The Bloody Chamber* 1979) to Cheryl Moch (*Cinderella, the Real True Story* 1985), from James Finn Garner (*Politically Correct Bedtime Stories* 1994) to Barbara Walker (*Feminist Fairy Tales* 1996) present dramatically different (and often wickedly humorous) versions of canonical fairy tales that foreground and critique their given ideological import.

A more effective reading of Woolf's use of "Sleeping Beauty" might acknowledge that the fairy tale is itself a changing, changeable commodity deeply involved with modernity. In this kind of interpretation, the fairy tale is not a locus of encoded "pure" meaning or nostalgic traces of authenticity, but rather a site of cultural dislocation, of radical instability. This instability is enabled by the convoluted history of the fairy tale's transmission and reception. It is the history and the number of versions of any given story that make an authentic or original or reliable fairy tale impossible to pin down.

According to this approach, I suggest that Woolf does not refer to one specific version of "Sleeping Beauty" in order to react against the modern world's corrupted values or the delimiting aspects of the fairy tale itself. Instead she uses the tale's shifting position in British culture to engage in an exploration of the subversive possibilities that inhere in such texts. For instance, one of the more popular forms of the stories in Woolf's time was the pantomime, which she attended more than once (*MOB* 144-145, 163). Though the performances were ostensibly geared towards an audience of children, the role of hero was played by a "principal boy," by a woman such as Vesta Tilley or Hetty King who read the lines while wearing a suggestively feminine costume (Herr 141). The gender confusion is obvious: while the spectacle of a woman wearing tights and showing off her legs in the Victorian era must have given men a thrill, the sight of a woman wooing another woman on stage—however much the lesbian dimension of the act was disavowed—must have given some women a few shivers too. The performance of the tale and the apparently incongruous staging of sexual roles opens up the interpretative possibilities of the narrative itself.

Woolf capitalizes on the range and potential reception of fairy tales in her society, and in a tactical use of the stories, explores how lesbian desire can refigure the fairy tale's significance. The image of Clarissa Dalloway's bedroom becomes central in Woolf's resistance to compulsory heterosexuality. As Schlack points out, the room is very much connected with the bower in which the Sleeping Beauty lies awaiting her Prince. "Like. . .a child exploring a tower" Clarissa ascends to her room, where she "pierce[s] the pincushion" with her hatpin as Sleeping Beauty pierces her finger with the spindle (*MD* 45). Her bed is a crucial image here and often associated with "a death-bed" (Tambling 149) where all nuns and virgins, those women to whom Clarissa compares herself, sleep (Lyon 117-118; Moon 155). As Emily Jensen writes, "So much for her personal, sexual self": lesbian experience must be disavowed in this society and replaced by the sleep of marriage (176). However, the solitude of her tower room is also a space of imaginative and indeed erotic possibilities, limited though they may be. It is in Clarissa's seclusion that she can reexperience the orgasmic moment: "a match burning in a crocus" (*MD* 47). She might be a Sleeping Beauty, frozen in her virginity, but as she says, she sleeps "badly" (*MD* 46). I suggest that this failure to sleep well, especially in light of her "failures" with Richard, signals her resistance to the pre-scripted role of a passive, waiting, heterosexual woman. In other words, Clarissa is a Sleeping Beauty whose unwillingness to sleep would have unnerved Walt Disney.

In Charles Perrault's version of "Sleeping Beauty," the teller lets us know that "the good fairy had beguiled her long slumber with pleasant dreams" (15). Perhaps coincidentally, just after the passage in which Woolf describes the room as the tower of the Sleeping Beauty, Clarissa engages in her erotic reverie about Sally Seton at Bourton. Here, Clarissa alters the staging of love's first kiss, and it is Sally who awakens Clarissa to her les-bian sexuality: "Sally stopped; picked a flower; kissed her on the lips. The whole world might have turned upside down! The others disappeared; there she was alone with Sally" (*MD* 52). This refiguration of the crux of the "Sleeping Beauty" plot becomes the key to Clarissa's perception of how the fairy tale and its gender roles are played out in this scene. Despite Peter's presence, Sally becomes the Prince by virtue of the kiss and by what Clarissa characterizes as her knightly behavior. Peter Walsh is only the inadequate heterosexual substitute for the more potent female gallant; Sally remains "unvanquished" (*MD* 53).

When the perspective shifts back to present-day, Clarissa takes up her green dress to mend a tear, almost as if to stabilize or sew herself back into her heterosexual role. But we're still in the world of the fairy tale where identity is rarely absolute or unchanging. "Sleeping Beauty" is refigured once more in the scene where Peter's fantasy of male mastery is expressed through his penknife, a truncated sword with which he tries to hack through Clarissa's defenses. Unfortunately for Peter, the "brambles" shelter rather than entrap Clarissa here (*MD* 65), and Clarissa changes her own fairy tale role. She becomes a kind of Prince Charming herself, matching him blow for blow. Where Peter plays with his pocket-knife, opening and closing it shut as if attempting to pin Clarissa down to a specific identity, Clarissa counters by opening her scissors. These are not only a potentially castrating weapon, but a tool that cuts and loosens the bonds of the character to whom she is sewn. Where Peter thinks her "too cold" (*MD* 64)—still asleep to his advances?—Woolf makes it obvious that Clarissa is in fact enraged by his presence. It is her anger that prompts her to rewrite not just the Sleeping Beauty role but the fairy tale itself:

> [Clarissa], taking up her needle, summoned, like a Queen whose guards have fallen asleep and left her unprotected (she had been quite taken aback by this visit—it had upset her) so that any one can stroll in and have a look at her where she lies with the brambles curving over her, summoned to her help the things she did; the things she liked; her hus-band; Elizabeth; her self, in short, which Peter hardly knew now, all to come about her and beat off the enemy. (*MD* 65-66)

When Clarissa feels that Peter is situating her as the passive consumer who internalizes cultural texts unthinkingly, she pulls out the stitches of one ver-sion of the fairy tale and creates a new one that fits her better. She resists his patriarchal privilege, subverting the gender roles of "Sleeping Beauty" and altering the plot and characters of the story itself. Instead of remaining the passive princess, she becomes an active queen, defending herself against the prince with her needle, thread, and scissors, defending herself by restitching the narrative.

Clarissa's manipulation of the threads of the plot of "Sleeping Beauty" undercuts gendered roles like hero and heroine, or prince and princess, in the novel. In this sense, the needle and thread point to the social construction of such textual positions and to their deconstruction and reconstruction at the hands of the sewer. Clarissa is alternately and simultaneously the princess who is still asleep in her attic room, the princess who awakens herself, the princess who is awakened to her lesbian desire by another prince-princess, and the princess who fights off the prince. Instead of an intertext that calms the novel down and that sews Mrs. Dalloway and *Mrs. Dalloway* into place, "Sleeping Beauty" becomes a site of slippage and a conduit for Clarissa's expression and experience of desire. Woolf shows in *Mrs. Dalloway* how the desire of a reader—Clarissa or Woolf herself—destabilizes the cultural encoding of "Sleeping Beauty" and reconfigures the significance of the fairy tale according to a different context.

Works Cited

Abbott, Reginald. "What Miss Kilman's Petticoat Means: Virginia Woolf, Shopping, and Spectacle." *Modern Fiction Studies* 38.1 (1992): 193-216.

Barrett, Eileen. "Unmasking Lesbian Passion: The Inverted World of *Mrs. Dalloway*." *Virginia Woolf: Lesbian Readings*. Eds. Eileen Barrett and Patricia Cramer. New York: New York UP, 1997. 146-64.

Herr, Cheryl. *Joyce's Anatomy of Culture*. Urbana: U of Illinois P, 1986.

Jensen, Emily. "Clarissa Dalloway's Respectable Suicide." *Virginia Woolf: A Feminist Slant*. Ed. Jane Marcus. Lincoln: U of Nebraska P, 1983. 162-79.

Lyon, George Ella. "Virginia Woolf and the Problem of the Body." *Virginia Woolf: Centennial Essays*. Eds. Elaine K. Ginsberg and Laura Moss Gottlieb. Troy: Whitston, 1983. 111-125.

Moon, Kenneth. "Where is Clarissa? Doris Kilman in *Mrs. Dalloway*." *Clarissa Dalloway*. Ed. Harold Bloom. New York: Chelsea, 1990. 147-157.

Perrault, Charles. "The Sleeping Beauty in the Wood." *Perrault's Fairy Tales*. Trans. A. E. Johnson. New York: Dover, 1969. 1-21.

Schlack, Beverly Ann. *Continuing Presences: Virginia Woolf's Use of Literary Allusion*. University Park: Pennsylvania State UP, 1979.

Squier, Susan. *Virginia Woolf and London: The Sexual Politics of the City*. Chapel Hill: U of North Carolina P, 1985.

Tambling, Jeremy. "Repression in Mrs. Dalloway's London." *Essays in Criticism* 39.2 (1989): 137-155.

Wachman, Gay. "Pink Icing and a Narrow Bed: *Mrs. Dalloway* and Lesbian History." *Virginia Woolf and the Arts: Selected Papers from the 6th Annual Conference on Virginia Woolf*. Eds. Diane F. Gillespie and Leslie K. Hankins. New York: Pace UP, 1997. 344-50.

Wicke, Jennifer. "*Mrs. Dalloway* Goes to Market: Woolf, Keynes, and Modern Markets." *Novel: A Forum on Fiction* 28.1 (1994): 5-23.

Woolf, Virginia. *Moments of Being*. Ed. Jeanne Schulkind. Sussex: Sussex UP, 1985.

——. *Mrs. Dalloway*. San Diego: Harvest/HBJ, 1985.

Zipes, Jack. *Fairy Tales and the Art of Subversion: The Classical Genre and the Process of Civilization.* New York: Routledge, 1991.

Zwerdling, Alex. *Virginia Woolf and the Real World.* Berkeley: U of California P, 1986.

Jane de Gay
"though the fashion of the time did something to disguise it": Staging Gender in Woolf's *Orlando*

It is well attested that Virginia Woolf's awareness of the potentialities of performance underlies the narrative and social criticism of *Between the Acts*; moreover, as Steven Putzel (438-40) and Penny Farfan (207-8) have shown, such an interest may be traced back to her theater reviews of the early 1920s. This paper aims to further this debate by showing that Woolf also exhibits a strong and informed interest in theatrical history, styles and conventions in *Orlando*. It will identify allusions to theater history that complement the well-documented references to literary and national histories in the novel, showing how Woolf uses them to investigate conventional constructions of gender and to explore ways of subverting them. *Orlando* displays what Farfan has identified as Woolf's awareness of theater's potential to "subvert, through its re-enactment of conventional dramatic plots, some of the long entrenched ways of seeing and patterns of interaction that help legitimate patriarchal authority." (209) As we will see, theatrical allusions appear at key moments in the novel where descriptions of action interrupt the flow of the narrative, disrupting or questioning conventions, particularly conventions of gender.

In exploring these issues, I build on the work of those scholars who, as Sally Greene has noted, have begun to "trace within Woolf's multivalent writing the essence of performativity," (354) in particular, Madelyn Detloff's work on performativity in *Between the Acts*. Performativity is the process whereby we enact and indeed are defined by the roles we play in everyday life: it has been theorized by Judith Butler as "the reiterative and citational practice by which discourse produces the effects that it names" (2). Butler argues that such a practice may be exclusionary (it defines what is acceptable by what is left out), but that the "violence" of exclusion might be overcome by parodying norms (Butler, 53). In *Orlando* Woolf interrogates the discourse of history, as purveyed by the biographer-narrator: a discourse which seeks to define and maintain a normative subject through time. Although Butler's work does not deal specifically with performance in the theatrical sense (Butler, 12), scholars have found her account of the reiteration and subversion of conventions highly relevant to what takes place in the theater. Thus, her work provides a suitable tool for investigating a novel which explores questions of gender performance, mainly (although not exclusively) through the medium of text.

The complexities of Woolf's treatment of performance in *Orlando* are illustrated in her allusion to Shakespeare's *Othello*, which Orlando watches as he plans to elope with Sasha. Here, Woolf uses an allusion to Shakespeare's work while engaging with his own paradox that "all the world's a stage" (*As You Like It*, 2.7.138): that "real" life is theater but that theatrical performances have their own reality, not least because they stir up real emotions. Woolf describes the audience at this performance as though they are in costume: "variously rigged out as their purse or stations allowed; here in fur and broadcloth; there in tatters with their feet kept from the ice only by a dishclout bound about them" (*O* 56). These costumes signify rank in theatrical terms—the dishcloth shoes even suggest the kind of makeshift costume used by Miss La Trobe in *Between the Acts*. However, Woolf shows that there is more to clothing than the conventions of representation, because we are also told that the way these people dress has been determined by economic forces ("as their purse . . . allowed"), and so clothing is indeed the visible manifestation of underlying economic realities.

Othello itself is defamiliarized in this passage. Woolf describes the set where *Othello* is performed as "something like our Punch and Judy show" and she signals the play iconographically by the unnamed figures of a "black man . . . waving his arms and vociferating" and "a woman in white laid upon a bed" (*O* 56). Woolf further breaks the frame by describing the actors tripping over steps and the audience becoming bored. As Herbert Marder (433) and others have pointed out, there are fruitful comparisons to be made between Woolf's writing and Bertolt Brecht's alienation effect. However, although Woolf exposes the mechanics of theater, she differs from Brecht (who wanted to create a theater in which the audience was not moved to empathy) by showing how theater does indeed provoke strong emotions. Orlando empathizes with *Othello* to the extent that the "frenzy of the Moor seemed to him his own frenzy, and when the Moor suffocated the woman in her bed it was Sasha he killed with his own hands" (*O* 57). Theater may be artificial, but something "real" takes place there, too; just as dress in ordinary life may seem superficial but also betrays realities. This paradox gives theater its subversive potential. Shakespeare becomes a touchstone for the paradox, and it is appropriate that he should make a cameo appearance at several points in the novel.

A concern to explore the troubled relationship between appearance and reality is also integral to Woolf's consideration of the performance of gender. This is seen when we are introduced to Orlando in the first sentence of the novel, as "He—for there could be no doubt of his sex, though the fashion of the time did something to disguise it" (*O* 13). Here, Woolf plays with gender ambiguities by suggesting cross-dressing: the protagonist is described as "really" male, but he borders on being a female impersonator because his clothing "disguises" his sex. This description is ambivalent, because in insisting that there is no doubt about *Orlando*'s gender, the narrator implies that there may well be doubt.

We can draw parallels between the boy Orlando's ambivalent gender and theatrical history, for female roles were played by boy actors in the period when this part of the novel is set. The narrator's description of Orlando as male but wearing a feminine costume may be compared with those moments in Shakespeare's plays when the female impersonator calls attention to his biological sex, such as in the epilogue to *As You Like It*. As Phyllis Rackin (36) points out, this is a profoundly ambiguous sequence, in which the "ambivalent figure" of Rosalind "refuses to choose between actor and character or between male and female but instead insists on the ambiguities" by identifying *her*self as "the lady" and *him*self as a boy ("if I were a woman") (5.4.198, 214). Woolf thus draws on the history of theatrical conventions to exploit the discrepancies between appearance and reality and, as in Shakespeare's comedies, to question the criteria by which society distinguishes between male and female.

The illustrations to *Orlando* open up a further dimension of Woolf's treatment of gender in performance. These may be seen as performances staged by Woolf, for they consist of portraits and photographs of real people used to play fictional characters, in other words, "cast" in the roles of characters from the novel. The boy Orlando's ambivalent gender is portrayed in the frontispiece to the first edition, which illustrates his visit to Queen Elizabeth, dressed in a "lace collar, waistcoat of taffeta, and shoes with rosettes on them as big as double dahlias" (*O* 21). This plate is half a portrait by Cornelius Nuie of the two sons of Edward Sackville, fourth Earl of Dorset. The painting was made in the 1630s, but Woolf uses it to illustrate Orlando's boyhood when "the sixteenth century had still some years of its course to run" (*O* 16). By shifting the historical setting for this portrait, Woolf ignores and thus subverts the Sackville family history which the painting was commissioned to support, and she also conflates the flamboyant fashions of the seventeenth century with Elizabethan stage conventions of cross-dressing.

Woolf continues to question the criteria for distinguishing between the sexes in the scene where Sasha is introduced. She is first seen from a distance as "a figure" which may be either "boy's or woman's, for the loose tunic and trousers of the Russian fashion served to disguise the sex" (*O* 37). While her costume is sexually ambiguous, her actions seem to categorize her as male (or at least, as not female), for "no woman could skate with such speed and vigour" (*O* 38). She is pronounced to be female (or at least not male) when seen in close-up, by virtue of her physical attributes: "no boy ever had a mouth like that; no boy had those breasts; no boy had those eyes which looked as if they had been fished from the bottom of the sea" (*O* 38).

The reference to breasts seems to mark Sasha as female, but even here there is room for sexual ambiguity, for the reference to her eyes and mouth do not mark her as female so much as ironically defend a logic that if Orlando, a boy, finds her attractive, then she must be a woman.

We can explore these scenes further by drawing on Butler's theories of gender performativity. Butler argues that the materiality of sex is constructed, but it is a construct we can barely think beyond. Butler notes, for example, that we become sexual subjects at the moment we are born, for the first thing said of an infant is: "it's a girl" or "it's a boy" (7-8). However, this interpellation of a subject as male or female involves the citation of gender categories which is necessary for maintaining the status quo, for norms are unstable and may be threatened with disruption by the "abject" subject who refuses to conform to gender expectations. The narrator's declaration of Orlando and Sasha to be male and female respectively is an act of interpellation, and, as we have seen, such naming is necessary because both figures threaten to subvert gender norms. Similarly, the narrator's logic that Sasha is female because the male Orlando is attracted to her also appears unfounded: it invokes but refuses fully to justify the convention which, as Butler notes, seeks to create a normal subject who is heterosexual. Thus the unruly bodies of Orlando and Sasha threaten to disrupt the conventional narrative the biographer is trying to construct.

Orlando's unruly body further disrupts gender norms in the sex-change scene. Here, Woolf stages a scene which interrupts the flow of narrative, again challenging the power of historical discourse to create a stable, normative subject. This scene also draws on a theatrical style which celebrates ambivalence and challenges fixed categories: the contemporary, seventeenth-century mode of the masque, which disrupted the divisions between social classes and between theater and reality, for wealthy patrons traditionally assumed disguises and took part in the pageant.

The sex-change scene satirizes Orlando's biographer by interrupting the narrative with performance. The narrator has until this point sought to pursue truths and to establish and maintain categories, but at the onset of the sex-change scene s/he becomes a participant-spectator in the drama. The sequence begins with the allegorical figures of Truth, Candor and Honesty joining the biographer in the study:

> Truth, Candour, and Honesty, the austere Gods who keep watch and ward by the inkpot of the biographer, cry No! Putting their silver trumpets to their lips they demand in one blast, Truth! And again they cry Truth! and sounding yet a third time in concert they peal forth, The Truth and nothing but the Truth! (*O* 134)

Here, a theatrical performance erupts into the narrative the biographer is trying to construct. Although the figures are apparently introduced metaphorically, metaphor swiftly modulates into narrated action in the form of the three blasts of the trumpet. The next sentence confirms this shift by plunging the narrator into the same performance space as Orlando: "At which . . . the doors gently open, as if a breath of the gentlest and holiest zephyr had wafted them apart, and three figures enter" *(O* 134). The use of the present tense suggests that the doors which open here are simultaneously those of the biographer's study and those of Orlando's bedroom. The worlds of Orlando and the narrator continue to be elided as the three female figures of Purity, Chastity and Modesty place veils over Orlando (representing the censors (Hankins 184)) and compete noisily with the three Gods who shout for truth.

The scene ends with the eruption of truth in the form of a momentary unmasking: "He stood upright in complete nakedness before us, and . . . we have no choice left but confess—he was a woman" (*O* 137). As in the sequence where Sasha is revealed to be a woman, there is a shaky attempt to use the physical body as evidence of a character's sex. Drawing on Butler again, we can see that Orlando becomes female by being called a woman; the stability of this naming is called to question because Orlando is still described as "he" (it is not until a page later that the narrator decides "for convention's sake" to start using the feminine pronoun). This suggests that gender categories are preserved only by convention.

The moment of the sex-change produces sexual ambiguity of a joyous and liberating kind. The narrator gazes longingly on Orlando's naked form: "No human being . . . has ever looked more ravishing" (*O* 138). Since we never truly know whether the narrator is male or female—the narrator claims "the immunity of all biographers and historians from any sex whatever" (*O* 220)—and since Orlando at this stage is female but still called "he," the moment celebrates sexual attraction which is liberated from considerations of gender, and thus from the fear of the abject.

A second kind of performance erupts into the narrative at this point, in the form of the illustrations. Woolf remarks on the similarities between a photograph of Vita Sackville-West masquerading as "Orlando on her return to England" and a painting of Lionel Sackville, First Duke of Dorset by Rosalba Carriera, labelled "Orlando as Ambassador": "The change of sex, though it altered their future, did nothing whatever to alter their identity. Their faces remained, as their portraits prove, practically the same" (*O* 138). This statement defends a theatrical logic that two actors may play the same part and be accepted as such, and that a man can be taken for a woman and vice versa. Yet the illustrations also threaten to betray theatrical convention as a travesty. The captions make a travesty of the portraits by describing them as something they are not, while the portrait of Sackville-West is a travesty of the earlier painting, for her pose, hair style and costume mimic and parody those of her ancestor. The two portraits demonstrate the instability of conventions, for while we suspend our disbelief in accepting these people as Orlando, the differences between them and the barely disguised appearance of Sackville-West in the photograph threaten to break the frame. Yet, the illustrations also point to a deeper "truth": that Sackville-West identified strongly with men and with her male ancestors in particular. Thus Woolf uses the discrepancy between appearance and reality to point to a deeply subversive truth about Sackville-West.

Although the part of the novel following the sex-change does not invoke theatrical history specifically, we can detect a continuing engagement with Shakespearean ideas about gender identity and gender confusion in Woolf's exploration of questions about what it means to be a woman and what it means to dress like one. Woolf's descriptions of clothing in this part of the novel present gender identity as culturally determined and insecure. Woolf suggests that gender is culturally relative when she notes that *Orlando* does not realize the effects of her sex-change until she enters a culture which imposes visual markers of the differences between men and women. She is barely aware of the change when wearing the androgynous costume of the gypsies, but becomes aware of the "perils and privileges" of her new status when she takes a ship home and has to dress as "a young Englishwoman of rank" (*O* 153). Although initially annoyed by her "plaguey" skirts, Orlando is surprised to find that she enjoys being treated as a lady. She feels "indescribable pleasure" when the captain offers to cut her a delicate slice of meat, provoking a sexual reaction: "birds sang, the torrents rushed" (*O* 155). Orlando is aware that this pleasure is obtained by "roundabout" means, by acting as men expect her to behave. As in the theater, a profound emotional effect is achieved by the pantomime of taking on the mannerisms and costume of a seventeenth-century female aristocrat. Thus the scene *both* exposes the artificiality and conventionality of gendered behavior *and* testifies to its far-reaching effects.

The scene in which Orlando cross-dresses as a man is reminiscent of multiple cross-dressings in Shakespeare, such as in *As You Like It* when Rosalind poses as herself while disguised as Ganymede. Describing Orlando wearing a suit from her days as a young man, the narrator temporarily reverts to calling Orlando "he," once again unfixing distinctions between the sexes. Orlando meets a prostitute and finds that, by playing the role of a man, she begins to experience "all the feelings which become a man" (*O* 217). This statement is ironic, because rather than becoming male in this scene, Orlando may be seen to experience a moment of lesbian attraction. By describing attraction to a woman as the "feelings which become a man," the narrator ironically asserts heterosexuality as normal and threatens to render lesbian experience invisible. As Judith Butler points out, the abject body is rendered invisible in conventional discourse because it does not conform to the norms which would make it intelligible (3).

Yet rather than endorsing the cultural invisibility of female intimacy, Woolf draws attention to its invisibility and uses this to subversive effect. Woolf tells us that, since Orlando has been both male and female, she can recognize that the prostitute is behaving as she thinks men expect her to behave. With this realization, Orlando throws off her male disguise, causing the prostitute to drop her feminine mannerisms: "it was remarkable how soon on discovering that they were of the same sex, her manner changed and she dropped her plaintive, appealing ways" (*O* 218). This scene reveals conventional "feminine" behavior as something acted out for men's benefit, but it also refuses to define what, if anything, lies behind the act. While noting that women behave quite differently in all-female company, Woolf insists that this behavior remains unreadable:

> it cannot be denied that when women get together—but hist—they are always careful to see that the doors are shut and that not a word of it gets into print. All they desire is—but hist again—is that not a man's step on the stair? All they desire, we were about to say when the gentleman took the very words out of our mouths. Women have no desires, says this gentleman, coming into Nell's parlour; only affectations. (*O* 219)

The passage suggests that there is an all-female subculture where female ways of behaving are validated but also remain independent of the play-acting which constitutes the cultural understanding of femininity. Woolf thus sketches out a reality behind appearances which is unreadable, but as a result subversive and secret.

Woolf takes to an extreme the idea of performance as something which hides women's experience in the scene where Orlando gives birth. Again, she evokes a contemporary theatrical style: the birth, which is set in the mid-nineteenth century, takes place during an interlude reminiscent of the Victorian music-hall, thus masking an event which Victorian prudishness would wish to suppress. The narrator evades describing the birth by cutting to a series of sketches of city life accompanied by music from a barrel organ, before simply reiterating the conventional statement that "Orlando was safely delivered of a son" (*O* 295). This highlights the cultural invisibility of women's physical experience by showing that childbirth lies beyond the conventions of representation.

Towards the end of the novel, there is a suggestion that women's exclusion from patriarchal representation may enable them to confound its categories: "the truth is that when we write of a woman, everything is out of place—culminations and perorations; the accent never falls where it does with a man" (*O* 312). The passage following this statement shows that the figure of Orlando refuses to be contained or constrained by the conventional male biographical narrative because she has many selves, forged by the many roles she has played. Orlando summons up her various selves, and each one enters as though fulfilling a stage direction (one is clumsy, one comes "skipping"), and each expresses a different point of view, as if contributing to a choral poem. The performance outlined in this closing phase (which even includes a song) complements the performance taking place in the novel's illustrations, in which three different people are "cast" as Orlando. The multiple selves evoked are secret and subversive for, we are told, they fall silent when Orlando talks aloud, entering into conventional discourse and assuming "what is called, rightly or wrongly, a single self, a real self" (*O* 314). The representation of Orlando's many selves in order to complicate the "normal" integrated singular identity may be read in terms of Butler's account of subverting norms by parodying them. However, in view of the Shakespearean influences discussed in this paper, Woolf's modernist sketch for a theatrical performance in this scene also may be seen to look back to the idea that each person plays many different parts during a lifetime, as suggested in Jaques' "seven ages of man" speech in *As You Like It* (2.7.138-65)—or even further back to the medieval morality plays where different attributes of a character, such as Everyman, were played by different actors. Thus Woolf invokes theater history in order to challenge the concept of the unified, normative subject that underpins historical and biographical discourse. This is an early example of the subversive use of performance history which she would put to even more radical effect in *Between the Acts*, as Melba Cuddy-Keane has demonstrated.

This paper has shown how Woolf invokes theatrical conventions and history as an integral part of her exploration of gender identity in *Orlando*: she uses these to question and expose the historical construction of gender, to disrupt conventions, and at times to posit ways in which it may be possible to think beyond gender. Furthermore, as we have seen, Woolf takes what we might call a directorial view, sketching out performances in her text, and conducting performances in the illustrations, in which the subversion of gender norms may be realized.

Works Cited

Butler, Judith. *Bodies that Matter: On the Discursive Limits of "Sex."* New York and London: Routledge, 1993.

Cuddy-Keane, Melba. "The Politics of Comic Modes in Virginia Woolf's *Between the Acts.*" *PMLA* 105 (1990): 273–85.

Detloff, Madelyn. "Thinking Peace into Existence: The Spectacle of History in *Between the Acts.*" *Women's Studies* 28 (1999): 403-33.

Farfan, Penny. "Writing/Performing: Virginia Woolf Between the Acts." *Text and Performance Quarterly* 16 (1996): 205-15.

Greene, Sally. "Introduction: Virginia Woolf in Performance." *Women's Studies* 28 (1999): 353-59.

Hankins, Leslie Kathleen. "*Orlando*: 'A Precipice Marked V' between 'A Miracle of Discretion' and 'Lovemaking Unbelievable: Indiscretions Incredible'." *Virginia Woolf: Lesbian Readings.* Ed. E. Barrett and P. Cramer. New York: New York UP, 1997. 180-202.

Marder, Herbert. "Alienation Effects: Dramatic Satire in *Between the Acts*." *Papers on Language and Literature* 24 (1988): 423-35.

Putzel, Steven. "Virginia Woolf and the 'Distance of the Stage'." *Women's Studies* 28 (1999): 435-90.

Rackin, Phyllis. "Androgyny, Mimesis, and the Marriage of the Boy Heroine on the English Renaissance Stage." *PMLA* 102 (1987): 29-41.

Shakespeare, William. *The Complete Arden Shakespeare*. General Ed.: Richard Proudfoot. London and New York: Methuen, 1985.

Woolf, Virginia. *Orlando*. San Diego: Harvest/Harcourt Brace Jovanovich, 1973.

Lisa Carstens
The Science of Sex and the Art of Self-Materializing in *Orlando*

Virginia Woolf's *Orlando* is about the natural fluidity of gender identity, or, correspondingly, about how culture falsely constructs gender as if it were not fluid but fixed, reductively, into either male or female. This, at least, is the position taken by a great deal of *Orlando* criticism across the past few decades, as when Sandra Gilbert asserts that in *Orlando* "costumes are selves and thus easily, fluidly, interchangeable" (405, her emphasis), when Francette Pacteau sees in *Orlando* a "displace[ment of] identity from the body to the costume" (81), and when Talia Schaffer reads gender in the novel as "an endlessly shifting intersection of sartorial signs that have no relation to any genital referent" (29). The fluidity of Orlando's gender role-playing, statements in the novel about how clothes "change our view of the world and the world's view of us" (187), and a change of sex that leaves Orlando "in every other respect . . . precisely as he had been" (138) would certainly seem to accord with a position that gendered selves are changeable performances with no essential grounds.

Yet, I think we can be misled by what is finally our and not Virginia Woolf's understanding of the ungroundedness of sexed identity. I do not dispute the view that Woolf rejects reductive notions of gender identity, but I see Woolf's play with questions of gender and identity to be much more closely aligned with the science and psychology of sex in her own day than with post-sixties concepts of gender. Putting Woolf back into her contemporary context highlights that Woolf insists not on the groundlessness of sex but on the forceful materiality of sex, even if it be a culturally mediated materiality. Woolf's emphasis on the material force of sex is important because it grounds her response to that force: she offers the material force of art as a counterforce to gender's power over cultural identities. She demonstrates art's counterforce not just within the story of Orlando but in the fascinating ways that she inserts her own body into the text of *Orlando*, materializing herself in the text in a way that extends her identity beyond conventional limitations.

The science of corporeal identity contemporary with Woolf's writing provides a context within which the apparent gender fluidity in *Orlando* emerges as a more complicated exploration of what sounds at first like the opposite: the corporeal materiality of sex. Orlando's gender fluidity is in fact quite compatible with early twentieth-century scientific accounts of sex identity. Between 1880 and 1910, the reproductive sciences, sexology, and psychoanalysis all accepted and developed variants of the theory that bodies are bisexually constituted (see, for instance, biologists Geddes and Thompson, sexologist Krafft-Ebing, psychoanalyst Freud), an idea Woolf echoes in *A Room of One's Own* when she hypothesizes that "there are two sexes in the mind corresponding to the two sexes in the body" (98). While critical debates have revolved around identifying the authorized perspective on gender in the novel, the narrator emphasizes this theory of internal bisexuality: "Different though the sexes are, they intermix. In every human being a vacillation from one sex to the other takes place, and often it is only the clothes that keep the male or female likeness, while underneath the sex is the very opposite of what it is above" (188). Woolf's imaginative development of this idea in *Orlando* confirms that she takes the narrator's explanation quite literally: she does not imply that the body is a neutral site that can be performed as man or woman, and certainly not at will; she implies that the mind is male *and* female, and that the body performs differently depending on which sexual mode demands expression and how historical conditions pressure particular gendered performances. While one could insist on the materiality of sex even if it were entirely socially constructed, Woolf does not trouble herself with that distinction, drawing instead upon the way in which a sexual difference relying upon a bisexual constitution already destabilizes any claim to natural and pure male and female identities. Rather than wholly socially-constructed, the gendered self is thus grounded in a biology that is an enabling multiplicity, as signaled in the choice of pronouns the narrator uses to describe Orlando's sex change: "The change of sex, though it altered *their* future, did nothing whatever to alter *their* identity" (138, emphasis added).

Notably, Orlando's special relationship to sex and gender is depicted as more exception than rule even in this novel. Orlando has a bisexual constitution that may be shared by all humans, but she is rare in her outright manifestation of that internal difference. As the narrator says of her, her "sex changed far more frequently than those who have worn only one set of clothing can conceive" (*O* 221). Woolf may be more like her contemporaries than like her late twentieth-century critics here, too, in subordinating the question of gender *per se* to the question, more pressing to the modernist writers of her era, of what sets an artist apart from the crowd. For, the character of Orlando is less a portrait of common gender fluidity than a portrait of the artist, where the artist is largely signified by exceptional gender fluidity or multiplicity.

As an artist Orlando is depicted as a kind of "third sex." The "third sex" is a phrase coined by novelist Théophile Gautier in his 1835 novel *Mademoiselle de Maupin* to describe a woman who, in loving another woman, could not be assimilated into the heterosexual matrix of man or woman. We could say that the third sex is the homosexual, but to do so would be to lose the "neither-and-both" complexity that both Gautier and Woolf attempt to articulate. Gautier's third sex is a culturally scandalous identity precisely because it cannot be assimilated; Orlando's artistic temperament is scandalous in strikingly similar terms. Indeed, the narrator recognizes both Orlando's sex change and his artistic temperament as obscene, literally aspects to keep out of sight: At the moment of Orlando's sex change, our ladies of Purity, Chastity and Modesty, and the narrator, shout "Hide! Hide! Hide!" (136), wishing to "spare the reader" the fact of Orlando's sex change by saying instead that "Orlando died and was buried" (134). In the same way, the narrator wishes he did not have to recognize in Orlando features of the artist that destroy Orlando's otherwise conventional promise: "Directly we glance at eyes and forehead, we have to admit a thousand disagreeables which it is the aim of every good biographer to ignore. Sights disturbed him; . . . sights exalted him" (15-16)–in other words, scandalously, Orlando sees the world through an artist's eyes and mind. Recognizing the obscenity of his compulsion to write, Orlando the man hides his writings because they are inappropriate for a nobleman; as a woman, she hides her writings because they are inappropriately intellectual and professional for a woman.

Orlando's artist quality is further made analogous to a third sex in the sense that it carries the same ambiguous androgynous character that marks Orlando's gender play—indeed, it could be said to stand for, if not stand as the material cause of, Orlando's androgyny. The same "disagreeable" eyes and forehead which signify Orlando's compulsion to "[take] out a writing book" (16) mark him at the same time as sexually ambivalent: he has "eyes like drenched violets," a very feminine portrait of male eyes, and a "brow like the swelling of a marble dome pressed between the two blank medallions which were his temples" (15)—a genitally-ambiguous figuration, with its "swollen dome" and "two blank medallions." We are reminded that in *A Room of One's Own* Woolf argues that to be an artist "one must be womanmanly or man-womanly" (104). Orlando is not man nor woman so much as artist, where artist is both—which is to say that the artist is profoundly bi-sexed, "bi-selfed," self-different.

If Woolf opens up the nature of identity (at least for the artist) to make sex, first, multiple and, second, a supporting rather than centrally-determining factor in the constitution of a self, she further opens up the horizons of gender identity through her play with how the very materiality of the body

41

promises extensions rather than reductions of agency. The artist's fluidity allows the artist, unlike the average citizen, to counter the material force of gender prescriptions with the equally material force of artistic self-extension. Woolf here seems to play with an idea similar to that introduced by one of her own doctors, Sir Henry Head. Head was a prominent London neurologist consulted by the Woolfs in 1913 (Bell v2 15). He is more famous for his contributions to a modern understanding of what he called the "postural body," also called the ego or the body-image, as an experientially-shaped and malleable sense of the self's boundaries and capabilities. In a 1920 collection, Head argues that the body keeps a running record of the ways it can move. Head uses the word "schema" to describe the standard of the body image as it is created and continually revised by the history of postures that the body performs. Our notions of our bodily selves could be described as the ongoing materialization of our experiences. Furthermore, our body-images are not limited to literal skin-boundaries but may take in objects such as eyeglasses and canes through which we extend ourselves into the world. Head writes, "It is to the existence of these 'schemata' that we owe the power of projecting our recognition of posture, movement and locality beyond the limits of our own bodies to the end of some instrument held in the hand. . . . Anything which participates in the conscious movement of our bodies is added to the model of ourselves and becomes part of these schemata; a woman's power of localisation may extend to the feather in her hat" (Head 606; Grosz cites a nearly identical passage from a 1911 article by Head and Holmes).

This record of experience constructs one's sense of one's body and of what it can do. Whether or not Woolf knew Head's work in this area, her consideration of how clothes predispose one to certain gendered limits shares provocative similarities. Woolf notes that "The man has his hand free to seize his sword; the woman must use hers to keep the satins from slipping from her shoulders" (188)—or to preen the feather on her hat, in Head's own example. Hence, "It is the clothes that wear us, and not we them" (188). Both literally and figuratively, the female body does not extend as far in space as does a man's, and so it does not know that it could. Yet Woolf also exploits the liberatory potential in this concept of malleable and extendable body-image. Woolf implies that, because every body contains at least two sexes (indeed, "two sexes are quite inadequate" [*AROO* 88]), the body *does* know that it could extend in ways that the limitations of the cultural male/female binary interdict. Hence, "It was a change in Orlando herself that dictated her choice of a woman's dress and of a woman's sex" (188). Woolf rejects a strictly socially determined model of identity in favor of a belief in a core, if multiple, self that seeks expression. As it expresses its multiplicity, it materializes and makes real the expansion of self that follows from an expansion of activity.

Although clothing exemplifies for both Head and Woolf one way in which the body-image extends itself artificially or technologically, Woolf, with her artist-protagonist, emphasizes another and yet more powerful way: through art. *Orlando*, of all Woolf's novels, offers art not just as a *figure* for the extension of self and authority but as the literal material extension of self. The novel *Orlando* represents art as the "root" of Orlando's material self in its play on the Oak Tree as both the title of the work of poetry that Orlando strives to develop across his 350-year progress as an artist and as a literal tree to which Orlando always returns to ground him/herself. In the first pages of the novel, Orlando flings himself at the foot of the oak tree because

> He loved, beneath all this summer transiency, to feel the earth's spine beneath him; for such he took the hard root of the oak tree to be; [. . .] he felt the need of something which he could attach his floating heart to; [. . .] To the oak tree he tied it [. . .] and he lay so still that by degrees the deer stepped nearer and the rooks wheeled round him and the swallows dipped and circled and the dragon-flies shot past, as if all the fertility and the amorous activity of a summer's evening were woven web-like about his body. (19)

In other words, the tree becomes a spine and suit of clothes that extends Orlando's body-image to the whole of nature, thereby endowing Orlando with its non-sex-specific creative fertility. If the oak tree metaphorically extends Orlando's identity, Orlando's poem of the same name does so more literally, in that Orlando's illicit passion for writing is what drives her to override naturalized laws of sexed identity. Indeed, commenting that, in vacillating between the two sexes, Orlando was "expressing rather more openly than usual—openness indeed was the soul of her nature—something that happens to most people without being thus plainly expressed" (189), the narrator would seem to be describing the difference between the artist and common folk. The openness of Orlando's soul is the boundary-breaking dimension that artistic mediation brings to conventional realizations of the self.

Sexual multiplicity is then just one aspect of the multiply-rooted self. Toward the end of the novel, Orlando the published author returns to the tree, and, again, "Flinging herself on the ground, she felt the bones of the tree running out like ribs from a spine this way and that beneath her. She liked to think that she was riding the back of the world. She liked to attach herself to something hard" (324). Just as Orlando shares the tree's hidden and extended roots, the self emerges in its attachments beyond a skin-bounded body. If the self is necessarily a multi-sexed self, it is also always a multi-localized self, a self produced and extended as self-externalization, the displacement of self beyond any closed boundaries.

In this sense, the dispersal of self is, ironically, the greatest extension of self, akin to Donna Haraway's portrait of the late twentieth-century cyborg as "a matter of fiction and lived experience that changes what counts as women's experience" (149). Woolf plays with dispersion as extension not only in the representation of Orlando as multiply-gendered artist but in the enigmatic weaving of herself into *Orlando*. The fact that *Orlando* is a playful biography of Vita Sackville-West was from the novel's beginnings an open secret, and is no less one way that Woolf writes herself into the narrative. But Woolf also places her body into this text through an intriguing use of calendar dates in the novel. For instance, the birth of Orlando's son occurs on the very date (March 20) that Woolf announced the completion of the first draft of *Orlando* to Vita (*D3* 176; Sackville-West 264). Since Woolf inserted this and other dates later, in the revision process (compare the Holograph with the final text), she self-consciously chose this date, implicitly identifying the birth of Orlando's son with the birth of *Orlando* as the child of her and Vita's intertwined lives. This mapping of their private correspondence onto a scene of sexual reproduction adds to the "scandalous" character of Orlando's childbearing, which the narrator treats with as much chagrin as he treated Orlando's sex change.

In another suggestive correlation of dates, Orlando's first trance occurs during the month in which Leonard read the *Orlando* draft for the first time (*D3* 183-84)—in other words, Orlando's "pause" occurs when Woolf herself had suspended writing. The date of Orlando's second trance ("Saturday the 18th," which correlates with February of 1928) is even more provocative. On that date in Woolf's life she recorded the following in her diary: "I had thought to write the quickest most brilliant pages in *Orlando* yesterday—not a drop came, all, forsooth, for the usual physical reasons, which delivered themselves today. It is the oddest feeling: as if a finger stopped the flow of the ideas in the brain; it is unsealed and the blood rushes all over the place" (*D3* 175). Quentin Bell notes that Woolf was in bed with influenza in mid-February (Bell v2 239), and Woolf alludes in her diary in March to having been fluish and headachey since February (*D3* 177). Yet, the language of blood suggests that Woolf may also have been put out by her own seven day trance, her menstrual period. (According to Hermione Lee, Woolf's periods were always disabling and frequently accompanied by depression [181].) If Orlando's trance corresponds with Woolf's period, the trance is an ironically fitting precursor to Orlando's sex change to woman. Either way, Orlando's pause expresses a pause in Woolf's writing process, making literal Woolf's claim, in *A Room of One's Own*, that "The book has somehow to be adapted to the body" (78). The novel emerges as an extension of Woolf's material life, expressing Woolf's physiological, social and sexual as well as her emotional experiences. One can read Woolf in *Orlando*, not in the superficial content but in the stops and starts, the interruptions and the ecstasies that are the writing process made manifest and the artist made art.

Obviously, the novel is not in this way sutured to her body, and, unless she's using it to swat flies, it does not take on the kind of instrumentality that Henry Head had in mind as extending one's body-image. Yet, in her description of the process of writing *Orlando*, Woolf shows herself to be existing differently in the world in relation to this very writing process. We could say that she not only adapts the book to her body but adapts her body to the book. She writes:

> [I] am launched somewhat furtively but with all the more passion upon *Orlando: a Biography*. . . . I walk making up phrases; sit, contriving scenes; am in short in the thick of the greatest rapture known to me; [. . .] the relief of turning my mind that way was such that I felt happier than for months [. . .] and abandoned myself to the pure delight of this farce; which I enjoy as much as I've ever enjoyed anything. (*D3* 161-62)

The way in which her rhetoric alternates between active and passive verbs—she "is launched," yet she walks, makes up phrases, contrives scenes, but yet again she "abandon[s]" herself to the farce—further portrays Woolf as writing "beside herself"—split between the conventional biological body (which sometimes, through accident of illness and sex, limits her agency) and the technological body of the book, which provides an entirely other imaginative domain through which to extend the body's agencies. It is in this sense that *Orlando* seems a particularly provocative illustration of how art is a mode of self-difference that, for Woolf, does not merely *represent* the subject but *materializes* the subject in powerful ways, and in ways that naturally resist the simple binary of conventional sexual difference.

Works Cited

Bell, Quentin. *Virginia Woolf: A Biography (*Volume One, *Virginia Stephen, 1882-1912;* Volume Two, *Mrs. Woolf, 1912-1941).* New York: Quality Paperback Book Club, 1992.

Freud, Sigmund. *Three Essays on the Theory of Sexuality.* 1905. Trans. and Rev. James Strachey. New York: Basic Books, 1962.

Gautier, Théophile. *Mademoiselle de Maupin.* 1835. Trans. Joanne Richardson. Harmondsworth: Penguin Books, 1981.

Geddes, Patrick and Arthur Thomson. *The Evolution of Sex.* London: Walter Scott, 1889.

Gilbert, Sandra. "Costumes of the Mind: Transvestism as Metaphor in Modern Literature." *Critical Inquiry* 7.2 (Winter 1980): 391-418.

Grosz, Elizabeth. *Volatile Bodies: Toward a Corporeal Feminism. Theories of Representation and Difference.* Bloomington: Indiana UP, 1994.

Head, Henry. *Studies in Neurology*, v. 2 (2 vols). London: Oxford UP, 1920.

Krafft-Ebing, Richard von. *Psychopathia Sexualis.* Trans. from 12th ed. by Franklin S. Klaf. New York: Stein and Day, 1965.

Lee, Hermione. *Virginia Woolf.* New York: Alfred A. Knopf, 1997.

Pacteau, Francette. "The Impossible Referent: Representations of the Androgyne." *Formations of Fantasy.* Ed. Victor Burgin, et al. London: Methuen, 1986. 62-84.

Sackville-West, Vita. *The Letters of Vita Sackville-West to Virginia Woolf.* Eds. Louise DeSalvo and Mitchell A. Leaska. New York: William Morrow and Co., 1985.

Schaffer, Talia. "Posing Orlando." *Genders* 19 (1994): 26-63.

Woolf, Virginia. *A Room of One's Own.* 1929. New York: Harvest/Harcourt Brace, 1989.

——. *The Diary of Virginia Woolf,* Vol.3: 1925-1930. Ed. Anne Olivier Bell with Andrew McNeillie. New York: Harcourt, 1980.

——. *Orlando: A Biography.* New York: Harvest/Harcourt Brace, 1928.

——. *Orlando: The Original Holograph Draft.* Transcribed and ed. Stuart Nelson Clarke. London: SN Clarke, 1993.

Diana L. Swanson
With Clear-Eyed Scrutiny: Gender, Authority, and the Narrator as Sister in *Jacob's Room*

Jacob's Room not only marks a turning point in Woolf's development of her particular modernist form and style but also in her ongoing consideration of gender and social authority. Vara Neverow and William Handley have in different ways analyzed the continuity between the critique of war and sexual inequality in *Jacob's Room* and Woolf's later political writing, especially *Three Guineas* and *A Room of One's Own.* Part of what I see Woolf doing in the 1930s is reenvisioning the social and political relations between the sexes in order to replace the daughter-father relationship with the sister-brother relationship as the paradigm for female-male social relations. A necessary prior step in this reenvisioning is the clear-eyed scrutiny of the brother by his sister. This important developmental step happens in *Jacob's Room.*

Is it not one of the uniquely complicated and confusing aspects of women's oppression that the oppressor is in the family? In *A Room of One's Own,* Woolf famously declares that just from the evidence of the front page of one daily paper "the most transient visitor to this planet . . . could not fail to be aware [. . .] that England is under the rule of a patriarchy" (33). I believe analysis of her work as a whole reveals the development of a vision of a more egalitarian social order figured in a familial metaphor. In previous work, I argued that in *The Years* and *Three Guineas* Woolf shifts the focus of the gaze of "the daughters of educated men" (*TG*) "away from the father to the political and social world," "the male-female relationship of concern becomes the sister-brother rather than the daughter-father relationship," and "the daughter begins to place herself on the same plane with men. She turns from looking up [at the father] to looking ahead, side by side with her brothers. She begins to take herself seriously as a political thinker and actor. She begins to envision a 'new world' (*TY* 422)" (Swanson 29, 31).

Woolf invokes Sophocles's Antigone in this metaphorical dismantling of patriarchy, using Antigone as a figure both for the damage done to daughters in the patriarchal family and the independent vision of which the resistant daughter is capable despite her oppression (Swanson 28). That Oedipus was not only Antigone's father but also her brother is suggestive. This fact can be interpreted to indicate that the brother in the patriarchal family is often a father-surrogate, that his position vis-a-vis the daughter is similar to the father's in power and authority, that the private brother becomes the public patriarch. But it also suggests an opening, a crack in the system, an opportunity for restructuring relations between women and men.

It is also suggestive that Antigone's so-called crime is to perform her brother's due burial rites against the decree of the city's ruler. Antigone's actions recognize her brother as a human being but Creon defines her actions as disloyalty to the state. I suggest we consider the narrator of *Jacob's Room* a modern Antigone come to bury the war dead. The narrator recognizes her "brother" dead in the Great War as a human being not a national ideal and thus refuses to participate in the idealization and reverence of the war poetry, memoirs, and biographies that came out during and after WWI. Alex Zwerdling states that the narrator's

> irreverence might well have seemed offensive to a generation of readers trained to think about the dead soldiers by the literature World War I produced. These works [. . .] convey a sense of high idealism or heroic indignation or romantic intensity [. . . .] They] treat the war dead with absolute seriousness [. . . .] /By contrast, Woolf's elegiac novel is persistently small-scaled, mischievous, and ironic. [Woolf] had an instinctive distrust for reverence of any kind, treating it as a fundamentally dishonest mental habit that made symbols out of flesh-and-blood human beings. (72-73)

As Judith Hattaway says, Woolf disliked "the way that [lives] cut short had been pressed into the service of national myth-making" (21). The citizens of England were called upon to mourn, memorialize, and glorify the fallen young men, but the narrator of *Jacob's Room* insists on sorrowing, scrutinizing, and satirizing. In "the conditions of [her] love" and "the manner of [her] seeing" the narrator is disloyal to patriarchal fictions and the patriarchal, militaristic state.

Many critics have noted that *Jacob's Room* is as much or more about the process and problems of observing Jacob than it is about Jacob, and the narrator is as central a character as is Jacob. I would refine these observations to say that the novel is as much about *women* observing Jacob as about observing Jacob, and the narrator is the female character who most sees through Jacob and most knows she doesn't know him. Many women look at and ponder Jacob over the course of the novel: Betty Flanders, Mrs. Norman in the train, Clara Durrant, Mrs. Durrant, Julia Eliot, Florinda, Mrs. Papworth who cleans for Bonamy, an unnamed hotel chambermaid, Julia Hedge the feminist in the British Museum, Fanny Elmer, Sandra Wentworth Williams. These characters are variously impressed, intimidated, intrigued, and attracted by Jacob. For the sake of brevity, I will concentrate here on the female characters of approximately Jacob's own age. Clara Durrant idealizes him, thinking "'You're too good, too good,'" "thinking that he must not say that he loved her" (63). She sees him as "unworldly" yet also "frightening" (71), and is reduced to a silent, hopeless longing, the words "Jacob, Jacob" echoing in her mind (166). Florinda says that Jacob is like one of the statues in the British Museum, and Julia Hedge, doing her research in the British Museum and wishing they'd left room for an Eliot or Brontë in the ring of men's names on the dome of the reading room, sees Jacob as one of the men in control of knowledge and the world: "she applied herself to her gigantic labours but perceived through one of the nerves of her exasperated sensibility how composedly, unconcernedly, and with every consideration the male readers applied themselves to theirs. That young man for example" (106). Fanny Elmer falls in love with him, impressed by "how little he said and yet how firm it was" and imagines herself keeping his home: "how childlike he would be, come in tired of an evening, she thought, and how majestic; a little overbearing perhaps; 'But I wouldn't give way'" (117). She is impressed too by his greater access to money: "And isn't it pleasant, Fanny went on thinking, how young men bring out lots of silver coins from their trouser pockets [. . .] instead of having just so many in a purse?" (117). She too perceives Jacob as firmly situated in the classical tradition, seeing Jacob in the statue of Ulysses at the British Museum. Desperate at his inattention, she at least briefly thinks of suicide. In short, Jacob's female peers see him through the lens of gender which magnifies and gives authority to Jacob's every move or silence, eroticizes his aloofness, control, self-absorption, and repression of emotion, and puts the women into a position of waiting and passivity.

Like the other women characters, the narrator feels both fear of and attraction to Jacob but unlike the others she sees the lens of gender as well as Jacob. During one of her discussions of the impossibility of ever completely knowing another person or conveying that knowledge in words, she points out

> the effect of sex—how between man and woman it hangs wavy, tremulous, so that here's a valley, there's a peak, when in truth, perhaps, all's as flat as my hand. Even the exact words get the wrong accent on them. But something is always impelling one to hum vibrating, like the hawk moth, at the mouth of the cavern of mystery, endowing Jacob Flanders with all sorts of qualities he had not at all [. . . . O]ver him we hang vibrating. (73)

So the narrator brings with her a consciousness of the effects of gender on reality and relationships and unlike the other women characters, the narrator takes an active part toward Jacob, vibrating above and darting in and out like a film camera operator on a boom, using this perspective and then that, sometimes commenting, sometimes letting the juxtaposition of pictures, of perspectives, do the work.

For example, she shows us Jacob, Bonamy, and their friends at Cambridge feeling indignant and up against the world: "one wants to write poetry too and to love—oh, the brutes! It's damnably difficult." But then she comments "but, after all, not so difficult if on the next staircase, in the large room, there are two, three, five young men all convinced of this—of brutality, that is, and the clear division between right and wrong" (44). She thus makes gentle fun of these privileged young men and points out their advantages of community and leisure. She then juxtaposes the scene in the Cambridge student rooms with a different picture that comes before her mind's eye: "the bare hills of Turkey—sharp lines, dry earth, coloured flowers, and colours on the shoulders of the women, standing naked-legged in the stream to beat linen on the stones. [. . .]But none of that could show clearly through the swaddlings and blanketings of the Cambridge night" (44). These young men who feel themselves to be in the center of the world cannot actually see much of the world, particularly parts of the world alien to them by culture and gender. While thinking of themselves as unappreciated Keatsian rebels, they are swaddled, babied, coddled. Cambridge, which sees itself as steeped in knowledge, worldly, from another perspective can seem provincial. This scene ends with the famous passages about Jacob feeling himself the inheritor of the civilization embodied and handed down by Cambridge; he looks "masterly" and as he walks back to his rooms, "the old stone echoed with magisterial authority" (46). But we have been prepared, if we've been paying attention, for the opening of the next chapter, which provides a significant contrast to Jacob's Cambridge sense of well-being, happiness, and security. Jacob and Timothy Durrant are on the yacht; they've argued about the right way to open a can of beef; Jacob broke the stove; the pages of Shakespeare stick together with salt water and eventually blow overboard. The leisure, serenity, well-being of Cambridge days depends on someone else doing the cooking and the cleaning, on someone else maintaining the material fabric of life so that reading the classics can go on smoothly and magisterially. With humor and without direct statement, the narrator has pointed out that Jacob's control, dignity, majesty, satisfaction depend on what he cannot see from Cambridge, on women beating linen, on hierarchies of gender, class, and nation.

In this manner, over the course of the novel the narrator shows us Jacob's unthinking privilege, his advantages, his schooling into the British masculinist and imperialist worldview, his misogyny, but also his idealism, his naivete, his beauty, his vitality and enthusiasm, his first experience of falling in love, his unsureness about his future career. And in the end, she leaves us with a sense of both his mysteriousness as an other and the pathos and waste of his death. Bonamy marvels "'What did he expect? Did he think he would come back?'" Mrs. Flanders, cleaning her son's room once again and for the last time, holds up Jacob's shoes and asks "'What am I to do with these, Mr. Bonamy?'" (176). No one can fill Jacob's shoes because no matter how typical of his sex and class he may be no one else is Jacob; we will never know whether or not Jacob would have been able to make a form through which to embody and live his individuality (*JR* 36).

Two articles in a recent issue of *Woolf Studies Annual* present contrasting views on the narrator of *Jacob's Room*. Catherine Nelson-McDermott argues that Jacob is "unflatteringly presented by the narrator because he is in training to be a patriarch" and that the novel is a parody that "holds up to ridicule many different aspects of the patriarchy" (84, 92). Sebastian Knowles, on the other hand, says that "Woolf's narrator is amused, and she is in love, and thus must abdicate the seat of narrative power. The 'our' of 'Such the conditions of our love' is a pronoun in transition, marking the move from a narrator in total power to a narrator unable to see [. . . .] The narrator's blindness is the blindness of a woman in love with a young man" (112). I argue that the narrator's relationship to Jacob is more complex and ultimately more transformative and challenging than either of these readings suggest. It is the voice of the sister, at once grieving, puzzling, criticizing, and understanding, who sees Jacob as the willing product of an elitist and patriarchal social system, as a deluded victim of that system, as a human being struggling for meaning, and as an always unknowable other. Her acknowledgement of Jacob's unknowability is a mark of respect, a refusal to delimit and objectify Jacob unlike the examiners at the University or the men in the Cabinet. This narrator is at once more critical and less judgmental than critics have made her.

The narrator of *Jacob's Room* is the precursor—or in Neverow's term a "sister/self"—of the narrator of *Three Guineas* who, as an every-daughter of educated men, addresses her brother directly and as an equal, who realizes her own agency and decides her own terms for participation in the public sphere. Through the critical yet loving narrator of *Jacob's Room*, Woolf deconstructs the power and privilege of the middle-class son/brother and his idealized image in the eyes of young women such as Clara or Fanny and of older women such as Mrs. Durrant or Sandra Wentworth Williams. She shows as well the price Jacob and men like him pay for accepting the privileges of and playing their parts in the patriarchal system. This critique is a necessary step in Woolf's reenvisioning of social authority and gender.

Works Cited

Handley, William R. "War and the Politics of Narration in *Jacob's Room.*" In Hussey, ed. 110-133.

Hattaway, Judith. "Virginia Woolf's *Jacob's Room*: History and Memory." In Dorothy Goldman, ed. *Women and World War I: The Written Response.* London: MacMillan, 1993. 14-30.

Hussey, Mark. "Living in a War Zone: An Introduction to Virginia Woolf as a War Novelist." In Mark Hussey, ed. 1-13.

Hussey Mark, ed. *Virginia Woolf and War: Fiction, Reality, and Myth.* Syracuse, NY: Syracuse UP, 1991.

Knowles, Sebastian D. G. "Narrative, Death, and Desire: The Three Senses of Humor in *Jacob's Room.*" *Woolf Studies Annual* 5 (1999): 97-114.

Nelson-McDermott, Catherine. "Disorderly Conduct: Parody and Coded Humor in *Jacob's Room* and *The Years.*" *Woolf Studies Annual* 5 (1999): 79-96.

Neverow, Vara. "Thinking Back Through Our Mothers, Thinking in Common: Virginia Woolf's Photographic Imagination and the Community of Narrators in *Jacob's Room, A Room of One's Own,* and *Three Guineas.*" In Jeanette McVicker and Laura Davis, eds. *Virginia Woolf and Communities: Selected Papers from the Eighth Annual Conference on Virginia Woolf.* NY: Pace UP, 1999. 65-90.

Swanson, Diana L. "An Antigone Complex? The Political Psychology of *The Years* and *Three Guineas.*" *Woolf Studies Annual* 3 (1997): 28-44.

Woolf, Virginia. (1922). *Jacob's Room.* NY: Harcourt Brace Jovanovich, 1950.

Zwerdling, Alex. *Virginia Woolf and the Real World.* Berkeley: U of California P, 1986.

Archives and Readers

Edward L. Bishop
From Frass to Foucault: Mediations of the Archive

Gerard Genette draws attention to the paratext, the thresholds we must cross before encountering the text itself, and which mediate our experience of the text. In the past I have spoken about the mediating experiences of dust jackets, of bookstores, and most recently of page design in manuscript transcriptions of Woolf. Here I want to open up the archive, to explore some connections between the theoretical writings of Derrida and Foucault and the actual archives we work in. Foucault says, "The archive is first the law of what can be said" (129). For me, the archive begins at a wine and cheese party, at an academic conference. Over the din of scholars consuming free wine, a young man shouted at me, "Why don't *you* edit *Jacob's Room*? She'll never let me back in."

He had just come from the Berg Collection in New York, where the curator, after discovering the young man was a graduate student, declared, "I won't have *my* material used for cheap theses," and punted him from the collection. Foucault was right: "The archive is first the law of what can be said."

Derrida would not have been surprised. Though he claims, "Nothing is less reliable, nothing is less clear today than the word 'archive'" (90), and cheerfully sets out to make it less clear in his book *Archive Fever*, he does begin with a helpful etymology. He reminds us that "archive" derives from *arkheion*: a house, a domicile, an address, residence of the superior magistrates, the *archons*, those who command. It is in their house that the documents or law were filed; and they have the power to interpret the documents. It is in this state of "domiciliation," this "house arrest" that archives exist. Also, the concept of the archive shelters in itself the memory of the name *arkhe*, but it also shelters itself from this memory which it *shelters*; which is the same as saying it forgets it (2). Thus the concept of the archive as the repository of law, watched over by those invested with the power of the law, is disavowed but inescapable. Further, Derrida points out, the archive occurs at the breakdown of memory (11). It is at the moment of forgetting that we archive. Even *The New Shorter Oxford Dictionary* now includes under "archive" as a transitive verb the meaning from computer work: to "transfer to a store of infrequently used files, or to a memory at a

lower hierarchical level (e.g. from disk to tape)." So archiving involves multiple paradoxes—it is to forget and to memorialize in the same act; it is to
preserve and to place under house arrest.

And this house is not an ordinary dwelling. Derrida was delivering his
lecture in Freud's house, a private home that had now become a museum.
The archive itself often marks the institutional passage of the documents
from the private to the public sphere (letters, diaries, notes—things not con-
signed originally to the published and public realm), and they now "inhabit
this uncommon place, this place of election where law and singularity intersect in *privilege*" (3). Indeed the space itself is usually a place of "privilege":
a physical space set off from the main library and with more luxurious
appointments, invariably with some kind of limited access to keep out the
rabble. You are a specialist, by intent or by interpellation, if you are there at
all. Woolf famously describes the moment of archival privilege in *A Room
of One's Own*: when the narrator tries to view the Thackeray manuscript,
"instantly there issued, like a guardian angel barring the way with a flutter
of black gown instead of white wings, a deprecating, silvery, kindly gentleman, who regretted in a low voice as he waved me back that ladies are only
admitted to the library if accompanied by a Fellow of the College or fur-
nished with a letter of introduction" (7-8). One must have documentation to
view the documents. The power of the archons asserts itself at the very
threshold of the archive. And the material itself is always already important,
simply by virtue of being in the archive. So privilege, law, and the power of
the archons are all implicit in the space and the action of the archive.

So how does that affect our actual practices in the archive, or the
research we produce? When we work in an archive there is the thrill of discovery, the excitement of the physical connection, of handling a document
that was actually "there." Yet there is also, as Robert Darnton warns in *The
Great Cat Massacre*, a temptation to treat archival documents as "hard
nuggets of irreducible reality," which the scholar "has only to mine out of
the archives, sift and piece together in order to create a solid reconstruction
of the past" (157)—like the student in *A Room of One's Own* "extracting
pure nuggets of the essential ore every ten minutes or so" (28). Darnton discusses the social conditions surrounding the production of archival
documents such as police reports. What I want to investigate are conditions
governing the production of the archive itself.

Pre-archival ordering

First, before material even gets to the institution it is ordered, or not, by
the author. Archivists make a distinction between a "collection of personal
papers" and a "personal archive." The University of Texas at Austin, for
instance, houses the Isaac Bashevis Singer Archive. The papers came to
them in a heap, in the order in which they were picked up from the piles on
the author's floor. That is a "collection of personal papers." Hugh Kenner,

on the other hand, sent and is still sending his papers carefully ordered. That is a "personal archive." Any of you who have worked with the papers of Virginia Woolf in New York or Sussex, and then encountered the meticulously organized Hogarth Press archives of Leonard Woolf at Reading will appreciate the difference.

As archivist Lisa Jones writes, "An archive cannot be read like a book. Its information [is] conveyed through both form and content [...] a writer's working papers show the physical process of thought" (n. pag.). Thus, "the physical disposition of the archive is part of the archive itself" (interview May 2000). The first rule of the archivist is basically, "Do no harm"—try to preserve the papers in the order in which they were found. However, the papers may come already ordered by the literary executor (which one archivist I interviewed referred to as literary "EXecutor" a telling slip). The executor may arrange them, withhold from them, or place time restrictions on their access. Or the papers may be selected by a book seller, so that what the archive receives is already a commercial product, a dealer's idea of what constitutes a definable and marketable archive. There is obviously potential for good as well as harm here. The dealer may be able to document and make connections that librarians would not. There is also the possibility of slicing and dicing to achieve maximum profit rather than maximum integration of the archive.

Transactions are not innocent on the part of authors either. The act of archiving conveys distinction, and may actively play a role in a writer's reputation. I learned of one author who gave his papers to an archive on the condition that the university press publish his next book. The apparently straightforward act of sending material to an archive is fraught with mediations. Woolfians of course know this better than anybody. Leonard was Virginia's first archivist, dispersing her papers in a manner that makes any exercise in genetic criticism a transatlantic enterprise. At the end of her biography, Hermione Lee draws our attention to the issue, and in *Woolf Studies Annual* 2000 Anna Snaith provides a fascinating glimpse into the ordering of the letters from readers of *Three Guineas*, but the saga of the Woolf archive is yet to be told

Archival ordering

Here is where Foucault meets frass. "Frass" is bug poop, important to archivists because from it you can tell what kinds of bugs you have, and what they are eating—pages, Morocco bindings, glue, etc. "The law of what can be said" can never be separated from the material practices of preservation and cataloguing. The physical processes may seem to have little to do with us as researchers (the unpacking of the papers, the examination for mold and insect infestation, the placement in Mylar and acid-free folders), yet they are fundamental determinants of the archive. Money is always a factor in the archiving process. "We must prioritize" said the archivist, and what gets preserved and catalogued depends upon the opinion of the archivists. If you are working on a minor figure you may be out of luck. Your writer may not have been deemed worthy, and left quietly to the bugs, with their archive of frass.

Further, to catalogue an item is already to pre-screen it; any description is like a publisher's blurb on the back of the book, it influences our reading. And the basic principles of organization can have profound effects. Consider the basic distinction between chronological and alphabetical order. In *Envisioning Information*, Edward Tufte's classic text of graphic design, he cites the Vietnam War Veterans Memorial in Washington D.C. and quotes a description of how Maya Ying Lin proposed listing by date of death rather than alphabetically: "chronological listing was essential to her design. War veterans would find their story told, and their friends remembered, in the panel that corresponded with their tour of duty in Vietnam. Locating specific names with the aid of a directory would be like finding bodies on a battlefield . . ." (43).

Initially some of the organizers disagreed, but when they examined the list, their thinking changed: there were over 600 Smiths; there were 16 people named James Jones. "Alphabetical listing would make the Memorial look like a telephone book engraved in granite, destroying the sense of unique loss that each name carried"(43). Roger Shattuck's fascinating essay "The Alphabet and the Junkyard" goes to the heart of this issue. Shattuck explores the difference between a dictionary and a thesaurus: Roget's *Thesaurus*, he says is an "aerial map of English," it describes "the overall topography of meanings projected by the language itself," a topography obliterated when an American lexicographer rearranged the *Thesaurus* into alphabetical order (35). The practice illustrates what Derrida calls "the violence of the archive itself, *as archive, as archival violence*" (7). He contends that *every* archive is at once *institutive* and *conservative*, revolutionary and traditional. It puts in reserve, it saves, but in an unnatural fashion, by making the law, or in making people respect the law.

In his book on visiting Anasazi Indian sites in the American southwest, *In Search of the Old Ones*, David Roberts talks about the problems of preserving the sites, how in the 1960s university researchers simply picked up all the shards from a given site and bagged them. But worse, a novice researcher came to a museum and took out bags of pottery shards from different sites, dumped them all together on a table and sorted them out by style, which immediately destroyed the provenance and the chronology of these shards (188). This is appalling. Yet any kind of ordering will be a kind of violence. If you alphabetize letters to Woolf or Joyce you will encounter a letter from X next to Y, even though the letters might be twenty years apart. On the other hand, looking at correspondence by years will reveal at a glance the growth and falling off of a friendship, like that between Woolf and Vita Sackville-West, which finally ended Woolf noted in March 1935 "as ripe fruit falls" (*D4* 287). Shattuck quotes Hugh Davidson who claims that, "Scientific order is logical, natural, and *forbidding*; while alphabetical order is illogical, conventional, and *inviting*" (33). The distinction is, as his title says, between the junkyard and the alphabet. This it seems to me is the problem of the archivist: to preserve the natural but forbidding order of the junkyard, so that we can appreciate the "topography of knowledge," and yet to provide access, to provide the unnatural but efficient ordering of the alphabet. The point is, however, her decisions will affect ours. What we encounter side by side in the archive will be a text itself, unrelated to the lived life of the document.

Further, there are institutional tensions within the archive: when someone tells you "I'm an archivist, not a librarian" or vice versa , we are talking about the two sides of the Mason-Dixon line. It was a librarian who told me that we must distinguish between an archive and collection of personal papers: "the latter comes in with no meaningful order," she said. It was a slip, but an interesting one, because for the archivist the lack of order is in itself meaningful. It will in fact be the starting point. The first time I visited an archive I still thought "provenance" was the capital of Rhode Island. Provenance is the place of origin, the "pedigree of previous ownership." For the archivist, "provenance" is all, and the inclination is to keep things in the original order. Archivists are working with material that has been declared "inactive." Librarians, working with material that is "active," are trained to distribute the material according to a pre-existing system—such as the alphabetically-ordered subject headings of the Dewey Decimal system or the Library of Congress codes. Unlike libraries, archives have no universal system of ordering. The different positions can have profound implications when you are dealing with something in the middle ground. As most of you know, the library of Leonard and Virginia Woolf is held at the University of Washington in Pullman. But you cannot see it. It is all there, but a few years ago the decision was made to treat it as a library, not as an archive. The collection was broken up and the books distributed according to their library classifications. The topography of the archive, to return to Shattuck's metaphor, was paved over. Happily, under a new curator, the collection is now being reassembled. Which brings me to…

the ordering of the archons

When I worked in the Berg collection, one of the junior librarians staffing the desk at lunch time asked me on my way out, "Have you felt the lash yet?"

The "lash" was the wrath of Lola, the terrifying curator who had denied the graduate student access to *Jacob's Room*. I was lucky. I never did "feel the lash" and in fact Dr. Szladits was very kind to me. But when I had a question about connections within the archive, which I felt she could answer, I approached a junior librarian first.

"Should I ask her, or would she tell me that's my job?" I asked.

"She'll tell you it's your job," he assured me.

The archivist can enable or inhibit. Bet Inglis at Sussex was knowledgeable and helpful, the clerks at the British Library manuscript room surly and uninterested. Regulations at the British Library prohibit you from having more than one manuscript at your desk at a time. I figured out that volume 3 of the *Mrs. Dalloway* manuscript was not really volume three at all, but the middle chunk of volume 2, only because somebody went to lunch and the staff member filling in did not know I already had a volume on my desk. When Foucault and Derrida write about the "law" of the archive, they may be speaking theoretically, even metaphorically, but the regulation is real, and the archons, the keepers of the law, are still very much a force. It is a subject awkward to talk about, difficult to quantify for footnotes, yet it would be good to have some way of making this visible. (I now read acknowledgements very carefully, and I suspect the most fulsome thank-you's designate the most prickly archivists. Genette has a fascinating section on the performative aspect of the dedication: by saying "I dedicate this book to So-and-So" you are also saying "I am telling the reader that I am dedicating the book to So-and-So"—and even "I am telling So-and-So that I am telling the Reader that..." There is always something oblique in a dedication, says Genette, and the economic function is never far behind [135].)

Foucault says the archive is a "system of functioning" (129); it is a set of institutional practices. This obtains at the most prosaic level. The best archives require all of their staff to work at least part of their time on the reference desk, so that you will have access to even the most senior curators. The point is, the archivist is not separate from the archive. Whereas you can happily work for months in a library without assistance, an archivist is an indispensable guide to the terrain of an archive. She will make cross-references for you that no finding aid ever will. There is no substitute for someone who knows the collection.

In his article "Text as Matter, Concept, and Action," Peter Shillingsburg speaks of the "difficulty in bridging the distance between concepts of works of art that are abstract, ideal, or mental with the material manifestations" of these contexts (42). What Shillingsburg does for text, we need to do for the Archive: to see it at once as matter, concept, and action—an abstract law, a set of social practices, and always, potentially, frass. I believe much of the exciting work on Woolf in this century is going to come out of the archive. We need a critical practice of the archive that reads the topography as well as the text, that traces the pre-history of the archive, and that interrogates the practices of the archons—a practice that succeeds in foregrounding the mediations of the archive itself.

Works Cited

Darnton, Robert. T*he Great Cat Massacre and other episodes in French Cultural History*. NY: Basic Books, 1984.

Derrida, Jacques. *Archive Fever: A Freudian Impression*. Chicago: Chicago UP, 1996.

Foucault, Michel. *The Archaeology of Knowledge and The Discourse on Language*. Trans. A. M. Sheridan Smith. NY: Pantheon Books, 1972.

Genette, Gerard. *Paratexts: Thresholds of Interpretation*. Cambridge: Cambridge UP, 1997.

Jones, Lisa. *The Isaac Bashevis Singer Archive*. Austin: Harry Ransom Humanities Research Center, 1996.

Roberts, David. *In Search of the Old Ones: Exploring the Anasazi World of the Southwest*. NY: Touchstone, 1997.

Shattuck, Roger. "The Alphabet and the Junkyard." *The Innocent Eye: On Modern Literature and the Arts*. NY: Farrar Straus Giroux, 1984. 32–39.

Shillingsburg, Peter L. "Text as Matter, Concept, and Action," *Studies in Bibliography* 44 (1991): 31–82.

Tufte, Edward. *Envisioning Information*. Cheshire, Conn.: Graphics Press, 1990.

Woolf, Virginia. *A Room of One's Own*. NY: HBJ, 1929.

Melba Cuddy Keane
Brow-Beating, Wool-Gathering, and the Brain of the Common Reader

October 1932 was a busy time for Virginia Woolf. At the beginning of the month, Leonard and Virginia attended the Annual Conference of the Labour Party, after which Virginia returned to work on the last part of *Flush*; on the eleventh, she broke off to begin writing, at extraordinary speed, the essay-novel that she was planning to call *The Pargiters*. The thirteenth saw the publication of *The Common Reader: Second Series,* and the end of the month, Woolf's writing—although not sending—a long letter to the *New Statesman*, subsequently and posthumously published as "Middlebrow."[1] It was also this month that Winifred Holtby's critical study of Woolf was released and reviewed.

At least two of these activities pose a challenge for any theories about the coherence of simultaneous events: how do we connect Woolf's location of herself, in her book of essays, as a "common reader" with her self-identification, in her letter on Middlebrows, as a "highbrow"? The question is intimately linked to our on-going debates about modernism's lack of accessibility: the alleged difficulty of modernist writing and therefore its aloofness, its supposed elitism, its opposition to "the masses." But the textual question of the relation between "common" and "highbrow" is inseparable from the *contextual* question of the meaning of "Middlebrow" in October 1932. At a time when Woolf was immersed in intense mental activity, the role of "intellectuals" was being hotly debated both on the radio and in print. "Middlebrow"—and perhaps all writing—comes out of a cultural context and we need to understand its meaning as a response

"Highbrow," "middlebrow," and "lowbrow" are keywords of the modernist period—that is, in Raymond Williams's sense, sites of contestation that expose prevailing cultural anxieties and identify what is at stake in disputes over cultural values. My question—and I think it was Woolf's question—goes behind the application of these labels to the discourse of the debate: who was doing the defining and in what terms was such definition being done? "Middlebrow," I have come to realize, is a densely intertextual essay—an extraordinary example of Woolf's engagement with other voices. Uncovering that dialogue reveals the competing discourses within Woolf's culture and demonstrates the significance of her writing as intervention in public debate.

On November 2, Woolf recorded that, in the midst of her incredible productivity on *The Pargiters*, she became "fire[d] up about Priestley and his priestliness" and dashed off an essay, only to suffer a subsequent collapse with rapid heart-rate problems on October 31 (*D4*: 129). The immediate stimulus for this essay was a series of talks on the B.B.C. under the general title, "To an Unnamed Listener"—in particular, J. B. Priestley's "To a High-Brow" on October 17 and Harold Nicolson's rebuttal, "To a Low-Brow," on October 24.[2] Since these talks became a subject for subsequent comment in the *New Statesman and Nation* on October 29, and since Woolf cast her views as a letter "To the Editor of the New Statesman," we can reasonably surmise that Woolf's letter was written sometime between the 29th and 31st. My argument here is that, in these intense and "incandescent" few days, the B.B.C. talks became a lightening rod for Woolf's broader cultural concerns. Innumerable things coalesced in her mind: the critical reception of her work, the social regulation of women's lives, cultural valuations of the intellectual, the prevailing controls and restrictions governing such public institutions as education and the radio—more precisely, the whole operation of public discourse in her time.

The puzzle that first proposed itself to me was why Woolf felt so compelled to respond to "Priestley and his priestliness"—to the extent of breaking off her writing of *The Pargiters*—when not only had Nicolson already done so but the *New Statesman* had celebrated Nicolson's victory. Mr. Nicolson, the review states, "took up the cudgels against Mr. Priestley and gave the low-brow a tremendous doing-down," showing "apparent enjoyment in trouncing his victim" (Critic 507). But this language itself suggests the source of disturbance: the *New Statesman* picks up and recirculates the discourse of battle with its vocabulary of "cudgels," "doing-down," and "trouncing." As Woolf wrote, "the Battle of the Brows troubles, I am told, the evening air"; the Battle of the Brows, her phrase implies, is one conducted by brow-beating.

Priestley's approach can be easily determined from the script in the B.B.C. archives and the published version in *John O'London's Weekly*. The style of his talk is informal, matey, and pugilistic; the unnamed listener—"my dear fellow"—is definitely constructed as male; and the gist of the message is to resist the stupid temptation to be a highbrow, to shape up and be "a man," and to join the speaker in going out for a drink. All the familiar clichés about highbrowism are rehearsed: that it sneers at popularity and can only admire what is liked by a small group; that it is divorced from ordinary life and characterized by affectation; that it is a product, as much as low-browism, of fashion and the desire to move in herds. It must have been particularly irksome to Woolf that Priestley fell back on a stereotypical notion that Leonard had already demolished as "a parasitic species of pseudo-highbrow" in his 1927 pamphlet *Hunting the Highbrow*; another source of annoyance might have been the hint of personal insult. One breed of highbrow, Priestley asserted, consists of "authors entirely without feeling, who write about human life as an educated *wolf* [my italics] might be expected to write about it" (ts. 5). But if we focus on discourse itself, we see a still more objectionable facet: the implied message is that there is nothing here worth the trouble of thinking about; we should all have a good laugh over the matter and take comfort in sensible views.

Nicolson's script has apparently been lost but his diary traces a fascinating history of its composition.[3] Though his talk was initially written before he heard Priestley, Nicolson rewrote it immediately afterward in angry rebuttal, only to have second thoughts: "Tuesday October 18. Work all morning on my reply to Priestley. Abuse him bitterly. Take the talk off in my pocket to drop it at the B.B.C. but then think better of it. The wireless is not there for scoring off people one dislikes." Nicolson rewrote the talk entirely, "toning down the attack," but even the revised version did not suit the B.B.C.: "Thursday October 20. . . . Joe Ackerley has telephoned to the effect that my talk will not do. I rewrite the whole thing." And still, the revised talk did not suit the listeners: "Thursday, October 27. . . . I get a batch of insulting letters over my last boradcast.[sic] Evidently I have hit the British public on the raw."

The excerpts from Nicolson's talk that I *have* been able to locate suggest that all his rewriting did indeed result in a more reasoned tone.[4] *The Yorkshire Post* devoted a long column to Nicolson's "lively wireless talk" on Anglo-Saxon anti-intellectualism, noting his question, "Has it ever struck you . . . that there is no equivalent for the words 'low-brow' or 'highbrow' in any language other than the English Language?" and his inference that "The Anglo-Saxon race is the only race in the world which openly distrusts the intellectual" ("Intellectual"). But although Nicolson speaks up for the neglected potentials of the Anglo-Saxon brain, he manages to imply its inactivity in his designated WASP listener. Driven by "herd instinct" and marked by "lazy intolerance," the low-brow, Nicolson warns, "will end by producing a race which, like the wasps, have no ideas at all." It would seem that Nicolson, too, adopted an oppositional, assertive style pleasing only to listeners who agreed with his views. What runs through the whole story is the polarization into sides.

In contrast, and characteristically, Woolf enters the fray at the foundational level, interrogating the discourse of the argument itself. Instead simply of defending the highbrow, she challenges her reader to scrutinize conventional thinking, beginning with the assumption that high, middle and low brow correspond to high, middle and low class. "I love lowbrows; I study them," Woolf writes, "I always sit next the conductor in an omnibus and try to get him to tell me what it is like—being a conductor" (178). Momentarily letting her readers slip into identifying lowbrow with working-class, Woolf then reverses direction by invoking a miscellany of occupations that makes any social categorization of lowbrow impossible: "In whatever company I am I always try to know what it is like—being a conductor, being a woman with ten children and thirty-five shillings a week, being a stock-broker, being an admiral, being a bank clerk, being a dressmaker, being a duchess, being a miner, being a cook, being a prostitute. All that lowbrows do is of surpassing interest and wonder to me." Having thus broadened the categorization of lowbrows to include both duchess and prostitute, Woolf then resituates the duchess, destabilizing any relation between brow and social position: "I myself have known duchesses who were highbrows," she continues, "also charwomen" (180). Interests are one thing; economics, another. We are warned not to confuse them.

Secondly, whereas the B.B.C. represented voices in neat binaries, Woolf undercuts such simplicity of opposition. Like Priestley, she groups highbrows and lowbrows together but instead of dismissing them as pawns of fashion, she recasts them as riders on galloping horses, each intent on a goal: the highbrows in pursuit of ideas, the lowbrows in pursuit of a living. Then, having suggested a division, however complementary, between people focused primarily on body or on brain, Woolf undercuts the viability of classification when it comes to what people do. Look, she says, at the lowbrows "lining up to get into the movies," fascinated to see what the highbrows can show them about their lives. If the art of the cinema depends on a symbiotic relation between highbrow production and lowbrow consumption, then cinema is a crossroads where highbrows and lowbrows meet. And, later in the essay, when she tells us that lowbrows write and are desirous of education, she acknowledges a lowbrow production as well as a lowbrow consumption of art.

In relation to Priestley and Nicolson, Woolf seems to be offering not so much an oppositional view as an alternative discourse. Pugnacious prose that badgers the listener to agree is countered by an elastic, pluralistic prose that challenges the reader to think. Ensconced binaries are disrupted by continuous reconfiguration. And Woolf performs even more complex discursive turns on a second essay by Priestley entitled "High, Low, Broad," published first in 1926 and republished in 1929. Like the B.B.C. talk, this earlier essay takes the discussion of brows as an occasion for the entertainment of those who share his views. After a laughing admission of the self-satisfaction in being like-minded people, Priestley proceeds to the joys of unabashed insult. From their superior position as "Broadbrows," writer and inscribed reader look down on both Highbrow and Lowbrow as sheep moving in herds to follow whatever fashion prevails: "Just as Low, you might say, is the fat sheep with the cigar from the City of Surbiton, so High is the thin sheep with the spectacles and the squeak from Oxford or Bloomsbury" (*Open* 165). Broadbrow, of course, is the only critical intelligence of the lot and the only one whose range of interest and experience takes in the whole of human life.

But whereas Priestley *claims* critical intelligence, Woolf *displays* it. She outperforms Priestley's abusive humor with a series of nimble-footed turns upon language that imply the more devastating criticism that middlebrow discourse displays a limited understanding of the nature of words. Woolf takes Priestley's conventional metaphor—sheep are easily led and behave in the same way—and, through extended word play, turns it back against himself. First, countering Priestley's typing of Bloomsbury with sheep-like behavior, Woolf introduces literal sheep to subvert his reductive geographical categorizing: "The hungry sheep," she writes, "did I remember to say that this part of the story takes place in the country?" (182)[5] Next, Woolf enacts a passage through the literal to re-turn the metaphorical, shifting the sheep, however, from a fashion-following herd to an expectant but disappointed reading audience. As she tosses Middlebrow's book out the window and "over the hedge into the field," "the hungry sheep look up but are not fed."[6] Woolf then layers her metaphor by drawing upon another conventional association but one whose irony performs a layered and self-reflexive turn. Demolishing Priestley's cliché liberates freer and broader processes of thought, imaged as "lapsing into that stream which people call, so oddly, consciousness, and gathering wool from the sheep that have been mentioned above" (184).

Wool gathering originally referred to a process of roaming a countryside and picking up the bits of sheep's wool caught on bushes and hedges; as early as the sixteenth century, however, it had become a metaphor for wandering fancies or idle speculation. And among its numerous pejorative uses is yet another possible intertext—an essay by Desmond MacCarthy the previous year, about which Woolf wrote, "Oh I was annoyed with Desmond's usual sneer at Mrs Dalloway—woolgathering"(*D4*: 42).[7] In *Orlando*, Woolf had already had ironic fun with conventional notions of wool-gathering, parodying the biographer's horror when faced with the task of describing a woman's thinking: "this mere woolgathering; this sitting in a chair day in, day out, with a cigarette and a sheet of paper and a pen and an ink pot" (241). In "Middlebrow," Woolf similarly challenges conventional associations, repossessing the sheep, and their wool, in her own terms. In the image of "gathering wool from the sheep mentioned above," language wobbles on the literal-metaphorical axis, with the radical implication that writing—the action of the roaming, scavenging brain—might just be practical, real work.

There's yet one further Priestlian intertext in "Middlebrow"—his column in the *Evening Standard* on October 13, in which in one fell swoop he covered Nicolson's *Public Faces*, Vita's *Family History*, Woolf's *Common Reader*, and Holtby's *Virginia Woolf.* What Priestley did here—and Woolf quotes him—was to translate Holtby's praise of Woolf's poetic qualities into a patronizing slur on novels "written by terrifically sensitive, cultured, invalidish ladies with private means" (11). Again working in binaries, Priestley contrasted such novels that "draw near to poetry" with those that "draw near to social history" and "cast a wider net."

In "Middlebrow," Woolf undercuts this last binary by writing allusive poetic prose with the bite of social critique. The "wider net" of Woolf's essay goes beyond Priestley's insult to challenge the Middlebrow discourse of the B.B.C.—renamed the "Betwixt and Between Company"—for the way it packages and polarizes controversy instead of promoting genuine dialogue. Remembering, too, Woolf's attendance at the Annual Conference of the Labour Party at the beginning of the month, we might note the economic and political ramifications in her charge that Middlebrow, driven by "earning enough to buy," displays a Capitalist materialism of unbridled acquisition, unlike the highbrow and lowbrow Socialist goal of earning "enough to live on" (183).

Woolf furthermore implicates a second public institution in Middlebrow discourse, although she draws it into her net more subtly than the B.B.C. One of the several examples she offers of Middlebrow are "people who call both Shakespeare and Wordsworth equally 'Bill'"(181). The implied lack of discrimination among writers, the chummy slap-on-your-back heartiness immediately suggest a reductive approach to literature but there is yet another, specific intertext here. In 1926, when Woolf reviewed Professor Walter Raleigh's letters, she was irritated by his slangy talk about "Bill Blake or Bill Shakespeare or old Bill Wordsworth," in which she heard the embarrassment of a man who dislikes having sentiments about English literature (*E*4 343; *L*3 242). In the same year that Raleigh was appointed to the Merton Chair of English Language and Literature at Oxford, for example, he wrote: "Bradley's book on Shakespeare is good . . . Even with it I can't help feeling that critical admiration for what another man has written is an emotion for spinsters" (Raleigh 1: 268).[8] As a teacher, Woolf suggests, Raleigh

63

exploits the popular appeal of the demagogue, lecturing instead of teaching students how to read; more dangerously, he typifies a general turn against intellectual interests, denigrated as effete and feminine, in favor of an aggressive, masculinized patriotism: "He drilled. He marched. He wrote pamphlets. He lectured more frequently than ever; he practically ceased to read. At length he was made historian of the Air Force. To his infinite satisfaction he consorted with soldiers" (*E4* 346). Behind Priestley's "don't be a highbrow, be a man," Woolf implies, lies an entire cultural discourse intimately connected with war.

The dense intertextuality of this essay thus becomes a web of searching cultural critique, exposing the complicity of unquestioning patriotism, capitalist values, media control of public discourse, and anti-intellectual complacency. Furthermore, the intricate play of Woolf's language emerges as a rhetorical technique for shifting positionality, destabilizing ideology, and putting the reader into active relation to the text. Woolf's supposedly difficult "highbrow" approach thus functions as an activist response to a pressing social need: the need to reject clichés, to shake off the nation's "priestliness," and to learn to think in flexible, relational, intelligent ways. The lines from her essay "Middlebrow" lead out into the public arenas of writing, broadcasting, and education, grounding her essay in public debate and demonstrating why, for her, common reader and highbrow were not oppositional terms. Although J. B. Priestley may be the immediate target of her satire, the proliferating allusions and slippages reveal her true antagonist to be not a person, or a group of people, but an entire discursive system. Middlebrow is a product of a mass—not popular—culture and of a masculinized institutional discourse that dogmatically interpellates the reader/listener into its own ideology. In contrast, the letter-essay "Middlebrow" shares with *The Common Reader* a respect for the reader's intelligence and the reader's intellectual needs. Ultimately, Woolf "draws near to social history" and "casts a wider net" by demonstrating how an education in wool-gathering is of more immediate and practical use to the brain of the common reader than the brow-beating of the educational system and the B.B.C.

Notes

[1] "Middlebrow" is the title Woolf planned to give to a revised essay version of the letter.

[2] The editorial note to Woolf's diary entry gives the date of Priestley's talk as October 10 (*D4* 129); however, through a comical mishap, his talk had to be rescheduled for the following week—on the same evening, as it turned out, that Vita Sackville-West broadcast her review of *The Common Reader*. I discuss Vita's broadcast, along with further elements in this cultural dialogue, in my forthcoming book.

[3] Excerpts are from Nicolson's unpublished ts. diary for 1932, pages numbered 84-91.

⁴ I managed to trace this article only after the conference, but it is crucial enough to warrant a brief gloss on my earlier suppositions about Nicolson's talk. I would like to thank James Codd of the B.B.C. Written Archives Centre and the Research and Study Library at the Leeds Central Library for their helpful assistance in my search.

⁵ Later, giving her "correct postal code" as "Bloomsbury, W.C.1," Woolf reinserts geography to restore the referent of "Bloomsbury" to material space.

⁶ I would like to thank Sally Greene for alerting me to the allusion here to *Lycidas*, another intertext discussed in my longer analysis.

⁷ "In the latest kind of novel—Virginia Woolf's, for example—events have become merely interruptions in a long wool-gathering process, a process, that is used chiefly to provide occasions for little prose poems, delightful in themselves" (MacCarthy 182). I would like to thank Todd Avery for providing me with the full text of MacCarthy's essay.

⁸ Woolf shortens this reference by quoting only from the second sentence and she does not make the point about the date.

Works Cited

Critic. "A London Diary." *New Statesman and Nation* 29 Oct. 1932: 506-07.

"The Intellectual Distrusted: Hon. Harold Nicolson and Anglo-Saxons: Talk to a 'Low-Brow.'" *Yorkshire Post* 25 Oct. 1932: 4.

MacCarthy, Desmond. "The Bubble Reputation." *Life and Letters* Sept. 1931: 174-92.

Nicolson, Harold. Diary 1932, ts. *The Vita Sackville-West and Harold Nicolson Manuscripts, Letters and Diaries from Sissinghurst Castle, Kent.* The Huntington Library, California, and other libraries. Britain's Literary Heritage. Brighton, Sussex: Harvester Microform, 1988.

Priestley, J. B. "High, Low, Broad." *Saturday Review* 20 Feb. 1926: 222. Rpt. in *Open House: A Book of Essays.* London: Heinemann, 1929. 162-67.

——. "Men, Women and Books: Tell Us More About These Authors!" *Evening Standard*, 13 Oct. 1932: 11.

——. "To a High-Brow." Ts. of broadcast 17 Oct. 1932, at 9.20 p.m: 1-6. B.B.C. Archives. Pub. in *John O'London's Weekly* 3 Dec. 1932: 712.

Raleigh, Lady, ed. *The Letters of Sir Walter Raleigh*, 1879-1922. Preface, D. Nichol Smith. 2 vols. London: Methuen, 1926.

Sackville-West, Vita. "Books of the Week." Rev. of *The Letters of D.H. Lawrence*, ed. Aldous Huxley, *Etruscan Places* by D. H. Lawrence, *The Common Reader: Second Series* by Virginia Woolf. *Listener* 26 Oct. 1932: 610.

Williams, Raymond. *Keywords: A Vocabulary of Culture and Society.* London: Fontana, 1976.

Woolf, Leonard. *Hunting the Highbrow.* London: Hogarth, 1927.

Woolf, Virginia. *The Common Reader: Second Series.* 1932. Ed. Andrew McNeillie. New York: Harcourt, 1986.

——. *The Diary of Virginia Woolf.* Ed. Anne Olivier Bell. 5 vols. New York: Harcourt, 1977-84.

——. *The Essays of Virginia Woolf.* 4 vols. to date. Ed. Andrew McNeillie. London: Hogarth, 1986-.

——. *The Letters of Virginia Woolf.* Ed. Nigel Nicolson and Joanne Trautmann. 6 vols. London: Chatto and Windus, 1975-80.

——. "Middlebrow." *The Death of the Moth and Other Essays.* 1942. San Diego: Harcourt Brace, 1970. 176-86.

——. *Orlando.* 1928. London: Hogarth, 1933.

Woolf and Other Writers

Nancy Knowles
Dissolving Stereotypical Cultural Boundaries:
Allusions to Virginia Woolf in Chitra Banerjee
Divakaruni's *Sister of My Heart*[1]

Like other women writers of Indian origin, Chitra Banerjee Divakaruni has frequently been criticized by Indians for the "troubling" characterization of the West as the place where "[. . .] Indian women can finally free themselves from the shackles of tradition [. . .]" (Daswani). While this positive characterization of the immigrant's adopted country may help to rationalize the immigrant's choice of self-exile (Pultar 49) and may evidence the immigrant's desire to build connections with her new culture (Wang 88), creating a utopia of Western culture, such critics argue, reifies cultural boundaries, stereotyping India as irretrievably patriarchal and the West as offering freedom from patriarchy. On an initial reading, Divakaruni's recent novel *Sister of My Heart* seems to embody these stereotypes and therefore earn such criticism: the novel chronicles the difficult arranged marriages of two Indian cousins, Anju and Sudha, who both eventually emigrate to the U.S. This trajectory reverses that of *Heart of Darkness* or *The Voyage Out*, British novels frequently discussed in a postcolonial context. In *Sister of My Heart*, citizens of a former colony travel to the West. If this journey reveals that they have left barbarism for civilization, then such a story risks reinscribing colonial values. Moreover, it oversimplifies the women's problems and choices.

The actual complexity of Anju's and Sudha's border crossings is illustrated by the novel's few but significant allusions to Virginia Woolf, which in such a non-European context perhaps demonstrate Brenda Silver's claim that "[. . .] Virginia Woolf is everywhere" (xv). In these allusions Woolf becomes an icon explicitly coded in terms of feminism and implicitly coded in terms of empire. This textual coding has little to do with Woolf herself—whether she had imperialist tendencies or not—and more to do with popular perception of her. My purpose here is not to analyze the icon itself but how that icon is deployed. In *Sister of My Heart*, Woolf-as-icon fails to fulfill its stereotypical promise as a symbol of liberation for all women regardless of culture; specifically, the allusions to Woolf ironically represent part of the reason Anju marries the wrong man. Thus, Woolf-as-icon is a metaphor for the West, "civilization," indicating it represents only a mythical answer to the problems of former colonies. When contrasted with the more positive allusions to the Rani of Jhansi associated with Sudha, these allusions to Woolf demonstrate that no culture can guarantee fairy-tale happiness, and women, particularly colonial women who may be tempted by circumstance to see the West as utopia, should not passively expect such utopia. Rather, all women must learn to build empowerment actively from the positive aspects of the cultures they encounter, including their own. They need to create what Henry Schwarz yesterday, in his discussion of Rabindranath Tagore and Satyajit Ray, called a "third space." This paper will first provide necessary background information about Divakaruni's *Sister of My Heart* and then analyze the Woolf allusions in contrast with the Rani of Jhansi allusions.

Divakaruni's *Sister of My Heart* is the story of two girls, Anju and Sudha, raised as close as sisters in a household of women. Anju and Sudha are opposites. Where Anju is practical, challenges tradition, enjoys reading, and hopes to travel, Sudha is beautiful, romantic, and conventional and likes clothes and storytelling. The girls are raised in what is nearly purdah for 1980s Calcutta society: they attend an all-girls convent school, and during their few social outings, they sit among the women. Their mothers also intend to marry them off in the traditional way, despite Anju's desire to attend college. Unfortunately, Sudha is already in love with a young man she met in an unapproved outing to the movie theater. Her plans to elope are foiled when Anju falls in love with the Indian-American man, Sunil, whom her mother has chosen; if Sudha were to elope, the scandal might ruin Anju's anticipated marriage. Instead, Sudha marries her mother's choice, Ramesh. Again misfortune courts them, as during the double ceremony, Sunil reveals his infatuation with the beautiful Sudha.

Neither marriage results in happiness. When Sudha finally becomes pregnant with a girl, her mother-in-law insists she have an abortion and her husband will not oppose his mother. Sudha, flouting convention, takes refuge with her family and is divorced for desertion. Although her girlhood love proposes to her, he doesn't really want Sudha's child, so Sudha refuses him and eventually comes to Anju in America. Anju, too, has marital difficulties. She loves Sunil, but imagines he is having affairs and is disturbed to find he expects her to be grateful to him for marrying her. When Anju becomes pregnant and Sunil discovers she has been secretly working at the campus where she takes classes, they fight, which results in a miscarriage for which Sunil blames her. These marital difficulties are complicated, because of Sunil's infatuation with Sudha, by Sudha's arrival in America at the end of the novel. The novel leaves this complication unresolved.

This summarized progression from India to America might easily be understood as a stereotypical reification of cultural boundaries where India manifests all the traditional Indian patriarchal restrictions under which Anju and Sudha suffer and where America promises possibilities not only for

Anju, who can work, take classes, and wear jeans, but especially for the divorced Sudha who would, along with her child, face discrimination in India. However, the novel doesn't treat this situation so simplistically. The allusions to Woolf demonstrate that it is dangerous for women to trust stereotypes of the dominant culture as means of self-empowerment. Rather than believing these myths, women must read culture critically in order to take an active role in choosing the most satisfying lifestyle.

As one might expect based on the stereotypical India-vs.-the-West dichotomy, Anju, the cousin who questions tradition and looks forward to a college education and international travel, is the one who values Virginia Woolf. Anju discovers Woolf's *A Room of One's Own* in the family bookstore and describes the book as having "the smell of distance, of new thinking" (118). Having been raised in the traditional way where "[. . .] a good woman is to offer up her life for others" (8-9) and "*the husband is the supreme lord*" (49), Anju is understandably inspired by Woolf's passion in *A Room*, Woolf's anger at women's "hav[ing] served all these centuries as looking-glasses possessing the magic and delicious power of reflecting the figure of man at twice its natural size" (35) and her ardor in believing Judith Shakespeare "would come if we worked for her, and that so to work, even in poverty and obscurity, is worth while" (114). Anju convinces her mother to buy a complete set of Woolf's novels for the store and then "devour[s]" them herself (118). For Anju, therefore, Woolf becomes an icon of all she dreams about her future—reading, education, and travel

However, Woolf-as-icon loses her stereotypical quality almost immediately, for on the same page that Woolf is introduced as Anju's passion, Anju also meets her future husband. Still unknown to Anju, Sunil enters the bookstore and asks immediately for any books by Woolf. Although Anju doesn't yet know he is her mother's choice for her, she is immediately attracted to him. She "bring[s] down the full set and start[s] extolling Woolf's virtues" (119). Sunil purchases the set, exchanging pleasant conversation and drawing Anju into discussion of "Mr. America," her mother's choice for her bridegroom. In the course of conversation, Anju wants to say, "'Don't go.' Or even, shamelessly, 'Marry me'" (120), and when Sunil reveals himself as "Mr. America," Anju can't believe her luck. And Sunil even seems to merit Anju's immediate affection, promising to fulfill her non-traditional dreams of education and travel if she will marry him. Despite the fact that Anju is attracted to this man, who seems to be kind and to have a sense of humor, this juxtaposition of Woolf and marriage is ironic. For Anju, and for many other women, Woolf represents the possibility of freedom and self-worth while marriage represents the possible threat of submersion of the self in the needs of others. Therefore, the enmeshing of the Western icon with the traditional patriarchal institution of marriage, regardless of its apparent benefits in this particular instance, already undermines the stereotypical dichotomy between India and the West. The promise of the West has become merely a seemingly better version of the tradition one finds in India.

In her immediate infatuation with Sunil, Anju accepts marriage without questioning whether it will truly fulfill her desires. She imagines that, although the marriage is traditionally arranged, Sunil will provide all the freedoms she associates with a westernized lifestyle, and she therefore romanticizes him in a very traditional way. Her whole-hearted conversion is expressed by another allusion to Woolf: "[. . .] I've traded in Virginia Woolf for Elizabeth Barrett Browning." Anju's statement implies not the Barrett Browning of *Aurora Leigh* but of the sonnets, "*How do I love thee?*" (132) Yet, this romantic sensibility metaphorically colonizes Anju's idea of Woolf. Because Sunil apparently enjoys Woolf, Anju thinks to herself, "Maybe we could even read Woolf together" (120), and "I look forward to the evenings when we'll read *To the Lighthouse* to each other" (121). Because of this romantic vision, she expects Sunil's constant sympathy. When she is day-dreaming during the wedding ceremony and is teased by onlookers as having forgotten him for another man, she imagines he will understand: "I expect no less of a man who loves Virginia Woolf" (150). Yet, shortly after this, Sunil reveals his love for Sudha in the midst of the wedding ceremony. Anju thinks, "His face is naked and open, like a house with no curtains. And because I'm so deeply in love myself, I recognize exactly what I'm seeing in there" (151). Anju continues with the remainder of the ceremony, her romantic dream shattered, and perhaps more devastatingly, her relationship with Sudha marred by jealousy. Where Woolf-as-icon had seemed to Anju to promise a healthy, happy relationship with Sunil according to a Western model of equality and respect, the Western image has actually trapped her into a conventional bond with all the associated problems.

It is only after Anju and Sunil have been living for a while in America that the final blow is delivered to Anju's dream-marriage; Anju discovers that Sunil is not really "a man who loves Virginia Woolf" (150) at all, and this discovery represents the tensions in their marriage. When Anju suggests they read Woolf together, Sunil refuses, saying, "'All that arty-farty stuff is not for me'" (188). When Anju presses him on the issue, wondering why he bought the complete Woolf set, Sunil reveals that Anju's mother had informed Sunil that Woolf was one of Anju's favorites before he'd come into the store, "[. . .] so [he] thought that would be a good way to start a conver-sation" and bought the set to make her happy (188). Thus, by excluding himself from what Anju always expected would be a mutual pleasure, he destroys the founding idea of Anju's marriage. His deception demonstrates that he wants the kind of relationship where he gives Anju the world and she is eternally grateful. Anju reflects, "Unlike some of the other Indian hus-bands I know, Sunil's always encouraged me to feel comfortable in America. He taught me to drive and introduced me to his colleagues at work. He bought me jeans and hiking boots, and when I said I'd like to see how I look in short hair, he said, 'Go for it!'" (187) Yet, after all these things, plus the travel and education that Anju has always dreamed of, he expects gratitude

(193). Gratitude is the basis of his pleasure in the relationship, and this forces Anju into a position of dependency. This dependency resembles a colonial relationship, as Sunil's nickname "Mr. America" perhaps signifies, where the one with symbols of power expects the one who eagerly wants those symbols to be grateful upon receipt. Rather than having accomplished her dreams for herself, Anju must thank someone else for them. This is the ultimate irony in the allusion to Woolf: Anju's faith in Woolf as a symbol of everything she desired has tricked her into an inappropriate, unhappy marriage. Thus, the allusion demonstrates that Western culture cannot simply erase colonial women's problems. Rather, women must begin to read cultures critically in order to negotiate the webs of power embedded in them. By taking this active responsibility for their own happiness, women can avoid the kind of trick Anju has essentially played on herself.

The allusion to Woolf that tricks Anju into an unhappy marriage is contrasted by an allusion to the Rani of Jhansi, who acts as a touchstone for Sudha similar to Woolf for Anju. The difference between the Western and Indian allusions is that, where Woolf-as-icon leads Anju astray, the image of the Rani empowers Sudha. Unlike Anju, Sudha has been anticipating becoming a wife and mother since childhood, and she sees her role in accomplishing that dream as primarily passive. Sudha romanticizes this passive role through the story of the princess in the palace of snakes who wakes to the kiss of a prince and loves him because he "tell[s] her about the magical universe of men" and "[w]hen she looked into his eyes, their dark center, she saw herself for the first time, tiny, and doubled, and beautiful. [. . .] Without him she'd never have known who she was" (86). Note the reduction of the woman here in comparison with the magnification of the man Woolf describes in *A Room*. It is this romanticism that Anju reverts to when she falls in love with Sunil. However, when Sudha's marriage threatens her unborn child, Sudha must change her self-conception. She can no longer be the sleeping princess trusting a prince to kiss her awake. Instead, Sudha turns to another Indian story, the tale of the Rani of Jhansi, which she recalls when viewing a video (225). In March of 1858, the Rani led a rebellion against the British who intended to annex the state of Jhansi because, according to their law, the maharaja, the Rani's husband, had died without an heir. However, the couple had adopted a relative, who according to Hindu law, should inherit. His inheritance had religious as well as political significance for the populace. The siege of Jhansi lasted two weeks, and when the city fell, the Rani escaped on horseback, rallied other Indian rulers, and captured the fortress of Gwalior. She died there on the battle's second day (Bois). By identifying with this legendary Indian woman, Sudha is able to brave traveling alone in public in order to escape from her husband's house. Fighting her way through the crowd at the Calcutta station, a man "grope[s] at [her] breast," and Sudha reports, "I swat his hand away furiously and kick at the ankles of a fat man blocking my path. [. . .] Maybe this is how the Rani

71

of Jhansi felt the first time she went to war" (243). Sudha's courage, her love for her daughter, and her success in reaching her family's house safely reaffirm her choice to leave her husband. When Sudha speaks to Anju on the phone after Anju has lost her baby, Sudha retells the Rani of Jhansi story, blending it with Anju's, reaffirming Anju's power and encouraging her to heal herself. In this way, the allusion to the Rani becomes not a trick, like the allusion to Woolf, but rather a source of power. And significantly this source of power is Indian, even anti-colonial, not Western.

Rather than reifying stereotypical cultural boundaries, the allusions to Woolf in Divakaruni's *Sister of My Heart* reveal the complexities of cultural difference. Anju's love of Woolf's writing is not a stereotypical portal to Western paradise but rather her excuse for loving and marrying a man for whom she is ultimately unsuited. The failed romance acts as a metaphor for the failure of Western values to meet the needs of former colonies. Paralleled by the novel's more positive allusions to the Rani of Jhansi, the allusions to Woolf dissolve cultural boundaries by demonstrating that the individual cultures themselves cannot guarantee a productive, happy life. This is particularly true of Western cultures in the postcolonial world. A woman must negotiate among aspects of culture, reading them critically and rewriting them for herself when necessary, in order to build a source of personal power.

Notes
[1] This title derives from an interview with Divakaruni quoted in Patel: Divakaruni says, "to me, the art of dissolving boundaries is what living is all about."

Works Cited

Bois, Danuta. "Lakshmi Bai." *Distinguished Women of Past and Present.* 7 June 2000 <http://www.netsrq.com/~dbois/bai.html>.

Daswani, Mansha. "Melodrama Fit for Bollywood." *South China Morning Post* 17 July 1999: 6. *Academic Universe.* CD-ROM. 19 July 1999.

Divakaruni, Chitra Banerjee. *Sister of My Heart.* New York: Doubleday, 1999.

Patel, Nilu N. "Chitra Banerjee Divakaruni." *Postcolonial Studies at Emory.* 4 Jan. 2000. <http://www.emory.edu/ENGLISH/Bahri/CBD.html>.

Payant, Katherine B. and Toby Rose, eds. *The Immigrant Experience in North American Literature.* Contributions to the Study of Amer. Lit. 4. Westport, CT: Greenwood P, 1999.

Pultar, Gönül. "*Jasmine* or the Americanization of an Asian: Negotiating between 'Cultural Arrest' and Moral Decay in Immigrant Fictions." In Payant and Rose 45-57.

Schwarz, Henry. "Cosmopolitan Modernism: Realism and Gender in Tagore and Ray." Woolf, Tagore, and Ray's *Charulata.* Tenth Annual Conference on Virginia Woolf: Virginia Woolf Out of Bounds. University of Maryland Baltimore County, Baltimore, MD. 9 June 2000.

Silver, Brenda R. *Virginia Woolf Icon.* U of Chicago P, 1999.

Wang, Qun. "Repositioning the Stars: Twentieth-Century Narratives of Asian American Immigration." In Payant and Rose 83-93.

Woolf, Virginia. *A Room of One's Own*. New York: Harcourt Brace Jovanovich, 1929.

Karin Westman
A.S. Byatt and "(V. Woolf)": Mapping a Misreading of Modernism

My query about A.S. Byatt's relationship to Virginia Woolf began when I happened upon Byatt's parenthetical formulation of Virginia Woolf—"(V. Woolf)"—in the essay "Still Life/Nature Morte" (*Passions of the Mind*, 1991). Commenting on the artistic project for that novel, Byatt states: "I am also resistant to the idea that the world hits us as a series of random impressions (V. Woolf) and that memory operates in a random manner. I wanted at least to work on the assumption that order is more interesting than the idea of the random [. . .]" (*Passions* 5). Wait a moment, you may be thinking (as I did): Isn't Woolf also interested in order, the order we live under and within, as well as the order we make of our lives as we process those "random impressions"? That catch phrase of literary modernism is certainly part of Woolf's polemical essay "Modern Fiction" and of her art, but a substantial quantity of Woolf's work explores what happens once the random impressions have entered the individual consciousness and how they may not be "random" but reflect structures of power. Byatt's curt reduction of Woolf's varied career to "random impressions" also struck me as odd for another reason: Byatt's characterization of Woolf seemed out of step with the innovative form and content I'd experienced in Byatt's own fiction.

Was Byatt's evaluation of Woolf, then, anomalous or representative? When not speaking about Woolf's *fiction*, Byatt does speak warmly about Woolf: about her theory of androgyny (at Morley College, 1985; qtd in Kenyon 61); about the need for women writers to have space to write ("I'd Rather Live Now" 23); and her claims in *AROO* about the importance of female friendships (Todd 189). However, after consulting interviews, essays, and even portions of Channel 4 transcripts, I soon realized that however much Byatt speaks of herself looking back to George Eliot, she does not see herself looking back through another mother of literature, Virginia Woolf. Further, however much Byatt may speak favorably of modernists Henry James, T. S. Eliot, Ford Madox Ford, and Proust (Todd 184), she rarely, if ever, mentions Woolf the novelist or Woolf the modernist in favorable terms. My paper today will therefore explore the rather vexed

73

relationship I see between A.S. Byatt's formulation of Woolf's modernism and the revisionist narrative strategies Byatt herself employs. First, we'll look at the narrative form and content of one of Byatt's recent novels; I will then offer some hypotheses which may help us account for Byatt's "mis-reading" of Woolf's modernism and her art.

Byatt's third installment of Frederica Potter's story in the novel *Babel Tower* (1996) encourages us to question, along with Frederica, the "mascu-line" modernist narratives of Lawrence and Forster. In their place, we are asked to value a feminist strategy built around multiplicity in story-telling and the "juxtaposed but divided" stories which affirm the self rather than subsume it to a masculine *grand recit*. Art and life converge in *Babel Tower* as the narrative investigates the opposing forces of individual freedom and institutional control during the 1960s, beginning with the written word. The struggle of Byatt's heroine, Frederica, to tell her tale to the divorce court in order to escape a disastrous marriage runs in counterpoint to the prosecution of the novel's inter-narrative, *Babbletower: A Tale for Children of Our Time*, under the Obscene Publications Act of 1959. If this latter "Tale," a dystopi-an satire heavily influenced by the Marquis de Sade, warns the reader against the excesses of individual desire, Frederica's "fantasy tale," as she calls it, warns the reader of the excesses of patriarchy lurking within the so-called freedom of the 1960s. We soon discover that Frederica is trapped within a cultural narrative of marriage which she thought to be her libera-tion—a narrative she's been expected to embrace since her youth, a narrative the law courts are ready to presume, and a narrative she is now clearly ready to put on trial: the myth of "Oneness" (315) propagated, among others, by Lawrence and Forster.

The bookish Frederica's love-hate relationship with D. H. Lawrence shapes her theoretical understanding and practical experiences of personal relationships throughout the first two volumes of her history, *The Virgin in the Garden* (1978) and *Still Life* (1985). At seventeen, the inexperienced Frederica tells her school teacher father that she finds Lawrence's *Women in Love* "corrupting and damaging" and "hopes Lawrence is lying," because otherwise she'd just kill herself now (*Virgin* 34). Extremely verbal herself, Frederica particularly dislikes how "people in Lawrence's novels love each other because of their unspeakable selves, their loins of darkness [...] They hector and gabble but they don't talk though he does, Lawrence does..." (*Virgin* 349-50). The hold Lawrence and his female characters have over Frederica's fertile imagination is intense, and its power is intensified by other literary works, by popular culture, and, notably, by her own father's beliefs. In questioning the abjection Lawrence and others expected her to desire, the now more experienced Frederica also develops, as we are told by the narrator of *Still Life*, a "skeptical mistrust of her father's undue respect for Leavisite 'values' and the 'life' located and propounded so easily in D. H. Lawrence" (196). For Frederica, rejecting Lawrence also means quite literally rejecting the Father—a feat she's not quite able to do when she chooses to marry Nigel Reiver, who fulfills the role of Lawrencian hero as he "takes [Frederica] beyond words, effortlessly and with skill" (42), attempting to persuade her that the "body," particularly the accompanying "Oneness" of sexual union, is "truth" (127).

The loss of self Frederica experiences in her marriage to Nigel Reiver prompts her flight from his moated grange in the countryside and her return to a life of language and the written word in London. While teaching Lawrence and Forster for an extramural class as she prepares for her divorce trial, Frederica discovers that their modernist narratives should be tried and convicted: the myths of divine "Oneness" and "Only connect!" which both authors claim to be the apex of personal relationships have not liberated but ultimately diminished the multiplicity of her body and mind. While *allusions* to Lawrence's books and theories have appeared in the two previous novels, it is in *Babel Tower* that Frederica engages directly with the texts themselves, parts of which are reproduced for the reader to ponder as well. As she works through excerpts of *Women in Love* and *Howards End*, tracing the Biblical cadences in the characters' desire to "experience an undifferentiated All" which "confuses and abolishes grammatical categories" (312, 313), Frederica realizes that she "[does not] want Oneness" (314), does not want "to be *fused* with someone else" (314). She rejects their modernist "myths of desire, the desire and pursuit of the Whole" (315) for a more dialogic "art" of "fragments, layers, tesserae of mosaic, particles" (315).

It is significant that Frederica arrives at this revelation not simply while preparing her lecture notes for class, but as she concurrently struggles and fails to convey her own fractured tale in legal linear prose for the divorce courts. Her failure to find value in either a masculine modernism or a masculine legal prose suggests a similarity between those realms of art and life, linking the modernist fathers to the law of the Father. As she experiments in private with an avant-garde, decoupage method she has chosen for her personal diary, "Laminations," Frederica realizes she need not cede authorial control to a central narrative voice, a patriarchal grammar. Keeping her ideas and herself "juxtaposed but divided" (315), Frederica feels that "it might be possible to construct a kind of plait [braid] of voices, with different rhythms and vocabularies" (463-4), which could represent the different "women" she contains: "a mother, a wife, a lover, a watcher" (463).

Frederica's goal echoes the concern we see so often in Woolf's diaries, essays, and fiction: to find strategies by which to break or bend the sentence and the sequence of narrative art, in order to communicate the self who lives under the powerful illusion of patriarchy. Unlike Rachel Vinrace of *VO*, Frederica's qualified success by the end of *Babel Tower* marks her resemblance to the narrator of *AROO* who questions the shadow of the egocentric "I" across the page, or to artists like Orlando and Miss LaTrobe who seek a narrative form which can better represent the multiple strands of self and of experience. The phrase "plait of voices" could, of course, describe Byatt's novel itself, as its title, *Babel Tower*, suggests. Byatt, like Woolf, pushes against a univocal narrative tradition towards a dialogic one, demanding readers' active responses to the narrative's varied voices. *Babel Tower*'s intertwining tales leave the reader considering the relationship between its many stories and the value of each: not only selections from Forster and Lawrence, but also from Tolkien's *Hobbit*, Frederica's legal account of her marriage to Nigel Reiver, her diary of "Laminations," and, most notably, substantial selections from Jude Mason's dystopian *Babbletower*. These "fantasy tale[s]" all nest within *Babel Tower*'s ostensibly "realist" but actually quite non-mimetic narrative frame; their presence offers alternative ways of experiencing and acting within the world, which the reader must evaluate and judge, with the assistance of the novel's third-person narrative voice. By emphasizing the telling of tales and how language matters in political and personal ways, A.S. Byatt presents multiple narratives to her readers with an ear towards the politics of narration and the teller of the tale—a Woolfian endeavor indeed.

How, then, do we reconcile Frederica's narrative rejection of a masculine and male modernism and Byatt's dialogic novel with Byatt's oft-repeated refutation of Woolf and her modernism in critical essays and interviews?

Hypothesis 1: Sibling Rivalry.

I offer this hypothesis because of Byatt's reticence on her relationship to her sister and literary rival, Margaret Drabble, and because this reticence has distinct narrative appeal. In the same *Guardian* article (Brace, "Who's the Greatest of Them All?"), as Margaret Drabble claims that she dislikes George Eliot and values Virginia Woolf, A.S. Byatt not only reasserts her long-standing favor for George Eliot but *also, in nearly the same breath, speaks against Woolf.* The sisterly and professional feud between Byatt and Drabble—played out in the public spaces of the press—dates at least to the ascendance of Byatt's star when she won the Booker Prize for *Possession* and the fall of Drabble's when she received unenthusiastic reviews for her domestic novels. We could even trace this feud as far back as their time together at Cambridge (Welsh, "Sister Act"; Leedham, "A.S. Byatt vs Margaret Drabble"). If Drabble helps Byatt define herself as an artist, then Woolf is very nearly exiled from Byatt's literary canon.

Hypothesis 2: Escaping the Body

This hypothesis bears a bit more weight than Hypothesis 1, in part because of Byatt's comments in several interviews. While Byatt is a self-identified feminist, she dislikes the label "woman writer," explaining that she writes to "escape" her sex, not to be condemned to its limits (Todd 186, 189). Fearful of feminist reviewers, theorists, and scholars who partition women writers off into separate courses, she worries that such segregation reiterates the closed canons of the past (Todd 186; Brace, "That Thinking

Feeling"). This concern finds public expression in her nom de plume. Her sex hidden within the initials A.S., Byatt seeks not just a Coleridgian artistic androgyny, I think, but a T.S. Eliot-like masculine presence within the still quite male ranks of the British literary establishment; her reputation is therefore built upon her works, not her sex, and she has gained a token status that allows her relatively free passage. Perhaps the reductive phrase "V.Woolf" should be read as a gesture of inclusion, from Byatt's perspective —a de-sexing of Woolf so Woolf, too, can escape the bounds of the material, female body. Yet the "V.Woolf" Byatt describes is criticized precisely for being too airy, too detached—all random impression, without order. The inclusive gesture, if it is one, is thwarted by Byatt's (mis) reading of Woolf's modernist art.

Hypothesis 3: F. R. & Q. D.

We will always have the Leavises, it appears—especially in the British university system, of which Byatt is a self-confessed inheritor (Byatt "Reading"; Kenyon 56; Kelly xii-xiii). For when Byatt reduces Woolf to the parenthetical "(V.Woolf)" and to Woolf's canonized statement on modernism in "Modern Fiction," Byatt restricts Woolf's theories of art to a view promulgated by critical voices of the 1950s and 1960s who constructed Woolf's modernism only in terms of that "luminous envelope,"[1] a mind seemingly divorced from a very material world of ideological apparatuses, and a narrative voice supposedly caught up in its own "solipsism" with no possible escape ("Accurate Letters: Ford Madox Ford," in *Passions* 93). When linking Woolf to modernism, Byatt does not speak of the Virginia Woolf of *AROO* or *TG* or *BTA*, but the High Modernist Virginia Woolf whose efforts in *TW* and in her essay "Modern Fiction" found disfavor with the Leavises.

However, Byatt's allegiance to the Leavisite "Great Tradition" is hardly complete, as we have seen in Frederica's rejection of Lawrence and Forster, two valued members of the Leavis and *Scrutiny* tradition. And though Byatt may value the artistic goals of George Eliot, one of F. R.'s "Greats," she also questions the hegemony of this tradition in her interviews and essays ("Reading," "The Last Word on Being British"). By placing the male and masculine modernists of that Tradition on trial in *Babel Tower*, and encouraging the reader to evaluate excerpts of their novels through Frederica's critical eye, Byatt clears a space for another model of art and of experience, divesting herself, to some degree, of her Leavisite inheritance.

Byatt's elision of Woolf—Woolf's absent presence within that space Byatt has cleared—illustrates more, I believe, than the willed persistence of a Leavisite viewpoint. Granted, Byatt's contribution to Tom Paulin's indictment of Woolf on the 1991 Channel 4 program "J'Accuse" found Byatt toeing the culturally acceptable Leavisite line: she aligned Woolf with the snobbery of Bloomsbury and criticized Woolf for her failure to depict working class people.[2] But does Byatt's anxiety of influence here reside with

Leavis, or with Woolf herself? Claiming just last year to find Woolf's modernist prose "frightening, like being caught in a mosquito net" (Brace, "Who is the Greatest of Them All?"), one wonders if *Woolf* provokes an "anxiety of influence" which the otherwise extremely self-conscious Byatt has yet to acknowledge.

The tension between Byatt's narrative art and her literary criticism not only speaks to the persistence of a reductive view of Woolf's modernism in the year 2000, when "Modern Fiction" is still most anthologies' short-hand way of including theories of modernist art, especially Woolf's. This contradiction in Byatt's work, I believe, reveals Byatt's own struggle to differentiate herself from a modernism she repeatedly (mis)assigns to Woolf, a struggle that takes place at the expense of Woolf's modernist, feminist legacy: Byatt's and Woolf's artistic, theoretical, even political goals intersect far more than they diverge. Byatt has yet to engage the more varied Woolf who exists beyond the "random impressions" of "Modern Fiction." She has been able to speak *against* Lawrence and Forster and even Leavis, but she has only gradually begun to speak *for* Woolf. In her most recent novel, *The Biographer's Tale* (published June 2000), the first-person narrator is an A.B.D. graduate student who has given up his study of postmodern literary theory for biography; in passing, he reminds us that Woolf wrote *The Years* as well as *The Waves*. Perhaps Byatt's misreading of Woolf's modernism *has* come full bloom and will now grow another way.

Notes

[1] See Regina Marler, *Bloomsbury Pie* (1997).

[2] See Silver, *Virginia Woolf Icon* (1999); Wilson, *Virginia Woolf and Anti-Semitism* (1995); Doan and Brown, "Being There: Woolf's London and the Politics of Location" (1995); and Shone, "The Blooming Group That Decries Woolf" (1991). For Byatt's comments, see the transcript of the Channel 4 program.

Works Cited

"Antonia Byatt in Interview with Boyd Tonkin." *Anglistik* 10: 2 (1999): 15-26.

Brace, Marianne. "That Thinking Feeling." *Guardian* 9 May 1996: T6.

——. "Who's the Greatest of Them All?" *Daily Telegraph* 23 November 1996.

Byatt, A. S. *Babel Tower*. NY: Vintage, 1996.

——. "I'd Rather Live Now." *Daily Telegraph* 30 Oct 1995: 23.

——. *Passions of the Mind*. 1991. NY: Vintage, 1993.

——. "Reading, Writing, Studying: Some Questions about Changing Conditions for Writers and Readers." *Critical Inquiry* 34 (1993): 4.

——. *Still Life*. NY: Vintage, 1985.

——. *The Virgin in the Garden*. NY: Vintage, 1978.

Doan, Laura and Terry Brown. "Being There: Woolf's London and the Politics of Location." *Re:Reading, Re:Writing, Re:Teaching Virginia Woolf*. Eds. Eileen Barrett & Pat Cramer. NY: Pace U P, 1995. 16-21.

Kelly, Kathleen Coyne. *A.S. Byatt*. NY: Twayne Publishers, 1998.

Kenyon, Olga. *Women Novelists Today*. NY: St. Martin's Press, 1988.

"The Last Word on Being British." *The Daily Telegraph* 12 September 1998: 6.

Leedham, Robert. "A.S. Byatt vs Margaret Drabble." *Sunday Times* 4 June 1993.

Shone, Richard. "The Blooming Group That Decries Woolf." *The Times* 30 March 1991.

Silver, Brenda. *Virginia Woolf Icon*. Chicago: University of Chicago Press, 1999.

Todd, Janet, ed. "A.S. Byatt." *Women Writers Talking*. NY: Holmes and Meier, 1983. 181-195.

Tredwell, Nicolas. *Conversations with Critics*. Manchester: Carcanet, 1994, 58-74.

Walsh, John. "Sister Act." *The Independent* 7 April 2000: 1.

Wilson, Jean Moorcroft. *Virginia Woolf and Anti-Semitism*. The Bloomsbury Heritage Series. London: Cecil Woolf Publishers, 1995.

Debrah Raschke
"It won't be fine" tomorrow: Doris Lessing's Struggle with Woolf

Lessing does not mention Woolf in her criticism or in her biography. Yet, particularly in Lessing's fiction, Woolf seems to be an absent presence—a position furthered by Ruth Saxton and Jean Tobin's essay collection, *Woolf and Lessing: Breaking the Mold*, which constitutes the main corpus of criticism addressing intersections between Woolf and Lessing. Not yet noted, however, are the connections between Lessing's *The Fifth Child* and Woolf's *To the Lighthouse* in which *To the Lighthouse* becomes an obsolescent solution to the contemporary world.

Lessing's *The Fifth Child* relays the domestic saga of Harriet and David Lovatt, who meet at a London office party where they are immediately drawn to each other's "unfashionable" and antiquated qualities, which subsequently set them apart from their more sexually swinging colleagues (3). They marry shortly after this, buy an old rambling house outside London where they attempt to sequester themselves from the problems of modern life. They bear four lovely children. However, the fifth child, Ben, threatens to destroy the domestic bliss Harriet and David have worked so hard to cultivate. Even while in the womb, Ben threatens to be different—hard kicks and jolts that frequently bring Harriet to tears. When he turns five, he tears a raw chicken apart with his hands and teeth, grunting and snarling in his pleasures (97). He then strangles a dog and cat. The older children are terrified of him, fearing that they will be his next victims. Finally, he causes so much disruption that David and Harriet decide to place him in an institution. Harriet, however, later recants and retrieves him, an act that causes her to lose everything—her marriage, her children, and her house. On the surface, this plot seems to have little to do with *To the Lighthouse*. Yet *To the*

Lighthouse seems to haunt this text, as if to suggest that Woolf's solutions to the modern world are impossible fantasies.

The text's spatial aesthetics, first of all, recall the crowded Ramsay household, where the children and various guests intermittently gather and disperse. Harriet and David, enacting their own "old-fashioned values," purchase a large Victorian house, which they hope to fill with lots of children. They first decide on four children, and then later, eight—the same number in the Ramsay household. Seeing themselves as the "centre of the family," Harriet and David pack their house with guests on holidays which then extend long after the official holiday is over. Easter had gone on for a week, Christmas for ten days, and on a regular basis, "one feast followed another" (19). There is also a key communal meal. Like the dinner table scene in *To the Lighthouse*, this eating scene seems to continue "indefinitely" (23). There are, as well, fifteen seated at this table (the same number of placings described when Mrs. Ramsay serves the Boeuf en Daube). Frederick and Molly, David's father and stepmother, "judging everything by the perspectives of Oxford" (23), dually don the position of a more affable Mr. Tansley. David, a bit of a loner who does not get the promotion he expected, recalls Mr. Ramsay. Harriet, as the one whose attention is always demanded, and as the core of all this, recalls Mrs. Ramsay.

Even the language of *The Fifth Child* at times has a Woolfian resonance, which is unusual since Lessing's writing rarely exercises the lyrical. One eating scene is described as follows:

> *Here, enclosed* in the hospitable kitchen, it was warm and steamy with the smell of soup. *Outside* was a blustering night. May. The curtains were not drawn. A branch stretched across the window: a spring branch, full of pristine blossom, pale in the twilight, but the air that beat on the *panes* has been blasted down south from some iceberg or snow-field (43).

This is the echo I hear:

> Now all the candles were lit up, and the faces on both sides of the table were brought nearer by the candle light [. . .] for the night was now shut off by *panes* of glass, which, far from giving any accurate view of the outside world, rippled it so strangely that *here, inside* the room, seemed to be order and dry land; there outside, there *outside* a reflection in which things wavered and vanished, waterily (97).[1]

In other words, *here inside* is safety and comfort—the smell of soup (or one might say order and dry land). *Outside* there is chaos and the threat of destruction—things that "wavered and vanished" or air that "beat on the panes." The phrase, "Time Passed," moreover, appears twice in describing Harriet's pregnancy with Ben, which is noteworthy both in the phrasing and in the positioning, since it is Ben who brings the chaos and destruction into the Lovatt family. The interpolated scenes in Lessing's *The Fifth Child* that recall *To the Lighthouse*—the old Victorian house, the gathering of guests, the central eating scenes, the number of children, the references to pools, mirrors and encroaching chaos, the reading of the fairy tale and its juxtapositions—it will be fine tomorrow— are too many for mere coincidence. The question is one of function.

The most discernible explanation lies in the critique of domesticity, which *The Fifth Child* could easily share with *To the Lighthouse*. It is clear from the beginning that Harriet and David's vision of Victorian bliss is a romantic fantasy. When they first meet at a party, they spot one another across a crowded room. Their house, located away from the city, promising a haven, albeit illusory, from the ever-encroaching sordidness of the world. The Ramsay household likewise is no breakwater. Although Mrs. Ramsay can and has been named goddess, hierophant, visionary, and artist, the domesticity over which this angel of the house reigns clearly has an edge to it. Although I would take issue with Mary Beth Pringle's suggestion that Mrs. Ramsay's soul is barren and that the dinner table scene reflects paucity, Pringle's point about the inhospitable domestic imagery is well-taken. A refrigerator is placed not in the kitchen, but in an Army and Navy catalogue (308), and the innocuous straw hats, flannels, ink-pots and paint-pots which litter the children's rooms mingle with bats, beetles, and the skull of small birds.

It seems thus that *The Fifth Child* simply reinforces the critique of domestic bliss that emerges as well in *To the Lighthouse*. But then, the question arises why kill the angel of the house all over again sixty-one years later. Lessing does share with Woolf a vexed relationship with her mother (see Saxton). That Woolf suffered from the loss of her mother at an early age and that *To the Lighthouse* enacts that loss is already well documented. Lessing likewise struggles with maternal loss, but in a different way. Noting that her mother "had not wanted a girl," Lessing remarks: "I knew from the beginning she loved my little brother unconditionally, and she did not love me" (*Under My Skin* 25). Thus, as Phyllis Perrakis suggests, *The Fifth Child* is a more "open" and "less repressed" working through the anger that emerges from a troubled mother-child relationship.[2]

Another explanation may lie in the class-conscious, if not semi-Marxist strain, that often underscores Lessing's works. In a rare interview Lessing comments on Woolf's writing:

> There's always a point in her books when I think, my God, she lives in such a different world from anything I've ever lived, I don't understand it. I think it is charming in a way but I feel that her experience must have been too limited, because there's always a point her in novels when I think, "fine, but look at what you've left out" (Rubens 32).

Thus, in *The Fifth Child*, David and Harriet's lifestyle emerges as charming, but also a bit parasitic. In other words, for Lessing, it becomes a class issue—who pays for such indulgences. And, in fact, David and Harriet cannot pay for their prolific lifestyle. It is David's father who pays for the mortgage and for part of the children's education. And although the Ramsays with their brood of eight are not dependent on anyone else's income, one could argue that for Lessing the issue extends into larger political realms. Rebuking her daughter for her prolific breeding, Dorothy, Harriet's mother comments:

> You want it both ways. The aristocracy—yes, they can have children like rabbits, and expect to, but they have the money for it. And poor people can have children, and half of them die, and expect to. But for people like us in the middle, we have to be careful about the children we have so we can look after them. (16)

Dorothy's argument, although pragmatic and economic, also pertains to eugenicist arguments that were rife during the late Victorian era to which Harriet and David seem so keenly drawn. Reflecting an Arnoldian stance of culture subduing anarchy, eugenicists at the turn of the century argued that middle and upper class breeding was a national obligation—a necessity for survival. As Laura Doyle in her analysis of the effects of eugenics on motherhood suggests, eugenics "helped to inspire a kind of racial panic among the professional middle classes of Western nations"(14). Mr. Ramsay perhaps reflects this when he ponders briefly on the dilemma of the large family, of how as a "father of eight children" he has "little choice," but is nonetheless "for the most part happy" (44). And in reflecting on his children nicknaming Charles Tansley "the little atheist," Mr. Ramsay remarks that Tansley (who came from a family of ten and a working class background), is not a "polished specimen" (66). As Christina Hauck suggests, Mr. Ramsay's internal debate, fraught with self-doubt and self-justification, evokes the national debate over the large family as fulfilling the necessity of empire and the small family as manifesting "evolutionary grace" (117).

These eugenic issues, although important, remain a backdrop in *To the Lighthouse* in that they compete with many other themes. In *The Fifth Child*, though, this issue takes near-center stage. Lessing seems to be enacting the criticisms she levies against Woolf's leaving too much out. Evoking all of the eugenic epithets, Ben, the child that disrupts the Lovatt family stability is described on various occasions as a "throwback," an "alien," a "Neanderthal baby," a "monster," and a "barbarian." He is the cultural Other, who in traditional eugenic terms, must be controlled and conquered, except, in this case, he is not an alien at all, but born into the host family. Specifically, *The Fifth Child* warns against the cataclysmic effects of exorcizing the Other, who is our own mirror. Not to recognize these patterns for Lessing becomes tantamount to succumbing to fairy tales.

Telling a fairy tale—is that what Lessing suggests Woolf is doing in *To the Lighthouse*? The twice repeated phrase "Time passed" (in the past tense) that marks Harriet's pregnancy with Ben and replaces the more fluid present progressive "Time Passes" in *To the Lighthouse*, in fact does suggest that the text's solutions are no longer viable in this more complicated contemporary world. A final interpolated scene in *The Fifth Child* emerges through the fairy tale that David reads to his son Luke and his daughters Helen and Jane, augmenting this suggestion. In Lessing's fairy tale, a brother and a sister venture into a magic forest where birds sing to them, bushes provide chocolate sweets, and pools provide, of all things, orange juice. At one point, the girl becomes separated from her brother and sits down by a pool of clear water where she searches for a fish that might tell her the way home. Instead she finds a girl's face looking straight up at her. She bears a strange and nasty smile and seems to be reaching toward the little girl to pull her into the water. At that moment, Harriet, recognizes herself in the image and cries out to David, "Stop—stop it! You are talking about me—"(45).

Like "The Fisherman's Wife" that Mrs. Ramsay reads to James, this fairy tale is told in pieces that mirror the ongoing diegetic narrative. Unlike Mrs. Ramsay, though, Harriet recognizes herself in the dark Other of the tale. Although Mrs. Ramsay recognizes that "people might say she was tyrannical, domineering, masterful" and although she wonders if she put too much pressure on Minta to make up her mind about marrying Paul (58-60), she remains virtually impervious to any connections between herself and the Fisherman's wife who would be King. The "Fisherman's Wife," concluding with "And there they are living still at this very time" (61), juxtaposes Mrs. Ramsay's pondering the eternal problems of suffering, death, and the poor, yet all the while saying "relentlessly" to all her eight children, "You shall go through it all" and to herself "They will be perfectly happy" (60). In other words, "it will be fine tomorrow"; and, of course, as it turns out, it is not fine tomorrow.

After the shock of the nasty girl trying to draw the child into the pond subsides in *The Fifth Child*, Dorothy, Harriet's mother, also tries to smooth things over. She states: "I know what happened." The little girl leaves the "nasty pool *at once*," runs down the path until she bumps into her brother. They take one another's hands, and they run "safely home" (45). In other words, it will be fine tomorrow. In response, David replies "absolutely," but he is smiling "ruefully" (45). And likewise in *The Fifth Child* all is not fine tomorrow. For Lessing in this text, as well as in others, it is catastrophic to take the pastoral fairy tale for the real.

On one level, Ben is a concrete and individualized manifestation of *To the Lighthouse*'s "Time Passes." Instead of nights "full of wind and destruction," the sea tossing and breaking itself, the "profusion of darkness" that nothing could survive (126-28), instead of these uncontrollable forces of nature that turn the Ramsay household into a ramshackle, there is Ben, who, in his own manner turns the Lovatt household into a ramshackle. Ben is the daily reminder of destructive forces, destructive people in our lives. No one character in *To the Lighthouse* functions in the quite same way—not the cranky Mr. Carmichael, not the judgmental Tansley, or the pessimistic Mr. Ramsay. All of these individuals may be difficult—but they are escapable. In response to Tansley's "Women can't write, Women can't paint," Lily on more than one occasion shifts the focus, asking herself, "Where can I move that tree?" And for a brief moment, there is coming together during the dinner table scene. Toward the end of his novel, Ben and his gang consume specularized violence as much as they consume food: "Shootings and killings and tortures and fightings: this is what fed them" (122). Lessing suggests that some situations or individuals may make the communion that emerges during Mrs. Ramsay's dinner impossible.

Lessing also suggests that these dark forces, which so define Ben, are in all of us. During one of David and Harriet's lovemaking sessions, their idyllic bedroom, that usually has the ambience of a pastoral garden, metamorphoses into what seems like a "black cave that had no end" (10). Later, the oldest of their two children, in rescuing a ball, joyfully engage in a kind of wild, primal dance. In *The Fifth Child*, like in many other Lessing works, there is a warning against a self-willed blindness that denies the Other and denies our own complicity in the social ills that plague our world. Moreover, the threat of our social order spiraling downward into a vortex of senseless violence probably does seem more real than a mother reading a fairy tale to her son, while her husband bumbles around saying "Someone blundered." The threat of children killing children in *The Fifth Child* probably seems more real than children breezing in and out of the house, while a house guest sits at the edge of the lawn painting a lighthouse. The take-out pizzas and quiches, the tacos, tortillas, and chili con carne that Ben and his friends consume are probably more familiar than Boeuf en Daube–what *is* Boeuf en Daube, my students invariably ask me.

To accept this picture is to accept Lessing's suggestion that *To the Lighthouse* attempts to create a dangerous illusory refuge. Beyond the obvious political complicity of the insensible forces of nature in "Time Passes" as being bound up with the forces of war—with the "gloom of cool cathedral caves where gold letters on marble pages describe death in battle" and with the bones that "bleach and burn far away in Indian sands" (127)— beyond the inextricable presence of the everyday in *To the Lighthouse*, (all of which are beyond the scope of this paper), *To the Lighthouse* is not at all the fairytale that *The Fifth Child* suggests that it might be. True, Ben as a phenomenon cannot be ignored—either as an undeniable part of the contemporary world or as a part of ourselves. Yet, in its relegating *To the Lighthouse* to the space of impossible fantasy, *The Fifth Child* seems to enact one of the more dismal fallouts of postmodernism's critiques of modernism. This critique becomes possible only through the processes of reduction—a delimiting of all extra-textual spaces to Mrs. Ramsay's vision that all will be fine tomorrow. Lessing, throughout her works, has critiqued systems of reason and has presented on several occasions other extra-textual spaces which open doors, rather than close them. Yet in this novel, there seems to be an attempt to contain within an objective system of signification all that escapes that system of signification. The result is that David's position of self-willed blindness moves toward apocalypse and Harriet's recognition of her own blindness leads to her losing everything. The epistemic result it seems to me is an entrapment within the culturally produced nonreal as the only real—a tyranny of culture that in disavowing all imaginary spaces nearly assures that the tyranny will continue. Lessing is most likely right in her belief that ignoring our ever-increasing social ills (everything that Woolf supposedly leaves out) ensures our destruction, but so does not attempting to rethink the culturally produced image or pattern. And the latter requires imaginative spaces—perhaps a purple triangle, which, in its mixture of red and blue, is both sacred and sexual, and which, in its openness of form, allows the reader the latitude of rethinking the image.

Notes

[1] Emphasis is mine in both passages.

[2] Also the phrase "Everyone needs a room" appears twice in Lessing's novel.

Works Cited

Doyle, Laura. *Bordering on the Body: The Racial Matrix of Modern Fiction and Culture*. New York: Oxford UP, 1994.

Hauck, Christina. "Why Do the Ramsays Have So Many Children?: Birth Control and *To the Lighthouse*." *Virginia Woolf: Emerging Perspectives. Selected Papers from the Third Annual Conference on Virginia Woolf*. Eds. Mark Hussey and Vara Neverow. NY: Pace U P, 1994. 114-20.

Kato, Megumi. "The Milk Problem in *To the Lighthouse*." *Virginia Woolf Miscellany* 50 (Fall 1997): 5.

Lessing, Doris. *Under My Skin: Volume 1 of My Autobiography, to 1949*. New York: Harper Colins, 1995.

——. *The Fifth Child*. New York: Random, 1989.

Perrakis, Phyllis. E-mail to author. 29 May 2000.

Pringle, Mary Beth. "Killing the House of the Angel: Spatial Poetics in Woolf's *To the Lighthouse*." *Virginia Woolf: Emerging Perspectives. Selected Papers from the Third Annual Conference on Virginia Woolf*. Eds. Mark Hussey and Vara Neverow. NY: Pace U P, 1994. 306-12.

Rubens, Robert. "Footnote to the *Golden Notebook*." Interview. *The Queen*. 21 August 1962.

Saxton, Ruth. "The Female Body Veiled: From Crocus to Clitoris." *Woolf and Lessing: Breaking the Mold*. Ed. Ruth Saxton and Jean Tobin. New York: St. Martin's 1994.

Woolf, Virginia. *To the Lighthouse*. 1927. New York: Harcourt, 1981.

Kathryn S. Laing
Chasing the Wild Goose: Virginia Woolf's *Orlando* and Angela Carter's *The Passion of the New Eve*

"The destination of all journeys is their beginning"
*(*The Passion of the New Eve *186)*

In her 1994 essay on Virginia Woolf, Anita Brookner and Angela Carter, Isobel Armstrong discusses the delayed reaction of women writers to Woolf's fiction, noting that: "when we put into her texts what, until very recently, was consistently left out of them, the categories of politics and sexual politics, it is also possible to see how novelists writing in the 1980s, in particular, have produced texts which resonate with hers" (Armstrong 261). Focusing specifically on the 1984 novel, *Nights at the Circus*, Armstrong discusses Angela Carter's response to the "dialectic of desire in Woolf's work, the source of both experiment and a sense of loss" (Armstrong 261), showing how her writing "comes out of the possibilities for bravura fantasy in *Orlando* (1928)" (Armstrong 258). Carter engages with *Orlando* in her earlier writing too, and in particular in *The Passion of the New Eve*, written prior to *Nights at the Circus* in 1977, and in a libretto, written but never performed, in 1979. I will argue in this paper that the earlier novel is, in part, a dialogue, even an oedipal debate with Woolf's *Orlando* and that Carter's appropriation, in true postmodernist fashion, and testing of themes and techniques in *Orlando* finally releases her from the bleaker vision of her earlier novels into the more liberating and playful idiom of *Nights at the Circus* and *Wise Children*.

In *Orlando* "androgyny, transsexualism, and transvestism call into question not just conventional assumptions about sexuality but, more importantly, conventional assumptions about language itself" (Caughie 79). It is these questions that remain challenging to late twentieth-century and early twenty-first century readers and writers alike. In *The Passion of the New Eve*, Angela Carter responds directly to Woolf's challenge, extending her own analysis of the subject in earlier novels and testing her own theories against Woolf's text. Carter, in her dystopian narrative, literalizes Woolf's fantasy of the man who becomes a woman—Orlando, traveler in space and time and across genders, becomes Evelyn, an Englishman in New York. Fleeing the city that has succumbed to chaos and abandoning his lover, Leila, Evelyn heads for the desert where he meets "Mother" and becomes Eve, not fantastically but painfully and scientifically. He learns femininity through the abuses of the misogynistic Zero and through a meeting with his screen idol, Tristessa. Eve, the newly made woman, discovers that Tristessa, the archetypal "idéale féminine," is a man masquerading as a woman. The violence that brings Tristessa and Eve together, making them "the great Platonic hermaphrodite" (148), leaves Tristessa dead and Eve abandoned and probably pregnant. Meeting Mother for one last time, undergoing a sym-

86

bolic return to the womb and discovering that "Mother is a figure of speech and has retired to a cave beyond consciousness" (184), Eve leaves America by sea.

While *The Passion of the New Eve*, with its titular conflation of Old and New testament narratives is, in one sense, a rewriting of the Genesis myth and the theory of origins, in particular, the origin of femininity, it is also a rewriting of *Orlando* in a postmodern context, and an acknowledgement of its own textual origins. The most concrete evidence that Carter was deeply interested in *Orlando* is of course clear in the posthumously published libretto, "Orlando: or, The Enigma of the Sexes" (*The Curious Room* 155-182). While she follows the Orlando story quite closely in the main text of the libretto, Carter reinterprets Woolf's narrative in the light of her own interests through the prologue. Here, in a dialogue between Orlando and his tutor, she introduces a version of androgyny, desire and "the enigma of the sexes" through a reference to Aristophanes and the myth of the hermaphrodite, divided into two by Zeus as punishment.

If, in the libretto, Carter implants her own theories into Woolf's text, Carter enacts a similar cross-fertilization in *The Passion of the New Eve*. The unnamed philosopher, John Locke, with whom Woolf takes issue over identity in *Orlando* (Burns 357) appears in the epigraph to *The Passion of the New Eve* ("In the beginning all the world was America"), at once highlighting its thematic connections and linking gender issues, according to Heather Johnson, to "a cultural and political economy of gender, race and sexual preference" (Johnson 168). The wild goose, hinted at through goose quills and feathers, that mysteriously appears and disappears in *Orlando* is perhaps recalled through "the Bird of Hermes" in *The Passion of the New Eve* (44), the bird that keeps returning, transmographied and symbolic. These can be read as traces of Carter's indebtedness and connectedness to Woolf's writing, and such a reading is countenanced by Carter's own admission in an interview in 1985 that "One of the snags is that I do put everything in a novel to be *read*—read the way allegory was intended to be read, the way you are supposed to read *Sir Gawayne and the Grene Knight*—on as many levels as you can comfortably cope with at the time" (Haffenden 86).

Through these implicit and explicit borrowings, I wish to consider the radical challenge and inspiration of Woolf's novel for Carter in three areas: demythologizing and motherhood, gender construction and the relation between sexuality, textuality and desire. "I am in the demythologizing business," Angela Carter wrote in 1983, "I'm interested in myths [. . .] just because they are extraordinary lies designed to make people unfree [. . .]. I wrote one anti-mythic novel in 1977, *The Passion of the New Eve*—I conceived it as a feminist tract about the social creation of femininity, amongst other things [. . .]" (Wandor 71). One of the main myths under attack in this novel is that of maternity and motherhood. "Mother," the grotesque and monstrous figure Evelyn encounters in the underground place known as Beulah, is a parodic construction of utopian and essentialist myths about motherhood: "She is the hand-carved figurehead of her own, self-construct-ed theology. [. . .] She was a sacred monster. She was personified and self-fulfilling fertility" (58-59).

Carter's attack on the myth of motherhood has an indirect, even uncon-scious connection with Woolf's writing. Both *The Passion of the New Eve* and *The Sadeian Woman* (a non-fiction work published in 1979) are cri-tiques of certain preoccupations in 1970s feminism, its essentializing tendencies (Bristow 17) and the popular "concept of androgyny that was briefly theorized and idealized" during this time (Rubenstein 115). It might be argued that some of these theories about androgyny were inspired by readings, or misreadings of *Orlando* and *A Room of One's Own*. In a more boldly speculative mode, I would argue that the obvious ambivalence regis-tered in *The Passion of the New Eve* is not only in relation to theoretical and philosophical representations of motherhood, but towards literary mother-hood too. In *A Room of One's Own*, Woolf famously suggests that "a woman writing thinks back through her mothers" (101), back through a female lit-erary line that is both supportive and enriching. In *The Passion of the New Eve*, Carter both acknowledges its matrilineal inheritance and tests it too. This testing and acknowledgement is most evident in central concern with the construction of femininity and gender identity.

Into the narrative of the metamorphosis of Evelyn into Eve, a collage of different narrative genres such as pseudo-medical documentation and sci-ence fiction, Carter inserts a direct reference to the fantastical masque during which Orlando becomes a woman. I quote from *Orlando* "But here, alas, Truth, Candor, and Honesty, the austere Gods who keep watch and ward by the inkpot of the biographer cry No! Putting their silver trumpets to their lips they demand in one blast, Truth!" (*O* 129). Following "Mother's" medical scrutiny of the newly born Eve, Carter's narrative shifts into a different mode, one that is parodic and allusive: "Prompt on cue, trumpets and cym-bals crashed off-stage; when she visited me as the goddess, clad only in her fringe of dugs, I was still overawed, and trembled" (77). At once fore-grounding its own intertextuality and indebtedness, Carter hints at her rewriting of Orlando's transformation, Orlando's vacillation, for her own purposes. Splitting Orlando's transsexualism and transvestism into two, Eve and Tristessa, Carter makes her own analysis of the cultural construction of femininity and gender performance, anticipating, as many critics have sug-gested, the theories of Luce Irigaray and Judith Butler.

Following Orlando's transformation from man into woman, the narrator declares that "in every other respect, Orlando remained precisely as he had been. The change of sex, though it altered their future, did nothing whatev-er to alter their identity" (*O* 133). Orlando only begins to feel her sex affecting her identity when she returns to England in the eighteenth century and she begins to experience society's expectations of her as a woman. The narrative is slippery at every turn and the famous debate about clothes and identity, about the "vacillation between one sex to the other" (*O* 181) that follows has been suggestive for feminist critics and novelists alike. Woolf's text resonates, almost uncomfortably, with Carter's much more brutal investigation of the relation between sex, gender and identity. When all the transformative surgery is over, Evelyn is assured that "A change in the appearance will restructure the essence" (68). Once Tristessa has been unmasked he talks of the methods of concealing his masculinity, noting that: "when the years passed and my disguise became my nature, I no longer troubled myself with these subterfuges. Once the essence was achieved, the appearance could take care of itself" (141). Like Woolf, Carter posits different possibilities for the formation of identity. But Carter refuses the playfulness of *Orlando*, its suggestive pluralism, and fixes the fluidity in its focus on femininity. When Evelyn, now Eve, looks into a mirror s/he "saw Eve; I did not see myself. I saw a young woman who, though she was I, I could in no way acknowledge as myself, for this one was only a lyrical abstraction of femininity to me, a tinted arrangement of curved lines" (74). Eve views herself through male eyes: "I was the object of all the unfocused desires that had ever existed in my own head" (75). Through Eve's troubled doubleness, Carter unravels a thread from the weave of Woolf's complex text and reworks it into a violent and nightmarish version. Eve becomes feminine firstly through scientific reconstruction, through Mother's indoctrination program (videos, pictures, lectures and so on), and through her treatment in Zero's harem. If, according to Isobel Armstrong, "What really ensures the fixing of sexuality [in *Orlando*] is the masque of purity (which is at the same time a masquerade) overseeing Orlando's change of sexual identity" (Armstrong 273), what fixes Eve's is brutalization and violation: "I had spent three months as a wife of Zero. It was as savage an apprenticeship in womanhood as could have been devised for me [. . .]. The mediation of Zero turned me into a woman" (107-108).

This is just one example of Carter's consideration of femininity as construct, Tristessa, Eve's other, being the most extreme version. As Sarah Gamble notes: "While Tristessa's act of self-creation hints at a multiplicity of potential gender identities, the being she chooses to become is nevertheless created out of her own essentialist notions of 'woman'" (Gamble 126). Tristessa alone cannot embody the vacillation of the sexes imagined by Woolf. Her consummate performance of the feminine is ultimately imprisoning and life-denying. Eve's negotiation of her acquired femininity is portrayed with more ambivalence by the end of the novel, partly because it is through Eve that the relation between sexuality and textuality is explored most fully.

Like *Orlando*'s narrator, whose "narrative speculations are only engendered, after all, by Orlando's change of sex in the direction of femininity" (Bowlby 48), Eve attempts to come to terms with her transformation and impending motherhood through the act of narration itself. Where Woolf overtly and playfully suggests the connections between gender identity and language through the metaphor of clothing (Burns 349), Carter introduces the imagery and iconography of alchemical philosophy into her novel. The "alchemical narrative and its emphasis on metamorphosis" is a key "metaphor for the negotiated experience of gender identity" in the novel (Johnson 169-170). While Johnson suggests that "Carter's emphasis on the language that structures alchemy effects a kind of demythologizing of the alchemical narrative itself" (Johnson 169), it also highlights the novel's self-reflexivity, its concern with language and textuality. The language and imagery used by the alchemist philosophers, air, water, earth, fire, nigredo, amber, pervade the novel, generating a unifying pattern and a lyricism that runs against the grain of the brutality and violence of the narrative. The alchemical imagery also constantly refers to other texts, those of the alchemist philosophers, Greek and Roman mythology, and ultimately, they refer to Evelyn who becomes Eve, a blank text, both literally and metaphorically, onto which femininity is imprinted.

In *Orlando*, the narrative of a would-be biographer in pursuit of his/her elusive subject, who is and is not feminine, and Orlando, who has always been haunted, haunted by her quest for the self and for a language to express that self, finds an intriguing echo in Carter's text. Eve's narration emerges not only out of a quest for her own sense of identity, what it means to become Eve, but also out of a sense of loss and desire, figured early in the narrative by the alchemical image of the bleeding white bird. Evelyn sees this alongside a print of a hermaphrodite holding a golden egg in the Czech alchemist's apartment in New York. During his sojourn in the desert, Evelyn encounters an injured and dying bird, "the Bird of Hermes, the bleeding bird of the iconography of the alchemists" (44). Following the sexual union between Eve and Tristessa and Tristessa's murder, Eve is literally haunted: "At night, dreaming, I go back again to Tristessa's house [. . .]. He himself often comes to me in the night, serene in his marvelous plumage of white hair, with the fatal red hole in his breast; after many, many embraces, he vanishes when I open my eyes" (191). Significantly, Carter retains the centrality of this image in her Orlando libretto. In her notes on the first draft, she describes a white eagle which flies away the moment it is given as "the perfect image of a love gift", and in a second draft, Sasha is described as "the winged bird that flies away; a variant of AMOR, the unachievable" (*The Curious Room* 506). Orlando flings words like nets after the wild goose, but she is only left with "an inch of silver—six words—in the bottom of the net" (*O* 299). This "curious residue of language" (Burns 359), the remains of desire, is, in Carter's text, potentially consoling. It gestures towards a new beginning, or at least a new narrative in the final line: "Ocean, ocean, mother of mysteries, bear me to the place of birth" (191). Carter's novel ends with a return to the image of maternity conflating birth and creativity unexpectedly (Johnson 180). Such an ending both looks forward to her later novels, and back to *Orlando* and the juxtaposed births of both of a son and a book.[1]

The wild bird that traverses and flies beyond Woolf's text returns us to ever more richly textured readings of *Orlando* through those writers inspired by the chase.

Notes

[1] These double births are now the subject of renewed critical interest. See, for example, Marylu Hill, *Mothering Modernity: Feminism, Modernism, and the Maternal Muse* (New York: Garland, 1999).

Works Cited

Armstrong, Isobel. "Woolf by the Lake, Woolf at the Circus." *Flesh and the Mirror: Essays on the Art of Angela Carter*. Ed. Lorna Sage. London: Virago, 1994: 257-278.

Bowlby, Rachel. "Orlando's Vacillation." *Feminist Destinations and Further Essays on Virginia Woolf*. Edinburgh: EUP, 1997: 43-53.

Burns, Christy L. "Re-Dressing Feminist Identities: Tensions Between Essential and Constructed Selves in Virginia Woolf's *Orlando*." *Twentieth Century Literature*. 40.3 (1994): 342-364.

Carter, Angela. *The Passion of the New Eve*. London: Virago, 1977.

——. "Notes from the Frontline." *On Gender and Writing*. Ed. Michelene Wandor. London: Pandora Press, 1983: 69-77.

——. "Orlando: or, The Enigma of the Sexes." *The Collected Angela Carter: The Curious Room: Plays, Scripts and an Opera*. Intro. Susannah Clapp. London: Chatto & Windus, 1996: 155-182.

Caughie, Pamela. *Virginia Woolf and Postmodernism: Literature in Quest and Question of Itself*. Chicago: University of Illinois Press, 1991.

Gamble, Sarah. *Angela Carter: Writing From the Front Line*. Edinburgh: EUP, 1997.

Haffenden, John. *Novelists in Interview*. London: Methuen, 1985.

Johnson, Heather L. "Unexpected Geometries: Transgressive Symbolism and the Transsexual Subject in Angela Carter's *The Passion of the New Eve*." *The Infernal Desires of Angela Carter: Fiction, Femininity, Feminism*. Eds. Joseph Bristow and Trev Lynn Broughton. London: Longman, 1997: 166-183.

Rubenstein, Roberta. "Intersexions: Gender Metamorphosis in Angela Carter's *The Passion of the New Eve* and Lois Gould's *A Sea-Change*." *Tulsa Studies in Women's Literature*. 12:1 (1993): 103-118.

Woolf, Virginia. *A Room of One's Own*. New York: Harcourt Brace, 1957.

——. *Orlando*. New York: OUP, 1992.

Jane Lilienfeld
"Something I've Been Meaning to Tell You": Alice Munro as Unlikely Heir to Virginia Woolf

Can one hypothesize, as some Canadian critics do, that female is to male as periphery is to Empire (Fraser xviii-xix; Irvine 50-51)? Materialist feminists working in Postcolonial studies have long argued that women occupy relative positions of privilege within systems of gender, race, and colonial domination (Donaldson 34). Posthumously, the figure of Virginia Woolf, anti-imperialist, cast an ambiguous yet not disempowering shadow over the dominion/ated writer, Alice Munro.

The Virginia Woolf whom Alice Munro first encountered in 1953—the year of Queen Elizabeth II's coronation—was nuanced and many-sided. However, as a socialist pacifist feminist, Woolf was disparaged by much of the British intelligentsia. The Leavis's view of her, certainly, excoriated Woolf's elite class status, underpinned, they insisted, by her co-ownership of the Hogarth Press and, to them, her uncomplicated access to the opinion-shaping power wielded by the male homosocial elite of the Bloomsbury Group (Marcus 76, 79, 92).

In 1953, newly married to a young man from a well-off family, Alice Munro was living what she herself termed a double life. Like Woolf, Munro had begun writing as a young girl, telling interviewers later that "I always did value myself terribly, but I had to pretend I didn't for the purpose of dis-guise" (qtd. in Ross 17). Once married, with children, settled "in the [Vancouver] suburbs, I went on [. . .] living two completely different lives [. . .] I worked out a way of living by pretending to be what people wanted me to be [. . .]" (Munro, qtd. in Ross 19). When first encountering Virginia Woolf and works about her, Munro appears to have had a complicated response to this symbol of the prominence of British writing (qtd. in Rasporich 9-11), under the shadow of which was written what readers and writers of it alike later came to call "Can Lit," Canadian literature (Atwood 11, 29).

What would Munro have been likely to read? By 1953 all of Woolf's novels, many of her stories, *A Room of One's Own*, *Three Guineas*, four books of essays and criticism, and familiar essays published in popular mag-azines were available, and Leonard Woolf's edition of his wife's *A Writer's Diary* was published in 1954. For Munro, writing is a natural outgrowth of reading (Ross 42-44), and at this period Munro read omnivorously, acknowl-edging—among others—the influence of American Southern women's stories (Howells 8-9). Munro had access to literature through her jobs in a University and then public library, but it was in a subversive female friend-ship, rather than the library, that Munro discovered Woolf. Munro and a woman friend—on the surface, ordinary housewives and mothers living in suburban Western Vancouver—

would spend every Tuesday afternoon [. . .] drinking coffee and smok-
ing until we were dizzy. [. . .] We read all the books by and about D. H.
Lawrence, Katherine Mansfield, the Bloomsbury Group, and then we
would get together and we'd talk with incredible excitement (Munro,
qtd. in Rasporich 9).

Following Lawrence and Mansfield, Virginia Woolf is not named, but subsumed into the Bloomsbury Group, appearing to signify that which Munro
could never be: established, upper class, British. Did Munro feel more
aligned with Lawrence, from a working class family, and Mansfield,
Australian rebel against wealth and bourgeois respectability?

Feminist scholars brilliantly debate the vexed personal and literary relations between Mansfield and Woolf; a brief paper cannot represent the
extensive scholarly discourse that shaped my tentative conclusions (*D2* 225-
227; Smith). While both Mansfield and Woolf textualize the female body (a
central preoccupation of Munro's fiction), below I will suggest that Munro
learned from Woolf how to disguise and disperse narratorial voice through a
multi-layered discourse that filters female experience through plots representing random circumstance.

Alice Munro's paternal forebears were impoverished Scots farmers who
in 1818 emigrated to the British territories in Canada. In 1850, they obtained
"crown lands" in the Huron Valley bush (Ross 27-28); that is, lands obtained
from indigenous tribes by the subterfuges of colonial practices, were ceded
to them in return for a token sum. Even after two generations, however, their
descendants lived a disadvantaged rural existence. As Munro could have
discovered in reading about Woolf, Leslie Stephen's forebears, too, had
begun as industrious Scots colonists; but Stephen's grandfather had emigrated to the West Indies, and with his return and subsequent attachment to
the abolitionist Wilberforce elite, his fortunes had risen (Annan 6-7).
Woolf's paternal and maternal forebears had profited in money and status
from a colonial system in which Munro's ancestors, with much less success,
had found themselves inscribed.

As white women aware of living under governments devolving from
colonial power, Woolf and Munro were themselves oppressed while also situated in relative privilege vis à vis indigenous peoples. Much poorer than
Leslie Stephen, who had objected to his daughter Virginia's attending university, Robert Laidlaw, Alice Munro's father, strictly enforced the separate
spheres inhabited by his son and daughter. Munro was expected to perform
the rigorous housework required on the family's failing fox farm while her
brother did farm chores and roamed the outdoors (Rasporich 8). Munro's
education was further curtailed by the family's poverty, and only hard work
in the inadequate rural schools had enabled her to earn a minimal two-year
scholarship to the University of Western Ontario. Not having the money to
continue her education when the scholarship expired, Munro had left college

and married (Ross 49-50). Like Virginia Woolf, personal experience and political observation had made Alice Munro a feminist writer.

It seems unlikely that Munro would have wholly subscribed to the Leavis's view of Woolf. Refusing to reduce literature to ideology (Munro, qtd. in Ross 85), Munro might have gathered strength from Woolf's manifesto as promulgated in "Modern Fiction." There and in Woolf's stories and novels she would have learned Woolf's methodologies. Through complex and freighted skeins of allusion rather than political pronouncements, Woolf's narratives represent a feminist, anti-imperial world-view, one skewering Patriarchal institutions' on-going class and racial domination (Marcus 38, 42, 132-133). Both Munro and Woolf satirize traditional marriage plots in order to make central that which had heretofore been seen as peripheral, focusing on the seemingly random happenstance of daily life, on human relationships and consciousness rather than on external events (*CR*1 149-153). Both deploy a multi-situated, polyphonic narration to represent fictions of women who, while seemingly entrapped in Patriarchal settings, circumvent circumstance. Although Woolf is best known for novels and Munro for stories, in fact, both writers trouble generic boundaries. Munro's recent works are novellas (Howells 11), and Woolf's experiments in form emerged from her short stories (*D*2 13-14).

Munro's short story "How I Met My Husband" is a feminist critique of the romantic view of marriage, presented through a combination of retrospective first person narration and disguised narratorial commentary couched in free indirect discourse. The setting in Ontario, Canada is a large house on land that used to be a rural farm but is fast becoming suburbanized. The suppressed native claims to this tract of land shimmer almost visibly in the background,[1] creating a palimpsest through which are visible subtle variations on colonization.

Munro constructs her plot from incidents in a working class Canadian life constricted by gender. The protagonist Edie's growing awareness of her own sexuality is mapped onto her service as hired help in a middle-class professional household immediately after World War II. Raised in dire rural poverty, Edie had received only a 37 out of 100 on her first-year high school exams and subsequently had left school, facing limited opportunities. The improbable—but entirely believable—appearance of a bush pilot named Chris who lands his small plane near her employers' property leads to a plot which juxtaposes Edie to three older women, separated from her by minute variations in social class, yet united by facing gender inequities. The recognition scene forces Edie to acknowledge that she is a younger version of Alice Kelling, Chris's rejected fiancée. Munro contravenes a reader's expectations of romance, freeing Edie not by seduction, but first by Chris's lost erection (Munro 60) and then by Edie's recognition of female solidarity and agency.

Waiting by the mailbox for the promised summons from Chris, Edie smiles at the mailman daily for many months in happy anticipation of the letter that never comes. Ironically, the mailman thinks she is attracted to him. Having acknowledged her sisterhood to Alice Kelling—both are duped and rejected by Chris—Edie can accept the mailman's offer of marriage, understanding that her "prince charming" came, not in an airplane, but in the mail truck (Munro 64-65).

He is not a sexually attractive man, but he is a member of a family with a good reputation in those parts, a steady worker, with a government job, and a pension plan: "He always tells the children the story of how I went after him by sitting by the mailbox every day, and naturally I laugh and let him because I like for people to think what pleases them and makes them happy" (Munro 68). Shaping unanticipated events to meet her needs, Edie circumvents the cultural conscription into Romance, living comfortably ever after.

I see Virginia Woolf more than Katherine Mansfield as a foremother of this story. Seduction, female jealousy, and traditional romance are mocked; economic consideration as partial cause of female sexual choices is subtly suggested. Events occur in retrospect, making narrative voice more central than dramatic confrontation. Consciousness is primary, and its revelation is methodologically Woolf's. The story's multi-layered narrative voices demonstrate mastery of one of Woolf's greatest legacies, the depiction of a multi-situated polyphonic narrative voice, weaving together personal and cultural memories with the narrative present, past times, and varied settings. Like Virginia Woolf, "Munro [. . .] includes the experiences of the intervening years implicitly in the tones and attitudes of the narrating voice [. . .] creating dimensional resonance like the echoes of memory within the reader's mind" (Moss, qtd. in Rasporich 160). And like Woolf (*D3* 106-107), Munro's polyvocal narrative voice is the result of conscious intervention: "It's so difficult to write a story within the voice of a woman who is not very articulate [. . .] to get the narrator to do something analytical [. . .] will have to be given in a very oblique way [. . .]" (Bonneti). Hence, in both Woolf and Munro's works, "time shifts and shifts in narrative perspectives unsettl[e the fiction . . .] multiple and often contradictory meanings have room to circulate in structures of narrative indeterminacy" (Howells 11).

Now recognized as one of the greatest of Canadian writers, often called the equal of Chekov, Alice Munro has been forced to emerge from her youthful disguise (Ross 91). Munro has repeatedly told the truths of the female body, insisting on her right to voice that which Woolf urged women to fictionalize (Munro, qtd. in Rasporich 21-22, *P* xxxvi-xxxix). As native and postcolonial voices gain increasing prominence in Canadian fiction (Moses and Goldie xix-xxix), Munro's oeuvre—with its development of tasks Woolf left for others to realize—will serve, perhaps as Woolf's may have served for Munro, as a compelling force to be resented and emulated, for that is how one may inadvertently serve as an inspiring embodiment of "the mother country."

Notes

[1] These native claims may be glimpsed in the reader's mind from the anti-hero's airplane in which Edie never flies. Gillian Beer argues that the airplane is a trope of colonial domination. For a discussion of Munro's awareness of native claims to the landscape her forebears pioneered, see Howells 105-113.

Works Cited

Annan, Noel. *Leslie Stephen: The Godless Victorian*. 2nd ed. New York: Random House, 1984.

Atwood, Margaret. *Survival: A Thematic Guide to Canadian Literature*. Toronto: Anansi, 1972.

Beer, Gillian. "The Island and the Aeroplane: The case of Virginia Woolf." *Nation and Narration*. Ed. Homi K. Bhabha. New York: Routledge, 1990. 265-290.

Bonetti, Kay. *Interview with Alice Munro in Clinton, Ontario*. Videocassette. APR, 1987.

Donaldson, Laura E. *Decolonizing Feminisms: Race, Gender, & Empire-Building*. Chapel Hill: U of N Carolina P, 1992.

Fraser, Wayne. *The Dominion of Women: The Personal and the Political in Canadian Women's Literature*. New York: Greenwood Press, 1991.

Howells, Coral Ann. *Alice Munro*. Manchester: Manchester U P, 1998.

Irvine, Lorna. *Sub/Version*. Toronto: ECW Press, 1986.

Marcus, Jane. *Virginia Woolf and the Languages of Patriarchy*. Bloomington: Indiana UP, 1987.

Moses, Daniel David and Terry Goldie, eds., *An Anthology of Canadian Native Literature in English*. 2nd ed. Toronto: Oxford U P Canada, 1998.

Munro, Alice. "How I Met My Husband." *Something I've Been Meaning to Tell You, Thirteen Stories*. New York: Penguin/Plume, 1974. 45-66.

Rasporich, Beverly J. *Dance of the Sexes: Art and Gender in the Fiction of Alice Munro*. Edmonton, Alberta: U of Alberta P, 1990.

Ross, Catherine Sheldrick. *Alice Munro: A Double Life*. Toronto: ECW Press, 1992.

Smith, Angela. *Katherine Mansfield and Virginia Woolf: A Public of Two*. New York: Oxford UP, 1999.

Woolf, Virginia. *The Diary of Virginia Woolf*. Ed. Anne Olivier Bell and Andrew McNeillie. 5 Vols. New York: Harcourt, 1977-84.

——. "Modern Fiction." *The Common Reader, First Series*. Ed. Andrew McNeillie. New York: Harcourt, 1998. 146-154.

——. *The Pargiters by Virginia Woolf: The Novel-Essay Portion of* The Years. Ed. Mitchell A. Leaska. New York: NY Public Library, 1977.

Orientalism/Colonialism

Chene Heady
"Accidents of Political Life": Satire and Edwardian Anti-Colonial Politics in *The Voyage Out*

In recent years, *The Voyage Out*, with its alluring South American setting, has become a popular subject for postcolonial criticism. Most major schools of postcolonial criticism have offered some analysis of the novel. June Cummins, for instance, persuasively connects the novel's anticolonialism with its feminism, noting complicated discrepancies and correspondences between patriarchy's attempts to quantify and conquer Rachel Vinrace and its treatment of indigenous peoples. Kathy Phillips uses the insights of Marxist criticism to suggest that the work's anticolonialism and feminism are both connected with and possibly derived from its critique of capitalism (xix, 53). Other critics have discussed *The Voyage Out* in terms of such important and popular postcolonial topics as the imperial gaze or hybridity. However, there is one major question which postcolonial critiques of the novel have failed to persuasively address. No one has convincingly explained why Richard Dalloway is funny. Nearly every study of *The Voyage Out* grants that Dalloway, who is sketched in sweeping, sarcastic terms, is a figure of anticolonial satire. However, the postcolonial critics have failed to identify anything particularly amusing about him.

Yet in *The Voyage Out*, Woolf is a funnier writer and better satirist than has been generally realized. Postcolonial criticism has failed to find the more amusing elements of the novel's anti-imperial satire for two primary reasons. One (though this principle admits obvious exceptions), jokes tend to be on the surface of a text, so deconstructive techniques will generally read past them. If, as Freud said, jokes reflect the subconscious, it is still the conscious mind that tells them. Secondly, and more importantly, topical humor often registers only in the cultural frame in which it was written. Postcolonial theory and Marxist theory, for all their insights, have failed to find the better jokes on empire in *The Voyage Out* because the Woolf who wrote these jokes lived in a colonial rather than postcolonial age and was politically closer to the Liberal party than to any form of socialism, Marxist or otherwise. As a critical symbol of imperialist capitalism, Richard Dalloway has been a figure more ponderous than funny. But read as a mockery of the imperialism of the Edwardian Conservative party, Richard Dalloway is savagely comic, the butt of a systematic and incisive satire.

My analysis of *The Voyage Out*'s cultural context assumes that the work is as unique among Woolf's novels ideologically as it is stylistically. As many critical works fail to make this distinction, it is necessary to begin by locating the novel as precisely as possible within both the unique political climate of its era and within its author's singular response to this climate. *The Voyage Out* is Woolf's only Edwardian novel, begun in 1907, after the sweeping Liberal victory in the 1906 parliamentary elections, and finished in March 1913, prior to the beginning of World War I and the collapse of the Liberal party (cf. Lee 323). Counter to the garden-party image of the Edwardian period fostered by Vita Sackville-West, the Edwardian era was a time of intense political tension and debate, especially on issues of empire. For every Kipling lauding the empire there was a Chesterton declaring the empire to be a "parasite," "not merely an occasional wrong to other peoples, but a continual feebleness, a running sore, in my own" (*Works* 29 480, *Works* 4 91). The Boer War of 1899 to 1902, in which the empire had to resort to vast expenditures and hideous atrocities to defeat a handful of South African rebels, had caused many Britons to wish for the abandonment of the empire and a return to a Little England. The empire was also losing money, for it was costly to maintain and possessed no particular trade advantages (Bernstein 54). As the colonies were each free to determine their individual trade policies, they had no real incentive to buy manufactured goods from the mother country rather than from the United States or Germany.

These issues were played out in the crucial General Election of 1906. As the imperialist novelist John Buchan admitted, "The name of 'empire' stank in the nostrils of the electorate" in 1906 (qtd. in Hunter 109). In this election, the Unionist vision of "Imperial Preference"—a protectionist trade policy designed to increase imperial profitability—and the Unionist legacy of the Boer War were soundly rejected by the electorate in favor of the Liberal vision of free trade and a consolidated, if not a smaller, empire (cf. Bernstein 54). Woolf characterizes the Tory businessman Willoughby Vinrace as both an imperialist and "a Strong Protectionist" (158), thereby aligning his politics with a defeated Edwardian Conservatism (Woolf 158). The Liberals remained in power in the two much closer elections of 1910, which were contested mostly over the connected issues of Irish Home Rule and the reform of the House of Lords. The Liberal party, then, was in power throughout the writing of *The Voyage Out*, making it reasonable to read the novel as a record of (to use George Dangerfield's term) "Liberal England." Most importantly for our purposes, Liberal opinion favored a devolution and localization of imperial power in both economics (free trade) and govern-ment (local democracy) (Bernstein 166-72). In both England and the colonies, power was, ideally, to devolve on individuals in a rather libertari-an fashion. Models for implementing these principles ranged from that of

the Little England faction, who demanded the abolition of empire altogether, to the moderates who desired a limited imperial reform, with most
Liberals falling somewhere in the middle (Bernstein 13, 168). Though the
Liberal party ruled throughout the last half of the Edwardian period, the
party was increasingly prone to internal conflict and legislative inaction. To
give just one instance, in the wake of the 1906 election Conservatives such
as Kipling feared the dismemberment of the empire, but the Liberal party's
range of opinion on the subject kept it from taking any action beyond a few
minor reforms (Hunter 168). As Dangerfield has argued, the perhaps illusory Liberal vision of a just, harmonious society was faced with the harsh
realities of regional and class conflict, and could not respond (7-8). After
World War I, the Liberal party entirely collapsed and gave way in the twenties to the Labour party. Consequently, Woolf's other novels were written in
a markedly different political context.

The Voyage Out clearly situates itself within the political debates of
Liberal England. London is in a "ferment" over a General Election resem-
bling those of 1910; the "Irish members" are "brawling" in parliament;
Willoughby Vinrace attacks the Liberal Prime Minister Asquith (Woolf 96,
114, 158). Woolf references even the late Edwardian worries about the direction of the Liberal Party. When Terence Hewet imagines attending a London
dinner party upon his return to England, he cannot help but also imagine the
diners "talking about the state of the Liberal party" (Woolf 243). Hewet's
dinner party could have been held in Bloomsbury. Patrick Brantlinger
asserts that during and after World War I Bloomsbury turned increasingly
toward political radicalism of a socialist and anti-imperialist variety, but
admits that prior to the war the group more or less unanimously espoused a
"liberal humanism" (150). Maynard Keynes supports this assertion, remembering "the early Edwardian days" of Bloomsbury as days of "undisturbed
individualism" (61). The common Edwardian contrast of Socialism with
Liberal individualism confers a definite political meaning on Keynes' assertion (cf. Masterman 2). If Brantlinger does not proceed to discuss *The
Voyage Out* in Liberal terms, this is only because, in a strange exception to
his generally fine historical scholarship, he dates *The Voyage Out* from its
World War I-era date of publication (1915) and not from its pre-war date of
completion (March 1913) (Brantlinger 150; cf. Lee 323).

Kathy Phillips' arguments against the idea that Edwardian Bloomsbury
and the Edwardian Woolf were Liberals, made throughout her chapter on
The Voyage Out, also fall on some hard historical soil. Even Leonard Woolf,
Bloomsbury's greatest political radical, did not begin his turn from
Liberalism to socialism until well into 1912, and he was not actively
involved in any socialist movement until the summer of 1913 (Lee 322-23).
Further, Leonard's socialism was, at this point, the Fabian socialism theo-
rized by the Webbs, whom Virginia usually hated, and popularized by H. G.
Wells, her future literary antagonist (Rose 149). Fabian socialism is largely

synonymous with Edwardian socialism, as the Fabians controlled the Edwardian Labour Party (Dangerfield 228). Fabian socialism imagined a future socialist Utopia gradually attained through social engineering performed by a chosen bureaucratic class. Fabianism was a mechanistic system which envisioned people as simply the sum total of environmental forces. Most importantly for our purposes, most Fabians were also imperialists, seeing centralized empires both as more efficient than localized self-government and as transitional steps toward the socialist world state (Rose 129). As should be apparent, the line between Conservative and Fabian could grow quite thin on issues of empire. In fact, from 1903 to 1908, the socialist Webbs hosted a discussion group called the "Coefficients," whose ultimate aim was "to unite imperialist Liberals and reforming Conservatives in a Party of National Efficiency" (Rose 131). Similar plans were proposed by the former Little Englander Lloyd George in 1910 (Dangerfield 38, Shannon 428). As we shall see, Woolf alludes to these coalitions in *The Voyage Out*, with no small amount of satire and repulsion. Woolf's historical location, literary circle, individualism, and hatred of empire, combine to place *The Voyage Out* solidly in a Liberal context.

As we should then expect, *The Voyage Out*'s jokes on imperialism are precisely the jokes of Liberal anti-imperialism, the jokes of free trade, democracy, and individualism against an empire in need of protectionism, bureaucracy, and authoritarianism. Richard Dalloway is mocked not as a figure of "capitalist imperialism," but as a self-deluded Conservative who cannot see that the height of empire is over, and that a Liberal devolution of power must follow. Even the means by which the Conservative politician Richard Dalloway enters Willoughby Vinrace's ship (and, therefore, the plot of the novel) is itself a mockery of Conservative imperialism. Home Rule for Ireland was the most controversial imperial issue in the Edwardian epoch, supported by Liberals, bitterly contested by Conservatives. As Home Rule was repeatedly passed by the Commons and vetoed by the Lords, the Liberal attempt to remove the Lords' veto power over legislation itself became an imperial issue. Dalloway forces his way onto the boat via his connections with the Lords, using the shipping magnate Lord Glenaway to pressure Willoughby Vinrace (Woolf 39-40). As Vinrace says, "Mr. Richard Dalloway seems to be a man who thinks that because [. . .] his wife's the daughter of a peer, they can have what they like for the asking" (Woolf 38-39). At the very least, the passage reflects a suspicion of the Lords. The Lords have too much power, and it literally forces the Conservative politician onto a colonial expedition.

Richard Dalloway's primary comic trait is his tendency toward self-delusion. This trait is often missed by critics who see him as an image of Britain's dominant political system. In both Dalloway's mind and Kathy Phillips' analysis, Dalloway and his kind do rule the world; the only point of disagreement between them is whether or not this is a fortuitous arrangement (Phillips 54-59). It is my assertion that Dalloway is deluded rather than dominant, as the narrator's initial sketch of him suggests. Richard Dalloway is, we are told, "unable for a season, by one of the accidents of political life, to serve his country in Parliament" (Woolf 39). In short, he lost his last election. Since the Conservatives lost every election between 1906 and 1915, it is unlikely that Dalloway's defeat is a mere "accident of political life." But Dalloway, the narrator implies, refuses to face such unpleasant facts and attributes his defeat to sheer chance. Dalloway's tendency toward optimistic self-deception is also present in his often discussed imperial fantasy of English "continuity," in which he imagines a world-conquering "line of conservative policy, which went steadily from Lord Salisbury to Alfred" (Woolf 51). Phillips sees this passage as reflecting the pervasive nature of British imperialism, embodied especially in the work of the "present" imperialist Lord Salisbury (54). I suspect that the joke, though, is that the Conservative Prime Minister Lord Salisbury, who led England in the Boer War, was not "present," as Phillips has it, but was, rather, dead. Salisbury had died in 1903 and his party had been defeated in 1906, largely due to public disgust with the Conservative imperial policy of Salisbury and Balfour. If, as a significant number of political references suggest, the book is set in 1911 (cf. Phillips 62-63), then Dalloway has simply blocked out the last eight years, and is fancifully living in the company of dead men. Given that Salisbury is dead and that applying either the term "conservative" or "imperialist" to the Saxon king Alfred is a ridiculous exercise, we can conclude that Dalloway's "continuity" has no real origin and no real continuance. It is entirely and comically imaginary.

Having been turned out of Parliament, but wishing to maintain a sense of political importance, Dalloway then goes on a kind of fact-finding mission to Europe and Africa. Abroad, Dalloway encounters only new illusions. He avoids all real dangers—"a disease" in the East and "typhoid" in Russia—and instead safely tours French factories in the hardly objective company of their owners (Woolf 39). Next, in what seems a clear attack on the imperialist Robert Louis Stevenson's Pyrenees travel book *Travels with a Donkey*, Mr. and Mrs. Dalloway ride mules in Spain, " for they wished to understand how the peasants live" (Woolf 39). Richard Dalloway, for all his talk of world empires, is as deluded about the world at large as he is about the will of his constituents. Thus, when he boards Vinrace's ship as part of his fact-finding mission, Richard is already lost in a thick comic fog of self-deception. His later comment that "[a]fter the labours of legislation, I deserve sleep" is true in more senses than he realizes (Woolf 62).

Once on board, Richard Dalloway begins to enunciate a mechanistic political philosophy resemblant to both Fabian socialism and certain varieties of conservatism. Dalloway's political philosophy, almost the inverse of libertarian Liberalism, is succinctly expressed in his "ideal": "Unity. Unity of aim, of dominion, of progress" (Woolf 64). In a conversation which oddly anticipates the essay "Mr. Bennett and Mrs. Brown," Rachel contrasts Dalloway's mechanistic vision of people and politics with the picture of a hypothetical "old widow, in her room somewhere, let us suppose, in the suburbs of Leeds" (Woolf 66). Like the novels of Arnold Bennett and H. G. Wells, Dalloway's political philosophy falls short precisely because it mistakenly treats the individual simply as a product of material and social forces. His paternalistic legislation may cause Rachel's hypothetical widow in the suburb of Leeds to have "a little more tea, a few lumps of sugar" but "Still, there's the mind of the widow—the affections; those you leave untouched. But you waste your own" (Woolf 66). Anticipating the counterarguments of both Wells and Bennett against Woolf, Richard replies to this criticism by insisting that Rachel's individualism minimizes the extent to which individuals are constructed by government and environment. "The state [is] a complicated machine" of which "we citizens are parts," Dalloway asserts; in other words, politics control if the widow has less tea, and if the widow has less tea, it does harm her soul (Woolf 66). Rachel, however, simply cannot think in these mechanistic terms, cannot imagine her "lean black widow, gazing out of her window" as also "a vast machine [. . .] thumping, thumping, thumping"(Woolf 66). Significantly, Wells, while ambivalent at times about the empire, had been one of the most ardent imperialists in the Coefficients (Hunter 117). The similarities between Woolf's critiques of literature and her critiques of political philosophy are far from coincidental. As Dalloway complains, Rachel's decision to reject his mechanistic system in favor of the primacy of the individual, identifies her, despite her lack of any conscious political philosophy, as a "young Liberal" (Woolf 66).

Richard Dalloway's comically unsuccessful attempts to force his philosophy on the ship's passengers culminates in his attempt to force himself physically on Rachel Vinrace. Dalloway's pick-up line—"Have you ever read Burke?"—immediately establishes this scene as unique in the literature of seduction (Woolf 75). Dalloway is the ultimate conservative seducer, attempting to force Rachel to simultaneously submit to his authority and to agree to read Burke's defense of legitimacy (Woolf 75). As Woolf seems well aware, here her satire becomes so extreme as to border on farce. When told of the scene, Helen Ambrose immediately recognizes its comic nature. As the narrator informs us, Helen "had to keep her lips from twitching" as the traumatized Rachel "poured out [her story] abruptly with great seriousness and no sense of humour" (Woolf 80). The narrative trajectory of Rachel's story underscores the scene's farcical satire: "We talked about politics. He told me what he had done for the poor somewhere [. . . .] He kissed me" (Woolf 80). Helen seems to get the last word on Richard. He is "pompous and sentimental," a "silly creature" (Woolf 80). His day has passed, and he poses no real danger for Woolf's characters and no real help for Britain's empire.

However, Woolf's comedy is too consistently dark to permit such a tidy resolution of the tensions embodied in the figure of Richard Dalloway. Both his remark that "I call myself a Conservative for convenience sake [. . .] But there is more in common between the two parties than people generally allow" (Woolf 67) and his later talk of "coalition governments" (Woolf 77) threateningly conjure up the schemes of Lloyd George and the Webbs to unite all imperialists in a seemingly invincible party of empire. Worse, if Dalloway has failed to seduce Rachel Vinrace, he has seduced Willoughby. While still on ship, Dalloway remarks that Willoughby Vinrace is "the kind of man we want in parliament" and suggests that indeed "we shall see him in Parliament" (Woolf 73-74). In short order, Dalloway's vision becomes Willoughby's vision. As he remarks to Helen concerning both his goal and its origin, "all this is tending to Parliament, Helen. It's the only way to get things done as one wants them done. I talked to Dalloway about it" (Woolf 86).

Following Dalloway's exit, Willoughby becomes the book's model of what a revived Conservatism would mean for both England and the colonies. When the ship reaches South America, Willoughby separates from the main party to attend to his business affairs. Following this, he writes Helen Ambrose "half a page about his own triumphs over wretched little natives who went on strike and refused to load his ships, until he roared English oaths at them" (Woolf 196). Besides providing a wonderfully ludicrous mental image, the picture of Vinrace swearing at colonized strikers is quite topical. The British "Industrial Peace" which, despite losses in real wages, prevailed from 1893 to 1910 was broken in 1911, first by Welsh mining strikes then, more devastatingly, by the London dock workers' strike (Dangerfield 260). The dock workers' strike of August 1911 paralyzed the nation, as goods could neither be shipped nor received. Food spoiled, coal could not reach its destination, and life in London began to grind to a starved out halt. Rather than settling with the workers, the shipping magnates notoriously and repeatedly demanded that troops be loosed upon the strikers and the goods delivered by force (Dangerfield 262). Winston Churchill, the Liberal in charge of the Interior, refused to employ force (as he had done against striking Welsh miners), and the dispute was worked out by arbitration, much to the annoyance of the owners (Dangerfield 261-62). Despite the shift in locale, Willoughby Vinrace's status as the owner of "one of the largest shipping businesses in Hull" (Woolf 158) connects his behavior towards his strikers with that of the major shipping magnates in the dock strike. In Woolf's darkly comic vision, though Dalloway's hour has passed, the danger remains that he will be reincarnated in a more violent and crass form in Willoughby Vinrace. Willoughby's true offense as a colonialist is, ironically, that he treats the indigenous people exactly as shipping magnates treat their English workers. One suspects all too well how he would "get things done." An England of Willoughbys would be as mechanistic and authoritarian as an England of Dalloways. In both England and the colonies, the individual would be crushed, and mechanism would rule. Woolf's satire on Richard Dalloway ends indeterminately. Having savagely depicted both the folly and brutality of the Conservatives, she leaves the question of whether this system will remain defeated or revive with the reader.

In "Mr. Bennett and Mrs. Brown" Woolf warned us of the dangers of abandoning the attempt to understand individuals in favor of subsuming the individual under deterministic or Utopian schemes. Similarly, as critics we must fight the temptations to subsume the earlier Virginia, a Liberal master of the broad topical joke, under the later political radical and experimentalist artiste who fits more easily into some critical paradigms. Liberating the early Woolf from her own long later shadow enables us to see in Woolf both a greater artistic range than she has usually been acknowledged to possess, and a distrust of empire deep enough to survive and transcend major changes in political philosophy. In short, if we are to truly understand Woolf as a writer and as an opponent of empire, we must "never, never" lose sight of the early Virginia.

Works Cited

Brantlinger, Patrick. "'The Bloomsbury Faction' Versus War and Empire." *Seeing Double: Revisioning Edwardian and Modernist Literature*. Eds. Carola Kaplan and Anne Simpson. New York: St. Martins P, 1996. 149-70.

Bernstein, George. *Liberalism and Liberal Politics in Edwardian England*. Boston: George Allen and Unwin, 1986.

Chesterton, G. K. "The Daisy as Imperial Symbol." *The Collected Works of G. K. Chesterton, Volume 27*. Ed. Lawrence Clipper. San Francisco: Ignatius P, 1986. 479-84.

——. *What's Wrong With the World. The Collected Works of G. K. Chesterton, Volume 4*. Ed. James Schall. San Francisco: Ignatius P, 1987. 33-220.

Cummins, June. "Death and the Maiden Voyage: Mapping the Junction of Feminism and Postcolonial Theory in *The Voyage Out*." *Virginia Woolf: Texts and Contexts: Selected Papers from the Fifth Annual Conference on Virginia Woolf*. Eds. Beth Daugherty and Eileen Barrett. New York: Pace UP, 1996. 204-9.

Dangerfield, George. *The Strange Death of Liberal England*. 1935. New York: Capricorn Books, 1961.

Hunter, Jefferson. *Edwardian Fiction*. Cambridge, Massachusetts: Harvard UP, 1982.

Keynes, John Maynard. "My Early Beliefs." *The Bloomsbury Group: A Collection of Memoirs, Commentary and Criticism*. Ed. S. P. Rosenbaum. Toronto: U of Toronto P, 1975. 48-64.

Phillips, Kathy. *Virginia Woolf Against Empire*. Knoxville: U of Tennessee P, 1994.

Rose, Jonathan. *The Edwardian Temperament: 1895-1919*. Athens, Ohio: Ohio UP, 1986.

Shannon, Richard. *The Crisis of Imperialism 1865-1919*. London: Paladin, 1976.

Woolf, Virginia. *The Voyage Out*. 1915. New York: Harcourt, Brace, Jovanovich, 1988.

Steven Putzel
Virginia Woolf and British "Orientalism"

The famous 1910 *Dreadnought* Hoax has, of course, inspired a great deal of critical comment. It is an example of Woolf's youthful adventurousness, of early Bloomsbury camaraderie and iconoclasm, and of her life-long criticism of British patriarchal imperialism. In another study, I have drawn on the incident as an example of her performative, even theatrical interests. Like all aspects of Woolf criticism, the incident defies simple analysis. Certainly, convincing the British Admiralty that Anthony Buxton was a visiting Abyssinian Emperor traveling with his entourage, finagling a military escort aboard the H.M.S *Dreadnought*—the most powerful battleship of its day and flagship of the British fleet—touring the ship, inspecting the Honor Guard, and then leaking the whole story to the press made a laughing stock of the British Navy and demonstrated the group's contempt for the imperial war machine. I am not at all sure, however, that we should be too quick to fully agree with Kathy Phillips when she speculates that "Perhaps Woolf already had begun to see the common cause uniting women in a patriarchy and colonized people in an Empire" (Phillips 248). Even the young Virginia Stephen is "against Empire," but the hoax also acts as an early example of Woolf's own complicity with the Orientalism of her time and culture.

Only a few months after Woolf's tour of the *Dreadnought*, Arthur James Balfour delivered a speech to the House of Commons outlining his suggestions for Britain's future policies toward Egypt. Edward Said, who defines Orientalism as "a way of coming to terms with the Orient that is based on the Orient's special place in European Western experience" (1), views this performance as a clearly articulated British view not only of Egypt policy, but of attitudes toward all of the colonies in the East and in Africa. In short, Balfour and the other politicians of his time outline the familiar patriarchal attitude that Egypt, India, Indochina, Malaya are all better off under British rule, that they are, in fact, historically incapable of self-rule (Said 31-46). Said demonstrates that western orientalist attitudes were not a nineteenth century phenomenon, tracing them back at least to Aeschylus's *The Persians* and Euripides' *The Bacchae*. The East is irrational, sprawling, amorous, insinuating danger and decadence. Although the well- known application of this orientalist theory to the works of Kipling, Conrad and Forster may not be as straight forward as Said suggests, the theory becomes even more complicated when applied to Woolf.

In fact, this Orientalism is to a large extent synonymous with British (or American) attitudes toward "the other," toward terra incognita in general. In Woolf's work, journeys to Egypt, India or to South America have much the same effect on her characters. Woolf's own brief 1907 *TLS* review of Charlotte Lorrimer's *The Call of the East* demonstrates both Lorrimer's romantic Orientalism and Woolf's somewhat ambivalent attitude toward

Lorrimer's perspective. Woolf praises the evocative descriptions of the Chinese and Japanese landscape, but she seems to understand that the descriptions are dreamy and romantic. The review shows that the young reviewer is seduced by the "orientalist" idea of the inscrutable eastern face and the eastern ability to "enjoy simple things—the shadow of the trees at noon and the insect humming on a summer's night" (131). But Woolf recognizes that Lorrimer's descriptions of the people are necessarily flawed. Lorrimer's attempt to empathize with the Japanese mother who has lost her child cannot be fully successful. Here is Woolf's (Virginia Stephen's) own orientalist comment: "The spectator's attitude is courteous, and she would like to help: but how? She is puzzled; she does not understand. The most she can do is to write down the actions in the little drama reverently, to notice all that is fair and quaint and different, and to believe that beneath the decorous surface there is the 'deep underlying poetry' of Oriental faith" (131).

In her essay, "Death and the Maiden Voyage: Mapping the Junction of Feminism and Postcolonial Theory in *The Voyage Out*," June Cummins cautions against any monolithic reading of Woolf's or her character Rachel Vinrace's colonial view: "Like Woolf, [Rachel] occupies neither a totally oppressive nor completely victimized position" (Cummins 205). Cummins has in mind critics such as Andrea Lewis and Suzette Henke who have discussed the way Rachel's (and perhaps Woolf's) "colonial gaze" dehumanizes the natives. In fact, I am reminded that even Jane Marcus, who has argued convincingly in support of Woolf's anti-imperialist credentials, notes that Woolf's description of a "'very fine negress'" in *A Room of One's Own* (55) is evidence of "Woolf's part in the Orientalism of modernism" (Marcus 149).

To add to the complexity of the questions of Woolf's Orientalism, let's return for a minute to the *Dreadnought* Hoax photograph. Clearly the group demonstrates the gullibility of the British Navy and the way its imperialist, orientalist attitudes blind it; the officers see what they expect to see. Nevertheless, the greasepaint, beards, turbans, jewels and Adrian Stephen's Swahili mixed with garbled Greek and Latin present a kind of minstrel show, and reflect the group's romanticized, orientalist view of how an Islamic African prince looks and acts. In addition, the Hoax demonstrates that the Empire readily accepts the "foreign" *signifiers* while demonstrating a profound ignorance of the *signifieds*. For example, the officers take in strange sounding words and they read "language," rather than "jibberish"; they see trousers and read male; and they see official, officious, confident behavior and read patriarchal royalty. In fact, the navy embraces theatrical, performative signs as though they were reality. The over coded theatrical signs presented by these Bloomsbury players neutralize knowledge that should have helped the officers detect the scam; these officers certainly knew Latin and perhaps even some Greek, but they failed to detect what should have been familiar words cribbed from Homer and Virgil.

In some ways the escapade reminds me of my British nephew's imitation of the accent and dialect of the ubiquitous Indian shop keeper; when we enact stereotypes we are at least to some extent complicit in those stereotypes. Woolf and her friends knew that their "Abyssinians" were a theatrical construct made up of stereotypes or signs, but how well did they themselves understand these signs? Their own ignorance of Africa and the Middle East, their own orientalist attitudes inform their performance. The Orientalism of the naval officers, the hoaxers, and of the British tourists in *The Voyage Out* is a product of what Louis Althusser calls "ideological state apparatuses" or ISAs. Our schooling, religious training, language, theatrical entertainment, literature, art, etc. form a complex system that over determines any knowledge we obtain through any one of the institutions in the system, making such learned constructions as stereotypes seem natural, and making the acquired reading of these signs also seem natural. Woolf's own growing awareness that this over determination subsumes even seemingly neutral institutions into the service of the white, middle class British patriarchy will eventually lead her to recognize that the subjection of women is inextricably linked to the "subjection" (as Althusser employs the term) of all people within the governing ISA (182). It will not be until *Three Guineas* and the immanence of a second World War that Woolf will fully tie women's resistance to their interpellation as "*subjects*" to the resistance of colonists, thus allowing her to become less complicit in the ideology of empire.

In an early work such as *The Voyage Out*, Woolf is still criticizing narrow British attitudes without the realization that she too is subject to interpellation by the ideological state apparatus; she had not yet raised the call for an "Outsider's Society," through which individuals might resist interpellation by the dominant ISA. As Patrick McGee puts it in his commentary on *Three Guineas*, "Woolf's antipatriarchal rhetoric, though it may employ figures drawn from the culture it opposes, does not simply repeat that culture" (McGee 98). So, while Woolf's depiction of South American culture is clearly a critique of British patriarchal colonialist attitudes, her description (and lack of description) also reflects her own still entrenched romantic conception of distant places. *The Voyage Out* begins with a view of London, the imperial center of the world. As Mr. and Mrs. Ambrose, genteel, scholarly, refined members of London's leisured middle class, walk along the Embankment, they are surrounded by angry drones, denizens of the empire's government, who "looked small–decorated with fountain pens, and burdened with despatch-boxes"; they "had appointments to keep, and drew a weekly salary . . ." (*VO* 9). After retreating to a cab and passing through Piccadilly Circus, Mrs. Ambrose is startled to discover "that after all it is the ordinary thing to be poor, and that London is the city of innumerable poor people" (*VO* 12).

Contrast this view of London life with the novel's only description of the South American natives. When a group of British tourists, including Mrs. Ambrose and Rachel, steam upriver to catch a glimpse of a native village,

> they observed the women, who were squatting on the ground in triangular shapes, moving their hands, either plaiting straw or kneading something in bowls . . . . The women took no notice of the strangers, except that their hands paused for a moment and their long narrow eyes slid round and fixed upon them with the motionless inexpressive gaze of those removed from each other far, far beyond the plunge of speech (*VO* 284).

The ISA of the British women separates them from these other women, just as the same ideological apparatus had separated Mrs. Ambrose from the poor London women. Meanwhile, one of the tourists "engaged in talk with a lean majestic man, whose bones and hollows at once made the shapes of the Englishman's body appear ugly and unnatural" (*VO* 284). To Rachel, the scene is atavistic, timeless, innocent. These English tourists "felt themselves treading cumbrously like tight-coated soldiers among these soft instinctive people" (*VO* 285). Here the tourists', even the women's, identity with imperial military colonialism is explicit, along with an unmistakable orientalist, romanticized, even Rousseauian view of the "natives." All of these binaries—time-bound/timeless, tight/soft, male/female, British/native —are momentarily connected by the intersecting gaze, the stare from British to native women and from native to British women. This connection affects each of the tourists differently, somehow shaking their certainty, perhaps causing a momentary questioning of their cultural assumptions.

The reader's response to the episode must be equally complex. The authorial narrator herself seems caught up in the romantic vision, focusing on the tourists' reactions rather than on the native women themselves. Although the gaze is mutual, the narrative and the British gaze still seem to objectify "the Other." Of course, in typical British fashion, the visitors see themselves as the norm and the natives as "the Other," even though they are the visitors, the outsiders. The scene fills Rachel with a sense of human frailty and perhaps serves as a premonition of the fatal disease that she contracts soon after her return to the villa.

Apart from this one trip upriver, the British tourists spend their time in an enclave and life-style that mimics England. They sit at tea in their club-like hotel, they pursue each other romantically, and they attend Anglican service. (A trip to British resort destinations in Spain, Portugal, Santorini, Kalamata, etc. today will still reveal much the same transplanted culture—with the addition of Fish & Chips shops reflecting the altered class status of the contemporary traveler.) Curiously, when the Anglican minister, Mr. Bax, delivers his sermon, he sounds much like Said's Mr. Balfour; the British tourists "owed a duty to the natives." He adds that a friend had assured him "that the success of our rule in India, that vast country, largely depended upon the strict code of politeness which the English adopted towards the natives" (*VO* 231). Of course, Rachel, along with Woolf, is appalled by this reductive, paternalistic view. But what does Rachel's indignant, even furious response mean: "How can they—how dare they—what do they mean by it—Mr. Bax, hospital nurses, old men, prostitutes, disgusting—" (*VO* 233)? Is she disgusted with the platitudinous paternalism, or is she disgusted by the thought that there is brotherhood between her kind and miserable wretches in the Spanish town and throughout the world?

Surely there is a powerful critique of paternalistic colonialism here. But Woolf seems more interested in this novel and in her other works in what this colonialism has done to the British than in what it has done to native populations. For example, she is more interested in the metonymic relationship between colonialism and the Western institution of marriage than she is in the lives of the native women who meet the visitors' collective gaze. In fact, many of Woolf's British characters abroad become indolent, corrupted by the languid clime. When Rachel herself succumbs to some strange tropical disease and languishes toward death, the local Spanish American doctor, Rodriguez, is a cliché, a product of British snobbery. He speaks "execrable French," he makes furtive little movements, and Hewet, Rachel's very British fiancé, notes Rodriguez's "insignificance, his dirty appearance, his shiftiness, and his unintelligent, hairy face" (*VO* 337-38). The narrative voice does nothing to mitigate the view of Rodriguez as a shiftless incompetent, in contrast to the middle-class European doctor who eventually (and too late) intervenes.

The British patriarchal colonialism in South America kills Rachel, as imperial India will later kill Percival in *The Waves* and will ruin Peter in *Mrs. Dalloway*. As early as her farcical play, *Freshwater*, Woolf has George

Frederick Watts, her representative of British paternalism, send Ellen Terry off to Bloomsbury with the following exhortation: "In that polluted atmosphere spread your doctrines, propagate your race, wear trousers." He adds, "there will come a day when the voice of purity, of conscience, of high-mindedness, of nobility, and truth, will again be heard in the land" (82). So Bloomsbury is where one goes to break free from the constraints of the Empire and where women can obtain what has been the prerogative of men. In contrast, Mr. and Mrs. Cameron pack up and are off, accompanied by their caskets, to die in India: "We go to seek a land less corrupted by hypocrisy, where nature prevails. A land where the sun always shines. Where philosophers speak the truth. Where men are naked. Where women are beautiful. Where damsels dance among the currant bushes . . ." (83). Julia Cameron, who was related to Woolf, is certainly a sympathetic character. But aren't currant bushes English rather than Asian? Once again, here is a somewhat less overtly violent, more romanticized, yet still deadly side of Orientalism. Whereas the Irish looked westward to the mythical Tir-na-nog for their other-world paradise, the British look both East and West to subsume other cultures into their military/economic empire and to be subsumed by the exoticism of "the Other"; the Camerons' "paradise" is an India that has been reconstructed to suit British sensibilities.

Those who survive their stint in the colonies to return to the Motherland, can never really leave the colonies behind. The patriarch of three generations in *The Years*, Colonel Abel Pargiter lounges in his club with "men of his own type, men who had been soldiers, civil servants," men who revive "with old jokes and stories now their past in India, Africa, Egypt"(*TY* 4). Thus their memories are reordered into jokes and stories, constructed experiences, through which they retroactively impose structure and meaning on multivalent experiences that they almost certainly did not understand at the time. The Colonel stares with "blue eyes that seemed a little screwed up, as if the glare of the East were still in them; and puckered at the corners as if the dust were still in them" (*TY* 5). He is partially blinded by his colonial experience, and what vision he has left is still tinged with sediments of Empire. After a lifetime of building and defending this Empire, now "there was nothing to do." Again, the colonies have sapped the colonist, relegating him to the inactivity of the Club which has been built with wealth stripped from the colonies.

In *The Waves*, which Jane Marcus and others see as Woolf's most complete critique of British imperialism (Marcus 142), Bernard describes a party whose inner circle are of Colonel Pargiter's class. "[S]ome lady . . . leads one into a private alcove and admits one to the honour of her intimacy." Here is the conversation of Empire: "What is to be done about India, Ireland, or Morocco? Old gentlemen answer the question standing decorated under chandeliers." Bernard and, of course, Woolf, realize that this ordering of the world through empire, the "orderly and military progress," is "a convenience, a lie" (*TW* 254-55). The idea that condescending British Orientalism is a product of the ideological state apparatuses gives way here to the reality of what Althusser calls the "repressive state apparatuses" (144-45) in which the colonized are coerced into accepting the social norms of British society.

Perhaps Woolf's clearest attitudes toward colonialism and empire can be found in two of her final works, *Three Guineas* and *Between the Acts*. Before relinquishing the last of her "three guineas" in the cause of "culture and intellectual liberty" and to "prevent war . . . by protecting the rights of the individual; by opposing dictatorship; by ensuring the democratic ideals of equal opportunity for all" (*TG* 100), Woolf insists on understanding what these concepts mean in British society. Woolf infuriated many in the establishment with her implication that Hitler, Franco and Mussolini were not the only dictators and tyrants, that "He [the dictator] has widened his scope. He is interfering now with your liberty; he is dictating how you shall live; he is making distinctions not merely between the sexes, but between the races" (*TG* 102). Since "Our country" has treated women as slaves "throughout the greater part of its history," women are "outsiders," for whom "Our country" has no meaning. Woolf now clearly recognizes and articulates an idea that she was striving for in all the works mentioned so far, that paternalism and imperialism are analogous, and she extends the analogy to equate imperialism with German, Spanish and Italian fascism. She knows, however, that she has "imbibed, even from the governess, some romantic notion that Englishmen, those fathers and grandfathers whom she sees marching in the picture of history, are 'superior' to the men of other countries." In other words, she recognizes her own complicity, her own participation in the Orientalist attitudes and outlooks. She further laments that even after checking the claims of the rulers against "the testimony of the ruled—the Indians or the Irish," some patriotism, "some ingrained belief in the intellectual superiority of her own country" remains (*TG* 108).

Woolf sees that the only possible solution to the violence and war inevitable under patriarchal imperialism is for women to identify with the colonized and to act upon the reality that woman is the "other," the "outsider." Neither Rachel Vinrace in *The Voyage Out* nor her author could have proposed "the Outsiders' Society," in which each member "will bind herself to take no share in patriotic demonstrations; . . . to absent herself from military displays, tournaments, tattoos, prize-givings and all such ceremonies as encourage the desire to impose 'our' civilization or 'our' dominion upon other people" (*TG* 109). The older Woolf has shed Rachel's ambivalence, and the connection between the oppression of empire and the oppression of women is complete.

By the time Miss La Trobe produces the pageant of English history in Woolf's final novel, *Between the Acts*, the voice of patriarchy, colonialism and empire is unambiguously that of Budge, a Hyde Park traffic cop. The "repressive state apparatuses" of empire are clearly delineated and then forced upon the unsuspecting, genteel, and very British audience in the final scenes of the pageant. The appropriately named Budge tirelessly directs "*the traffic of 'Er Majesty's Empire. The Shah of Persia; Sultan of Morocco; or it may be 'Er Majesty in person; or Cook's tourists; black men; white men; sailors, soldiers; crossing the ocean; to proclaim her Empire; all of 'em Obey the Rule of my truncheon*" (*BTA* 161-62). Although war planes over the spectators' heads attest to the imminent danger from Nazi tyranny, Woolf is more concerned that her audience recognize the tyranny within its own culture. When Budge outlines the dangers to the Empire, he concentrates not on unruly colonists, but on women: "*The ruler of an Empire must keep his eye on the cot; spy too in the kitchen; drawing-room; library; wherever one or two, me and you, come together. Purity our watchword; prosperity and respectability.*" Here Budge sounds very like George Frederick Watts in *Freshwater* when he sends Ellen Terry on her way. What is new here, however, is Woolf's explicit link between colonial enslavement and the enslavement of women at home. Through Budge, his author Miss La Trobe, and her author, Virginia Woolf slam British Orientalism with a swipe at Kipling, one of the most blatant participants in the orientalist ideology and apologists of Empire: "Let 'em sweat at the mines; cough at the looms; rightly endure their lot. That's the price of Empire; that's the white man's burden" (*BTA* 163).

Woolf has come a long way from the youthful antics of the *Dreadnought* Hoax. Although her attitudes toward "other" lands remain essentially orientalist, she learns to recognize that she is a product of the patriarchal colonists whom she criticizes. The layering of viewpoints has become more complex. She moves from colonists and tourists misreading *signifiers* and *signifieds* toward a deconstruction of the colonial experience with a focus on how readers interpret the signs of Empire. Characters remain more than ever unaware of the economic, linguistic, political baggage they carry, but Woolf and her readers bear the full weight that comes with the recognition that the oppressive structure of institutions close to home directly lead to the oppressive structures that threaten those homes.

Works Cited

Althusser, Louis. "Ideology and Ideological State Apparatuses." *Lenin and Philosophy and other Essays*. London: New Left Books, 1971. 127-86.

Caughie, Pamela. *Virginia Woolf and Postmodernism: Literature in Quest and Question of Itself*. Urbana: U of Illinois P, 1991.

Cummins, June. "Death and the Maiden Voyage: Mapping the Junction of Feminism and Postcolonial Theory in *The Voyage Out*." *Virginia Woolf: Texts and Contexts: Selected Papers from the Fifth Annual Conference on Virginia Woolf*. Ed. Beth Rigel Daugherty and Eileen Barrett. New York: Pace UP, 1996. 204-10.

Henke, Suzette. "De/Colonizing the Subject in Virginia Woolf's *The Voyage Out*: Rachel Vinrace as *La Mysterique*." *Virginia Woolf: Emerging Perspectives: Selected Papers from the Third Annual Conference on Virginia Woolf*. Ed. Mark Hussey and Vara Neverow. New York: Pace UP, 1994. 103-08.

Lewis, Andrea. "The Visual Politics of Empire and Gender in Virginia Woolf's *The Voyage Out*." *Woolf Studies Annual* 1 (1995): 106-19.

Marcus, Jane. "Britannia Rules *The Waves*." *Decolonizing Tradition: New Views of Twentieth-Century Literature*. Ed. Karen R. Lawrence. Urbana: U of Illinois Press, 1992. 136-62.

McGee, Patrick. *Telling the Other: The Question of Value in Modern and Postcolonial Writing*. Ithaca and London: Cornell U Press, 1992.

Phillips, Kathy. *Virginia Woolf Against Empire*. Knoxville: U of Tennessee Press, 1994.

Putzel, Steven. "Virginia Woolf and 'The Distance of the Stage." *Women's Studies* 28 (1999): 435-70.

Said, Edward, W. *Orientalism*. New York: Pantheon Books, 1978.

Woolf, Virginia. *Between the Acts*. 1941. New York: Harcourt Brace [Harvest], 1970.

——. Rev. of *The Call of the East* by Charlotte Lorrimer. *The Times Literary Supplement* (April 26, 1907): 131.

——. *Freshwater: A Comedy*. Ed. Lucio P. Ruotolo. New York: Harcourt Brace [Harvest], 1976.

——. *A Room of One's Own*. 1929. New York: Harcourt Brace [Harvest], 1991.

——. *Three Guineas*. 1938. New York: Harcourt Brace [Harvest], 1966.

——. *The Voyage Out*. 1920. New York: Harcourt Brace [Harvest], 1948.

——. *The Waves*. 1931. New York: Harcourt Brace [Harvest], 1959.

——. *The Years*. 1937. New York: Harcourt Brace [Harvest], 1965.

Genevieve Abravanel
Woolf in Blackface: Identification across *The Waves*

By invoking the image of Woolf in blackface, I mean to address both the historical instance of Woolf in blackface in 1910 and the structure of cross-cultural and inter-racial identification, if not literally blackface, in her 1931 work, *The Waves*. As an early twentieth-century meditation on subjectivity and, following the analyses of Jane Marcus and Kathy Phillips,[1] a response to the imperial politics of its cultural moment, *The Waves* is capable of revealing the ways in which the white, metropolitan subject has been produced by circumatlantic fantasies of race. I will attempt to show how a climate of racial identification helps to shape the subjective and libidinal economies of the characters, as well as how ornamental motifs of cultural difference, including the circulating figures of "turbaned men" (75), structure the work itself. But before turning to an examination of *The Waves*, I would like to consider the stakes of Woolf's own moment as a turbaned man, especially in light of the recent critical reticence in the interpretation of her performance.

In January of 1910, disguised in dark makeup and a beard, wearing a turban and an African robe, the eighteen-year old Virginia Stephen joined her brother and four male friends posing as members of an Abyssinian court in order to trick the officers of a British naval ship, the H.M.S. *Dreadnought*, into taking them on a ceremonial guided tour. The consequences of the prank were somewhat predictable: the admiral and officers of the *Dreadnought* were the objects of public amusement; the men of the Cambridge crowd were reprimanded in private bouts with members of the crew. The consequences for Woolf studies have been less predictable. The image of Woolf in drag and blackface, a combination that echoes the minstrel performances that had made their way to England by the mid-nineteenth-century, seems capable of disturbing a strictly uniform image of Woolf as a champion of humanist concerns. In what is perhaps the telling instance of conflicted sentiment about the incident, Barbara Christian in 1994 styles the hoax as a "protest" (176), although it appears from several accounts not to have been politically nuanced beyond its vague disrespect for the British navy.[2]

While this act may not have been political in the manner that Christian hopes, it seems worthwhile to ask what the political content of such a gesture might be. Critical work on the most recognizable genre of racial cross-identification, minstrelsy, most often concerns white male performance of blackness and sometimes femininity, as in Eric Lott's now classic study, *Love and Theft*. The common nineteenth-century practice of white men playing black women on stage has led Jennifer Brody to surmise, "The practice of blackface cross-dressing—white males impersonating black women—in minstrel shows may also be read as a form of miscegenation. Taking on the body of a 'black' woman, the white man unites with or perhaps expresses his own repression of blackened femininity" (83). What would it mean to understand the eighteen-year-old Woolf on a lark with her brother as displaying her repression of blackened masculinity? For the writer who would go on to produce *Orlando* (1928), such an instance of gender fluidity seems entirely plausible. Yet not only the gendered but also the racial aspects of her impersonation can further our understanding of her social and political positions. Of late, the image of Woolf in the hoax has had a somewhat limited critical circulation, including an appearance in Peter Stansky's work on Bloomsbury and a quick cameo in Susan Gubar's recent book, *Race Changes*.[3] While Gubar helpfully reminds us that the Cambridge crowd's act must be taken in part as an expression of "racial privilege" (35), the hoax in general has not been subject to the kind of scrutiny that one might expect. I would suggest that it may be the desire of critics to identify *with Woolf* as committed to humanitarian, egalitarian politics that has somewhat circumscribed inquiries into her disturbing racial performance.

Of course, what has come to be called the *Dreadnought* Hoax was not a minstrel performance, not the explicitly transgressive overlay of whiteness with blackness, but an elaborate attempt to pass for African. Such an attempt relies on both the metropolitan fantasies of Africa that led to pieced-together costumes and made-up rituals and the easy susceptibility of the naval officers and crew to these signs of "authenticity." Blackface minstrelsy as it traveled from America to England can be clearly understood as a transatlantic product of nineteenth-century fantasies of race; yet the successful staging of the *Dreadnought* Hoax aboard a naval ship seems almost emblematic of the trade in fantasies of racial behavior as not only coming from the British colonies but as reworked and returned to shipboard as commodities of the metropolitan imagination. Strikingly, though perhaps not entirely coincidentally, racial fantasies are woven into movement across the ocean in few modernist texts as pervasively as in *The Waves*. Claiming Anglo-American modernism as a literary movement committed to the performance of race, Michael North notes, "Linguistic imitation and racial masquerade are so important to transatlantic modernism because they allow the writer to play at self-fashioning" (11). While Woolf may seem a somewhat less likely candidate than American expatriates such as Stein, Eliot, and Pound for transatlantic influence, *The Waves* is a text with minstrel inclinations, one in which racial imagery comes repeatedly to represent, or even explicitly to costume, the white bourgeois subject.

Twenty-one years after passing for an African man on the deck of the H.M.S. *Dreadnought*, Woolf published *The Waves*, in which the alternating monologues of six white characters, or perhaps of a single presence, are framed by images of the ocean. Between the monologues, the interludes feature interchangeable images of culturally marked bodies—in particular "turbaned men" (75)[4]—as momentary figures for the changing waves. Woolf's own youthful stint as a turbaned man has not led her to describe the inner lives of these figures. While the Britons rhapsodize in solipsistic ecstasy, the turbaned men of the interludes never speak and they circulate as something close to an ornamental motif. Since *The Waves* is a meditation on the self, in the context of 1930s Britain, Ann Laura Stoler's suggestion that "bourgeois identities in both metropole and colony emerge tacitly and emphatically coded with race" (7) may be helpful here. While certain portions of *The Waves* can quite plausibly be read as critiques of Empire,[5] the work also harbors an impulse that is more participatory than critical. For all that Woolf shared Leonard's call for an end to imperialism in *Empire and Commerce in Africa*,[6] *The Waves*, with its exotic motifs, is also working within the cultural assumptions of its imperial moment. In this way, *The Waves* is able to display what Stoler's account of colonialism, despite its meticulous historical groundwork, does not emphasize in its archive: precisely the fantasies of race, the performed and performative moments when identities are grafted, one to the other, and identifications occur.

Such a moment takes place near the end of *The Waves* when Bernard offers a more complete answer to the relentless self-query of the characters—"Who am I?" (288)—than he was able to produce in his youth: "There is the old brute, too, the savage, the hairy man who dabbles his fingers in ropes of entrails; and gobbles and belches; whose speech is guttural, visceral—well, he is here. He squats in me" (289). While this self-description as "savage" recalls the Freudian id more than any cultural identity,[7] it is important to remember that Freud's own work, such as the 1913 *Totem and Taboo*, often theorized general psychic principles from the lives of "those whom we describe as savages" (1). Bernard's unabashed identification of his inmost self as a "savage" rewrites his sexual impulses in implicitly primitivist terms. This formulation becomes clearer when Bernard continues: "That man, the hairy, the ape-like, has contributed his part to my life [. . .]. He has brandished his torch in murky by-streets where girls suddenly seem to shine with a red and intoxicating translucency. Oh, he has tossed his torch high! He has led me wild dances!" (290). With the image of the "torch," Bernard's inner savage here follows the classical Freudian symbolism that Woolf blatantly draws on from time to time, perhaps most notably in *A Room of One's Own*. But the passage seems also to embody Stoler's suggestion that "an implicit racial grammar underwrote the sexual regimes of bourgeois culture" (12). Here I would suggest that the very fact that the word "savage" is not attached to any particular racial or cultural group, but has been translated into a discussion of sexual impulses, suggests the extent to which racial otherness can be seen to underwrite sexuality. It is as if the system of racial signs, or the racial grammar, is performing a description of sex so thoroughly that one register is momentarily able to pass for the other. While there is a substantial difference between Woolf's performance of racialized masculinity and Bernard's troping of his own masculinity in racial terms, it seems that Stoler's assumption is born out by Bernard's tendency to rephrase the primal, in the Freudian sense, as the primitive.

Lest it seem that the code word, "savage," has been altogether emptied of its racial content by becoming a descriptor for sexuality, it is worth turning to what may be the most striking instance of racial identification in *The Waves*. At the farewell dinner for Percival, Louis and Rhoda imagine the currents of flirtation at the table in this way:

> 'Horns and trumpets,' said Rhoda, 'ring out [. . .]. There is a dancing and a drumming, like the dancing and the drumming of naked men with assegais.'

> 'Like the dance of the savages,' said Louis, 'round the campfire. They are savage; they are ruthless. They dance in a circle, flapping bladders. The flames leap over their painted faces' (140).

Here the transformation of the characters into dancing savages translates their sexuality into primitivist performance. Dancing with "painted faces," the characters follow the form of minstrelsy in a manner that recalls Woolf's own blackface performance in the 1910 hoax. Although it may be objected that the performance in *The Waves* is above all metaphorical—that the characters don't actually paint their faces and dance in a circle—it is worth recalling Diana Fuss's definition of metaphor as the very figure of psychic identification. As Fuss puts it, "Metaphor, *the substitution of the one for the other*, is internal to the work of identification. . . . The Greek metaphora, meaning transport, immediately implicates the transferential act of identification in the rhetorical process of figuration" (5-6, emphasis in original). The figures of the savages dancing in a circle can be understood to be the product of a transatlantic exchange that trades in images which reify colonial fantasies, traveling not only from continent to continent but across Woolf's phantasmatic waves. The waves themselves are crafted precisely out of such cultural fantasies: the turbaned warriors and turbaned men do not simply ornament the interludes; they are metaphorical figures for the waves themselves. To pun on the title, if "turbaned warriors" are figures for the waves in the interludes, they can also be taken as figures for *The Waves* the literary work, in a set of metaphorical equivalences that weaves cultural difference into the surface of the work itself.

The colonial import of these fantasies can hardly be overlooked; the waves are, after all, metonymic for Britain's imperial reach. Yet the echoes of circumatlantic fantasies of race, fantasies that allude not only to the British colonies but also to the Americas, can be heard in the passage quoted above. When Rhoda describes the dancing and drumming, she alludes most obviously to a distant imagined jungle; yet in the twenties in England, while Woolf was writing *The Waves*, dancing and drumming characterized few locales better than the London jazz club. As Eric Hobsbawm notes of Britain in the teens and twenties, "Jazz made its way and triumphed, not as a music for intellectuals, but as a music for dancing" (267).[8] While the case for *The Waves* as a work of British-*American* transatlantic modernism is not often made, images of racialized characters playing "horns," "trumpets," and "drums" recall few musical forms more readily than jazz.[9] When Rhoda notes that "Their horns spill blue smoke" (140), her description evokes a jazz performance as much as a fantasy of colonial spaces.

In *The Waves*, images of Africans, Indians, and unidentified islanders circulate in totemic fashion; the addition of African-Americans to such a list only emphasizes the equivalent exchange value of otherness in this particular circumatlantic trade. While Woolf's cultural politics may range from anti-imperial sentiment to patent exoticism, what *The Waves* most persistently reveals is not a commitment to any one political stance. Rather, it displays the vast range of cultural images and fantasies, with reference to the modern British colonies and even the US, that structures the identifications of its white characters. The protagonists of *The Waves* could be said to be six characters in search of an other, but capable only of trading in racial and cultural images that function as costumes, guises, and styles for the self. Woolf's great tribute to subjectivity, then, needs to be taken in part to reveal the inextricability of images of racial otherness to an interwar British meditation on the self. Woolf's youthful prank takes advantage of the easy availability of racial disguise; her 1931 work reveals that metaphors of racial disguise have become integral to her vision of British subjectivity. Whether or not *The Waves* is directly responding to the problematics Woolf encountered in the *Dreadnought* Hoax, the text leads its characters into fantasies that resemble racialized performance, a position with which Woolf could well have been able to identify.

Notes

[1] Jane Marcus, "Britannia Rules *The Waves*." *Decolonizing Tradition*, Ed. K. Lawrence (Urbana: U of Illinois P, 1992). Kathy Phillips, *Virginia Woolf Against Empire* (Knoxville: U of Tennessee P, 1994).

[2] Barbara Christian, "Layered Rhythms: Virginia Woolf and Toni Morrison," *Virginia Woolf: Emerging Perspectives*, ed. Mark Hussey and Vara Neverow (New York: Pace UP, 1994). Christian calls the Dreadnought Hoax, "a protest against British policy in Africa" (176 fn4). Yet according to the separate accounts of Adrian Stephen, who organized the prank, and of Quentin Bell, frivolity rather than protest was the order of the day. See Adrian Stephen, "The Dreadnought Hoax," *The Bloomsbury Group*, ed. S.P. Rosenbaum (Toronto: U of Toronto P, 1975) 6-17 and Quentin Bell, *Virginia Woolf: A Biography* (New York: Harvest, 1972) 157-158.

[3] Susan Gubar, *Race Changes: White Skin, Black Face in American Culture* (New York: Oxford UP, 1997). Peter Stansky, *On or about December 1910: Early Bloomsbury and Its Intimate World* (Cambridge: Harvard UP, 1996).

[4] The turbaned figures recur in the interludes: "The waves drummed on the shore, like turbaned warriors, like turbaned men with poisoned assegais" (75) as well as "the sea which beat like a drum that raises a regiment of plumed and turbaned soldiers" (109).

[5] See Marcus and Phillips.

[6] Leonard Woolf, *Empire & Commerce in Africa: A Study in Economic Imperialism* Westminster, Labour Research Dept.; London, Allen & Unwin, 1920.

[7] See Gillian Beer, *Virginia Woolf: The Common Ground* (Ann Arbor: U of Michigan P, 1996) for a discussion of the above passage in relation to primary desires.

[8] See chapter 22 of Hobsbawm's *Uncommon People: Resistance, Rebellion, and Jazz* (London: Weidenfeld and Nicolson, 1998).

[9] While there has been much critical attention to the musicality of *The Waves*, comparisons tend toward Wagner, Satie, and especially the late Beethoven quartets that Woolf listened to during the months of writing *The Waves*. See Peter Jacobs, "Virginia Woolf and Music," *The Multiple Muses of Virginia Woolf*, ed. Diane Gillespie (Columbia: U of Missouri P, 1993) 234-236.

Works Cited

Brody, Jennifer DeVere. *Impossible Purities: Blackness, Femininity, and Victorian Culture*. Durham: Duke UP, 1998.

Christian, Barbara. "Layered Rhythms: Virginia Woolf and Toni Morrison." *Virginia Woolf: Emerging Perspectives*. Ed. Mark Hussey and Vara Neverow. New York: Pace UP, 1994.

Gubar, Susan. *Race Changes: White Skin, Black Face in American Culture*. New York : Oxford UP, 1997.

Freud, Sigmund. *Totem and Taboo*. Trans. James Strachey. New York: Norton, 1950.

Fuss, Diana. *Identification Papers*. London: Routledge, 1995.

Hobsbawm, Eric. *Uncommon People: Resistance, Rebellion, and Jazz*. London: Weidenfeld and Nicolson, 1998.

North, Michael. *The Dialect of Modernism: Race, Language, and Twentieth-Century Literature*. Oxford: Oxford UP, 1994.

Stoler, Ann Laura. *Race and the Education of Desire*. Durham: Duke UP, 1999.

Woolf, Virginia. *The Waves*. San Diego: Harcourt Brace Jovanovich, 1978.

Philosophical Approaches: Politics, Phenomenology, Ethics, Physics

Michèle Barrett
Reason and Truth in *A Room of One's Own*: A Master in Lunacy

Virginia Woolf's *A Room of One's Own* elaborates two clearly separable meanings of that slippery word, "truth". As we know well from the opening paragraph, the duty of a lecturer is "...to hand you ... a nugget of pure truth to wrap between the pages of your notebooks and keep on the mantelpiece for ever" (*AROO* 3). This rendering down of "truth" to its essence is fully recognizable in the move from nugget to a more liquid metaphor. By chapter two, truth has taken the form of an "essential oil," a "pure fluid." It is the distillation of disinterested scholarship:

> . . .an answer was only to be had by consulting the learned and the unprejudiced, who have removed themselves above the strife of tongue and the confusion of body and issued the result of their reasoning and research in books which are to be found in the British Museum. If truth is not to be found on the shelves of the British Museum, where, I asked myself, picking up a notebook and a pencil, is truth? (*AROO* 23)

This kind of truth is the traditional academic one. Woolf contrasts her fruitless and frustrating morning in the British Museum reading room with the experience of the student sitting next to her. Clearly the beneficiary of an Oxbridge training in research methods, he is copying from a scientific manual and grunting with satisfaction as productively he gathers up "pure nuggets of the essential ore every ten minutes or so." This search for truth, the academic route towards "the truth" (even Truth perhaps), is treated by Woolf with heavy irony. Here as elsewhere in her writings, her attitude towards professional academic life was critical in the extreme. She systematically refused all academic recognition such as honorary degrees, and claimed that she "would rather sit in a cellar or watch spiders than listen to an Englishman lecturing" (*L6* 167). Woolf's heavily critical treatment of "the truth" as seen by academia was premeditated, rather than an outburst of spontaneous annoyance. A comparison between the draft of the manuscript and the version that she published indicates that some of these laden comments, belabouring the critical tone, were added as revisions in the cold light of day.[1] Whilst it is in *Three Guineas* that the ridiculous pomposity of academia is most eloquently derided, Woolf's private papers are a mine of acerbic comment too. In *A Room* the most entertaining example of this long running joke for Woolf is the arch: "I do not believe that even the Table of Precedency which you will find in Whitaker's *Almanac* represents a final order of values, or that there is any sound reason to suppose that a Commander of the Bath will ultimately walk into dinner behind a Master in Lunacy" (*AROO* 95).

There is, of course, a second conception of 'truth' in *A Room of One's Own*, as in Woolf's other writings. It is internal truth as opposed to externally validated truth, and it most definitely is not treated with irony. Woolf's own view of truth concerns the integrity of the writer, and the "inner light" by which it is judged. It is about making the truth visible. Writerly truth is about enabling a vision be seen, "whole and entire," by the reader. To add to the many formulations of this in Woolf's essays, let us note here the way that she puts this in *A Room of One's Own*:

> What one means by integrity, in the case of the novelist, is the conviction that he [sic] gives one that this is the truth. Yes, one feels, I should never have thought that this could be so; I have never known people behaving like that. But you have convinced me that so it is, so it happens. One holds every phrase, every scene to the light as one reads—for nature seems, very oddly, to have provided us with an inner light by which to judge of the novelist's integrity or disintegrity. Or perhaps it is rather that Nature, in her most irrational mood, has traced in invisible ink on the walls of the mind a premonition which these great artists confirm; a sketch which only needs to be held to the fire of genius to become visible. When one so exposes it and sees it come to life one exclaims in rapture, But this is what I have always felt and known and desired! (*AROO* 65-66)

This visual metaphor is central to Woolf's conception of truth. Truth is not learning, it is not a cognitive operation; it is making reality visible. Reality is thus fixed, made permanent, by the writer, so that ". . .one sees more intensely afterwards; the world seems bared of its covering and given an intenser light" (*AROO* 99). I have distinguished here two conceptions of "truth" in Woolf's thought. First there is "the truth" as a meretricious and ill-fated search for academic knowledge, and opposed to this there is the genuine "truth" of the writer's imagination. These two conceptions recur through Woolf's writings, albeit expressed in *A Room* with elegant economy in the contrast between flat-footed scholars and those who "live in the presence of reality." On the rival claims of history and fiction, Woolf declared that "where truth is important," she preferred to write fiction (*P* 9).

The meanings of the term "reason" in *A Room of One's Own* are, perhaps, more difficult to unravel.[2] There is a conception of "reason" used at the beginning of the text which could be seen as analagous to Woolf's notion of "the truth." The "age of reason" is invoked in the description of the endowments of Cambridge colleges—vast quantities of wealth devoted, first in "the age of faith" and then in "the age of reason," to the establishment of this seat of learning. While the medieval church and monarchy had originally poured gold and silver into the foundations of Cambridge's colleges, it was the later beneficiaries of trade and industry who supplied the money for the libraries, chairs and fellowships. Being products of the age of reason, they financed laboratories and observatories too; hence "the splendid equipment of costly and delicate instruments."

It is worth noting that Woolf was by no means anti-science in her general outlook. She points out that Margaret Cavendish, Duchess of Newcastle, should have been given a microscope and taught to "reason scientifically;" that George Eliot should have spread beyond fiction to history or biography "when the creative impulse was spent" (*AROO* 56, 61). Most timely of all, what Chloe and Olivia share, in the closing parable of *A Room*, is a *laboratory*—they are trying to find a cure for anaemia. In the right context, and with recognition of the complementarity of reason and vision, Woolf is neither anti-reason nor anti-science.

The "age of reason," we are told, informs the spirit of the famous lunch in the first chapter of *A Room*. The material comforts described here provide the opportunity not for some flashy brilliance of conversation, but for "the more profound, subtle and subterranean glow which is the rich yellow flame of rational intercourse" (*AROO* 10). Woolf is here describing what feminist philosophers have subsequently elaborated and analysed—the silently masculine nature of this "rational" intercourse—this age of reason that so unreasonably excludes half the human population.

The "age of reason" is frequently thought of in terms of the principles of the philosophical "rationalists," who believed that "the general nature of the world could be established by wholly non-empirical demonstrative reasoning,"[3] in particular, the most frequently invoked name is that of René Descartes (1596-1650). In this context, what can we make of Virginia Woolf's remark "The human frame being what it is, heart, body and brain all mixed together, and not contained in separate compartments as they will be no doubt in another million years, a good dinner is of great importance to good talk" (*AROO* 16). Is this a premeditated assault on the Cartesian separation of mind and body? According to Roger Poole, Virginia Woolf, having married an arch-rationalist, was then stuck with a husband who exemplified the *cogito ergo sum* of Descartes—in direct conflict with her own more phenomenological and inclusive world view.

Roger Poole rightly draws attention to the conflict between the meaning of intellect for Virginia Woolf, which allowed a place for intuition and feeling, and the prevailing "Bloomsbury" ethos of a relentless exclusion of anything illogical. In today's terms, "Bloomsbury," as defined by the men who spoke for it, was emotionally illiterate. Poole says that "To read Leonard Woolf's volumes of autobiography is to breathe in the aroma of the very fine flower of the Bloomsbury rationalist-reductive consciousness. He was its very exemplar, its paragon, its nonpareil. . . .And nowhere is this self-imposed set of limitations more evident than in those pages of his autobiography where he writes of his wife's 'insanity.' It very often looks as if the rationalist mind, because of its very presuppositions about views which 'could not be justified rationally,' deliberately refuses to see what, to a less blinkered intelligence, is strikingly obvious" (Poole 63).

Virginia Woolf's comment on the indivisibility of "the human frame" was geared to her argument that we all need a good dinner if good talk is to follow, but it is nonetheless tempting to read more into it. Woolf pointed to a future a million years hence, when heart, body and brain will have separate compartments. Less than a hundred years later, the theme of implanted or "prosthetic" memory is already elaborated in detail in science fiction films such as *Blade Runner* and *Total Recall*. More seriously, her cheeky reference to the "mind-body dualism" often associated with Descartes, points to a more general—and more fundamental—distance from rationalism as a doctrine. In the manuscript version we can see from the cancelled passages that her first thoughts were to roll up the brain with the emotions (and even with love, sex and insomnia) in a way that her rationalist friends would have found very alarming.

> But the truth is this: <The> Human ~~nature is~~ frame being what it is, ~~not made up of body in this here and brain, there heart & in wit, affection, there, but & heart the affection, the emotions, in another compartment, since on the contrary, the heart & body and brain are all~~ all in one, body & brain & heart <the emotions> all mixed up if you together—though in a more perfect state they will <not in separate compartments as they will be in a million years or so> doubtless be seperated—as things are, at the moment, if one has not dined well, first one is ~~tired & then one is~~ one cannot think well, & then one cannot love well, & finally one cannot sleep well. . . (*Women and Fiction* 26)

At this point it is worth parenthetically clarifying the over-used expression "mind-body dualism." The mind at the center of the famous *cogito* has been much misrepresented in the popular recycling of the so-called "Cartesian self." Descartes argued that "thinking" was the basis of human as opposed to divine knowledge and that "the mind" could be distinguished from the body. But "thought," for Descartes, included the imagination and, crucially, the *senses*. In his *Meditations* he writes quite clearly that "By the term 'thought,' I mean everything which is in us in such a way that we are immediately conscious of it. Thus all operations of the will, intellect, imagination, and the senses are thoughts" (*Meditations* 85). Although Descartes was seeking to distinguish between the "soul," "mind" or "thinking thing" and the body or "physical thing," he certainly does not attempt this in terms of a crude split between the sensual and the cognitive. In answer to his own question "*What is thought?*" he replies:

> By the word "thought" I understand all the things that we are aware of as occurring in us, insofar as we are aware of them. Thus not only understanding, willing and imagining but even sensing is the same as thinking in this context. For if I say "I see or I walk, therefore I exist," and if I understand this as referring to the seeing or walking that is done by the body, the conclusion is not absolutely certain because, as often happens during sleep, I can think I see or walk even if I do not open my eyes and do not move from where I am and even if, perhaps, I had no body. But if I understand it as the sensation or awareness of seeing or walking, since it then refers to the mind which alone senses or thinks that it sees or walks, it is obviously certain.[4]

Descartes' thinking may be puzzling to us in allowing for a hypothetical out-of-body epistemology, but it is a long way from his careful formulation to the "dualism" of mind and body regularly spotted in critical and cultural theory. That Virginia Woolf here distances herself from such dualism and endorses an integrated "humanist" position, does not necessarily imply any rigidly "anti-Cartesian" logic in her approach. Nevertheless, Woolf reverts to this theme later in *A Room*, insisting that "nothing whatever is known" about the mind. Pressing home an imaginative critique of the famous *cogito*, she conjures up the "masterful" I that appears frequently in her novels. The I as "shadow," as "dark bar," invoked here by Woolf is the self as logical and pedagogic: reason characterizes this conception of the modern, rational, self, and this is noted by Woolf as implicitly masculine. ". . . (T)he worst of it is that in the shadow of the letter 'I' all is shapeless as mist. Is that a tree? No, it is a woman. But. . .she has not a bone in her body, I thought, watching Phoebe, for that was her name, coming across the beach. Then Alan got up and the shadow of Alan at once obliterated Phoebe."[5]

To pull this thread to a conclusion, we can say the first sense in which Woolf uses the notion of reason in *A Room of One's Own* registers the historical decline of religious faith and the rise of an "age of reason," where an implicitly masculine rationalism is the dominant mode, and comments sceptically on the separation of a faculty of reason (called by Descartes the "natural light of reason") from the general make-up of the human being.

A Room of One's Own contains, however, a far more punchy and direct critique of reason than its meditation on rationalism and the self. I want to look at the way in which Woolf deals here with the *irrational*, with *unreason*.

During Woolf's day at Cambridge, we find the controlling grip of "reason" breaking down as early as at lunch-time. The "rational intercourse" facilitated by good food and wine, does not even outlast her post-prandial smoke. In the absence of an ash-tray [improbable, in 1928], our protagonist is knocking her cigarette ash out of the window when she spots an ". . . abrupt and truncated animal padding softly across the quadrangle:" it is a Manx cat, the tail-less species recognised throughout the country as native to the Isle of Man (hence Manx). Woolf's version of what she called "Freudianism" makes an appearance at this point, as she says that the sight of the creature "changed by some fluke of the subconscious intelligence the emotional light for me." The cat, as well as the narrator we are told, is questioning the universe: ". . .something seemed lacking, something seemed different. But what was lacking, what was different, I asked myself, listening to the talk?" (*AROO* 10).

In order to answer her own question Woolf says she has "to think myself out of the room, back into the past, before the war indeed," where "Everything was different." The passage that follows is structured around a repetition of the phrase "before the war," "before the war indeed" first appears as barely noticed, turns to the proposition that "before the war" people would have said the same things but they would have "sounded different," and moves onto the form of a question—was Tennyson's *Maud* what men and women were "humming" before the war? The energy generated by the repetition of "before the war," in a variety of grammatical constructions, is resolved in Woolf's abrupt response to why we have now stopped "humming."

"Shall we lay the blame on the war? When the guns fired in August 1914, did the faces of men and women show so plain in each other's eyes that romance was killed?" (*AROO* 13). The ensuing comment constitutes a dense reflection on the nature of truth and illusion, again using a relentless repetition of the words themselves: "illusion" appears six times in one paragraph, "truth" four. Woolf poses the question of the war as one of truth or illusion—was the rational intercourse of the pre-war culture an "illusion," and the war had "put truth in its place?" The passage is dense (and much amended, "erased," crossed through in the manuscript version, where Woolf airs more comment on the death of romance, on mothers sending their sons to the war, and on the post-war drop in the birth rate). It is dense because it is carrying so many cross-cutting meanings: truth and illusion, truth and reason, the unconscious (in the figure of Jane Harrison), and the impact of the war on life in general. It evokes in the reader Woolf's own account of the irrelevance of the representational conventions of the pre-war period: for us "those conventions are ruin, those tools are death," a formulation that speaks precisely of the "ruin" and "death," by the war itself, that brought about this change (see Barrett, "Great War").

Any criticism of men is here implied delicately. Later in *A Room* Woolf was to articulate it more directly, and of course in *Three Guineas* the connection of war to masculinity emerges as a manifesto. An interesting aspect of this nexus of issues around reason, masculinity and war can be seen in Woolf's account of her enraging trip to the British Museum library. The unconscious, Freudian psychoanalysis, is again invoked, this time somewhat more directly than via what Woolf at times likes to call the "subconscious." Here she says, of a sketch she has made, ". . .it is in our idleness, in our dreams, that the submerged truth sometimes comes to the top. A very elementary exercise in psychology, not to be dignified by the name of psycho-analysis, showed me. . ." (*AROO* 28-9). What is revealed was that she was angry, as indeed were the patriarchal professors whose views on women she was studying. The interpretation of her drawing allows Woolf to let in the "submerged truth" of anger—the "red light of emotion" rather than the "white light light of truth" (*AROO* 30).

Woolf's approach to the connection between war and masculinity turns on a recognition that although "reason" is claimed for the masculine, men do not—in practice—behave rationally at all. They are not driven by reason, but in Woolf's own words—by instinct, desire, rage. Woolf's reference to the First World War in this is direct: she speaks of frontiers and poison gas. She suggests that men are driven by instinct that they cannot control. Like the hopelessly irrational Mr Jex-Blake in *Three Guineas*, who could just about cope with his daughter getting a job as long as she wasn't actually paid for it, these fellows were suffering from destructive instincts of angry possessiveness. It is ironic that Woolf here represents men as driven by instinct and emotion, as being irrational and uncivilized.

> great bodies of people are never responsible for what they do. They are driven by instincts which are not within their control. They too, the patriarchs, the professors, had endless difficulties, terrible drawbacks to contend with. . . .True, they had money and power, but only at the costs of harbouring in their breasts an eagle, a vulture, for ever tearing the liver out and plucking at the lungs—the instinct for possession, the rage for acquisition which drives them to desire other people's fields and goods perpetually; to make frontiers and flags; battleships and poison gas; to offer up their own lives and their children's lives. . . .These are unpleasant instincts to harbour, I reflected. They are bred of the conditions of life; of the lack of civilization, I thought. . . . (*AROO* 35)

Woolf's understanding of the cause of war—the "possessive instinct" that wants other people's land and goods—may be referred to lightly in this passage, but appears in the manuscript in more startling terms: "killing one's sisters and cousins in order to get it from them," deleted from the final published text (*Women and Fiction* 60). The reference to men killing their sisters refers ostensibly to a desire for land, but is very curious as a deflection of the expected "brothers." In the case of the 1914-18 war, it was of course true that so many of Queen Victoria's children had married into European royal families, as to make Woolf's remark literally appropriate. It is tempting, however, to associate Woolf's unexpected reference to sisters with a recent new emphasis on the relationship of sibling conflict and military conflict:

Juliet Mitchell's *Mad Men and Medusas: Reclaiming Hysteria and the Effects of Sibling Relations on the Human Condition.*

Mitchell offers an explanation of both the murderous rage of war, and the tendency for violence to be sexualized in wartime. The book, a magisterial rewriting of psychoanalysis (despite its populist title), argues that Freud himself repressed lateral sibling conflict, and hysteria, in favour of the "vertical" parental Oedipal model. That the extent of male hysteria, so evident in the psychic carnage of the 1914-18 war, did not lead to a revision of the Freudian model was an opportunity missed to correct the imbalance of the psychoanalytic corpus. Mitchell puts forward an account of sibling rage, jealousy and envy (at displacement, and a consequent sense of emptiness) that she applies to the very murder of one's peers that is sanctioned in war. The attribution of hysteria principally to women has occluded its general significance as a sibling-related unconscious formation characteristic of both sexes, whether heterosexual or homosexual. Mitchell suggests that a recognition of the inevitably sexual character of unconscious "possession," thought of laterally rather than generationally, sheds light on the apparently inevitable sexual violence associated with war.

Mitchell's book has an import, in both its implications and importance, for psychoanalysis that is far beyond the concerns of this paper. It deploys, however, one argument that has a specific bearing on an aspect of 'unreason' discussed here. Mitchell suggests that psychoanalysis can be described, if misleadingly as ". . .an anti-Cartesian science," in that Freud provided an explanation of the mind-body connection of the hysteric (*Mad Men* 205). Mitchell's point brings us neatly back to the "anti-Cartesian" impetus found in Virginia Woolf—her rejection of the extreme rationalism of which the idea of "mind/body dualism" is both cause and symptom.

Woolf's use of the term "reason" in *A Room of One's Own* registers both the importance of the war as the source of her disillusionment with "the age of reason," and a recognition of the salience, for her, of the unconscious (read in a wilfully "loose" manner from Freud). Woolf's approach to "reason" is fully in line with the more general reaction against rationalism that was engendered by the experience and aftermath of the 1914-18 war. The huge numbers of "shell shocked" soldiers, including officers, had a destabilizing effect on assumptions about personality, masculinity and medicine. In addition, the war brought a massive revival of forms of irrationality such as spiritualism, and a general flourishing of superstition and myth of all kinds.

Virginia Woolf's treatment of these issues is best known in her portrayal of the shell-shocked Septimus Warren Smith in *Mrs Dalloway*. This figure —according to Woolf's own diaries—represents an "insane truth" spoken in the novel. I have suggested elsewhere that Septimus, and this "insane truth" that Woolf created him to make visible, can usefully be thought of in terms of Michel Foucault's account of the widening split between reason and unreason in western culture (*Imagination* 189). Woolf is here fighting the "monologue of reason" that Foucault describes, as well as the ratiocination of her Bloomsbury friends.

Earlier in *A Room*, Woolf had described the taxonomic capacities of Cambridge, where ". . .they are so adept at putting people into classes and fixing caps on their heads and letters after their names" (*AROO* 95). To finish, let us invoke again the wonderful character who has, or indeed, is a "Master in Lunacy" (a degree in madness, a qualification in fooling), and consider his place in the procession (is it to be before or after the Commander of the Bath?). A banal attempt at improbable order, and a rationalization of the unruly, are here exposed as, laughably, the wrong kind of truth. This glancing sideswipe of *A Room* is completely in accord with its formal argument: to reiterate Virginia Woolf's preference for the truth of the writer over the reason of the academic.

Notes

[1] Invoking the methodical reader next door who had organized (his) material under lettered headings, Woolf reports that her own notes were "the wildest scribble of contradictory jottings" (*Women and Fiction* 44). To which she added in the final text "Truth had run through my fingers. Every drop had escaped" (*AROO* 27).

[2] ". . .this text ravels the crossed threads of history and fiction." Peggy Kamuf ("Penelope" 185)

[3] This formulation is from the *Fontana Dictionary of Modern Thought*, entry on "rationalism" (by Anthony Quinton) London, Fontana, 1977 p525.

[4] *Meditations* 114 The real problem here is that Descartes can conceive of a disembodied soul; the profoundly religious flavor of his writing tends to be ignored by those promoting his position as a "rationalist" theory of the self.

[5] *AROO* 90. Jane Goldman has pointed out that the metaphor is drawn from a Copernican model: masculine enlightenment casting women in shadow, as in an eclipse, whilst at the same time construing Phoebe (the moon) as an alternative source of light (17).

Works Cited

Barrett, Michèle. "The Great War and Post-modern Memory." *New Formations* 41 (Autumn 2000) 138-157.

——. *Imagination in Theory: Writing, Culture, Words and Things*. New York: NYU Press, 1999.

Descartes, René *Meditations and Other Metaphysical Writings*. Trans. D. Clark. London: Penguin 1998.

Goldman, Jane. *The Feminist Aesthetics of Virginia Woolf.* Cambridge: Cambridge U P, 1998.

Kamuf, Peggy. "Penelope at Work: Interruptions in *A Room of One's Own*," in *Virginia Woolf*, edited by Rachel Bowlby. London: Longman Critical Readers, 1992.

Mitchell, Juliet. *Mad Men and Medusas: Reclaiming Hysteria and the Effect of Sibling Relations on the Human Condition.* London: Allen Lane, 2000.

Poole, Roger. *The Unknown Virginia Woolf.* Cambridge: Cambridge U P, 1978.

Woolf, Virginia. *A Room of One's Own* in *A Room of One's Own/Three Guineas.* Edited with an introduction and notes by Michèle Barrett. London: Penguin Classics, 2000.

——. *Women and Fiction: the Manuscript versions of* A Room of One's Own. Edited by S. P. Rosenbaum. Oxford: Blackwell, 1992.

——. *Letters* Vol. 6. Edited by Nigel Nicolson. London: The Hogarth Press, 1980.

——. *The Pargiters.* Edited by Mitchell A. Leaska. London: The Hogarth Press, 1978.

Laura Doyle
The Body Unbound: A Phenomenological Reading of the Political in *A Room of One's Own*

"But," Woolf opens *A Room of One's Own*, "you may say, we asked you to speak about women and fiction." This opening "but" signals many to come, and it characterizes a contrapuntal movement in the essay that I will argue is phenomenological as well as rhetorical, with political import.[1] In her introductory remarks, Woolf explains that she has taken "the subject which you have lain on my shoulders" and, because it is impossible to address it directly, she has "made it work in and out of [her] daily life"—an ambulatory life full of bodily turns, twists, and interruptions (*AROO* 4). In shaping her essay to this movement, Woolf explores the pivot in the body's world-relation that Maurice Merleau-Ponty calls "chiasmatic," wherein a body inhabits itself through its surround, turns inward by way of its exteriority, and often hovers (interrupt-ably) at the pause or hinge between these aspects of being. Repeatedly exposing us to motions of turn and counter-turn attended by physical interruption, Woolf reveals how the pivot or hinge inherent to this chiasmatic embodiment both opens the self to the world and allows for the world's interpellation or invasive calling-out of the self. As several critics have argued, Woolf's shifting style is a rhetorical mode with political implications;[2] but, as I'll explore, this shifting entails a phenomenological movement by which Woolf manipulates her reader's as well as her own positionality. In this way she realizes a relation between politics, ontology, and aesthetics. The contrapuntal form of the essay is Woolf's unbinding of the body by way of self-interruption and self-slippage. It is an enactment of a self that is not one.

1

In Merleau-Ponty's words, "I am from the start outside myself and open to the world."[3] That is, whether I like it or not, I come *to* myself from *out-* side myself. Because I hear myself from inside and outside, because I am a phenomenon that touches herself from without with her own touching hand, I live on a pivot, a turn, a "but." I am here looking out at the screen but also here faced with the screen and the room. In Merleau-Ponty's phenomeno-logical description, "the body . . . is not itself a thing, an interstitial matter, a connective tissue, but a *sensible for itself*."[4] It is a sensible for itself via the world it inhabits for, "our body is a being of two leaves, from one side a thing among things and otherwise what sees and touches them" (*Visible* 137). Thus "when one of my hands touches the other, the world of each opens upon the other because the operation is reversible at will" and *this* is so "because they . . . are the hands of the same body" and they belong to the same world. (*Visible* 141). Within the "circle of the touched and the touch-ing" (*Visible* 143), neither the sameness of the one body nor the difference of the two touching parts but rather both of these together give access to a world—literally a span of time and space—within this circle. Each body is in this sense two bodies, or "two leaves"—or a kind of double helix where two opposite sides of one ribbon touch and describe a circle of time and space.

Or, rather, in the case of the animate human body, these two sides *almost* touch, *almost* close into a circle, and this almostness is equally essen-tial to the possibility of worldness. For at the moment when the body verges on closure with itself, closure of the "circle of the touched and the touching," there is what Merelau-Ponty calls a "brief torsion." That is, "If my left hand is touching my right hand, and if I should suddenly wish to apprehend with my right hand the work of my left hand as it touches, this reflection of the body upon itself always miscarries at the last moment: the moment I feel my left hand with my right hand, I correspondingly cease touching my right hand with my left hand" (*Visible* 9). There is always a différance or non-coincidence (an écart) at the heart of this meeting between a body and itself. There is always a "shift," a "spread," a "hiatus" as Merleau-Ponty says, "between my right hand touching and my right hand touched" (*Visible* 148). The slippage moment is the hyphen, we might say, in the word "self-touch-ing," the fulcrum of Woolf's opening word, "But," which signals a need for leverage, a distance to be arced. It is what Merleau-Ponty calls the chiasm, thus comparing it to the rhetorical form in which parallel sentence parts invert, as in "the trees bent down, up swept the snow," or, in a usage that draws repetition and semantics into the reversal, "When the going gets tough, the tough get going." In these examples, as in the body's self-relation, the reversal feels like correspondence but depends on a shift in position and, in the latter, a semantic tension between one word's double meanings.

Yet this non-correspondence is not, Merleau-Ponty argues, "an ontolog-ical void, a non-being" (*Visible* 148). For him, the impossibility of self-closure in the chiasm—the hyphen, the comma—prompts not merely a Derridian condition of infinite reversal or deferral but also a pressure and a fullness, a state of anticipation and possibility, even a desirous reaching.

This slippage in meaning, in my being, *is* my being, my moving, and my caught-upness in a world and a future. It is my opening toward others, for I live all of this *with* others. I look to others to hear what I have heard myself say. I am turned implicitly, in body, toward others, who may give me myself by touching me, and by seeing me return my seeing to me, allowing me to know myself as palpable, visible, and thinkable. And finally this slippage may even be, as Woolf seems to grasp, the very condition of thinking, of projecting and envisioning, for my imagination can reach across the hinge or gap that my hands cannot.

In sum the chiasm generates the continuous, volatile arena of encounter we habitually call the real, that which Woolf calls "the world of reality" in *A Room* (118), and what, in her fiction, she renders as the carnation seen in common, the unharmonious choral knowing. We might think here of the moment when Lily Briscoe and William Bankes walk together through "that break in the thick hedge" early in *To the Lighthouse*. Entering through this *break, together* they see the bay as a "pulse of color" and together they feel "a common hilarity, excited by the moving waves" (*TTL* 20). They share a world and the sensations it provokes. But then both also feel in its wake "some sadness," they muse on separateness and loneliness, and Woolf's narrator uses a touch of chiasmatic syntax to explain the point of divergence between them that also connects them in the feeling of sadness. She says they register "some sadness—because the thing was completed partly, and partly because distant views seem to outlast by a million years (Lily thought) the gazer and to be communing already with a sky which beholds an earth entirely at rest" (*TTL* 20). Initially, we may understand the clause "the thing was completed partly" to mean that the thing—the picture of the bay they share—was partially completed, was incomplete. Woolf conjures this feeling in us, and allows this provisional meaning. But as we cross over into the second half of the sentence, the position and meaning of "partly" change: the picture *is* complete, and this very completion and closure explains, "partly," their experience of sadness. Here the word "partly" belongs to two orders of meaning at once, mirroring the same doubleness in Lily and William, who belong at once to themselves and to each other, to the now and to the future, to the visible and the invisible. Yet all the while it is *this* world that carries them; it launches and holds adjacent their separate, thinking bodies. Lily and William live a chiasmatic, intercorporeal relation to one another and to the world that brings them *to* each other, and all of these relations are predicated on a principle of "partly," on a world of intercorporeal contingency.

In this corporeal way, we each continue but never complete the ongoing circle of the touching and the touched for each other. We come to ourselves through others, partly, and through ourselves we come partly to others. While thought may be what Merleau-Ponty calls the "lining and depth" of "the sensible" (*Visible* 149), its inward extension, other persons may be thought's horizon, its outward extension. In our very capacity to approach from outside and to interrupt each other, we *intercede* for each other in an ontological, embodied sense. Woolf captures this paradoxical, incomplete interdependency in her reference to what she calls "the spot the size of a shilling at the back of the head which one can never see for oneself" (*AROO* 94). She seems to understand that there is an ontological blind spot, or point of nonclosure and unknowability, inherent in our embodiment. She suggests that there are gender blind spots and that men and women can supplement each other's blind spots. Indeed, our engagement with others may be prompted by this backside, this blind spot of ours that draws us toward those who can see and inhabit it for us. What Merleau-Ponty calls this "incessant escaping" of myself from myself entails an ontological opening or leakage into the world that allows others to re-turn myself partly to me. My incompleteness creates my turning outward and forward into space and time and thought—with others. It is in this radical way that "I am from the start outside myself and open to the world."

Yet this meeting of the self as something already-in-the-world, this coming to the self "from without" as well as within yet never completely, leaves us vulnerable. Here enters and exits power. In so far as we are turned to ourselves *through* it, the world can take up our bodies according to its own interests, can *occupy* us like a foreign power and make violent our knowing of ourselves. As Woolf remarks in *A Room*, "the world [can] sa[y] [to women] with a guffaw, Write? What's the good of your writing?" and can bear down with the weight of "an enormous body of masculine opinion to the effect that nothing could be expected of women intellectually" (55-6).

Woolf intuits, in other words, how the chiasmatic processes of embodiment leave a perilous opening for what Marxist theorist Louis Althusser calls "interpellation"(162).[5] He develops the idea of interpellation as a kind of societal calling out by which the self becomes a social subject as it is called to occupy or answer to a certain position in the social order. For Althusser, this hailing of the self into social subjectivity occurs immediately—one is always already called out—so that one identifies one's position in the ideological order with one's *self*. Bringing together the insights of Althusser and Merleau-Ponty reveals how corporeal self-relation is a circle with a loophole, how that loophole is the outsideness of oneself that belongs to the world: and how interpellation enters *here*. This is the "here" that structures Woolf's essay and troubles yet launches her thought.

2

The calling-out by society, and its choreographing of our motions, is central to the spatial design of *A Room of One's Own*. As Woolf enters the street in Chapter Two to wend her way to the Library of the British Museum, she experiences the rush and pull of the metropolis: "London was like a workshop. London was like a machine. We were all being shot backwards and forwards on this plain foundation to make some pattern" (*AROO* 26). The Library, too, silently issues its orders to whomever may enter: "The

British Museum was another department of the factory. The swing-doors swung open; and there one stood under the vast dome, as if one were a thought in the huge bald forehead which is so splendidly encircled by a band of famous names. One went to the counter; one took a slip of paper; one opened a volume of the catalogue" (*AROO* 26). As if one were a thought in the head of patriarchal culture, one walks the paths, thinks the thoughts, laid out there.

Or, one takes a detour and uses a decoy, by playing with the doubled, other-tilted relation to oneself. Woolf foregrounds the very body that marks her as female and in need of relocation and policing, and she objects to these interruptions; yet meanwhile she uses them as opportunities to *move* and so embrace the unfixability and motility of this ambidexterous body. She joins a kind of dance with these interruptions.

As we saw, Woolf explains that she has taken the "subject which you have laid upon my shoulders . . . and made it work in and out of my daily life" and in her lecture/essay aims to "develop *in your presence* as fully and freely as I can my train of thought" (*AROO* 4, emphasis added). She continues this placement of herself before her audience by situating us with her on the bank of a river, where she meditates on women and fiction. She conjures a Romantic scene of "willows weeping in perpetual lamentation" with her self "lost in thought" (*AROO* 5), but hers is not the Romantic tradition of a transcendent self in which nature's outside mirrors the self within and so enables the poet to surpass both time and nature. In her world, the self fades as if it had never been, for "the river reflected whatever it chose of sky and bridge and burning tree, and when the undergraduate had oared his boat through the reflections they closed again, completely, as if he had never been" (*AROO* 5). Nonetheless, the world's indifference to the undergraduate's and to her presence makes *possible* her imaginary departures, her lostness in thought: "There one might have sat the clock round lost in thought." Like Lily, Woolf observes the world's indifference, which is lonely but also sustaining; the world's autonomy frees the body even as it provides its literal ground. It is this simultaneous situatedness and lostness, the luxury of being lost inside the self yet still inhabiting a world, that Woolf moves us into in this opening scene.

Seated here, within the chiasmus of world and person, Woolf's thinking "let[s] its line down into the stream. . . . until—you know the little tug—the sudden conglomeration of an idea at the end of one's line"—and suddenly Woolf finds herself on her feet: "It was thus that I found myself walking with extreme rapidity across a grass plot." We move with her rising momentum, catching up, as she does, with her own body's movements—until just as suddenly "a man's figure rose to intercept me" (*AROO* 5-6). The Beadle blocks her way in a spectacle that offers a precise allegory of the promise and danger of chiasmatic embodiment. Because thought is not separate from body but rather is "its lining and its depth" (*Visible* 149), a thought is interrupted when a body is blocked. Woolf momentarily loses her capacity to come to herself *via* the world she is lost in, she loses the world and loses her thought.

Yet throughout the essay, Woolf's lostness in and of thought moves her continually, dialectically, back into the world; she renders dramatically the way that thought attaches to movement, it sways with the water and then propels her across the turf; and even an abrupt diversion sends it off down another path. Thought is, in Woolf and Merleau-Ponty alike, "the invisible *of* this world, that which inhabits this world, [. . .] its own and interior possibility" (*Visible* 151, emphasis in original). Thought and body are sustained in chiasmatic relation to one another. By displaying before us the shared radical of thought and body Woolf challenges the very assumption that authorizes the Beadle to reprimand her—that body and thought do *not* cohere, especially not in a woman. In *A Room*, Woolf repeatedly insists on their co-herence—"the human frame being what it is, heart, body and brain all mixed together" (18). She stresses the inextricability of book from body (81), the intermingling of the prosaic and the poetic (46), the material and the imaginative (43-44), the economic and the artistic (112).

Yet, she repeatedly enacts the shocks that result from this vulnerable reversibility of thought and body. After recovering from the Beadle's interruption, she decides to go and study the manuscript of William Thackeray's *Esmond* stored in the Oxbridge library, taking us by the arm to lead the way. Thinking as she walks about the question of "what is style and what is meaning, a question which—but here I was actually at the door to the library itself" (*AROO* 7)—she abruptly follows this innocent interruption with another: "I must have opened [the door], for instantly there issued, like a guardian angel barring the way with a flutter of black gown instead of white wings, a deprecating, silvery, kindly gentlemen, who regretted in a low voice as he waved me back that ladies are only admitted to the library if accompanied by a Fellow of the College" (*AROO* 7-8). The first arrival of the world, in the form of the library, constitutes what we might consider a productive collision of thought and body: one that defines the relation between her style and meaning, and through which she creates for her readers a fluctuating real that encompasses thought and things. But Woolf juxtaposes this generative meeting of thought and body against an obstructive one, in the form of a silvery gentleman, whose presence overtakes and cancels Woolf's. In effect he takes the door—the world—right out of her hands since, in seeing him, she realizes she "must have opened it." Her action belongs to him before she realizes she has done it. The first encounter is dialogically corrective to thought in the sense that it brings pressure and presence—the library itself—to bear on its questions: it offers answers though they lead to other questions. The second leads, at least momentarily, to anger and cursing, to another lost minnow of thought—yet also, as Woolf manages it, back to a physicality entwined with musing, for now she turns to follow the music she hears.

When Woolf arrives at Fernham in the next chapter—and all of her chapters situate us in places, libraries, restaurants, lecture halls—she brashly flaunts her power to imagine the world, the place, on her own terms and through her own body. She begins by transforming her October day into a Spring day in order to capture the odd "making" energy in this world, for that evening at Fernham "there was something odd at work."

> It was the time between the lights when colours undergo their intensification and purples and golds burn in window-panes like the beat of an excitable heart; when for some reason the beauty of the world revealed and yet soon to perish (here I pushed into the garden for, unwisely, the door was left open and no beadles seemed about), the beauty of the world which is so soon to perish, has two edges, one of laughter, one of anguish, cutting the heart asunder. The gardens of Fernham lay before me in the spring twilight, wild and open [. . . .] somebody, but in this light they were phantoms only, half guessed, half seen, raced across the grass—would no one stop her? [. . .] All was dim, yet intense too, as if the scarf which the dusk had flung over the garden were torn asunder by star or sword—the flash of some terrible reality leaping, as its way is, out of the heart of the spring. For youth—
>
> Here was my soup [. . . .] It was a plain gravy soup. There was nothing to stir the fancy in that. (*AROO* 17)

Woolf suspends us in a hovering moment, between day and night, where again the real and the reflection become coterminous, purples and golds have an existence that reappears in window-panes and this passing-over creates a pulsing like an excitable heart that in turn excites the heart of the writer and so, too, the reader. All aspects of this world are reversible and attached like a Jacob's ladder, like the chiasm.

Woolf moves into this garden of the real, interrupting herself to say that there was no one to interrupt her here: and this move epitomizes the strategy we have been witnessing. In naming the near-constant threat of interruption and interpellation even in its absence ("no beadles seemed about"), she calls us out into a mode of suspension that will carry us past coercive interruptions, for we must live through her parenthetical words, her syntactic interruptions that mimic yet displace his absent one, to get to the beauty of the shimmering garden. In doing so, she enables us to feel all the more acutely in answer to the question, "will no one stop her?"—that, No, no one will. For even if coercive interpellation takes advantage of the uncertainties, the "shift," the spread," the anticipatory states of the intercorporeal body, Woolf nonetheless refuses to throw out the baby with the bath water—that is, she refuses to reject uncertainty, contingency, interruption, and suspension even when they are tyrannized by the forces of convention, decorum, and patriarchy. She refuses to shut down. This is a difficult way of being; it means embracing a world filled with beauty that too soon perishes, a world with two edges, one of laughter, one of anguish, that cut the heart asunder. She chooses risky suspension in the precarious hammock of the world. She calls forth the phantoms and their terrible reality.

Such a meeting of the world also includes coming face to face, rudely, with "plain gravy soup." Woolf's fantasy collides with plain gravy soup served in a homely red brick building and in this moment she makes us collide with the fact that she has been inside this building throughout her entire fantasy, which in turn may feel to us like the world has been torn asunder by the flash of a sword. Her fancy, "wild and open" like the garden, has all along wandered within the confines of a building whose plainness, she has shown, is a function of patriarchy, of men's fear of women. Yet even though at the level of content Woolf has exposed this encasement of her fancy and her body, at the level of form she has counteracted this enclosure by her abruptness, which interrupts and surprises *our* reading bodies and so calls *us* out into a turning, a moving on, a break in the wall. In other words, this interruption is exactly at once a deflation and a liberation of fancy, a stealing back of the powers of interruption in order to re-create the ontology of suspension that is our openness to the world. Woolf forces us to live the tragic arc of the Daedalian fall from the sky, to live in the flight of being, despite the threat of exposure and entrapment it presents.

3

In the closing pages of *A Room*, Woolf moves her audience through a final series of turns and counter-turns. At one point she even chides herself after a rapid series of clauses beginning with the word "but": "'But' ⁀ . . I had said 'but' too often. One cannot go on saying 'but.' One must finish the sentence somehow, I rebuked myself" (*AROO* 104). Nonetheless the essay closes in a crescendo of "buts." She considers abruptly ending her essay, "but" she says, "the pressure of convention decrees that every speech must end with a peroration" (*AROO* 114). She accordingly attempts to provide one, guided by the principle that

> a paper read by a woman to women should end with something particularly disagreeable. *But* how does it go? What can I think of? The truth is, I often like women. I like their unconventionality [an unconventional insertion in a peroration that is supposedly conforming to convention]. I like their subtlely. I like their anonymity. I like–*but* I must not run on in this way. [. . .] Let me adopt a sterner tone. Have I, in the preceding words, conveyed to you sufficiently the warnings and reprobation of mankind?" (115, emphasis added).

Her closing pages thus weave in and out, continuing the disjunctive, sinuous, suspenseful mode the essay has cultivated throughout.

Yet Woolf does circle back again and again in her closing remarks to one particular point, one that crucially informs her method: "that our relation is to the world of reality and not only to the world of men and women" and that it is by thinking "of things in themselves [that] the opportunity will come and the dead poet who was Shakespeare's sister will put on the body she has so often laid down" (*AROO* 118). Woolf's practice makes us feel that our relation to men and women unfolds *through* the world of things, through the real that we are suspended in as both dialectical selves and intercorporeal others. Anticipating our concern with the term "reality," she asks: "What is meant by reality? It would seem to be something very erratic, very undependable—now to be found in a dusty road, now in a scrap of newspaper in the street, now in a daffodil in the sun. It lights up a group in a room and stamps some casual saying. It overwhelms one walking home beneath the stars and makes the silent world more real than the world of speech—and then there it is again in an omnibus in the uproar of Picadilly" (*AROO* 114). Of course all of these descriptions center on physicality but I would suggest that reality, as rendered by Woolf's aesthetic practice, is less *in* any one of these things than it is in the movement Woolf creates between them, the imagined reaching from one to the other *as if* one could encompass them but the very sharpness of the juxtapositions Woolf builds between them conveys that one can't: that the experience of their co-divergence is reality, and that to inhabit the spaces of divergence between things is the only way to know their commonality. As Woolf says in praising her audience for their differences from her, "In a question like this truth is only to be had by laying together many varieties of error" or in other words, truth, or reality, is a gathering of contingencies, imaginings, and intercorporealities that will always move in suspended tension with one another.

This reality, this phenomenality, is "resonant and porous; it transmits emotion without impediment; it is naturally creative, incandescent and undivided" (*AROO* 102). It is a "new type of being, a being by porosity, pregnancy, or generality, and [the person] before whom the horizon opens is caught up, included within it. The body and the distances participate in one same corporeity or visibility in general, which reigns between them and it, and even beyond the horizon, beneath [the person's] skin, unto the depths of being" (*Visible* 149). The first description belongs to Woolf, the second to Merleau-Ponty. Both implicitly testify that the body is not a wholeness that patriarchy or racism or homophobia or colonialism interrupts and splits against itself; rather, the body interrupts itself; the body moves in the span, on the hinge of its own non-closure. Domination doesn't block closure, it blocks non-closure. Hegemony succeeds by using a chiasmatic ontology against itself and so shutting it down. It aims to fix the body, to interrupt, intimidate, and then hold it on *its* terms, according to its rules. It steals from the person her or his power, or willingness, to extend the self across uncertainty and to risk encounters with the world. This is what Woolf wants to give back to her audience. Not safety. She fancies that the risk of continuous chiasmatic living is the only defense against coercion. And that art, to be political, to resist clichés and coercions, must among others things live in the lurch, beat the beadle to the opening, or meet him at the opening.

4

This leap into the opening—recalling Clarissa's "plunge" into the open air at Bourton (3), and the clerks who make "flying leaps into the mud" on the first page of *The Voyage Out* (9), and Katherine Hilbery's "leap" in the first scene of *Night and Day* "over the little barrier of the day" (9), and of course the leap into and out of the boat James Ramsay awaits for ten years—these kind of leaps launch Woolf's fiction as well as her essays. I even venture to suggest that Woolf's practice reflects a larger pattern in the experimentalism of early twentieth-century fiction, an inclusive one that would include those minority or marginalized or working-class writers who might seem traditional at first glance. For it seems to me that a broad range of "modernist" texts dramatize a certain kind of movement, and stumbling, not only of characters' bodies but also of narrators' voices. Many characters in modernist works travel across boundaries and mix dictions and cultural conventions in their experiences as expatriates, "half-breeds," or immigrants, or in their wanderings as Prufrock, Molloy, Cogewea, Bloom, Clare Kendry, Kabnis, Hanneh Breineh, Joe Christmas, or Isabelle Archer. And the voices that narrate these stories move us into the blind spot at the back of their characters' perambulating heads—even as the narrators, we are quietly invited to note, operate from their own blind spots, which a reader or community of readers may in turn enter from the backside, or unwittingly overlook. But this is speculation. I leave it as an opening in the ongoing conversations about Woolf and modernism.

Notes

[1] After writing this paper, I discovered Judith Allen's wonderful piece, "The Rhetoric of Performance in *A Room of One's Own*," in which she, too, notes the abundance of "but" clauses in Woolf's essay, including in its opening. Allen's emphasis on Woolf's "oscillation" that "repudiates a fixed stance" (293) and calls for "openness, for contradictions, and a certain wildness" (292) also accords with my reading which, however, extends the argument into the realm of the phenomenological in order to consider the implications of Woolf's mode for a rethinking of mind and to establish its engagement with processes of interpellation.

[2] In addition to Judith Allen, for discussions of Woolf's shifting strategy in *A Room*, see Sally Greene, Melba Cuddy-Keane, Nancy Hynes, James L. Hoban, and Peggy Kamuf. Kamuf's emphasis on Woolf's self-interruption compares closely to mine, yet again I aim to supplement these rhetorical or deconstructive feminist readings with an emphasis on the part the body plays in the drama of interruption. My reading shares the spirit of Jane Goldman's in *The Feminist Aesthetics of Virginia Woolf*, in which Goldman sees Woolf's "writing practice" as a "material intervention" in the Bergsonian "flow" of phenomena (5-6). This stands in contrast to critics such as Jean Long and Julie Robin Solomon who see Woolf's "awkward breaks" as signs of her conciliatory, self-censoring stance in this essay (although Solomon convinces me that Woolf does *unconsciously* short-circuit in her discus-

sion of Brontë and Austen). Of course, Lucio Ruotolo and Rachel Blau Duplessis have both written key studies of Woolf's creative use of interruption.

[3] Merleau-Ponty, *Phenomenology of Perception*, 456.

[4] Merleau-Ponty, *The Visible and the Invisible*, 135, emphasis in original.

[5] Althusser borrows from the use of the term in government, whereby the proceedings of a government chamber are *interrupted* so that a minister can be questioned.

Works Cited

Allen, Judith. "The Rhetoric of Performance in *A Room's of One's Own*." In *Virginia Woolf and Communities*. Eds. Jeanette McVicker and Laura Davis. New York, NY: Pace U P, 1999: 289-96.

Louis Althusser, *Lenin and Philosophy and Other Essays.* London: New Left Books, 1971: 162

Blau Duplessis, Rachel. *Writing Beyond the Ending: Narrative Strategies of Twentieth-Century Women Writers*. Bloomington: Indiana U P, 1985.

Cuddy-Keane, Melba. "The Rhetoric of Feminist Conversation: Virginia Woolf and the Trope of the Twist." In *Ambiguous Discourse: Feminist Narratology and British Women Writers*. Ed. Kathy Mezei . Chapel Hill: U of North Carolina P, 1996: 137-171.

Goldman, Jane. *The Feminist Aesthetics of Virginia Woolf: Modernism, Post-Impressionism, and the Politics of the Visual*. N Y: Cambridge U P, 1998.

Greene, Sally. "Virginia Woolf and the Courtier's Art: The Renaissance Wit of *A Room of One's Own*." In *Virginia Woolf and the Arts: Selected Papers from the Sixth Annual Conference on Virginia Woolf*. Eds. Diane F. Gillespie and Leslie K. Hankins. NY: Pace U P, 1997: 292-301.

Hoban, James L. "Rhetorical Topoi in *A Room of One's Own*." In *Re: Reading, Re:Writing, Re:Teaching Virginia Woolf*. Eds. Eileen Barrett and Patricia Cramer. NY: Pace U P, 1995: 148-54.

Hynes, Nancy. "The Chameleon Voice and Classical Structure in *Three Guineas* and *A Room of One's Own*." *Virginia Woolf: Emerging Perspectives*. Ed. Mark Hussey and Vara Neverow. NY: Pace U P, 1994: 140-46.

Kamuf, Peggy, "Penelope at Work: Interruptions in *A Room of One's Own*." *Novel*. 16 (1982): 5-18.

Long, Jean. "The Awkward Break: Woolf's Reading of Brontë and Austen in *A Room of One's Own*." *Woolf Studies Annual*. 3 (1997): 76-94.

Merleau-Ponty, Maurice. *Phenomenology of Perception*. Trans. Colin Smith. New Jersey: The Humanities Press, 1962.

——. *The Visible and the Invisible*. Trans. Alphonso Lingis. Evanston: Northwestern U P, 1968.

Ruotolo. Lucio. *The Interrupted Moment: A View of Virginia Woolf's Novels*. Palo Alto CA: Stanford U P, 1986.

Solomon, Julie Robin. "Staking Ground: The Politics of Space in Virginia Woolf's *A Room of One's Own* and *Three Guineas*." *Women's Studies: An Interdisciplinary Journal* 16 (3–4, 1989): 331–47.

Woolf, Virginia. *The Voyage Out*. New York: Harcourt Brace Jovanovich, 1948.
———. *Night and Day*. New York: Harcourt Brace Jovanovich, 1948.
———. *Mrs. Dalloway*. New York: Harcourt Brace, 1981.
———. *To the Lighthouse*. New York: Harcourt Brace, 1981.

Justine Dymond
"The Outside of its Inside and the Inside of its Outside": Phenomenology in *To the Lighthouse*

In chapter IV of the first section of *To the Lighthouse*, Virginia Woolf offers us a philosophical challenge. The artist Lily Briscoe has "asked [Andrew] what his father's books were about. 'Subject and object and the nature of reality,' Andrew had said. [. . .] 'Think of a kitchen table then,' he told her, 'when you're not there'" (23). Lily Briscoe takes up the challenge in a literal sense by imagining a very specific "scrubbed kitchen table [. . .] lodged now in the fork of a pear tree" (23). Though Woolf portrays this intersection of artistic sensibility and philosophical pondering in a humorous manner, her novel can be seen as a serious consideration of "subject and object and the nature of reality" through an artistic and narrative medium.

In order to examine the novel's philosophical dimensions, I have turned to the work of two phenomenologists, Maurice Merleau-Ponty and Emmanuel Levinas. Both philosophers eschew the notion of a mind/body split. As Elizabeth Grosz notes in *Volatile Bodies*, "Merleau-Ponty begins with a fundamental presumption, not of a Cartesian dualism of mind and body but of their necessary interrelatedness. He claims that phenomenology wants to understand the relations between consciousness and nature and between interiority and exteriority" (86). It is that fundamental presumption and the way in which its challenge to the mind/body split reorients our notions of self, other, and language which compels my analysis. What I find particularly useful about reading the work of Merleau-Ponty and Levinas alongside Woolf is the way in which their theories of corporeality resonate with her concerns with the nature of reality as an intersubjective experience. This resonance between phenomenology and Woolf's text particularly occurs as the intercorporeality of reader and text emerges from the materiality of her stylistics, that is, as I will show, the physicality produced by the very syntax of her prose.

In this paper I will show how Woolf's *To the Lighthouse* enacts the phenomenological challenge to the inside/outside dichotomy as theorized by Levinas and Merleau-Ponty. I will argue, using the vocabulary of these phenomenologists, that Woolf's narrative explores orientation towards the *other* as constitutive of a fluid subjectivity, therefore putting into question what constitutes the boundary between the subject and the other, and between the self and what we conventionally see as the world outside the self.

The "Incarnate Mind" and the "Fundamental Phenomenon of Reversibility"

Both Merleau-Ponty and Levinas describe consciousness as an embodied phenomenon. Levinas uses the term "incarnate mind" to describe the interrelatedness of mind and body. He writes, "The body is the fact that thought is immersed in the world that it thinks and, consequently, expresses this world while it thinks it" (40). The image of the Möbius strip, the one dimensional figure eight that exists as one surface and yet manages simultaneously to be three-dimensional in space, may be helpful in understanding Levinas's notion of the "incarnate mind." In other words, thought emerges from the physical and sensual experience of being but that experience is also constituted by thought; mind and body are inseparable and indistinguishable, the mind always incarnate, the body always experiencing the world as expressed in thought.

In *The Visible and the Invisible*, Merleau-Ponty uses the term "the flesh" to describe embodied consciousness. For Merleau-Ponty, perception arises from "the thickness of flesh between the seer and the thing" which "is constitutive for the thing of its visibility as for the seer of his [sic] corporeity; it is not an obstacle between them, it is their means of communication" (135). The "flesh" also expresses, as Grosz explains, a "reflexivity, that fundamental gap or dehiscence of being that Merleau-Ponty illustrates with a favorite example, the 'double sensation,' an example that clearly illustrates the various gradations between subjectivity and objectuality" (100). Merleau-Ponty's often quoted example of the subject's left hand touching its right hand illustrates the body's ability to be both sentient and sensible, as well as the body's inability to perceive itself perceiving:

> If my left hand is touching my right hand, and if I should suddenly wish to apprehend with my right hand the work of my left hand as it touches, this reflection of the body upon itself always miscarries at the last moment: the moment I feel my left hand with my right hand, I correspondingly cease touching my right hand with my left hand. (9)

In this example, Merleau-Ponty illustrates the "chiasm," or "fundamental phenomenon of reversibility," that is, the way that the body experiences itself as both sentient and sensible at the same time but not in a manner complete unto itself. It is this "chiasm" that allows Merleau-Ponty to claim that being is not solipsistic since existence is not an unbroken circle of self-referentiality.

The example of the left hand touching the right hand is fundamental to Merleau-Ponty's notion of "intercorporeity." He argues that if a being can experience itself as both subject and object of its own touch (though not simultaneously; thus the "chiasm" of the self touching itself), "why, when

141

touching the hand of another, would I not touch in it the same power to espouse the things that I have touched in my own?" (141). Thought is thus born in the possibility of the subject's imagining the perception of another sentient being. Merleau-Ponty writes that the body is "fascinated by the unique occupation of floating in Being with another life, of making itself the outside of its inside and the inside of its outside" (144). Merleau-Ponty suggests that it is the physical presence of the other which provokes thought, though thought originates in the body that speaks "I." With this argument, Merleau-Ponty can conclude that no ideas exist without "carnal experience" (150), what Levinas calls the "incarnate mind." As Merleau-Ponty shows, such a phenomenon of reversibility upsets the dichotomy of inside/outside; our subjectivities are therefore not so easily distinguishable from the horizon in which our incarnate minds arise. But it is not just the outside—the horizon of objects—that provokes thought; the desire to know the inside of that outside, to press "through into those secret chambers" (51), as Lily Briscoe puts it, gives the impetus to thought.

"One With the Object One Adored"

In *To the Lighthouse*, the artist Lily Briscoe is concerned with the question of a center, a central object around which to orient the perspective of her painting. She confronts the "uncompromising white stare" (157) of her canvas and "all the difference in the world between this planning airily away from the canvas, and actually taking her brush and making the first mark" (157). The novel ends with the solution to Lily's problem of the gap between planning and execution: "With a sudden intensity, as if she saw it clear for a second, she drew a line there, *in the centre*. It was done; it was finished" (209; emphasis added). Though this passage contains a tone of certainty, we must note the hesitancy in the phrase "*as if* she saw it clear for a second" which suggests that though Lily finds a center to orient her painting's perspective, that center is not a certain one.

A similar sense of an elusive center occurs through the novel's point of view. In Part I of *To the Lighthouse*, "The Window," the narrative weaves in and out of several perspectives as the characters circle around the Angel in the House, Mrs. Ramsay. Sometimes the shifts in perspective occur within a single sentence, as in the following:

> She [Mrs. Ramsay] knitted with firm composure, slightly pursing her lips and, without being aware of it, so stiffened and composed the lines of her face in a habit of sternness that when her husband passed, though he was chuckling at the thought that Hume, the philosopher, grown enormously fat, had stuck in a bog, he could not help noting, as he passed, the sternness at the heart of her beauty. (64)

The consciousnesses of the characters interconnect within paragraphs and sentences, and in their focus on the central figure of Mrs. Ramsay. These interconnected moments also happen through shared metaphor, as when, at dinner, both Mrs. Ramsay and Lily Briscoe think of sailing imagery to describe others, without voicing their thoughts aloud (84); or through a shared object of perception[1], as when Lily and Mr. Bankes watch the waves on the beach and "both felt a common hilarity, excited by the moving waves" (20). In short, the narrator of "The Window" works to weave together the consciousnesses, the insides, of the novel's characters.

Though the narrator of the novel moves fluidly in and out of characters' consciousnesses without barrier, the characters themselves, most notably Lily Briscoe, cannot realize such an ease of movement inside the consciousness of others; the body creates a barrier. Nonetheless, Lily attempts to reach "the chambers of the mind and heart" of Mrs. Ramsay by physical intimacy:

> What device for becoming, like waters poured into one jar, inextricably the same, one with the object one adored? Could the body achieve, or the mind, subtly mingling in the intricate passages of the brain? or the heart? Could loving, as people called it, make her and Mrs. Ramsay one? (51)

The word "one" takes on a heightened and permutating sense, appearing three times in three different meanings, as a numerical distinction ("one jar"), as a sense of unity, and as an indefinite pronoun ("one with the object one adored"). It is certainly in the second sense that the word "one" carries the most weight, since it also echoes the novel's recurring concern with marriage, the metaphorical joining into one of two people. But the way the word "one" in this particular passage slips around in meaning forecasts the impossibility of unity through language. Furthermore, the difficulty of knowing "one thing or another thing about people, sealed as they were" (51) in their bodies also creates a barrier to unity with the other. This mini-melodrama of Lily's unsuccessful attempt to mingle with Mrs. Ramsay's inner being, that is, the self Lily sees as existing in the interior of the body, provokes questions about the body as a possible conductor of, and a barrier to, knowing the other.

Here, we can see how Woolf's text resonates with Levinas's notion of the "incarnate mind" and Merleau-Ponty's "fundamental phenomenon of reversibility." It is in both hers and Mrs. Ramsay's corporeal being that Lily desires to *be* in Mrs. Ramsay's consciousness. Lily's melodramatic moment is not pure tragedy then, since it is in the going *toward* Mrs. Ramsay, though Lily is always frustrated in reaching her, that Lily and we begin to see the possibility of being "one with the object one adored." Furthermore, it is through physical intimacy with Mrs. Ramsay that Lily perceives her desired object perceiving; in other words, Lily exists in this moment in Merleau-Ponty's "gap" where she sees that subjectivity and objectuality have the possibility of reversing.

This "fundamental phenomenon of reversibility" occurs on yet another level in the text. The language on the page, the *body* of the text, produces an intersubjectivity, or in Merleau-Ponty's terms, an "intercorporeal being," where the textual body interweaves the insides of several consciousnesses, including the reader's. Coming to the page, I desire, as Lily does, to know the *other*, though the language, like the body, creates a slippery barrier: Am I *one* with Woolf's thoughts by means of intimacy with her textual body, or am I *one* who can only desire to be *one* with the other?

Intercorporeality With No Bodies

The question of "being one with the object one adored" and the fluidity of subjectivity implied in intercorporeality becomes complicated by the middle section of *To the Lighthouse*, "Time Passes." The narrative voice in this section seems to have no perspective through which the narrator perceives things. Furthermore, this bodiless voice also narrates a place where no *body* exists, where "loveliness reigned and stillness" (129):

> What people had shed and left—a pair of shoes, a shooting cap, some faded skirts and coats in wardrobes—those alone kept the human shape and in the emptiness indicated how once they were filled and animated; how once hands were busy with hooks and buttons; how once the looking-glass had held a face; had held a world hollowed out in which a figure turned, a hand flashed, the door opened, in came children rushing and tumbling; and went out again. (129)

Like a ghost, the narrator of "Time Passes" reminds us of what once existed. The central perspective of this section is a veritable absence for which the narrator longs. However, even as Woolf tries to empty her text of human presence, the things that remain suggest the presence of people through the animation of their absence: clothes and mirrors and doors imply bodies, hold the traces of human presence, and thus betray the text's desire for "one."

More importantly, the narration *stylistically* embodies the communal absence of the Ramsays. As Woolf's narrator disconnects perception from the body's physical orientation in the world, the omniscient narrator's prose takes on a shapely presence, an embodiment through style. The prose in the above passage has a quality of "rushing and tumbling" out in a myriad of directions then ending abruptly, like a door suddenly closing. In other passages, Woolf's prose unfolds or, conversely, burrows into itself, revealing more information in succeeding or embedded clauses and appositive phrases, as in the famous parenthetical passage wherein we learn of Mrs. Ramsay's death: "[Mr. Ramsay, stumbling along a passage one dark morning, stretched his arms out, but Mrs. Ramsay having died rather suddenly the night before, his arms, though stretched out, remained empty]" (128). Thus, the narration embodies the movement of absent bodies in the text, again creating an absent center in the narrative. With no orienting perspective, no line to draw a clear center of vision, Woolf asks, what exists in the world of objects with no body to perceive them? Does Woolf then attempt through her disembodied narrator to see things without the "factual presence of other bodies" which Merleau-Ponty claims produces thought?

The narrator both perceives and experiences the world of "Time Passes" in a corporeal state. The body's sentient self, its thickness, represented by the textual wandering of the prose, enables the world of things to be, at the same time that it is *by* those things that the text traces the movement of human bodies. In this way, Woolf's narration enacts Levinas's seemingly paradoxical notion of the "incarnate mind" that thought arises from the body's interaction with the world, a world that exists for the being as expressed in thought. And, as Merleau-Ponty shows, the sense of the self as inextricable from the world, which in turn constitutes the self, belies the fiction of the interiority/exteriority dichotomy. Furthermore, in the act of reading, our sense of our interior subjectivities is shaped by a textual body, such as Woolf's novel, which makes us "the outside of its inside and the inside of its outside."

Notes

[1] In *Bordering on the Body: The Racial Matrix of Modern Fiction and Culture* (New York: Oxford U P, 1994), Laura Doyle uses the term "intercorporeal narrative practice" to describe the use of objects as pivots between consciousnesses in *To the Lighthouse*.

Works Cited

Grosz, Elizabeth. *Volatile Bodies: Toward a Corporeal Feminism*. Bloomington: Indiana U P, 1994.

Levinas, Emmanuel. *Basic Philosophical Writings*. Eds. Adrian T. Peperzak, Simon Critchley, and Robert Bernasconi. Bloomington: Indiana U P, 1996.

Merleau-Ponty, Maurice. *The Visible and the Invisible*. Evanston: Northwestern U P, 1968.

Woolf, Virginia. *To the Lighthouse*. New York: A Harvest Book/Harcourt Brace & Company, 1955.

Todd Avery
Talking with the Other; or, Wireless Ethics: Levinas, Woolf, and the BBC

This paper is part of a larger study of the Bloomsbury Group's and other modernists' involvement with the early British Broadcasting Corporation; it is motivated by my curiosity about the nature of the conjunction between the following four elements: Victorian and twentieth-century ethical philosophy, late-Victorian and early-twentieth-century cultural theory, radio as a techno-cultural phenomenon, and Virginia Woolf as an active participant in the formation of modern mass culture. The question that I will address is implied by my subtitle, in which Virginia Woolf meets the BBC and the philosopher Emmanuel Levinas in a perhaps unlikely combination. The question is this: What, from the perspective of moral or ethical philosophy, was the nature of Virginia Woolf's involvement with the BBC, where she broadcast three times during the 1920s and 1930s? A corollary question is this: How might a clearer understanding of Woolf in the context of radio broadcasting foster a fuller awareness of the nature of Woolf's ethics?

I'm especially interested in how the Bloomsbury broadcasters negotiated the moral imperative behind early public service broadcasting in Britain, and used the BBC as a platform for the promotion of their own ethical beliefs. Much has been written about the influence of G. E. Moore's *Principia Ethica* (1903) on Bloomsbury values, with his valorization of conversation and aesthetic enjoyment as the two greatest ethical "goods." Less is known about other influences on Bloomsbury's ethical values. But I think that there is some truth in Kate Whitehead's slightly facetious suggestion that "Bloomsbury" is a misleading moniker for this group of friends and public intellectuals who were also early radio celebrities (121). A comprehensive study of Bloomsbury at the BBC may help us to understand Bloomsbury's ethics in general and Virginia Woolf's ethics in particular more fully than we currently do. One way to begin such a study is to locate Bloomsbury's—and Woolf's—talks in the context of the BBC's mission to elevate British morality through the promotion of a cultural ideal rooted in the work of Samuel Taylor Coleridge, John Henry Newman, and Matthew Arnold, and of a moral ideal that can be found in the writings of F. H. Bradley, T. H. Green, Leslie Stephen, Thomas Henry Huxley, and other ethical philosophers of the later nineteenth century.

The founders of the BBC, most notably the Corporation's first Director-General, John Reith, explicitly invoked the Arnoldian definition of culture as "the best which has been thought and said in the world" (*Culture and Anarchy* viii) when forming public service broadcasting as a technocultural medium in the national public interest. Following Arnold's prescription for national health, these self-described cultural and moral arbiters wanted to establish the BBC as a microcosm of "*the State*, or organ of our collective best self, of our national right reason" (58, italics in text). They did this by trying to impose a type of sonic architecture on British culture and society that would, they hoped, hail radio listeners to moral conformity through radio talks and other broadcasts. As Reith explained to a Parliamentary Committee on broadcasting in 1924, two years after the British Broadcasting Company took to the airwaves, the BBC had an ethical obligation to the nation, and to the idea of nationalism more generally. Reith's desire for national unity also involved an effort to structure broadcasting as a vehicle for what Thomas De Quincey and Coleridge respectively called "alloquium" as opposed to "colloquium" and "*one*versazione" as opposed to "*conver*-sazione"—talking to rather than with others (Simpson 49).

One of Reith's fundamental ideological assumptions was that public service broadcasting in Britain, as opposed to the American model of privately owned, commercial broadcasting, should not to pander to public taste, but uplift it in the interest of national coherence and stability. In this connection, I think of Ruskin's famous dictum from the 1860s, "Taste [. . .] is the ONLY morality" ("Traffic" 234). Reith's obsession with national coherence combined with his evangelical enthusiasm to form a quasi-fascistic directorial manner. Indeed, photographs of Reith from the 1920s show him as the masculine type Virginia Woolf would later associate with tyrants and dictators: "he is Man himself, the quintessence of virility, the perfect type of which all the others are imperfect adumbrations. He is a man certainly. [. . .] his eyes glare. His body, which is braced in an unnatural position, is encased in a uniform" (*TG* 142). Some critics saw the fledgling BBC as a benevolent autocracy, a sort of Platonic state ruled by a philosopher-king. But among some BBC employees in the 1930s, Reith was rather less than affectionately known as "Mussolini." Reith conceptualized culture as a whole and broadcasting itself as allies in a fight against the anarchic habit of "doing as one likes." He explained in a school lecture in 1922, just after he was hired by the BBC, that culture should "divert into useful channels" potentially "wrongly used energies" (qtd. in LeMahieu 144). As an agent of culture and morality, the BBC was "to make the nation as one man" (Reith 217)—or one family—under a decidedly paternal head.

This vision for broadcasting had deep roots in late-Victorian moral philosophy. Reith's invocation of the late nineteenth-century's dominant conception of culture recalls the moral views of a host of eminent Victorian philosophers. In his argument for the absolute moral rightness of a paternalistic society, Reith's position, translated into the terminology of ethical philosophy, amounts to a "deontological" approach to morality similar to that embraced by the Oxford idealists Bradley and Green, and the evolutionists Huxley and Stephen. Deontic ethics is a branch of ethics that focuses on such concepts as obligation, responsibility, and duty. Reith, who believed he had been called by God to the BBC's helm (Giddings 155), surely would have agreed with Green's belief that individuals' duties and responsibilities ought to coincide with those of "the institutions in which the progress of the divine spirit has thus far embodied itself" (qtd. in Schneewind 402). Reith also would have found sustenance in Bradley's notion that the purpose of ethical philosophy was to provide a theoretical basis for existing moral values, in Huxley's insistence that one subsume one's desires to moral conventions in order to combat the anarchic forces of both nature and society, and in Stephen's celebration of the family as the foundation of national moral and social health.

Bloomsbury's opinions on the moral underpinnings of the Reithian imperial project may be discovered in many of their radio talks, letters, diaries, essays, and novels (e.g., *Orlando*). Forster's *Commonplace Book* contains one of the Bloomsburyans' most savage attacks on the BBC's moral ideals:

> You can't understand life or live properly without the help of God, you can't believe in God unless you believe in Christ, you will find what Christ taught and was in the Bible, you can't read the Bible properly without the help of God, but you can't believe in God unless you believe in Christ, you will find what—[sic] So spins the 24 hour record on the BBC. (131)

From the standpoint of ethical philosophy, the relationship between the Bloomsbury broadcasters and the Reithian BBC may be figured as a contest between conceptions about the common good. Reith articulated the common good to a reified ideology of paternal nationalism. For the Bloomsburyans, to the contrary, the good was part and parcel of a politics that valorized both intimacy and internationalism and contested nationalist ideals; their ethics may be described as aretaic or "virtue ethics" (from the Greek *aretai*, "excellences"—and perhaps even, in Emmanuel Levinas's compelling concept, "ethics as first philosophy." Virtue ethics focuses on questions of individual character; it sees goodness as a condition that may be attained outside of the prescriptions of moral rule, and through the (quasi-aestheticist) cultivation of moral virtues like magnanimity and generosity, and intellectual virtues like contemplative wisdom and intelligent judgment. Levinas' idea of "ethics as first philosophy" involves the notion that ethics precedes existence—or that one exists in proportion to the fullness of one's response to "the singular otherness of the other person," and the degree to which one "provokes inventive responses to other persons" and works to "bring about a more widespread alteration in intersubjective behavior" (Attridge 30, 24).

The very style of address—conversational, intimate, inventively provocative—that the Bloomsburyans pioneered during the 1920s and 1930s challenged John Reith's moral and cultural authoritarianism. The originally unified Talks Department was divided in the early 1930s, under pressure from some Talks producers, into the categories of "popular" and "serious" talks with corresponding modes of address (Cardiff 33-4). Subsequently, literary broadcasters—"radio personalities who offered mild diversion or solace rather than information" (34) —found themselves inhabiting an institutional space within which it was possible to develop subtle forms of critique of the BBC's deontic moral underpinnings. To speak intimately or conversationally about literature was also to repudiate reified moral norms, and to foster the cultivation of ethical and intellectual virtues by implying that the ultimate ethical value of literature lay not in its ability to introduce a reader—or listener—into the cultural empyrean where, in

Arnold's phrase, the will of God prevails (xxxii-xxxiii), but rather in what the individual reader makes of the work.

In Virginia Woolf's 1937 broadcast on "Craftsmanship"—just as in such *Common Reader* essays as "Notes on an Elizabethan Play," "Modern Fiction," "The Patron and the Crocus," and especially, "How Should One Read a Book?"—this "virtue ethical" approach to reading and writing combines with a sort of Levinasian adjuration to respect words' "singular otherness" and counters a "deontic" view of cultural productions. In this talk, she argues that the ethical value of our relation to words resides in how successfully we both resist the temptation to "lay down laws for such irreclaimable vagabonds" and respect words' "liberty," their "thousand" nonutilitarian "possibilities" for speaking the truth. "It is the nature of words," she says, "to mean many things." They are not intrinsically "useful;" they do not speak "God's or gospel truth;" nor do they speak "home truth;" rather, they speak what Woolf calls "literary truth" (868)—and to recognize this type of truth is a demanding endeavor: to do it, readers and writers must assiduously cultivate their responsiveness to words' "various" and "strange," but above all, "loving" relations with other words in sentences (868). "In reading," Woolf says, "we have to allow the sunken meanings to remain sunken, suggested, not stated; lapsing and flowing into each other like reeds on the bed of the river" (868). In short, we need to participate in a conversation with words, to lapse and flow into them as they do into us. To learn this responsiveness is to cultivate a "diabolical power" (868) of resistance to the utilitarian employment of words as conduits of moral and cultural absolutes. It is also to celebrate what Levinas calls "the facing of a face"—the ethical and by extension, political "summons" into a type of relationship in which "the proximity of my fellow [. . .] is the responsibility of the I for another" ("Philosophical" 186, italics in text). To accept this (in Levinas's opinion, *impossible* but necessary) summons is, finally, to love, and by loving to make a breach "in the barbarism of being, even if no philosophy of history"—or indeed, of ethics—"guarantees us against the return of barbarism" (187).

Virginia Woolf broadcast three times; she gave solo talks in 1929 ("Beau Brummell") and 1937, and participated in a broadcast discussion in 1927 with Leonard Woolf, on the question, "Are Too Many Books Written and Published?" Compared to the other Bloomsbury broadcasters, her involvement in radio was minimal. In attempting to understand the nature of this involvement, one may argue, with Leila Brosnan, that Woolf's participation in broadcasting "reveals the complexities of cultural and class dynamics, the Foucauldian network of power that politicises and historicises the mechanics of textual production, often submerged in purely textual approaches to literature"(165). From Brosnan's perspective, Woolf is an interesting case study in how radio, "the symbol of new popular and mass culture" (164), enabled willing high modernists to cross seemingly impassable boundaries between high and mass culture and to participate in "a process of democratising the accessibility of art" (164-5). Woolf's broadcast on craftsmanship certainly testifies, too, to her employment of radio to diffuse to a mass listening public some of the best that was being thought and said in Britain in the 1920s and 1930s. But it also shows her as an ethical theorist in an age threatened by a fresh eruption of the "barbarism of being." For in "Craftsmanship," as in *Three Guineas*, whose composition she interrupted to write it, Woolf promotes a social ideal based in the manifestly ethical demand to resist, as words resist, "ceremony and convention," to "create beauty" as words create beauty, to "belong"—as words do—"to each other," to "fall [. . .] in love" as words fall in love, and in the final analysis, to "survive" (869).

"Craftsmanship" was published in the *Listener* on 5 May 1937 (and reprinted in *DM* and *CE*). That issue also contained articles, letters, and transcribed talks on such topics as "The Future of Cricket," "What Birds' Eggs Teach Us," "Hedgehogs as Weather Prophets," "The Christian Social Movement," "Nutrition and the Housewife"—and "Freedom and Progress for All," by Winston Churchill. Churchill's featured article is a paean to Empire, a celebration of "the duty which stands first" (850)—namely, to support the maintenance of a military power sufficient to preserve the British Empire, the most "wonderful association of human beings [. . .] in history" (849). That duty, Churchill says, "stands first because without it no other duty can be done" (850). For Woolf, to the contrary, one's first duty is to recognize the intrinsic interrelatedness of words and readers—the ways that meaning and value emerge from this structural relation. In the responsibility implied by this recognition lies Woolf's own version of the Levinasian notion that "ethics precedes existence"—as well as her desire for what Levinas calls "the authentic relationship with the Other; it is discourse and, more exactly, response which is this authentic relationship" (*Ethics* 88). Out of this desire, as Woolf writes, we "tempt words"—and by extension, each other—"to come together in one of those secret marriages which are perfect images and create everlasting beauty" (869). Woolf seems to hope that, from behind the microphone in a soundproof booth in Broadcasting House, she has connected with her listeners in just such a marriage. Otherwise, she fears—"Time's up! Silence" (869)!

Works Cited

Arnold, Matthew. *Culture and Anarchy*. New York: Macmillan, 1923.

Attridge, Derek. "Innovation, Literature, Ethics: Relating to the Other." *PMLA* 114:1 (January 1999): 20-31.

Brosnan, Leila. *Reading Virginia Woolf's Essays and Journalism: Breaking the Surface of Silence*. Edinburgh: Edinburgh UP, 1997.

Cardiff, David. "The Serious and the Popular: Aspects of the Evolution of Style on the Radio Talk, 1928-1939." *Media, Culture & Society* 2:1 (1980): 29-47.

Churchill, Winston. "Freedom and Progress for All." *Listener* Vol. XVII, No. 434 (5 May 1937): 849-50, 887.

Forster, E. M. *Commonplace Book*. Stanford: Stanford UP, 1987.

Giddings, Robert. "John Reith and the Rise of Radio." *Literature and Culture in Modern Britain, Volume 1*: 1900-1929. Ed. Clive Bloom. London: Longman, 1993. 146-66.

LeMahieu, D. L. *A Culture for Democracy: Mass Communication and the Cultivated Mind in Britain Between the Wars*. Oxford: Clarendon, 1988.

Levinas, Emmanuel. *Ethics and Infinity: Conversations with Philippe Nemo*. Trans. Richard Cohen. Pittsburgh: Duquesne UP, 1998.

——. "The Philosophical Determination of the Idea of Culture." *Entre Nous: On Thinking-of-the-Other*. Trans. Michael B. Smith and Barbara Harshav. New York: Columbia UP, 1998. 179-87.

Reith, John. *Broadcast Over Britain*. London: Hodder and Stoughton, 1924.

Ruskin, John. "Traffic." *Unto this Last and Other Writings*. Ed. Clive Wilmer. London: Penguin, 1985. 233-49.

Schneewind, J. B. *Sidgwick's Ethics and Victorian Moral Philosophy*. Oxford: Clarendon, 1977.

Simpson, David. *The Academic Postmodern and the Rule of Literature*. Chicago: U of Chicago P, 1995.

Whitehead, Kate. "Broadcasting Bloomsbury." *The Yearbook of English Studies*. London: The Modern Humanities Research Association, 1990. 121-31.

Woolf, Virginia. "Craftsmanship." *Listener* Vol. XVII, No. 434 (5 May 1937): 868-9.

——. *Three Guineas*. New York: Harcourt/Harvest, 1966.

Michael Whitworth
Porous Objects: Self, Community, and the Nature of Matter

In January 1897, the young Virginia Stephen saw a man and a woman reduced instantaneously to skeletons. I refer not to a previously unrecorded hallucination, but to the occasion when she, Vanessa and Adrian went to a lecture on the Röntgen rays: "we were shown," she recorded, "photographs of normal hands and diseased hands, a baby, and a puppy—and a lady and gentleman from the audience had their hands photographed" (*PA* 9-10). The metaphorical themes of solidity and transparency run throughout Woolf's work, and are very often shaped through elements of a scientific discourse. This connection has been unduly neglected, but in pursuing it here, I don't wish to treat that particular x-ray exhibition of 1897 as a unique point of origin. To do so would be to underestimate the full extent of the x-ray as a popular sensation in the period from its discovery in December 1895 through to the end of the nineteenth century. The x-ray was the subject of articles in the popular press and in the generalist periodicals (e.g. Swinton). These articles were frequently illustrated with images of skeletons (Tsivian 82-84): although radioactivity was believed by some to be a vital, life-creating force, and although its dangers were not fully appreciated, the association of the x-ray with death was present from the outset. Unlike later popular scientific sensations—relativity, for example—x-ray photography allowed the general public to experience the sensation at first hand, if you'll excuse the pun. In 1898, Joseph Conrad met an x-ray pioneer in Glasgow and had a photograph taken of his own hand (Conrad 2: pl.1). So, even if Woolf hadn't been to the 1897 lecture, she would have been familiar with the phenomenon.

X-ray photography provided striking images which implicitly questioned the idea of solidity, but technology was at this time running in advance of theory, and the theorisation of the atom developed gradually from the 1890s onwards, reaching a significant moment of synthesis in 1911 with Rutherford's theorisation of the "porous" or "solar" atom (Eddington 1). This theorisation and its popular versions supplement the x-ray imagery with a vocabulary of spacio solidity and transparency find themselves contrasted. In the x-ray images, if flesh was paradoxically both visible and transparent, at least bone and iron remained reassuringly solid; in Rutherford's model, the paradox extended its scope to encompass the entire material world. While ideally, from the perspective of the history of science and ideas, one might wish to maintain the distinction between the two periods of theorisation, for the purposes of the present essay, I don't think the distinction essential: the effect of Rutherford's work was to enrich the vocabulary available to Woolf for thinking about solidity.

The cultural importance of the scientific developments from 1895 to 1911 has been neglected, I think, because the later quantum mechanical themes of uncertainty and complementarity were more explicitly the subjects of philosophical reflection: the writings of Bohr and Heisenberg provide a more familiar point of departure for the humanist scholar than do the popular accounts of Röntgen rays or the Rutherford atom. This is unfortunate, not least in the case of Woolf, because the metaphors surrounding matter, solidity and atoms are of such widespread cultural importance. They are, in Lakoff and Johnson's terms, metaphors we live by: metaphors of solidity can be used to express confidence in facts, theories and personalities, as well as figuring forth our feelings about an environment which is limiting or oppressive. However, to deliver these metaphorical phrases of their philosophical content requires tentative reconstructions, speculative movements, and imaginative leaps; these will always run the risk of misconstructing the text, distorting it, or leaping over the edge.

The nature of matter is most obviously relevant to Woolf on account of her designation, in 1919, of Bennett, Wells and Galsworthy as "materialists"

(*E3* 32), and her development of this idea in "Mr Bennett and Mrs Brown" (*E3* 384-89) and in "Character in Fiction" (*E3* 420-38). If one examines these canonical essays alongside others such as "On Re-reading Novels" (1922; *E3* 336-46), a picture emerges in which the mimetic solidity of the Edwardian novelists is challenged by an aesthetics of fluidity and transparency. The challenge is not completely clear cut, as Woolf also sees the x-ray as a metaphor for reductiveness, but throughout these essays the dualism is structured in terms derived from science.

From a wider cultural perspective, our concepts of the atom provide metaphors for the concept of individuality, and vice versa. Moreover, the interactions of atoms are often spoken of as if they were the interactions of individuals in crowds. The Newtonian concept of the individual as having qualities independent of the system within which it moves broadly corresponds to the seventeenth-century concept of the bourgeois individual (Freudenthal 115-16). The porous atom, and the atom surrounded by a field of force, model a very different kind of individual, one without clear boundaries, and model a very different kind of group relationship, one of invisible interfusion and interdependency. This model, I propose, was very congenial to Woolf.

I'd like to start with *To the Lighthouse*. The novel explicitly refers to the x-ray, using it to picture Lily's ability to perceive Tansley's motivation (*TTL* 99). The reference is not in itself terribly interesting, but it lends some textual authority to a further investigation of the theme, by indicating that there was not a complete break from the Virginia Stephen of 1897 to the Virginia Woolf of 1927, nor between the two cultures; metaphors can be easily remembered for nearly thirty years, and can be transported over disciplinary boundaries. More worthy of attention are images of transparency.

In "The Window" section 13, Lily Briscoe notices the Ramsays watching Prue and Jasper on the lawn, and perceives the scene as an epiphany: "so that is marriage, Lily thought, a man and a woman looking at a child throwing a ball" (*TTL* 79-80). In this moment of transformation the characters are said to acquire an "outline," and to become "sharp-edged and ethereal and divided by great distances"; for a moment, "it seemed as if solidity had vanished altogether" (*TTL* 80). To be simultaneously sharp-edged and yet ethereal may seem paradoxical. Other modernist writers, notably Pound and Lewis, associated sharp edges with sculptural solidity. However, Woolf's apparently paradoxical position was anticipated by x-ray images, and she consistently develops it in her work. In "Mr Bennett and Mrs Brown," Woolf had declared that "character" in the novel had lapsed into "shapelessness" on account of the materialist excess of Bennett. Her generation of novelists needed to "sharpen its edges" once again (*E3* 387), yet such a sharpening does not imply the return to solidity that the vorticists would have sought.

In this instance, the vanishing solidity expresses the miraculousness of epiphany without denying the everyday material ordinariness of the participants. The language of physics allows Woolf to think "poetically and pro-saically at one and the same moment" (*AROO* 45). But when Mrs Ramsay thinks about matter, this meaning is supplemented by another. As she goes upstairs at the end of the dinner party, she tries to clear away the "chatter and emotion" and reach something more permanent. This she achieves by think-ing of the continuity of the generations, in a way that affects her sense of the house's physical fabric:

> she felt [. . .] that community of feeling with other people which emo-tion gives as if the walls of partition had become so thin that practically [. . .] it was all one stream, and chairs, tables, maps, were hers, were theirs, it did not matter whose, and Paul and Minta would carry it on when she was dead. (*TTL* 123)

Woolf had already explored the idea of "community of feeling" in *Mrs Dalloway*, centrally in the relationship of Septimus and Clarissa, but that novel's allusions to the new physics reinforce the sense of community only in a general sense. Septimus's description of the flesh being "melted off the world" could be a description of an x-ray photograph (*MD* 74), though as Barri Gold argued in her paper, it also co-ordinates well with the question of heat death. If the world can lose its solidity, then one might infer that the social and physical barriers which separate Septimus's world from Clarissa's might also break down; but the novel does much less to encourage this asso-ciation of ideas than do the later works. It is clear that Woolf's treatment of the theme of community is not absolutely dependent on scientific concepts, and throughout her work it owes as much to the French unanimist school of writing, and also to Bergsonian theories of the self (McLaurin). However, the unanimists retained a vestigial religious vocabulary, in which "souls" moved through a world without walls; "souls" is ubiquitous in McCarthy and Waterlow's translation of Jules Romains's *Mort de quelqu'un*. Woolf's appropriation of the new physics allows her to create a more distinctly sec-ular account of the self.

In *The Years* (1937), Woolf returns to the idea of the "walls of parti-tion," in this case the walls constructed by Victorian patriarchy. The novel's metaphors of opening doors and windows are supported by more subtle ref-erences to the nature of matter; if the idea of "pargetting" reminds us that appearances of solidity can be deceptive, so too does modern physics. Woolf inscribes historical ironies into the 1908 chapters, in the scene where Eleanor considers her lack of education:

> But what vast gaps there were, what blank spaces, she thought leaning back in her chair, in her knowledge! How little she knew about anything. Take this cup for instance; she held it out in front of her. What was it made of? Atoms? And what were atoms, and how did they stick togeth-er? The smooth hard surface of the china with its red flowers seemed to her for a second a marvellous mystery. (*TY* 126)

What we have here is a variant on Woolf's technique of compression, whereby a character's thoughts are juxtaposed with an external object which the reader can interpret as an ironic commentary. In this variant, the thoughts comment ironically on the external object: the real answer to Eleanor's question comes in the very characterisation of her knowledge. The "vast gaps" and "blank spaces" of her knowledge resemble Rutherford's 1911 conception of the "porous" atom. The reference to Eleanor's chair provides an additional clue, through the philosophical tradition of referring to tables and chairs as types of the perceivable material world. As Russell points out in the introduction to *The ABC of Atoms*, tables and chairs "seem to present an unbroken surface," and we think "that if there were too many holes the chairs would not be safe to sit on" (Russell 7). While a collocation of "chair" and "atom" alone would not point with any great certainty to popular science, accompanied by the phrase "blank spaces" the terms recover much of their scientific meaning.

Eleanor perceives the hardness of the china as a surface quality, and this relates her scientific questions back to pargetting and to the family masquerade. Here the historical irony comes into play: to ask how atoms "stick together" before Rutherford had broken them would have been surprising. To some extent we are encouraged to view Eleanor as prescient, but we might also be inclined to read the question about atoms as a displaced question about Edwardian family life. Such a family can only "stick together" by virtue of being "boxed up together," as Martin later puts it (*TY* 180). Thinking about atoms allows Eleanor to displace family questions into an emotionally neutral space, and allows Woolf to inscribe historical ironies into Eleanor's questions. The reader who knows that atoms contain "vast gaps" may well expect the Pargiter family to mutate or break up in some way. If we take "sticking together" to refer to the cohesion of subatomic particles into atoms, then we can anticipate that the disintegration of the unstable Pargiter family atom would liberate the repressed energies of the Pargiter children.

Eleanor's characterisation of her knowledge as containing "vast gaps" furthermore invites the reader to reassess metaphors of solidity as applied to knowledge and literary form. It raises the suggestion that the solidity of "solid" knowledge can itself become confining. Eleanor's uncertain, exploratory mode seems ironically to contain the correct answers, without creating the intellectual closure of solid knowledge. This creates a minor embarrassment for someone trying to conclude a paper: we talk of arguments in terms of matter; we talk of the "bare bones" of an idea which can be "fleshed out," we talk of a "watertight" argument, and we expect someone to "wrap up" a presentation as if it were a parcel with a gift inside. If this paper is a body, it welcomes your x-rays. If it is an atom, please emulate Rutherford and bombard it with alpha particles.

Works Cited

Beer, Gillian. *Virginia Woolf: The Common Ground*. Edinburgh: Edinburgh UP, 1996.

Conrad, Joseph. *Collected Letters* ed. Frederick R. Karl and Laurence Davies. 5 vols. to date. Cambridge: Cambridge UP, 1983-96.

Eddington, A. S. *The Nature of the Physical World*. Cambridge: Cambridge UP, 1928.

Freudenthal, Gideon. *Atom and Individual in the Age of Newton: On the Genesis of the Mechanistic World View*. Tr. Peter McLaughlin. Boston Studies in the Philosophy of Science 88. Dordrecht: D. Reidel, 1986.

Henderson, Linda D. "X-Rays and the Quest for Invisible Reality in the Art of Kupka, Duchamp, and the Cubists." *Art Journal* (Winter 1988): 323-340.

Lakoff, George and Mark Johnson. *Metaphors We Live By*. Chicago: U of Chicago P, 1980.

McLaurin, Allen. "Virginia Woolf and Unanimism." *Journal of Modern Literature* 9 (1981-82): 115-122.

Romains, Jules. *The Death of a Nobody*. Tr. Desmond McCarthy and Sydney Waterlow. London: Howard Latimer, 1914.

Russell, Bertrand. *The ABC of Atoms*. London: Kegan Paul, Trench, Trubner, 1923.

Swinton, A. A. C. "Photographing the Unseen." *Cornhill Magazine* 26 (o.s. 73) (1896): 290-96.

Tsivian, Yuri. "Media Fantasies and Penetrating Vision: Some Links Between X-Rays, the Microscope, and Film." *Laboratory of Dreams: The Russian Avant-Garde and Cultural Experiment*. Ed. John E. Bowlt and Olga Matich. Stanford: Stanford UP, 1996. 81-99.

Woolf, Virginia. *Mrs. Dalloway*. Ed. Stella McNichol. London: Penguin, 1992.

——. *A Passionate Apprentice*. Ed. Mitchell Leaska. New York: Harcourt Brace Jovanovich: 1990.

——. *A Room of One's Own*. Harmondsworth: Penguin, 1945.

——. *To the Lighthouse*. Ed. Stella McNichol. London: Penguin, 1992.

——. *The Years*. Harmondsworth: Penguin, 1968.

Reading and Teaching
A Room of One's Own

Brenda R. Silver
Virginia Woolf://Hypertext

To begin with a familiar question: But, you may say, we asked you to talk about *A Room of One's Own*—what has that got to do with Virginia Woolf and hypertext? Like Woolf's deconstructive play on the meaning of the words "women and fiction" in her text, the conjunction of Virginia Woolf and hypertext produces a link that can take us in many different directions. It might, for example, lead to a discussion of Woolf's narrative strategies and their anticipation of hypertexts. Or it might lead to a discussion of Woolf's narrative strategies, formulations of what a "woman's writing" might be, and recent hypertext fictions, by both women and men. Or it might lead to a discussion of the ways in which Virginia Woolf becomes a figure for hypertext, particularly when we put "Virginia Woolf" in quotation marks: when we turn her into Virginia Woolf icon and link her, in a metonymic move that crosses the multiple definitions of icon today, to the internet.[1] Or it might lead to the intersections among all of these paths, which, branching out in multiple directions, nevertheless cross each other at key points, plunging us into a metaphoric web.

Like Woolf, I am most interested in the last possibility, and like Woolf, I know that in pursuing it no "conclusion" will be possible, just as there is no conclusion or closure in hypertext, and hence no "nugget of truth." Instead, all I can do is offer you some speculations about *A Room of One's Own*'s conjunctions not only with hypertext (defined most simply as "nonsequential writing—text that branches and allows choices, best read at an interactive screen"; "a series of text chunks connected by links which offer the reader different pathways" [Nelson O/2]), but with recent attempts to theorize its socio-political potential. Proceeding in a hypertextual fashion, my itinerary will take me through a number of links that trace connections, even as they open up spaces for what Michael Joyce, hypertext writer and theorist, calls structures "for what does not yet exist" (*Of Two Minds* 42).

The opening node or screen or lexia or writing space[2] of my hypothetical hypertext consists of a picture of Arnold Schwarzenegger. The pervasiveness of Schwarzenegger, cultural icon *par excellence*, prompted two of his fans who happened to be academics, Louise Krasniewicz and Michael Blitz, to create a hypertext and an argument about it premised on the actor's role as marker of "the postmodern condition of our culture at the end of the century" ("Dreams.Hypertext.Arnold"), a condition, they argue, best experienced through hypertext and the Internet. The impetus for their own hypertext project on Arnold was not just the amount and diversity of materials they had collected—the "drawers and basements full of notebooks and videos and scribbled napkins and e-mails"—but their belief that these so-called "supplementary materials" "lead us through our subjects better than a tight, logical, proper argument" ("Why We Did Not Produce" 259).

Having admitted these materials into their project, they continue, "in good deconstructive form, the supplementary material, the supporting evidence, will not stay in its place and it is the exchange of center and periphery that becomes so fascinating" ("Why We Did Not Produce" 260). For them, hypertext provided a "medium in which to grow this strain of culture we were abbreviating with the name, 'Schwarzenegger'" ("Dreams.Hypertext. Arnold"); it became a way to examine "the detours or interconnections between the personal, embodied nature of information and the larger, cultural, context where the narratives of our research have to reside," for hypertext, they note, "is a cultural circumstance made of detours" ("Why We Did Not Produce" 260).

Next node; *detour* provides the link. Visually the node might consist of an abstract image, a zigzag line, or, more concretely, a switchback railway line, a metaphor Woolf uses to describe the effect of reading Mary Carmichael's prose in *A Room of One's Own* (81). Here we take a step back in time to the late 1970s, early 80s, when feminist critics turned to *A Room of One's Own* as a textual exploration and inscription of women's relationship to writing. Although the essay, because of the doubleness of its arguments about women and writing, can be and has been used to support radically divergent perspectives, what interests me now are the deconstructive readings that take doubleness as their starting point in order to emphasize the prevalence of detours, digressions, interruptions, and ruptures in the text. Here we can choose from a number of links. The first takes us to Mary Jacobus's 1979 essay "The Difference of View," a reading of the difficulties and possibilities confronting women as they enter into writing itself. *A Room of One's Own* enters her narrative as an example of the "opting for rupture and possibility, which can [. . .] make women's writing a challenge to the literary structures it necessarily inhabits" (34). The scene she chooses to illustrate her point involves a double disruption: the scene in which Woolf, by citing and criticizing the "awkward break" produced in *Jane Eyre* by Brontë's angry intrusion into her novel, simultaneously allows the anger to disrupt her own text. As Jacobus puts it, Brontë's text "opens up a rift in [Woolf's] own seamless web" (35).

Remember the web: I'll come back to it. Now, though, I want to choose a link that takes me from Jacobus's essay first to Rachel Blau DuPlessis's chapter on "Breaking the Sentence; Breaking the Sequence" in her 1985 book *Writing Beyond the Ending*, then to Ellen Friedman and Miriam Fuchs's collection of essays on women's experimental fiction, *Breaking the Sequence*, and from there to Barbara Page's essay on "Women Writers and the Restive Text: Feminism, Experimental Writing, and Hypertext." All of these posit a feminine textual practice that, although not limited to women writers, permeates women's writing: a practice characterized as a "poetics of rupture and critique" (DuPlessis 32). The phrase comes from DuPlessis, who links it to the narrator's well-known description of Mary Carmichael's novel, "First she broke the sentence; now she has broken the sequence" (*AROO* 81), breaks, DuPlessis argues, that reveal the fictionality of both dominant narratives and social structures. The terms that Friedman and Fuchs use to describe the "radical forms" in women's experimental writing that rupture "patriarchal fictional forms" and produce "alternate fictional space[s]" are more specific: "nonlinear, nonhierarchical, and decentering" (3-4). These same terms take Page directly to hypertext. The writers Page describes, whether their medium is print or electronic, are "leery of the smooth, spooling lines of type that define the fictive space of conventional print text and delimit the path of the reader," articulating instead "alternatives to linear prose. The notion, for example, of textuality as weaving [. . .] and of the construction of knowledge as a web that has figured prominently in the development of hypertext has also been important in feminist theory, though for rather different purposes" (112).

A Room of One's Own enters Page's argument not so much as a formal structure as an inspiration, offering both print and hypertext writers an image of "the individualist woman writer" seeking "a place where she can concentrate her attention and do her work" and a model for "re-membering our foremothers" (132). Judy Malloy's hyperfiction *it's name was Penelope* is Page's example of the first; Shelley Jackson's *Patchwork Girl*, another hyperfiction, her example of the second. But Woolf also makes another appearance in Page's text: in an essay by Carole Maso, a theorist and writer of lyrical print novels, who consistently claims Woolf and Gertrude Stein as her stylistic precursors. Woolf, Maso tells us, "implies that the writer may have to write notebooks rather than masterpieces. Notes instead of coherent, authoritarian, beginning, middle, and end, thesis and conclusion pieces" (Maso 29). What Maso is after is "room . . . for the random, the accidental, and the associations and shapes that arise from allowing accidents to happen" (Maso 27).

At this point if I were to click on the word *hyperfiction* we might find ourselves in Michael Joyce's now classic *afternoon: a story*, where Virginia Woolf makes a number of explicit appearances. Instead, both Maso's evocation of *notebooks*, with its link back to Krazniewicz and Blitz's decentering *supplement*, and the mention of Malloy's *Penelope* take me, in a movement that can be figured as a turn, to my next node, Peggy Kamuf's 1982 essay

"Penelope at Work: Interruptions in *A Room of One's Own*," which uncannily anticipates rhetorics of hypertext. But first, another *turn*, this one linked to the concept of the turn itself, and a detour to Terence Harpold's early essay on narrative digression in hypertext that begins: "Digression, detour, swerve, split, cut—I'm going to apply several names to the narrative turns of hypertexts. The idea that is common to all of these names is that turning is a circular process that is also divisive: a turn toward a destination is also a turn away from an origin; [. . .] The different names for that turn describe not only a trajectory but also the contour of a place that you never get to" (171), one that can be figured as a fissure or gap. In such a topography, Harpold notes, where "detours" are what the text is *"about"* (172), one can easily lose one's place; one can get lost.

Turning back now to Kamuf's argument, which, although concerned with women's writing, leads more in the direction of social structures and power than literary forms. For Kamuf, Penelope's nightly unweaving of the web she had woven during the day—the labor that, having been excluded by her son from male spheres of power, Penelope performs by being where she should not be: in her work room rather than her bedroom—serves as a metaphor for women's entrance into power: an interruption or disruption of masculine power and discourse by women's art that works in part by covering over its own actions. This process of raveling, Kamuf argues, a term that like Freud's *heimlich* contains its opposite, *unraveling*—this process of making something plain or clear even as it entangles or confuses it—also characterizes Woolf's narrative strategies in *A Room of One's Own*. The opening establishes the trope: the question that rather than being answered is immediately subject to deferral or deflection by the introduction of the narrator's fiction; "asked to explain," Kamuf notes, "the narrator promises an answer once she is through spinning out her story. But this narrative sets off from a doubling back, or a crossing out in which a meaning, a sense of direction gets lost" (7). As we have seen, an apt description of hypertext.

The zigzag pattern Kamuf traces in *A Room of One's Own*, the repeated turns toward a new direction occasioned by the interruptions of the narrator's thoughts—and here Kamuf evokes the beadle, the Oxbridge librarian, and the encounter with Professor von X in another library—becomes a methodology, one in which, confronted with women's exclusions from libraries and the histories they contain, the narrator turns to fiction, "[raveling] the crossed threads of history and fiction" (9). The scene Kamuf uses to make her point is the narrator's story of what happens when the "great man of letters" leaves his study or library and enters into another room, the drawing-room perhaps, a scene, Kamuf writes, that "has no place in the history and the biographies of great men which one may consult. It is thus invented, but to take the place of what is missing in the scholar's medium. In other words, the encounter with a supplemental difference takes place as fiction in history. Or rather, it takes place in a mode which has as yet no proper name"

(14). The reference here is to Woolf's oft-cited description of what is needed: a "supplement to history[,] calling it, of course, by some inconspicuous name so that women might figure there without impropriety" (*AROO* 45). "When it acts to restore a missing scene in history's self-narrative," Kamuf continues, "Woolf's text catches history at a loss for words, interrupted in its train of thought. What is restored here, then, is not simply some unrecorded moment in the history of power but an interval, a hiatus where power has momentarily broken off its discourse" (14).

At this point Kamuf enters into an argument that once again reads like a description of hypertext: "In order to figure such an interval or interruption, Woolf's text creates a passage leading out of the library and into another room" (14-15). This passage, I suggest, functions like a hypertext link; more accurately, perhaps, it represents the interval or gap that ensues after you click on a link: the blankness that takes over the screen as one set of words or images fades away and another takes its place. If the passage links or connects the two rooms, then, it simultaneously opens up a space that destabilizes the hierarchical power relationship between them. It also suggests once again that in traversing that passage or link one might lose one's direction, get lost.

Turning once again; here, web provides the link to my next node, one that takes a different line on hypertext and power: Mark Hussey's essay on Virginia Woolf and hypertext, "How Should One Read a Screen?," which is in part a warning against conflating the two. Evoking two terms widely used in connection with hypertext, Hussey registers his resistance: "For readers of Virginia Woolf, imagery of web and net is obviously seductive. [But] in the brave new world of hypertextual reality," he asks, "what would be the place of Woolf's version of *reading*" (251), a version inseparable from power structures themselves? For Hussey, and I am radically simplifying his far more complex argument, the process of reading that Woolf privileges, like the book itself, posits a *reader* who stands in contrast to the *user* or *receiver* implied by the "'media model' . . . of electronic processing discourse" (255). Woolf's "version of reading," he argues, "with its emphasis on rhythm, silence, and space, on creating meaning not only from the words on a page but also from what is *not* on the page" (263), produces a reader capable of reading between the lines. Hypertext, he counters, despite its rhetoric of "[making] the absent present, [causing] a dynamic *process* to be enacted within the frame of the screen, before our eyes" (260), is, because of its reduction of words to code and the fact that all our choices are fixed by the encoder, far more limiting.

To which I would respond, yes and no, for webs and nets, as I've been suggesting throughout this talk, consist not just of threads or lines that connect one node to another, but of the gaps or spaces or intervals that the threads produce, and these gaps or spaces can become the starting point for positing other concepts of power and/or social structures. My link here is our understanding of the link itself. As I noted earlier, just as the passage that runs from library to drawing room in *A Room of One's Own* simultaneously figures and deconstructs the difference between two sites of power, the link, theorists have argued, simultaneously connects and undoes connections. In the process, it reconfigures the metaphor of the web itself. In fact, much of the discussion about links is a discussion about rhetorics and metaphors: what metaphors we use to talk about the new, still hybrid, technologies and how these metaphors figure their limits and possibilities.

At this point, and in the time left, I can only list some of the issues motivating recent debates about the rhetorics of hypertext and the models they provide for social spaces. For one thing, there is a debate about the link itself: whether one figures it in terms of the connections between points or nodes, or whether one privileges the gaps between them. One produces hypertext as a reticulated network; the other, as a fabric riddled with holes. Other theorists, drawing on Deleuze and Guattari's distinction between striated and smooth social spaces, have put a different spin on the debate. Here, striated space, conceived as a system where "'lines and trajectories tend to be subordinated to points: one goes from one point to another,'" becomes associated with a social system that is "State-oriented and static" (Nunes 62, 63); striated space, Stuart Moulthrop writes, "manifests itself in hierarchical and rule-intensive cultures, like the military, the corporation, and the university" (303). In contrast, smooth space, where "'the points are subordinated to the trajectory'" (Nunes 62), is associated with a social system that is fluid and dynamic, one characterized by transformation and becoming. When linked to other of Deleuze and Guattari's formulations such as rhizomes, lines of flight, nomadism, and deterritorialization, smooth space becomes a model for alternative social structures. Moulthrop identifies some of these as "ad hoc or populist political movements, cooperatives, communes, and some small businesses, subcultures, fandoms, and undergrounds" (303).

So where are we? We have several choices. Clicking on *fandoms* would create a turn from smooth social spaces back toward Arnold Schwarzenegger, Virginia Woolf, and their intersections with the World Wide Web, another entity often placed on the side of smooth space. Alternatively, clicking on *nomad* would turn us toward the hyperfiction *Patchwork Girl*, where the narrator known as Patchwork explains her rejection of traditional forms in both writing and life in terms of nomadism: "instead of fulfilling a determined structure, I could merely extend, inventing a form as I went along. This decision turned me from a would-be settler to a nomad" ("what shape"). In a note on this passage, Barbara Page directs her readers to the writings of theorist Rosie Braidotti, who, "adapting Deleuze and Guattari for feminist purposes," has claimed the figure of the "nomadic subject" for feminism (134).

But for now I want to make a different move, one that turns back toward *A Room of One's Own*, toward the passage or link between the library, with

162

its bound books, its histories, and the drawing room, a room or space that the narrator tells us is both multiple and without words: "whole flights of words would need to wing their way illegitimately into existence before a woman could say what happens when she goes into a room" (87). This turn also constitutes a turn away from the utopian vision seemingly promised by smooth spaces, including hyperspaces, to the recognition that the distinction between smooth and striated is constantly being undone. As Deleuze and Guattari themselves make clear, these spaces do not exist as a set of opposites; instead, they "'exist only in mixture: smooth space is constantly being translated, transversed into a striated space; striated space is constantly being reversed, returned to smooth space'" (Moulthrop 316). Moreover, as Moulthrop recognizes, the utopian rhetoric of hypertext grounded in metaphors of rhizomes and deterritorialization is highly problematic. Hypertext systems, looked at critically, do not effect "a transition from reductive hierarchies to polyvalent networks" (310).

Confronted with this reality principle, Moulthrop posits two responses: one, to return to the library, to book culture and theoretical writing, giving up all ideas of hypertext as a form of resistance; the other, "to leave the library and to develop an ideological critique of hypertext through a practical engagement with the medium" (312)—his preferred path. Here, hypertext, perceived as a transition and not a terminus, as a "hybrid, smooth-striated" medium and domain (Moulthrop 317), becomes, in Jay Bolter's terms, a writing space. Approached from this direction, hypertext—like the space Penelope opens within the constraining power structures as she shuttles back and forth between the bedroom and the workroom, undoing her weaving; like the spaces opened up by the detours and digressions characteristic of *A Room of One's Own*'s nomadic narrator; and like the space of the passage from library to drawing room—hypertext, to repeat, can become a space for structures that do not yet exist.

At this point I want to stop making turns and evoke Michael Joyce's dictum about closure in hypertext: "When the story no longer progresses, or when it cycles, or when you tire of the paths, the experience of reading it ends" (*afternoon*, "work in progress").

Notes

[1] For a preliminary exploration of Virginia Woolf icon on the web, see Silver, "World Wide Woolf."

[2] All of these terms are used to describe the individual segments of text and/or images that comprise a hypertext.

Works Cited

DuPlessis, Rachel Blau. *Writing Beyond the Ending: Narrative Strategies of Twentieth-Century Women Writers*. Bloomington: Indiana UP, 1985.

Friedman, Ellen G. and Miriam Fuchs. "Contexts and Continuities: An Introduction to Women's Experimental Fiction in English." *Breaking the Sequence:*

Women's Experimental Fiction. Eds. Ellen G. Friedman and Miriam Fuchs. Princeton: Princeton UP, 1989. 3-51.

Harpold, Terence. "Threnody: Psychoanalytic Digressions on the Subject of Hypertexts." *Hypermedia and Literary Studies*. Eds. Paul Delany and George Landow. Cambridge, MA: MIT Press, 1991. 171-84.

Hussey, Mark. "How Should One Read a Screen?" *Virginia Woolf in the Age of Mechanical Reproduction*. Ed. Pamela L. Caughie. New York: Garland, 2000. 245-65.

Jackson, Shelley. *Patchwork Girl by Mary/Shelley & Herself*. Eastgate Systems. Software, 1995.

Jacobus, Mary. "The Difference of View." *Reading Woman: Essays in Feminist Criticism*. New York: Columbia UP, 1986.

Joyce, Michael. *afternoon, a story*. Eastgate Systems. Software, 1990.

——. *Of Two Minds: Hypertext Pedagogy and Poetics*. Ann Arbor: U of Michigan P, 1995.

Kamuf, Peggy. "Penelope at Work: Interruptions in *A Room of One's Own*." Novel 16.1 (Fall 1982): 5-18.

Krasniewicz, Louise, and Michael Blitz. "Dreams.Hypertext.Arnold// Narrative-Metaphors-Analogies." URL: http://www.sscnet.ucla.edu/ioa/arnold/arnoldwebpages/dhaessay.htm. 15 Aug. 2000.

——. "Why We Did Not Produce 'Dreaming Arnold Schwarzenegger' as a Book, Several Articles, an Encyclopedia, a Video, an Annotated Bibliography, and a Museum Installation (or, Did We?)." *American Quarterly* 51.2 (1999): 258-62.

Malloy, Judy. *its name was Penelope*. Eastgate Systems. Software, 1993.

Maso, Carole, "Notes of a Lyric Artist Working in Prose: A Lifelong Conversation with Myself, Entered Midway." *American Poetry Review* 24:2. (March/April, 1995): 26-31.

Moulthrop, Stuart. "Rhizome and Resistance: Hypertext and the Dreams of a New Culture." *Hyper/Text/Theory*. Ed. George P. Landow. Baltiimore: Johns Hopkins UP, 1994. 299-319.

Nelson, Theodor H. *Literary Machines*. Swarthmore, Pa: self-published, 1981.

Nunes, Mark. "Virtual Topographies: Smooth and Striated Cyberspace." *Cyberspace Textuality: Computer Technology and Literary Theory*. Ed. Marie-Laure Ryan. Bloomington: Indiana UP, 1999. 61-77.

Page, Barbara. "Women Writers and the Restive Text: Feminism, Experimental Writing, and Hypertext." *Cyberspace Textuality: Computer Technology and Literary Theory*. Ed. Marie-Laure Ryan. Bloomington: Indiana UP, 1999. 111-36.

Silver, Brenda R. "World Wide Woolf." URL: http://www.press.uchicago.edu/Misc/Chicago/757463.htm. 15 Aug. 2000.

Woolf, Virginia. *A Room of One's Own* (1929). San Diego: Harcourt, 1989.

Lois J. Gilmore
"She speaks to me": Virginia Woolf in the Community College Classroom

Although the title of this paper states "She speaks to me," it should read "and me...and me...and me," the echo of an open-ended voice. One of my students spoke those words one day as she was working on the refinement of her research paper topic. Brandie's voice expressed the awe and wonder of a woman who had had a revelation, a woman who had found a connection to someone and something she had not known existed. Her words were a powerful revelation to me, too, as I wondered what had happened in that moment to both of us. Why was this insight so profound for her? Where did it come from? What would happen from that moment on? Why Bucks County Community College? Why Virginia Woolf? What is so powerful to connect an elitist woman of the British intelligentsia with a young college student at an American public, open-admission community college? Why, indeed. I believe it is the transformative power of Virginia Woolf that is so profound as to touch the heart of this young woman as so many of us who know Woolf. In her book *Virginia Woolf Icon* Brenda Silver identifies this power and underscores the spirit of this conference:

> Virginia Woolf has proved too powerful an image to remain in any one location. The men who still control so many of the organs of the "intellectual" sphere may think they have contained her, fixed her into positions that make her safe or dismissible, but like all boundary-dwelling, border-disrupting figures, Virginia Woolf continually escapes, returning in both old and new guises. (75-76)

This paper raises the questions that confront the community college teachers and students as Virginia Woolf moves "out-of-bounds," appearing and disappearing in expected and some unexpected spaces.

Virginia Woolf's presence on the community college campus is both predictable and surprising. It is clear that Virginia Woolf's intelligence and spirit exist in the community college classroom. Bucks County Community College is located directly outside Philadelphia; the county runs along the Delaware River from the densely populated, multi-cultural lower county to the rural and economically elite, generally white, population of the upper county. The student body is drawn from all groups (geographical, age, economic, ethnic, racial, academic) in the county, but it is mostly white, mostly middle class, mostly academically struggling, including many first-generation college students. The community college with its open enrollment policy, first generation college students, diverse student body, a huge number of students with jobs, and variety of both academic and occupational programs obviously manifests what Brenda Silver calls the democratization of education in the nineteen sixties (105). Bucks was part of these efforts to enable a growing population around Philadelphia to have access to higher education with a high school or equivalence diploma, regardless of high school performance and at a cost that would open the door to economic and social improvement.

The fundamental issue of textbooks in many cases drives the content of most courses, particularly in the community college where both the instructors and students are keenly aware of the economic limitations inherent in our students' situations. Introducing alternative material into the classroom requires attention to copyright law, cost to students, and duplicating costs to the institution. It can be done, and is done, but is difficult. Does it make a difference whether the students read "Kew Gardens" or the "Death of a Moth"? Does it make a difference whether students read *A Room of One's Own* in toto or in excerpts?—within the context of a thousand years of British literature? I would argue that it does because the limited range of Woolf's work available to the instructors limits the intellectual opportunities of our students.

A survey of textbooks for the writing courses reveals very little Virginia Woolf, even in texts where her presence would be expected; her limited, repetitious representation in the form of only one or two pieces of fiction and her absence are astonishing. At Bucks every degree-seeking student must take two sequential courses: English Composition I (the standard freshman composition) and English Composition II, which includes instruction in the research paper and an introduction to literature. Many textbooks for English Composition I do not include Virginia Woolf in the selections of expository writing. Virginia Woolf's expository work is not deemed worthy, current, necessary. Why? One reason put forth by Houghton Mifflin publishing representatives may be high permission costs; however, Woolf is represented in *The Dolphin Reader*, one freshman composition text. Unfortunately, no member of our composition faculty uses this text. In the context of so many different and varied essays included in these texts, it would seem logical to suppose that the reason for the exclusion of Woolf might lie in the publishing world and in the pressures on educational consultants. Publishers will respond to demand: what sells? Obviously, Woolf does not sell in this venue; she is not deemed useful for the instruction of essay writing. I cannot answer why Woolf is so glaringly absent from a forum where she would present a model of argumentative and expository skill. Does anybody miss her?

Woolf does not fare substantially better in textbooks for English Composition II. Although full-time instructors can choose whatever texts they want, the adjunct instructors must choose between two texts, neither of which contains Woolf: Barnet, et al, *An Introduction to Literature* (11th ed) and Birkerts, *The Evolving Canon* (2nd ed). As the Writing Program Director and Comp II instructor, I am ashamed to say I just assumed the inclusion of Woolf. After all, isn't her place in literature assured? Prentice Hall's *Literature and the Writing Process* (5th ed), *The Norton Introduction to Literature* (7th ed), and *The Bedford Introduction to Literature: Reading, Thinking, Writing* (5th ed) do not provide Woolf's work for study at the composition level. Two recent editions of textbooks do represent Woolf. St. Martin's *Literature: Reading and Writing the Human Experience* (1998) provides an excerpt of *A Room of One's Own* entitled "What if Shakespeare had had a sister?" in a section called 'Culture and Identity.' Prentice Hall's publication suitable for this course *Literature and Society: An Introduction to Fiction, Poetry, Drama, Nonfiction* (3rd ed) ambitiously announces on the glossy back cover that it "provides an extensive, varied, and innovative introduction to four literary genres." Here Woolf appears in the "Women and Men" subdivision of the non-fiction section.

These two texts illustrate some of the problems I see in the *when* and the *how* of Woolf's representation in the community college, especially when her work is excerpted—some might say cannibalized. The Prentice Hall text provides only a small portion of the original work and superficial questions asking the students about facts, Woolf's thesis, the relationship of the work to their own lives, leading them into personal reflection rather than into critical thinking (Arras 678-79). On the contrary, the chapter-ending questions in the St. Martin's text interrogate Woolf's work in terms of writing—how she explains, links her ideas to history, sets up problems, develops argument, and writes with style. Further, the questions ask the students to make connections to other writers in the text by speculating on what Woolf would think. Finally, the questions force students to think about cultural attitudes and the portrayal of women and men in Western fiction (Abcarian 923). The contrast here in how Woolf is handled in the two texts illustrates the problem of whether we treat her work superficially or delve into the depths of her thinking. Who's afraid of Virginia Woolf in the community college?

Against those of us who fight so hard to include Woolf in our curriculum because her value in teaching the beauty of her writing and critical thinking is incalculable, the absence of Woolf in the texts we use presents a difficult problem. Yet, in this course we can encourage students to explore Woolf in their individual research projects. Many of us have been gratified by the students' response to her as they delve into aspects of Woolf's work. I have heard responses like Brandie's as the students awaken to a new awareness of their own lives and experiences through Woolf's words.

The literature texts available for such courses as short fiction, the novel, survey of British literature, women's studies, and a new course for this fall, Introduction to British Women Writers, offer more selections of Virginia Woolf, but there are serious limitations to even these opportunities. Two short fiction texts used at Bucks contain the same—and only—story "Kew Gardens": *The Norton Anthology of Short Fiction* (shorter 5th ed) and *Short Fiction: Classic and Contemporary* (1999). Another frequently-used text contains no Woolf at all: X. J. Kennedy's *Introduction to Fiction.* Short fiction is one of our most popular courses with three to five full sections each semester. It would take a dedicated instructor to sound Woolf's voice there. The text used for the second semester British literature survey contains a good sampling of Woolf, given the nature of this course—the requirement that both the nineteenth and twentieth century be covered. The sixth edition of the Norton anthology contains "The Mark on the Wall," "Modern Fiction," the full text of *A Room of One's Own*, "Professions for Women," "Moments of Being and Non-Being" from *A Sketch of the Past*, and "The Legacy." The editors of the new 7th edition of this text have obviously not seen a need to add to these selections; however, the new *Longman Anthology of British Literature* (1999) contains an excerpt from *Mrs. Dalloway*, "Mrs. Dalloway in Bond Street," an essay published in *Harper's Magazine*, December 1929, "The Lady in the Looking-Glass: A Reflection," and excerpts from *A Room of One's Own*, *Three Guineas*, and *The Diaries*. Under a section entitled "Perspectives: Bloomsbury and Modernism" three of Woolf's letters—to Vanessa Bell (concerning their perceptions and writing), to Gerald Brenan (concerning writing) and to Vita Sackville-West (concerning *Orlando*)—are included. The Longman gives instructors an opportunity to broaden the scope of Woolf, to discuss writing, to place her in the context of modernism, and to humanize her as a woman writing at a particular time and place, of history, and for permanence

It is not surprising that the best representation of Virginia Woolf lies in Gilbert and Gubar's text *The Norton Anthology of Literature by Women* to be used in the new Introduction to British Women Writers course at Bucks. These editors provide an excellent choice for introduction to the students: essays "22 Hyde Park Gate," "*Jane Eyre* and *Wuthering Heights*," "A Woman's College from the Outside"; "Professions for Women," a short excerpt from *A Room* (the Shakespeare's Sister segment); and fiction "The Death of the Moth" and "Slater's Pins Have No Points" from *Moments of Being*. I have planned this course to begin and end with Woolf: introducing the students to issues of women's writing that Woolf deals with so beautifully in *A Room of One's Own* and *Orlando*, then focusing on *To The Lighthouse* or *Mrs. Dalloway* and other pieces of fiction in the latter part of the course.

Where does Virginia Woolf reside in the community college classroom? Given the limitations of the tools we use and the feasibility of adding books to our students' already heavy economic burden, why is it so important to make such an effort to include Woolf in the curriculum? It was, after all, possible to sit through classes in modernism at Lehigh University, University of California, Riverside, and so many other places and not hear Woolf's name during the sixties, seventies, eighties, and, sadly, the nineties. It is possible at Bucks County Community College to sit through a survey of British literature and not learn of any women writers. Indeed, I spoke to several professors in the Language & Literature Department who do not include

Virginia Woolf in the curriculum with limp rationale like: "I tried a story and it did not go well," "I am not an expert in Woolf," "Woolf is too difficult for the community college students," "There isn't enough time or space in the course to include her." It seems that these instructors are afraid of Woolf for a variety of very questionable reasons.

What is the struggle and why is it worth it for so many "Other" dedicated professors to make a space for Virginia Woolf? For Susan Darrah, Chair of Language & Literature, Woolf represents for us a place to open up the curriculum, to disrupt the traditional periodicity, to dislocate and expand the patriarchal view of modernism as we stand in the way of a canon perpetuating itself. Given the tools we must work with, we can increase the volume rather than silence Woolf's voice in *A Room of One's Own* as "clearly as if she had just spoken yesterday. Woolf allows us to disturb the view of a fragmented world that perhaps has not fallen apart and how we perceive it" (Darrah). It is the notion of who we are and who our students are that drives us to search for places to open up the community college classroom to the beauty of her work and the life of the artist. We believe it is our obligation to share this beauty.

How and why, then, does Virginia Woolf speak to the community college student? Another way of asking this question is "Why do our students feel spoken to?" Most of the students in the classroom have never been exposed to Virginia Woolf. Virginia Woolf is a complete revelation to them. Brandie Holland-Zimmerman, who chose Woolf as her research focus in Comp II, connected to the person of Virginia Woolf who had accomplished so much as she struggled through so much adversity: Brandie said, "I felt a sense of accomplishment for her and myself. How brilliant a woman she was, a woman who would not let herself be beaten down by everything in her childhood and in her life. I connected to her concept of androgyny in *Orlando*, my paper focus, as a way to find her balance, her own sexuality, to live with what's inside of her. She spoke to me with her brilliance, her powerful voice." Like so many of our students Brandie vaguely knew of Woolf's existence through a bookmark birthday present, one of Silver's icons, but she had learned nothing of her in high school. Like so many of our students Brandie feels angry that she was cheated out of Virginia Woolf in the study of the men—of Hemingway, of Shakespeare—when Woolf has "so much to offer women in an equally brilliant and powerful way." For her, it is definitely "worth it" to introduce Woolf in the community college classroom. Community college students *deserve* introduction to Virginia Woolf precisely because they have not been exposed to her and may never meet her again. My students tell me that they will carry her with them into their lives whether they continue college or leave the academic world.

Where does the voice of Virginia Woolf flourish in the community college classroom? She flourishes in the power of her voice to open up the world of beauty and thought, as well as in the power of the instructors to

169

believe in her and to find a way to include her in the synergy of the community college classroom. Indeed, we believe that it is our obligation to open her work to the students.

Works Cited

Abcarian, Richard, and Marvin Klotz, eds. *Literature: Reading and Writing in the Human Experience.* Shorter 7th ed. NY: St. Martins, c. 2000.

Annas, Pamela J., and Robert C. Rosen, eds. *Literature and Society: An Introduction to Fiction, Poetry, Drama, Nonfiction.* 3rd ed. Upper Saddle River, NJ; Prentice Hall, 2000.

Darrah, Susan. Personal interview. 22 March 2000.

Holland-Zimmerman, Brandie. Telephone interview. 25 March 2000.

Silver, Brenda R. *Virginia Woolf Icon.* Chicago: University of Chicago Press, 1999.

Karen L. Levenback
Teaching *A Room of One's Own* in the New Millennium: The War Continues

I proposed this paper—and the messianic title of it—as I was anticipating the first meeting of "Virginia Woolf: The Years Between the Wars," a course with the following aim: "To consider selected works of Virginia Woolf written in the years between the Great War and World War II so as to come to terms with her experience of war as a civilian and response to its representations. To trace Woolf's growth and development as a modern writer, as a woman, and as a theorist of war." This class, I think, offers lessons that may be taken into the new millennium, having to do with the teaching of *A Room of One's Own*. Much of what this paper is about is how new developments in technology can help us to teach little recognized and barely appreciated themes and concerns of *A Room of One's Own*, in the case of my class—the Great War.

The class had eleven registered students—seven women and four men—all but a few English majors or minors (another was a women's studies major, one a philosophy major, one in creative writing), all of whom had read Woolf, and all but a few were upperclasspersons. One of the few, Katie Marts, an English major but (believe it or not) a first-year student at the university, responded to an offer to the class to combine a term paper assignment with one that might be delivered on this panel at this conference. Katie, whose paper follows, will be telling you more of what followed—and how our efforts continued after the semester was over, though given her modesty, I feel sure that she will neglect to tell you how much I learned from her and from the other students in the class.

"Virginia Woolf and the Years Between the Wars" met twice weekly, on Tuesday and Thursday nights, from 18 January until 2 May, and I offer the dating so as to provide a chronological context for our treatment of *A Room of One's Own* which we discussed on 14 and 16 March— immediately before spring recess. By the time we came to *A Room of One's Own*, we had become familiar with Woolf and her experience of the Great War, having seen videos, read memoirs, diary entries, short fiction, essays, novels. And, the students had already taken the midterm; hence we were beginning the second phase of the course, involving representations of the war in the years between the wars and the politics of memory these representations inform.

The development of Woolf studies and the extraordinary technological development since I last taught the class in 1990 offered new and interesting ways of looking at the texts and new approaches to their analysis—approaches that will undoubtedly be enhanced and altered in ways that only the most sophisticated of our colleagues and students can imagine. The Virginia Woolf CD-ROM, which was offered at a nominal cost during the semester, proved of immense value in ways that I will describe— and notwithstanding the fact that I never quite mastered the technology (and the fact that I remember Jim Haule asking me at an MLA meeting about the value of doing a *concordance* of Woolf—how far we've come, eh?). My introduction to the class on the first day reflected not only shifts in approach reflecting technological change and the richness it can bring to the classroom, but in our vision of Woolf as literary master and cultural icon. "The last time I offered a class on Virginia Woolf alone was in 1990," I said. "And I remember beginning the class by asking 'Who's afraid of Virginia Woolf?' largely because her iconization had begun in the sixties with the publication and production of Albee's play and more particularly with the movie upon which it is based. In the seventies, the women's movement began in earnest, and the biography by Woolf's nephew Quentin Bell was published, and Woolf's image first began to appear on t-shirts and coffee mugs. Today—the question is less a matter of who's afraid of Virginia Woolf than how the proliferation of Virginia Woolf in popular culture (as Brenda Silver argues in *Virginia Woolf Icon*) has transformed the writer into a star whose image and authority are persistently claimed or challenged in debates about art, politics, gender, the canon, class, feminism and fashion. Today the question for this class is who is Virginia Woolf, and how did she come to terms with the defining conflict of the twentieth century—as a civilian, as a woman, as a writer, as a theorist of war. And to do that we will read selected works of Virginia Woolf written in the years between World War I (The Great War— 1914-1918/1919) and World War II (more specifically the Battle of Britain in 1940, which saw the end of what populace and press called the *phoney war*,[1] and 25 January 1941, which saw the end of Virginia Woolf.)"

The approach and emphasis are important in part because students today, I found, no longer admit to being afraid of Virginia Woolf, whatever their notion of war in general or the world wars in particular. Iconization breeds familiarity, which may be more than name recognition and can induce disdain or contempt or ignorance. In this class, it aroused curiosity: students were perplexed, but willing collaborators in the class effort, seeking clues to delimiting iconic distractions and reading Woolf with a new focus. Nonetheless, this presented an additional challenge because students by and large have little historical background to and no first-hand experience of war. (The Gulf War, remember, occurred when most current undergraduate students were in elementary school.) Yet, as I learned and continue to learn when I teach the literature of war, students lacking war-consciousness are not without interest in what Milton Bates calls the "politico-poetics of the war story" (214). While the boundaries between combatants and civilians seem in some contexts to have become almost nonexistent (recent cultural and feminist critiques like *Women and the War Story* [Miriam Cooke 1996] and *The Wars We Took to Vietnam: Cultural Conflict and Storytelling* [Bates 1996] come to mind here), war stories and other representations of war (as Evelyn Cobley explains it [*Representing War* 1993]) remain concentrated on combatant experience.

Thus, the class began with a sense of subverting the reading process, as we attempted to see through Virginia Woolf's eyes, indirectly, and from a civilian vantage. I explained to the class that Mark Hussey once said to me that any class in Woolf is a class in reading Woolf: that is, how to read Woolf, who characteristically blurs the boundaries between genres, merging, for example, autobiographical and fictional styles. This becomes the more urgent, as I suggest in *Virginia Woolf and the Great War*, because Woolf's own voice changes as her war consciousness develops and in response to her own lived experience. Her first formal representation of the effect of the war may be inferred, as Katie Marts points out, in a close reading of *A Room of One's Own*.

In the class we were prepared to take advantage not only of critiques but of both different versions of Woolf's work and representations of it. In the second meeting of the class we viewed John Fuegi's *The War Within*, a documentary/cinematic introduction to Woolf, her circle, her times, her ethos, after which we consider her memoirs "A Sketch of the Past" and "Old Bloomsbury," and her diaries, selected critical essays, short fiction, and novels. Many of the writings are juxtaposed with holographic and typescript versions—and sometimes, as with *Mrs Dalloway*, holographic and early versions, as well as the film. Similarly, if less obviously, in considering *A Room of One's Own*, we used the video of the Eileen Atkins version, the text of which, fortunately, along with an interview of her, has been published in *Scenario: The Magazine of Screenwriting*. In regard to *A Room of One's Own*, this offers additional dimensions and layers and opens up new ways of appreciating the work, Woolf, and how she is represented.

Students may trace dimensions and layers through response sheets (two-plus pages for each work studied, due the day we begin to discuss a text) and verbal responses to a work. Although I leave response sheets open ended, I do provide a list of questions or topics that might be considered, and some students rely on these to get them started. The open-ended question/topic to *A Room of One's Own* is: 12. In reviewing *A Room of One's Own* for the Sunday Times (of London), Desmond MacCarthy said "[i]t is feminist propaganda, yet it resembles an almond tree in blossom"? Michèle Barrett believes this comment "captures something of the seductive charm of the essay." What is the point of *A Room of One's Own*—and what's the war got to do with it and what is "feminist propaganda"? The responses in my class were predictably varied—one student while finding the essay "overflowing with insights and gorgeous allusions," could not find "a strong presence of war"; another calls Woolf a "general calling to arms the female masses" and another believes that "Woolf is constantly pointing out binary relationships that guide our society." One student points to Woolf's "speculations on the importance of social illusions, implying that they are perhaps a major vehicle in the history of western civilization: 'mirrors are essential to all violent and heroic action'" (*AROO* 36). Several seize on androgyny, one or two on Tennyson and Christina Rossetti. Yet another finds reviews of the novel on amazon.com and takes four pages to respond to these—and does so on the verso of COURT TV stationery, which, he explains, is all that was handy at the moment of composition.

I shall let Katie Marts explain what she found helpful in coming to terms with the text, thereby suggesting doors that allow us to gain entry to it, but I will briefly mention two approaches to *A Room of One's Own* that might be modified and used to enrich the experience of the work in the new millennium:

1. My students found Rosenbaum's *Women & Fiction*, the manuscript versions of *A Room of One's Own*, useful in coming to terms both with Woolf's juxtapositions and with how syntactic and other signals inform Woolf's understanding of the war in 1928. Clearly, because *A Room of One's Own* is such a rich, varied, and difficult text, it is most important to have a handle on it before attempting a comparison with earlier versions. This I do by providing some historical background to the work and how it can be traced through both manuscript and typescript versions—several of which I share with the class. The history of the discovery of the Fitzwilliam manuscript in 1990 by Pat Rosenbaum does catch their interest—and suggest Potteresque mysteries of archival research, sans wizardry, if not serendipity. As Rosenbaum explains, the manuscript had first to be found as it was lost, filed under *Women & Fiction*, its earliest version, rather than *A Room of One's Own*, the text it became. The history of the writing of the texts is informed by the early versions—the economic reality facing women and their need for financial independence—and particularly women writers in the nineteenth century, with reference to the Married Women's Property Acts of 1870 and 1882, for example.

This takes us back to the response question—simply put—What is the point of *A Room of One's Own*—and what's the war got to do with it? What is "feminist propaganda"? In other words, what's it all about? The class sometimes suggests categories of enquiry as a start: economics; education; patriarchy; history; newspapers; facts/truth; writing; androgyny; and—war. Interestingly, in using *Women & Fiction* to inform and highlight the presence of the war in *A Room of One's Own*, one might first isolate and explore evidence of the war in the text, which can be done using the CD-ROM and explore whether this representation suggests Woolf's response to the war in 1928. One might also look at specific passages and suggest the effect of the changes—how it augments or adds another wrinkle to the complex patterning of the text. This is of particular interest to those who are embarking on the fascinating use of textual variants—part of what Brenda Silver among others calls versioning— and the loss of authorial authority.

2. The second device I use is the Masterpiece Theatre production of Eileen Atkins's version of *A Room of One's Own*, a truncated, dramatic "adaptation" (fifty minutes long) and Alistair Cooke's introduction to it. On the one hand, Cooke (whose women friends actually attended the lecture in 1928) draws our attention to the "preposterous condition" of five hundred pounds and represents Woolf as "not a professional practiced reader," unlike Eileen Atkins, who, he says, presents the "lecture artfully distilled." In fact, what Cooke calls "a seminal feminist tract" is improved upon in untold ways, presumably, the performance being "as memorable as it might have been if Woolf had been as fine and funny an actress as Eileen Atkins." What students are especially alert to, after reading and responding to the text and discussing it in class, are the omissions: no Manx cat, for example, and, even more to the point, no mention of the war. The anger, the trenchant irony, the deeply felt critique of social and literary values is there, yes. But, not politics—and no public figures like Mussolini and Napoleon. And, needless to say, no sense of Woolf's own growing war consciousness.

Recognition of what is missing in the video itself in turn leads to discussion of representation—how is Woolf being portrayed? How should/does this affect our vision of Woolf? What happens to "Woolf as a theorist of war" (Hussey, "Living," 3)? Isolating parts of the text that students (before this class) and Alistair Cooke and Eileen Atkins (consistently) are wont to overlook and considering them in relation to the experience of war offers a richer vision not only of Woolf but of history and war. It is in reading the texts and juxtaposing them with their representations that students who may admit to having been afraid of Virginia Woolf, no longer wonder why, and those who seek validation of their interest, are inspired to continue their exploration. It is at this point that they see that *A Room of One's Own* is not only related to the years between the wars, but to the new millennium, sometimes in ways not considered before, as Katie Marts makes clear.

Finally, this approach calls into question iconic notions of Woolf and alters the way she has been read before. At the same time, whatever resistance may be offered, it opens doors for the students to appreciate her in a historical context and her representations in popular culture. And so the war continues.

Note

[1] The term "phoney war" (sometimes capitalized) originated in the American press and was subsequently employed by the British to describe the relatively calm period militarily in northwestern Europe between September 1939 and May 1940. John Keegan refers to the "studiedly unserious flavour of soldiering in the British army" (Keegan 345) and on the home front it was called the "Bore War" (Turner 180).

Works Cited

"Adapting *Mrs. Dalloway*: A Talk with Eileen Atkins." *Scenario: The Magazine of Screenwriting*: 5.1 (1999): 159ff.

Atkins, Eileen. "*Mrs. Dalloway*: A Screenplay." *Scenario: The Magazine of Screenwriting*: 5.1 (1999): 125-156.

——. adapt. *A Room of One's Own*. By Virginia Woolf. Perf. Eileen Atkins. Masterpiece Theatre. Introd. Alistair Cooke. PBS. WCBH, Boston: 1990.

Bates, Milton J. *The Wars We Took to Vietnam: Cultural Conflict and Storytelling*. Berkeley: U of California P, 1996.

Cobley, Evelyn. *Representing War: Form and Ideology in First World War Narratives*. Toronto: U of Toronto P, 1993.

Cooke, Miriam. *Women and the War Story*. Berkeley: U of California P, 1996.

Fuegi, John. *The War Within: A Portrait of Virginia Woolf*. Directed by John Fuegi and Jo Francis. NY: Arthur Cantor Films, 1995.

Hussey, Mark. "Living in a War Zone: An Introduction to Virginia Woolf as a War Novelist." *Virginia Woolf and War: Fiction, Reality, and Myth*. Mark Hussey, ed. Syracuse: Syracuse UP, 1991: 1-13.

——, ed. *Major Authors on CD-ROM: Virginia Woolf*. Woodbridge CT: Primary Source Media, 1997.

Keegan, John. *The Book of War: 25 Centuries of War Writing*. NY: Viking Penguin, 1999.

Levenback, Karen L. *Virginia Woolf and the Great War*. Syracuse: Syracuse U P, 1999.

Silver, Brenda R. *Virginia Woolf Icon*. Chicago: U of Chicago P, 1999.

Turner, E. S. *The Phoney War on the Home Front*. London: Michael Joseph, 1961.

Woolf, Virginia. *A Room of One's Own*. 1929. San Diego: Harcourt Brace Jovanovich, 1957.

——. *Women and Fiction: The Manuscript Versions of "A Room of One's Own."* Transcribed and edited by S. P. Rosenbaum. Oxford, England: Blackwell, 1992.

Katie Marts
Opening Doors to *A Room of One's Own*

Virginia Woolf's writing should be approached with both eyes and ears open to her subtleties, word choices, and omissions. It is just as important to look for Woolf's meaning in what she doesn't say as in what is stated. Woolf dances with language in her writing, particularly when dealing with the subject of politics. Her approach to the Great War in *A Room of One's Own*, is such an example, often using irony and indirection. In the course, "Virginia Woolf: The Years Between the Wars" Professor Levenback stressed reading Woolf's work with sensitivity to the presence of war. An underlying and constant theme, the Great War plays an important and necessary role throughout the book. The method Woolf uses in addressing this to her audience is often subtle and subdued. By reading between the lines, understanding the environment in which she wrote, as well as having access to different versions of the text, we discover the effects of the Great War on Woolf and other civilians

Woolf experienced the Great War as a non-combatant. Hearing progression of the war through newspapers and bulletins, citizens were left to decipher for themselves what was occurring overseas. Woolf experienced the war indirectly and in turn relates the war using irony and indirection. This method represents the uncertainty of the effects of the Great War and is present in Woolf's passages throughout *A Room of One's Own*.

In studying *A Room of One's Own*, we learned to see the Great War through Woolf's eyes, and were encouraged to isolate references to the war so as to come to terms with its meaning and text. Professor Levenback suggested listing the references to the Great War in chronological order, therefore following Woolf in her own discussion of the war. This would help in developing final conclusions about Woolf's message and beliefs. I found that the war is present, and a core theme of *A Room of One's Own*. Woolf has an agenda in mentioning war. She begins the book questioning prewar and postwar life. She notices the differences and the changes, though they are undefined and unexplainable. Woolf then notes the role women have played in war, conscious of it or not, and the effect that has on perpetuating war. She concludes the book with a plea for women to take part in reality, no longer to sit passively allowing war to occur, and to raise their voices as women and as citizens.

War is a contradiction and Woolf battles with opposing thoughts and beliefs. Professor Levenback made clear that Woolf held not one particular belief, but many. Woolf was neither solely a pacifist nor solely in support of war. Instead, she strove to find the "razor-edge of balance" between the two, the same balance that she strove to find in all of life. Woolf's statements were often contradictory. Woolf is not only one thing, but a fabric of thoughts and beliefs.

Woolf begins early in the book with an awareness of the differences in life during 1928. She notes that something "seemed" lacking and something "seemed" different after the war. Unsure of exactly what had changed, she could only state with authority that "everything was different" (*AROO* 12). Woolf compares the postwar world to the world before the war. Woolf is certain of the changes in people and their interactions. Also wondering at the meanings and sounds of words before the war, Woolf questions the subtlety of inflection and purpose in statements before and after the war. She is aware of the subtle changes of life that were undoubtedly the effects of the Great War. Woolf represents the effects of the Great War by comparing modern poets with those of the nineteenth century. Exclaiming into the foaming waters, she wonders if two living poets could be as great as Tennyson and Christina Rossetti. Claiming it is impossible because the feeling of excitement and rapture that poetry excited before the war is feared and misunderstood in her contemporary life, Woolf relates the tension and loss of security in postwar life (*AROO* 14). The changes are subtle and Woolf, herself, looks beneath the surface and reads between the lines. The Great War has destroyed a sense of security, altering perceptions and interpretations.

Woolf is not only aware of the change in the sounds of words, but in what they represent. It is difficult to decipher truth from lies. The lines have been blurred. Woolf suggests that the Great War has destroyed illusions of the past and put truth in their place. Woolf is uncertain of the long-term effect of the war and demonstrates this by continually posing questions to the audience. In so doing, she indirectly strengthens her sense of what the war has done, as well as helping us to face reality. Woolf wonders if the blame should be placed on the war for killing romance and illusion. She continues questioning the reason we do not "praise the catastrophe" (*AROO* 15) that has put truth in place of illusions. These questions relate the uncertainty of life after the Great War. Questions of truth and illusion arise in a constant attempt to order and reconstruct life, which has been shattered by guns and by deaths.

Woolf juxtaposed contradictory images that also demonstrated the uncertainty of life after the war. She goes on to state, "The beauty of the world which is so soon to perish has two edges, one of laughter, one of anguish, cutting the heart asunder" (*AROO* 16). Laughter and anguish prevail throughout the book, as Woolf juxtaposes her innate pacifism with her recognition of the economic liberty war can offer to women. The war did allow women access to sources of income, which Woolf believes is necessary for women to have the "freedom to think of things in themselves" (*AROO* 39). Women, without income, have no luxury to protest a war that drastically impacts their lives. Woolf's juxtaposition of such images shows the difficulty in defining life after the war, and also represents Woolf's own battle with defining the effects of the war and her feelings towards it.

Virginia Woolf also shows the role women have played in war and the specific effects it has had on them. She states that women have been looking-glasses for men without which the glories of all wars would be unknown. Woolf claims it is necessary to change women's role towards the war and their involvement in it. Though she mentions a few women writers who have been able to write in spite of surroundings, she notes others' lack of ability to pull away from the drawing room writing table and the restrictions placed on subject matter. Captivity in the male world forces them to reflect the "heroic" deeds and actions of the men in their lives.

Woolf is also keenly aware of the experience and knowledge men gain from participation in war. Though she neither condones nor approves of the war, she does recognize the liberty and opportunities it provides. Women have a small base of actual war experience. They understand the torture of waiting for the news of their loved ones or what it feels like to lose a son. Yet in the eyes of society, this different yet powerful knowledge has little place. Woolf states that though women have had to submit to the social convention, young men have had the freedom to experience life, war, and opportunities, which supplied them with priceless wisdom to write books. Action gets published and rarely emotion. Ironically Woolf remarks in the voice of the male critics that, "This is an important book...because it deals with war. This is an insignificant book because it deals with the feelings of women in a drawing room. A scene in a battlefield is more important than a scene in a shop" (*AROO* 74). Woolf asserts that world and life experience is crucial to validation as an author.

Stressing the theme of the Great War, Woolf urges women to get involved. Woolf stands ironically in *A Room of One's Own*, as a general calling her troops into action. Declaring that women, "have never shaken an empire or led an army into battle" (*AROO* 112), she demands women realize that we "go alone" in life with no others to depend on. Woolf encourages women to see that their role in life belongs to "reality and not to the patriarchy of empire (*AROO* 114). Woolf firmly believes that the process of government must and can change, but will only do so if new voices arise. She concludes that women must assure their position as equal voices, writers, and thinkers, as well as use their independence to prevent future wars. Professor Levenback dispelled the myth that Woolf was not political. In fact, as Claire Tylee and others have shown, Woolf believed it right for literature to have a political effect (154). However, the irony is apparent in that the war brought both life and death. Women writers, as well as Woolf, were caught in a Catch-22. For, the thing that brought them opportunity also brought them suffering greater than any known before.

Professor Levenback supplied the class with copies of manuscript pages from *Women and Fiction*, which is Woolf's earlier version of the text, *A Room of One's Own*. In selected passages where war was mentioned, we compared the word choices and omissions that Woolf made in self-censorship. This exercise also helped in understanding Woolf's use of indirection. She would often condense her meanings and choose vagueness over explicit stating of an idea. She supplies a stream of questions to the audience rather than declaring opinions. The passage on page 15, which begins, "Shall we lay the blame on the war," is an example of her struggle to relate her message. In *Women and Fiction*, Woolf includes specific information and thoughts. She questions, "what sort of future will men & women produce when they have ceased to find each other romantic? <And the human race—> Fewer children were born in England last year than have ever been born before. . ." (20). She also refers to the war in *Women and Fiction*, as being made the "scapegoat" and wonders at the "part played in human affairs by illusion" (20). Woolf also uses many conditional words in her text demonstrating the difficulty in defining and explaining the true effects of war.

Woolf again shows clearly the presence of war in *Women and Fiction*, but she later removes this reference to war from *A Room of One's Own*. She states more precisely that women's role as a mirror to the men in her life is probably the reason for war as well as the reason leaders such as Napoleon and Mussolini insist on keeping women inferior. Edited by Woolf, it reads simply in *A Room of One's Own* that without women as a looking-glass for men, "the glories of all our wars would be unknown" (35). This self-censorship is an example of Woolf's indirection. She provides the backbone to her meaning and allows her audience to fill in the flesh.

Continually asking questions and masking anger and passion in a calm and reserved manner, Woolf shows the difficulty in understanding postwar society. I found it difficult to pinpoint exactly what Woolf believed or thought about the effects of the Great War. Yet Woolf might not have fully known how the Great War affected society and therefore might have often shifted views and feelings towards the war. She might find it impossible to define the impact of the war. Woolf was aware, however, that war had the ability to bring great opportunities to women and could open doors to experimental literature and thought through economic liberty. Yet that same war has enforced gender differences and kept women authors, scholars, and students from entrance into academic institutions.

A Room of One's Own shows the effects of World War I on society. In the course, "Virginia Woolf: The Years Between the Wars," Professor Levenback highlighted the importance the Great War had in Woolf's writing through holographic material, typescripts, and background information of the time in which she wrote. In *A Room of One's Own*, Woolf stands at the head of her army, and calls her battalion of women authors to partake in the war. She asks them to partake with pen, acquire independent income, and secure a room in which to think and thrive as independent and equal players in war's aftermath.

Works Cited

Tylee, Claire M. *The Great War and Women's Consciousness: Images of Militarism and Womanhood in Women's Writings*, 1914-64. Iowa City: U of Iowa P, 1990.

Woolf, Virginia. *A Room of One's Own*. 1929. San Diego: Harcourt Brace Jovanovich, 1957.

———. *Women and Fiction: The Manuscript Versions of "A Room of One's Own."* Transcribed and edited by S. P. Rosenbaum. Oxford, England: Blackwell, 1992.

Nancy S. Shay
'I'm Not a Feminist or Anything, But…': Teaching *A Room of One's Own* in High School

As a high school teacher speaking at an academic conference on Virginia Woolf, I feel a little bit like the tailless cat in Chapter 1 of *A Room of One's Own*. A high school teacher? What a queer animal, you may good-naturedly conclude, thinking how strange it is what a difference a tail makes.

Before I discuss the assignment we give our students and the responses it evokes, I should probably tell you about my school, students, and academic program. Richard Montgomery High School, in Rockville, Maryland was recently ranked among the top high schools in the nation based on the number of International Baccalaureate and Advanced Placement tests our students take. Our International Baccalaureate (or I. B.) program is highly selective and draws eight to nine hundred applicants from all over Montgomery County each year competing for just one hundred spots.

I have been teaching two of the four sections of senior I. B. English for the past three years with my colleague and mentor Susan Barrett who has been a vital force in creating and sustaining the integrity of the I. B. English program in our school. She, along with my predecessor, the now retired Betsy Butler, created the assignment that I will discuss today. Achieving the IB diploma in English requires the student to develop his or her own individual, critical stance when analyzing literature. Secondary sources are used infrequently. One of the aims of the IB program in English is to "encourage a personal appreciation of literature and develop an understanding of the techniques involved in literary criticism" in order to "promote in students an enjoyment of, and lifelong interest in, literature" (Language A1 Subject Guide). The culmination of the IB diploma in English is a four-hour exam taken in May of the senior year. Because Woolf writes so insightfully and persuasively about the art of the novel and literature in general, during the senior year, students read three works by Woolf in addition to *A Room of One's Own*—the essays, "How Should One Read a Book?" and "Modern

Fiction," and the novel *To the Lighthouse*. By the end of the year, they're either completely afraid of Virginia Woolf or reading as much of her work as they can.

When I joined my colleague Susan Barrett in teaching Woolf's *A Room of One's Own* three years ago, I had high expectations. Our students, all of whom were International Baccalaureate candidates, were phenomenally capable and motivated and still had something of the unfettered and incandescent quality of their minds intact. I anticipated my classes figuratively clasping hands in recognition that we were, as Woolf might suggest, "destroying illusions" about women's history and literature once and for all and "putting truth in [their] place." Which is why I was that much more disconcerted when I discovered that many of the young men and women in my classes at first responded to Woolf's text not with a sense of liberation or confirmation, but instead, hostility. Even students, both male and female, who saw something worthy of critical exploration in the text originally felt the need to hedge their enthusiasm by prefacing contributions with, "I'm not a feminist or anything, but...." Their initial responses to *A Room of One's Own* were characterized by what English professor Christine Farris described at the 1993 Conference on Virginia Woolf as a "resistance to feminism and feminist interpretation" and a "lack of understanding of the historical situations of women" (Farris 52). Over the years of teaching *A Room of One's Own*, I have seen otherwise insightful and knowledgeable students suggest that Woolf's claims about the historic subjugation of women are ungrounded, and I have witnessed numerous students squirm in discomfort when the "'f' word"—feminism—came up in class. Over the course of our discussion of the text, many students' opinions shift. It would be inaccurate to suggest that all of my students are transformed into feminists and become entirely enlightened about what Farris calls "the influence of history upon women," but many of them learn, if nothing else, the value of questioning the validity of their positions (Farris 52). And this, I think, they learn not only because of the text itself, but because the assignment gives them the freedom to assert their views, challenge one another, and reevaluate their positions. In both the work and the assignment, the process is perhaps as valuable as the product.

The pedagogical style of the assignment mimics Woolf's rhetorical approach to the text by decentering the authority of the teacher and, consequently, shifting the balance of power from the teacher to the students. Just as the essay encourages autonomy and independence for women, the assignment encourages the same for the student. After reading the whole work on their own, the students, in groups of four or five, prepare a single chapter in depth and conduct a panel discussion which the teacher moderates from the sidelines. All students prepare for their panel discussions by finding points on content and style that they think are worthy of exploration and elaboration. Categories that we offer for them to consider include: the appropriateness of style to content, the issues of logic or reason that they find pertinent, the application of Woolf's ideas to contemporary issues, the extent to which the student agrees or disagrees with specific ideas raised in the chapter, what the ideas in this chapter contribute to the structure of the work as a whole, and the effectiveness of the persona that Woolf creates to communicate her ideas. The students must illustrate and support their views carefully with the text and are evaluated on the four categories prescribed by the I. B. English curriculum: their use of language, their knowledge of the work, the quality of the presentation of their ideas, and their literary insight and response.

Woolf's approach to her subject lends itself well to the constructivist teaching methods we often use in our I. B. classes. In the constructivist classroom, teachers place themselves at the margins of the activities and encourage student examination of content and reflection on its meaning. Constructivism is based in part on the psychological theories of Piaget, who argued that knowledge resulted from the individual learner's ability to construct meaning and Vygotsky, who emphasized the importance of social interaction in the learning process (Hynds 256). The objective of constructivist teaching practices is to "place in students' hands the exhilarating power to follow trails of interest, to make connections, to reformulate ideas, and to reach unique conclusions" (Brooks 22). Teachers who formulate assignments along constructivist principles emphasize group work, value students as thinkers with emerging theories about the world, and privilege student questions over a strict adherence to teacher interpretation (Brooks 17).

In some ways, the speaker in Woolf's text engages in similar practices—she downplays her own importance while challenging the existing authority, encourages dialogue, asks open-ended questions, constructs relationships—and in so doing, plays the role of the constructivist teacher and learner. Her approach encourages readers to challenge presumptions about authority and gender, just as the assignment, based on constructivist principles, challenges "the long tradition of teacher as knower" (Hynds 260). Susan Hynds suggests that constructivist teaching "creates a space for those uncomfortable conversations that lead us to a new critical consciousness" (Hynds 262). In the constructivist classroom, students grapple with ideas, and the dissonance which accompanies their grappling yields rich examination of meaning.

Using a constructivist approach in the teaching of *A Room of One's Own* requires the students to examine their personal—and private—responses to the topics of women and literature. The assignment places the authority in the students' hands; no teacher will tell her what to think or why to think it, and by constructing meaning, the student is forced not only to take responsibility for her own learning, but to question everything she thinks she knows about the topic. As a model of instruction, of course it isn't revolutionary. But it is an unusual departure from the kind of instruction one typically finds in the high school classroom. Students find themselves dissecting constructions such as the classroom and the essay and reevaluating what they know about feminism, gender, and history. In so doing, many discover that the "essential oil of truth" is a slippery substance, one that can easily escape their grasp.

One of the first questions that arises about *A Room of One's Own* has to do with the issue of genre. "What is this?" the students ask because its style challenges their conception of the lecture or essay. In many of the students' minds, the work has no formal introduction, no linear development of ideas, and no satisfying conclusion to tie up all of the loose ends. Some students claim her approach is stereotypically female because she meanders, contradicts herself, and lets her emotions interfere with the clarity of her ideas. One girl said, "She's chosen herself to be a representation of women and so I want her to be logical about it. If she isn't logical, people will assume that there are no arguments to be made." Another student argued, "She doesn't use counterexamples and that weakens her argument . . . . If women can be better than men as she implies, they can also be worse. She doesn't say this." Frequently, students object to her use of fictional examples and bemoan the absence of concrete "proof," not recognizing that the absence of actual references to women writers is powerful evidence of women's literary and historical invisibility.

However, other students offer insightful explanations of Woolf's technique. One noted, "There are two levels to the book. On one level, she's very direct, and then there's the under-level, the novel type thing. That almost seems to be the more effective level; the subtle parts are more important." The student begins to demonstrate sensitivity to the distinctions between genres and the rich possibilities that emerge when forms of literature collide. Once the students recognize that the author's use of narrative in her essay doesn't invalidate her ideas, they begin to appreciate that the same Virginia Woolf who argued for a creative approach to the novel in "Modern Fiction" is herself taking the same unconventional approach to the essay.

Even though I realize that it isn't particular to high students, the students' negative reaction to anything that resembles feminism or a feminist perspective is curious to me. Twenty-five minutes into the first discussion of the text this year, the word feminism came up, and we stopped our analysis of chapter one to discuss what the word meant to us. It became clear that the negative connotations were the result of what students believed were "extreme" cases of feminism, like "women who run around hating men," one student said. I suspect that the reluctance to embrace anything feminist for the girl students had something to do with sexuality, and a fear, perhaps, that by claiming to be a feminist, one would be labeled a lesbian.

Back in 1979 Gloria Steinem explained why she believed that young women are more conservative, and therefore reluctant to participate in feminist activism. She explains that young women,

> haven't yet experienced the life events that are most radicalizing for
> women: entering the paid-labor force and discovering how women are
> treated there; marrying and finding out that it is not yet an equal part-
> nership; having children and discovering who is responsible for them
> and who is not; and aging, still a greater penalty for women than for
> men. (212)

Furthermore, many of my students have been fortunate enough to have been
raised by parents and educators who are familiar with the damages that are
perhaps unwittingly done to girls and young women in school settings.
Many of my students' parents and their teachers have read Mary Pipher's
Reviving Ophelia which addresses damages incurred by unforgiving and
unrealistic images of women in the media and educational settings, and
Myra and David Sadker's *Failing at Fairness* which outlines just how pervasive the gender gap is in our nation's schools. Adults familiar with these
works have gone to some lengths to undo harms created by the media and
unjust expectations and practices in the schools. Unfortunately, this has had
the effect, I think, of seeming to confirm to both our girls and our boys that
not only are they now equal, but that it has been so for many years.

Furthermore, the students are immune to the suggestion that although
their situation at our school seems just and equitable, it is very different from
the worlds of the academy and business that they will soon enter. Although
few students this year claimed, as did one boy, "the speaker in *A Room of
One's Own* fears that what men say about women is true [. . .] they truly
are the inferior sex," there were many who believe she exaggerates the conditions of women and the arrogance of men. They accuse Woolf of being
hypocritical because in her description and assessment of men, like
Professor Von X, for instance, she herself writes in "the red light of emotion
and not in the white light of truth" (Woolf 32–33). And for those students
who are sure that Woolf is justified in her anger and evaluation of male dom-
inated society but who aren't quite sure of all of the details in its historical
explanation, hedging prevails.

Their ignorance about women's history is attributable, in part, to the
fact that they haven't ever studied the concept of gender or women's history in school; consequently, it's difficult for them to construct persuasive
theories about why women didn't have rooms of their own and steady
incomes when Woolf presented her lectures and composed the book. In a
recent essay in the *Journal of American History*, two teachers at Phillips
Academy write about their experiences teaching gender in their high school.
Recognizing that "gender, taken as a cultural construct or a way of ordering
social and political life, does not yet have a regular place in the high school
curriculum," they combined forces to construct a course on gender history
in which they address scholarly examination of men's history and women's
history (Dalton and Rotundo 1716). Most schools, however, don't have such
a course. In order to remedy some of the difficulties we encounter teaching

A Room of One's Own, this summer I will be working with one of the IB history teachers in my school to construct a few lessons about women and education and women in the work force so that by the time students read *A Room of One's Own* in English class, they will have a more solid basis for evaluating the underpinnings of Woolf's argument. I hope that this will result in a deeper understanding of the text.

Although I haven't made this clear, many students truly enjoy reading *A Room of One's Own* in high school. One of my students this year wrote her college application essay about why it was the most influential book she had ever read. Others voluntarily joined my colleague and me for a lunchtime meeting of what we nicknamed "The Virginia Woolf Dream Team," a gathering during which we continued to discuss the text. One of my favorite lines in the book occurs at the end of Chapter 1 where Woolf writes, "…and I thought how unpleasant it is to be locked out; and I thought how it is worse perhaps to be locked in" (*AROO* 24). Teaching *A Room of One's Own* well in high school is about giving the students the power not only to unlock the text, but also to unlock closed minds, and, ultimately, to "think of things in themselves" and live wholeheartedly "in the presence of reality" (*AROO* 111, 110).

Works Cited

Brooks, Jacqueline Grennon, and Martin G. Brooks. *In Search of Understanding: The Case for Constructivist Classrooms*. Alexandria, Virginia: Association for Supervision and Curriculum Development, 1993.

Dalton, Kathleen M., and E. Anthony Rotundo. "Teaching Gender History to Secondary School Students." *Journal of American History* 86 (2000): 1715–20.

Farris, Christine. "Using Woolf to Teach Reading and Writing in Undergraduate Classrooms." In *Virginia Woolf: Emerging Perspectives*, ed. Mark Hussey and Vara Neverow, 52–8. New York: Pace University Press, 1994.

Hynds, Susan. *On the Brink: Negotiating Literature and Life with Adolescents*. New York: Teachers College Press, 1997.

Language A1 Subject Guide. Geneva, Switzerland: International Baccalaureate Organisation, 1999.

Pipher, Mary. *Reviving Ophelia: Saving the Selves of Adolescent Girls*. New York: Ballantine Books, 1994.

Sadker, David, and Myra Sadker. *Failing at Fairness*. New York: Charles Scribner's Sons, 1994.

Steinem, Gloria. *Outrageous Acts and Everyday Rebellions*. New York: Holt, Rinehart, Winston, 1983.

Woolf, Virginia. *A Room of One's Own*. San Diego: Harvest/ HBJ, 1981.

Woolf Through Other Arts

Suzanne Bellamy
Experiments in Constructing The Visual Field :
Conversations with Woolf and Stein and *Painting* The Waves

My experiment in the form of the Visual Essay has now ranged across four projects and over four conferences. I began with the Virginia Woolf print exhibition at New Hampshire (1997), then the collaborations with Isota Tucker Epes in painting and writing about *To The Lighthouse* and *The Waves* (1999, 2000) and now the exhibition and presentation "Conversations With Woolf and Stein" at Baltimore in 2000. Each phase has refined the process, giving equal weight to the intellectual and scholarly, and the more elusive creations from my studio, in printmaking and painting. I began with a general idea that I could explore Woolf's ideas on creativity and the creative process, moving from her influences, through biographical contexts and on to her most experimental texts. As with all such grand plans, the journey has been rather different and yet richly worthwhile to me personally. The ideas of dual creativity underpin this series of projects, from Woolf's lifelong conversation with her sister Vanessa Bell, from my own reading and visual research, and from the critically important work of scholar Diane Gillespie. It could be said that Gillespie's work forms the backbone of this whole experiment.

Conversations With Virginia Woolf and Gertrude Stein

Linking Woolf and Stein in conversation had its beginnings for me in the research I had done over many years on Virginia Woolf's place within the post-impressionist world of ideas. Gertrude Stein also lived within and worked off the edges of an art movement and she inhabited a world of painters, aesthetic theorists and passionate friends of the arts. It is known that Woolf and Stein met, that the Hogarth Press published Stein's essay *Composition As Explanation*, and that there was frisson between them. Here was a fruitful field of connection open to exploration. My goal was to focus on the work that specifically dealt with language, processes, and writing itself. I hoped to compare *Composition As Explanation* and Stein's other essays and lectures with Woolf's essays "The Narrow Bridge of Art" and "A Sketch of the Past." Of course this idea needed some preparation of the

186

ground. What resulted in the prints was more introductory, narrative, diplomatic, political, humorous. One cannot force two such women into forms preconceived and imposed. As with the previous work I had made on Woolf, I found myself drawn into a field of action where it was better to take advice than give it, and the participants opened all the doors.

My methods as usual were diverse. I read widely, helped especially again by Diane Gillespie who sent me the influential article "Woolfenstein" by Rachel Blau DuPlessis. In this work, DuPlessis strongly suggests that Woolf was influenced by Stein's ideas in writing *The Waves* particularly. My Stein reading of 20 years became more disciplined and I finally tried to sort out the difficult strands from Cezanne to Matisse to Picasso.

Setting up the creative meditation proved to be the most complicated part of the process. Sitting in my studio, I tried to bring Virginia and Gertrude together. From the start, this was problematic, and was going to take delicate diplomacy. They would not sit facing each other at all, and only over time did I manage to have them sit, à la café, across a table, slightly leaning towards conversation. Over a period of months this chill thawed as I took the view that the situation was not a comparison in any sense but a three-way exploration, myself included. The final rapprochement I will not forget, when Stein leaned across and offered her hand, and they shook hands at last. We were away !!!

In this initial series there are twelve Conversations. I offer here the briefest summaries of what are to be extended essays on each Conversation. It has become clear to me that this is a much bigger project than I first thought, and that this is the first part.

No. 1 SETTING THE SCENE: Still Life, Perception. Here the stage is created. They sit looking at pears on the table, each seeing something different. They discuss refraction, the nature of objects and the "real," cubism and prismatic light. They become a still life as they discuss the still life. The curtain rises.

No. 2 COLLISIONS: "Lying Under the Whole of Gertrude Stein." This print tells the story of their meetings and business transactions. Rejecting the manuscript of *The Making of Americans*, perhaps not ever reading it, Woolf wrote various letters to friends parodying Stein's weighty work, body and presence. Here Alice faces the backdrop of their own Parisian life as Gertrude hurtles through the air on her magical manuscript and Woolf deftly avoids being crushed. The subsequent Hogarth printing of *Composition As Explanation* testifies to a shift in position over the value of Stein's work and worth.

No. 3 CARS–POSITIONING gives each her vehicle, dangerous and beautiful. Stein, like Toad, is up for the contest, Woolf more reflective but

SETTING THE SCENE: Still Life, Perception.

COLLISIONS: "Lying Under the Whole of Gertrude Stein."

curious to move through the scene. Both wrote about cars, Stein composed to the sounds of her pistons, Woolf considered the nature of speed and the past on an evening in Sussex.

No. 4 RITUAL and DEEP RHYTHM concerns the different ways each writer draws upon forms and myths from the ancient and matriarchal worlds. The work of Gloria Feman Orenstein on Stein's use of the Seder ritual and Jewish iconography sits here with Woolf's involvement with the work and ideas of Jane Ellen Harrison. As with all the Conversations, this theme shows how there can be deep points of connection between these two women artists if certain doors are opened.

No. 5 PATTERNS: Repetition, Sentences, Words, Grammar. This print in particular deals with and embodies the actual processes of repetition and structure. I set up the printing block as an experiment in repetition of form, then subjected it to great downward pressure through the press. The result is clear—repetition subverts itself and shifts the frame. Although Stein writes more specifically about grammar and the sentence, they have strong points in common in this area. Stein's essays on the development of sentences and paragraphs can be richly compared with Woolf on Anon and Chaucer in particular.

No. 6 COSMOLOGY: Sun Moon Light Shadow places each in her direct relation to the cosmos, ideas and realities. More than absorbing the science of their day, each became part of her solar and lunar landscape, travelling in very different ways. We know from Alice that Gertrude used to lie in full sunlight with open eyes staring into the light. For me Woolf travelled more like the comets, in the eclipses and shadows of the heavens. In all the art work of these series, the ideas of eclipse, light and shadow are significant.

No. 7 BIOGRAPHY: Country, the Twentieth Century
Both Woolf and Stein lived lives where the boundaries of art and life merged, where as women artists their lives became the material of movements. Here they pre-empt those who sought to study them, as they discuss the idea of the twentieth century itself, its mythic potency for each of them in separate ways, the experience of being subjects of their own writing and the life writing each tried to reinvent. Basket listens, and wonders why Virginia's dogs are not here too. I tried so hard to have Pinker in the frame but it would not happen. I finally decided that this was because in the end the dogs were truly Leonard's.

No. 8 VISUAL GEOGRAPHY: Colors in the Field
This print floats upon a Picassoesque collograph of a broken frame. In

CARS–POSITIONING

RITUAL AND DEEP RHYTHM

abandoning the traditional narrative structure, and in radically different ways, Woolf and Stein choose what to illuminate with color. Their atonal experiments act here like spots on a stage.

No. 9 MASKS: Personas and Production explores the different ways each writer created a persona within the text, and within the life.

No. 10 OUTSIDERS: Porpoise, Cow, Patriarchy broadly considers the nature of each writer's feminism and sexual politics. Both clearly experienced lives outside mainstream predictabilities and lived with secrets. This is the debate about the degree to which each invented little and private languages, codes and jokes to explore sexual games and layers of erotic meaning, and the ways in which private life, lovers and lesbian experience informed their politics.

No. 11 USE EVERYTHING: Outside The Frame
Stein's marvellous invocation to use everything inspires this print, where the frame of reference is shattered; they consider each other no longer adversarily but as revolutionaries in the invention of new forms.

No. 12 LEGACY: "Not Since Lesbos. . ." is a print for the present. Rising above their curtain and stage, Woolf and Stein take on the harlequinesque joy of a circus act and float to the surface. Two hot air balloons bear them aloft, carried by the words of Woolf who mused that not since Sappho had there been conditions to produce great work among women artists and writers. In some recent perspectives, they have been named the two greatest lesbian modernists. What does this mean? What is their tradition? What is the legacy they each separately and together leave for women writing and fighting now ?

A Postscript.
Working each year with Isota Tucker Epes in collaboration on the painting projects has led me to expect a certain magical quality in our combinations. This year we painted *The Waves*. It had not been a book I had liked much but it was Isota's choice this time, and I embraced it heartily.

On the morning we set up the exhibition, something wonderful happened. Isota, her daughter Maria and I were hanging and organizing the paintings, prints and floor installation. It's my favorite time really, our time just with all the work, in an empty room.

Suddenly Isota dropped a bombshell.

"By the way, Suzanne, I forgot to tell you. I met Gertrude Stein."

With my complete attention, she told the story of being a young student at Bryn Mawr in 1936, when Stein visited to give a lecture. Stein would not come straight out onto the stage from the side and instead insisted on walking the full length of a marble floor up through the assembled crowd to the stage. It was a long walk and she was wearing espadrilles, a floppy sandshoe kind of thing. At this point Isota demonstrated the scene. She re-enacted Stein's long, slow, purposeful walk, especially the sound effects of those shoes, kaplunk kaplunk kaplunk. . . on and on all the way, in the otherwise total silence as the audience waited.

Maria and I were in the land of legends, and I know at that moment I felt in the presence of Stein as I never had before, reading her. Something in the sound of that repetitious cheeky walk did it, and the particular sharpness of Isota's memory of the event, and of Alice B. Toklas's moustache at the meal later, riveting to a seventeen year old.

Later, during my session talking about the Woolf and Stein print series, I asked Isota if she would tell the story again to the audience, as a way of illuminating the print on "Cars—Positioning." The sound of those shoes kaplunking across the marble hall brought to life all the stories about Stein sitting in the car writing to the sound of her pistons. It was pure jazz, syncopated rhythms coming across a sixty-five year bridge through the memory of a young student and into the Woolf conference. How that filled me with joy.

Works Cited

DuPlessis, Rachel Blau. "Woolfenstein." *Breaking The Sequence: Women's Experimental Fiction*. Eds. Ellen G. Friedman and Miriam Fuchs. Princeton: Princeton University Press, 1989.

Gillespie, Diane F. *The Sisters' Arts. The Writing and Painting of Virginia Woolf and Vanessa Bell*. New York: Syracuse University Press, 1988.

Orenstein, Gloria. "Decoding the Hieroglyphics of Feminist Matristic Subversion: Patriarchal Symbol Systems as Decoys. Gertrude Stein." *The Reflowering of the Goddess*. New York: Pergamon Press, 1990.

Isota Tucker Epes
A Lifetime With *The Waves*

The Waves has always been my favorite novel; to me, it is magical, adapting itself over and over to the changing stages of my life. I encountered it first in the summer of 1935, enjoying it so intensely I can still close my eyes sixty-five years later and smell the pungent pine trees that clustered around the sleeping porch of my family's cottage on Lake Champlain, for it was to this porch I retreated after luncheon to read undisturbed. After the first few pages, I became totally absorbed in the six characters Woolf suspended before my eyes, individuals unencumbered with the narrative trivia of most fiction, who revealed their thoughts in a sort of shared consciousness.

Here was a book that truly treated the reader as an adult, I decided in my youthful exuberance; I would give it a place of honor among my favorites and who cared whether anyone else liked it or not? Such a naive reaction would have been impossible even for a fifteen-year-old a few years later, but in the mid-thirties the average reader still regarded Woolf as a contemporary writer whom one was free to judge for oneself.

Before long, such readers had some surprises. First, Harcourt, Brace and Co. announced the upcoming publication of *The Years* toward the end of 1936. Shortly thereafter, The Literary Guild, a large, nationwide book-of-the-month club in the USA, chose this novel as one of its monthly selections for 1937, along with *Gone With The Wind* by Margaret Mitchell and *Of Mice and Men* by John Steinbeck. Actually, *The Years* was on the Best Seller List for a while and the idea that any reader was exploring an unknown author by perusing it was gone forever. Most of all, it seemed to those of us familiar with her earlier work a very puzzling choice.

Meanwhile, Hitler and his Nazi Party were steadily extending Germany's sphere of influence and confronting Europe with the inevitability of a second World War. At the height of the summer season in July 1938, Woolf published her pacifist tract, *Three Guineas*, with painful, though not unexpected results. It was sharply ridiculed by conservative critics and even some of her close friends such as Maynard Keynes and E. M. Forster repudiated its argument as misguided and unrealistic. On the other hand, to a college student like myself who had already been exposed to the Peace Movement in evidence on U. S. campuses at the time, it seemed welcome evidence of Woolf's intellectual honesty.

September 1938 brought the Munich Conference which for the moment quieted the fear of war in most people's minds, at least on the surface, but almost exactly a year later Hitler ordered his troops into Poland and World War II began. From then on, military service or civilian war work took over the lives of my British and Canadian contemporaries; and long before Pearl Harbor, members of my generation in the U. S., regardless of their earlier pacifist sympathies, were going into war production or into certain areas of Government service. I remember reading about Woolf's death in March, 1941 only a couple of months before I moved to Washington, D.C. to go in the newly-formed O.S.S. From then on for almost five years, I was involved with war work of one kind or another. For five dreary years indeed I had not stolen time to browse about my collection of favorite books, especially *The Waves* which began to provide an added sort of pleasure in the form of escape from frenetic group action into individual exploration in its purest essence.

By the time World War II had ended, I'm glad to say I had outgrown my childish possessiveness about *The Waves* and longed to have some solid, unbiased criticism to expand my understanding and appreciation of the novel and of its author's other writing. What developed in its stead was a peevish, ongoing struggle between two opinionated groups of academics, both British and American, who were far more interested in winning their contested argument than in fairly assessing a body of work. Dr. F. R. Leavis of Cambridge University led the pack of Woolf deriders deploring her lack of involvement with reality, while the opposition, whom I always think of as the Greenery-yallery Aesthetes, dwelt exclusively on her aesthetic purity. Both sides ignored her innovative style, her feminism, her pacifism, her intellectual depth, and above all, her superb sense of humor. The teapot tempest had a strangely dampening effect on the common reader, and I still had to carry my books off to a quiet place and go on reading on my own.

Finally in 1963, Grove Press published a small critical text, *Virginia Woolf* by A. D. Moody, which was notable for me because in its final chapter the author reviewed the long battle between the Leavis grumps and the Aesthete gang, closing with an analysis of the detrimental effect this squabble had had on Woolf's literary reputation in the two decades since her death (98-113). In any case, it seemed to clear the air and let the critics move on.

Happily for me, the real breakthrough in my search for solid critical analysis of Woolf's writing came just two years later when I discovered Jean Guiguet's *Virginia Woolf and Her Works* published in translation by Hogarth Press in 1965, three years after its original publication in France. Particularly able in his discussion of *The Waves* (280-302), Guiguet helped me perceive intellectually what I had sensed emotionally long ago from my first contact with the novel. Put in simplest terms, it is this: by eliminating the conventional concept of fictional reality from its structure, Woolf had turned the work into a sort of abstract play-poem into which the reader pours the world of his own imagination and experience, creating a whole new reality and identifying with each of the characters in turn as each is propelled through time by the insistent motion of the descriptive interludes.

It was, I became aware, because of the depth of involvement demanded of the reader that I had become so awed by the novel on my first clumsy reading. What a privilege at fifteen years old to be allowed to be present at the final meeting of the six friends at Hampton Court and to listen to Bernard's musings. "Here we could see for a moment laid out in front of us the body of the complete human being each of us failed to be but at the same time cannot forget. All that we might have been, we saw; all that we missed" (303). Yet how the meaning of that same passage expands and deepens as we mature and then move on toward life's close.

Surely it is the secret magic of *The Waves* that it lets its reader escape the boundaries of self and possess for a brief time a consciousness that is wholly objective in what amounts to a sort of temporary liberation from the bonds of personality. But what is far more remarkable, this time of liberation can and does return with each rereading, each time changed to fit the changed understanding of the reader.

The mid-sixties marked a reawakening of interest in Virginia Woolf, but no one was prepared for the outpouring of books and articles about the writer and her work, an outpouring which gathered momentum from decade to decade over the last thirty years. Younger academic associates cannot imagine what a joyous surprise it was for those of us who discovered her books back in the 1930s and who, shortly afterward, saw them bickered over or ignored for so long. Even in 1963, A. D. Moody wrote, "There is not much agreement at present about Virginia Woolf's standing as a novelist" (98). Today she is generally spoken of as one of the foremost literary figures of the twentieth century, and each time we aging fans hear the statement we cannot resist a blush of pride.

Perhaps because I felt the job of preserving and extending this writer's influence was now in far more competent hands than mine, when I retired from teaching English Literature in the mid-eighties, I turned to painting rather than to literary research. As a few of you may remember, a series of my Woolf paintings were exhibited at the Third Annual Conference on Virginia Woolf in 1993, and in 1999 at the Ninth Annual Conference, Suzanne Bellamy and I presented a painting project on *To The Lighthouse*. Having enjoyed both of these experiences, I was delighted when Suzanne and I decided to present yet another painting project at the Tenth Annual Conference based on my special favorite, *The Waves*.

During the period of painters' block that afflicts visual artists confronted with a blank canvas or a pressing deadline, I jotted down some notes on how I envisioned approaching this project. First of all, I proposed that I would paint six portraits of the six characters whose consecutive interior monologue provides the main structure of the novel. Each portrait was to be painted in acrylic paint on a gessoed surface 30" x 22". Then I outlined in one paragraph the chief characteristics of each of the six characters, notes that turned up when I started writing this paper so I include them here:

1. Rhoda is the fragile artist in each of us who is capable of amazing flights of imagination and sensitive to every nuance of experience, but who is eventually destroyed by her inability to deal with the mundane world.

2. Louis , like Rhoda, is an outsider but, except for being shy and insecure, is quite unlike her in his ambition for worldly success. He is the part of us greedy to be accepted by our peers, but condemned to an ongoing sense of isolation.

3. Susan is the part of us that wants to fall back on instinctual nature and in so doing to escape the complexities of human society. She tries to become the earth mother and to find serenity and simplicity in the sweep of fields, hills and sky but discovers these open spaces can also shut one up in a prison of solitude.

4. Neville is the egotist in each of us, always looking inward. Love of another for him is simply love of something as much like himself as possi-

ble to reinforce his own of sense of identity. Unable to enjoy his chosen career of scholarship, he is imprisoned in himself.

5. Jinny is the side of us that lives confidently in flesh and bone, a purely physical being. Everything in her world is two dimensional except her body which is the center of every space she inhabits. With her, movement is an art, a form of dance created in the beckoning of a finger or the flicker of an eyelid. There is something reassuring to us in her being, limited though she is, something that provides us with crucial energy.

6. Bernard is the middle-of-the-road side of our nature, the part of us that enjoys life, that sincerely likes his fellow man. A bit lazy, he has no desire to rock the boat but prefers to float along on the current. At the end of his life he learns, perhaps because he has not absorbed all of his energies in serious enterprise, that it will fall to his lot to close the last act of this abstract play-poem, to turn aging amiability into valor, and to ride into battle, his old heart pounding, against death itself.

After I finished making these notes, I put them away and went to work with my paints, letting the images go where they would and for four months having a blissful time in front of my easel. Finally in June, I wrapped up my portraits and took them to UMBC where my daughter Maria hung them in the gallery space set aside for our show. Suzanne Bellamy had already set up her fascinating abstract three-dimensional floor installation for *The Waves* project. Our separate versions couldn't have been more unlike, yet the two of them, together with Suzanne's series of prints on Gertrude Stein and Virginia Woolf which graced the opposite wall, made in my biased opinion, a truly challenging exhibit. In any case, this project was a most rewarding one for me because it gave me yet another way of exploring the novel I have been reading for sixty-six years.

Works Cited

Guiguet, Jean. *Virginia Woolf and Her Works*. Translated by Jean Stewart. London: Hogarth Press, 1965, rpr. New York: Harcourt Brace Johanovich, 1976.

Moody, A. D. *Virginia Woolf*. New York: Grove Press, 1963.

Woolf, Virginia. *Three Guineas*. London: Hogarth Press, 1938.

——. *To The Lighthouse*, New York: Harcourt, Brace and Co., 1927.

——. *The Waves*. London: Hogarth Press, 1931.

——. *The Years*. New York: Harcourt, Brace and Co., 1937.

Cultural and Material Woolf

Nicola Luckhurst
Photoportraits: Gisèle Freund and Virginia Woolf

> *The great portrait photographers are great mythologists.*
> Roland Barthes, *Camera Lucida.*

> *Please caption "Portrait" by Man Ray, not "photo."*
> Man Ray, letter of 1 June 1966 to Leonard Woolf.

The only color photographs of Woolf were taken in 1939, by the photographer Gisèle Freund. I first came across Freund's photographs when, leafing through a collection entitled *Die Frau mit der Kamera*, I saw the following—(Slide 1: Portrait of Virginia Woolf, 1939. *Photographer* plate 94)[1]—in color. I find this image haunting, and I know that it is powerful because it's not in black and white. Color seems to dispel the iconic quality that has increasingly accrued to Woolf's image; through it she becomes mortal, by which I mean that one senses her mortality. This image might be read as a heightened expression of the truism that, "All photographs are *memento mori*. To take a photograph is to participate in another person's [. . .] mortality, vulnerability, mutability" (Sontag 15).

On the next page of the collection is a photograph of Woolf's writing table taken almost thirty years later, at Rodmell—(Slide 2: Photo of Woolf's writing table, 1965. *Photographer* plate 100). A different kind of *memento mori*, the staging of this still life is curious. This is Woolf's desk, so the caption tells us, the writer's tools are carefully placed, the book lies open with the pen laid across, the chair is pushed back as if the author had just walked away. And yet—looking again—this careful placing is less the staging of a place of work momentarily left, than it is a memorial. In this "nature morte" all traces of the writer's work are erased, the table is highly polished, the inkwell clean and empty, the book is Woolf's diary, both pages fully written, and the flowers the clearest indication that this image is *in memoriam*. The table is placed on the terrace outside Woolf's writing hut, the grass fading upward into a white light, as if this scene were set at a threshold.

The producers of this second image are Gisèle Freund and Leonard Woolf. Other photos taken during this session feature Leonard reading Virginia's diary, and were used by him to illustrate his autobiography.

The following portrait (Slide 3: Leonard Woolf, 1965. *Photographer* plate 99) from this same session, was not used as an illustration but was reproduced in the collection, *Gisèle Freund Photographer* (1985). In it the only visible detail is what seems to be a candle set on a tripod. The blank, geometric background of this photograph, taken in Leonard Woolf's study on the first floor of Monk's House, is in striking contrast with the richly Bloomsbury settings of Freund's 1939 photographs of the Woolfs at Tavistock Square. The portrait centers on Leonard's isolation, his great age—more than that, he confronts the camera with his devastation. I believe that this photograph was taken in black and white.

There is a complex relationship between these two photo-sessions of 1939 and 1965. Virginia Woolf's response to the sitting for Freund is well known—her anger, her sense of violation. Yet Leonard Woolf invited Freund back, years later, to photograph not only himself, but also his wife's diary, the very text in which Woolf had accused the photographer. I want to work back through the images presented here towards a definition of Freund's photographic aesthetic, so as to revisit and illuminate the relationship between the two Freund-Woolf photo-sessions.

The portrait that I began by showing is part of the series taken at the Woolfs' home in 1939. In one image Woolf is seen, unusually for Freund's work, in profile. Several use a three-quarters pose. This shot is perhaps the most direct and animated of the series (Slide 4: Virginia Woolf portrait, 1939. *Photographer* plate 96). Although taken on the one occasion, Woolf changes her dress three times as if unsure as to how her face might best be framed. This seems to be the only indication of her part in the arrangements of this photo-session, and as such, it is interesting to compare with the far more extensive sequence taken by Freund in the same year of James Joyce for *Time* magazine (8 May 1939). Where Woolf's concern with framing suggests that she viewed the photographs as portraits, Joyce's concern with location and staging the involvement of others indicates that he had a different genre in mind: reportage. Joyce is shown as a writer, that is, engaged in writerly activity. By contrast, the photographs of Woolf were taken on condition that they would not be made public. The images would become part of Freund's collection of color photographs of writers, a collection which was at this time shown principally to other potential subjects, with the intention of persuading them, in turn, to join this pantheon of great European authors and intellectuals.

Freund and Victoria Ocampo, who provided the photographer with her entrée to the Woolfs, are the designers of this first photo sequence of 1939. Photography is also the connection between Ocampo and Woolf, who first met at a private view to an exhibition of Man Ray's photographs in London in 1934. Ocampo's friendship with Freund began in Paris at Adrienne Monnier's book shop, "La Maison des amis des livres," the venue for Freund's first showing of her portraits of writers on 5 March 1939, and the first exhibition of color photographs in France.

The exhibition took the form of a slide show. Freund had begun to use color in 1938, shortly after Kodak and Agfa first made it commercially available. But color film was prohibitively expensive, and the development of prints still more so, such that the reproduction of color photographs tended to be reserved for commercial purposes. Freund sent her negatives for development as slides. Even when developing the negatives as prints became feasible, Freund would continue to favor projection. In the first major retrospective of her work in Paris, 1968, Freund was concerned to light the photographic prints on display so as to simulate the effect of projection: "the light was concentrated exclusively on the illumination of the photos" (*Portrait* 132). Thus, color might differently inform our notion of the icon, taking us back to the rich oils of Byzantine devotional images. Or, focusing instead on the use of light and projection, we might see the writers, as did Adrienne Monnier, as stars of Freund's silent screen: "light plays the role of a sculptor [. . .] the movie-star type of enlargement here finds its very raison d'être" (119).

Freund's first exhibition was, then, a slide-show, described on the invitation printed by Monnier as a "a permanent projection of portraits of writers in the medium of color photography by Gisèle Freund." Simone de Beauvoir, one of the writers present, described the event as follows:

> On a spring day in 1939, Gisèle Freund invited us to Adrienne's bookshop to see her portraits [. . .] projected in color upon a screen. The place was crowded with famous writers. I don't remember who was there; what has stayed eternally in my mind, however, is the sight of [. . .] the screen glowing in the darkness, and the familiar faces bathed in beautiful color [. . .] All the consecrated authors as well as the new talents with a still-uncertain future drifted across the screen before our eyes. The camera had captured them with a precision which was often cruel [. . .]

> Ours was no Golden Age, as I am the first to admit, not being a believer in lost paradises [. . .] But I keep an ardent memory of those days [. . .] With their contradictions and their turbulence, the thirties had an extraordinary character, for they were, at one and the same time, a flowering and a decline. (ix)

Looking back at these photo-portraits we recognize the faces of great writers: Freund's collection has become a literary who's who of the 1930s. If most of the images are familiar, color alone still has the potential to surprise and, perhaps only in the case of Woolf's portrait, to shock. What remains *striking* is the charged and ambiguous significance of the event: for the projection was at once a performance—of the new medium of color photography; a commemorative categorization—the collective representation of the generation of pre war European writers; and, finally, a large color advertisement for the new literature which the gallery, that is the bookshop, promoted.

The ambiguity is heightened by the fact that Freund was not only a photographer but also a student of sociology and aesthetics. Her pioneering thesis, *La photographie en France au dix-neuvième siècle* (published by Monnier in 1936) describes the rise of photography as "the democratization of the portrait." Freund had planned, also with Monnier, a book on the face of the writer. The publication was prevented in the first place by the expense of color reproduction, and subsequently by the war. But it is interesting to speculate about the kind of book which Freund, at this stage more an academic than a photographer, and Monnier, bookseller and publisher, might have produced. Would its bias have been sociological or commercial, a catalogue to an exhibition of the faces of avant-garde writers held in a bookshop which specialized in their work?

Both these connections, the commercial and the sociological, are latent in Freund's projection; either might have informed the book Monnier was unable to publish. Yet I believe that neither was intended; indeed, that Freund later went to some lengths to deny their potential.

For someone so knowing about photography, Freund assumes an attitude of great naivety in her taking of literary portraits. Her passion for the human face led her to reject the profession of portrait photographer. Commercial portrait photography, Freund claims, demanded a compliance with conventions which necessarily compromised the integrity of the image: "I would have had to bow to [the] taste [of the clientele] and do retouching, which was the reason I had always refused to earn my living as a portrait photographer" (*Photographer* 182). Paradoxically, Freund made this decision in the 1930s, the decade in which the use of the author's photograph to advertise books became common (Richardson 295), as is strikingly illustrated by the exceptions to her decision—her portrait of André Malraux commissioned by the publishers, Gallimard, and her cover photo and reportage of Joyce for *Time*. When, in later years, her literary portraits do enter the marketplace (in book form), Freund claims that their value is itself literary, her assumption being that curiosity about the writer's face is stimulated by reading their work—"the face is a mirror-image of the inner personality; the faces of writers and artists seemed to me particularly interesting, because their creative ideas move us most deeply" (*Fotografien* 117)—this is the very inverse of the promoter's desire that the writer's face will turn the consumer into a reader (see Boscagli and Duffy).

Freund, then, became a photojournalist and kept separate her photographs of writers. Her decision to describe her career as split between reportage (to make a living) and the portrait (a non-commercial pursuit) together with her insistence that the portraits sprang simply from her passion for the face of the creative artist seems to be a way of staking out the integrity of her aesthetic. But this distinction also has a curious parallel in Freund's work as writer, where she keeps her *knowing* texts—whether photographically knowing, her academic work on the history of photography, or politically knowing, her photojournalistic writing—apart from those which describe the literary portraits and consist of autobiographical anecdote and/or literary quotation.

200

By turning to those knowing texts, in particular her thesis on photography, of 1936, and bearing in mind what might be termed the great naivety of Freund's literary portraits, we can begin to understand what is at stake for her photographic practice and aesthetic.

For the Freund of *La Photographie en France au dix-neuvième siècle*, photography is the expression of democratization, and the portrait is key to the history of its development. Her sociological approach, rigorous to the point of dogmatism, precludes the discussion of aesthetics: art is simply the expression of the society that produces it. "In order to reveal these relations between art and society," she writes, "the sociological method must refrain from any judgement relating to aesthetics" (*Photographie en France* 4). But there is a pause in the relentless development and method of the thesis, namely the discussion of the period between the invention of photography and its mass production. This, Freund argues, stating what has become a commonplace of photographic criticism, was the Golden Age of the photographic portrait (*Photographie et Société* 49),[2] its key figure, Nadar. "His work," writes Freund, casting aside methodological caution, "can claim to be art, because like all true art, it is disinterested" (43).

> The fascination of Nadar's first plates is arresting.[3] These faces are watching, almost talking to you, with a degree of life that is gripping. The aesthetic superiority of these images lies in the overwhelming importance of the physiognomy; the position of the body merely serves to draw out the facial expression. Nadar is the first to discover the human face with the camera. The lens plunges into the very intimacy of the physiognomy. What Nadar pursues is not the external beauty of the face: he is attempting above all to draw out the expression that is characteristic of the subject. (42)

Aesthetics here is born of a charged encounter between the viewer and the human face. If Freund herself refrains from "looking" at photographs in the course of her survey, these images will not allow themselves to be passed by, to be packaged theoretically; they demand to be looked at, stopping the viewer. Nadar's aesthetic of photo-portraiture is as compelling to Freund as theorist as it is to Freund, photographer. Her phrase, "aesthetic superiority," is, of course, the moment at which she most clearly moves from sociological, materialist analysis to aesthetics, and enters her forbidden territory. From this transgression and cumulatively in Freund's discussion of Nadar's work there emerges a defense and definition of her own aesthetic of photo-portraiture.

The alignment I am suggesting between Freund and Nadar is also found in the material context of the photographers' work. Nadar's atelier became, Freund describes, the meeting place for the intellectual élite of Paris, where he enjoyed "personal and friendly relations with the subjects of his photographs" (42); that the "relationship between the photographer and his model was as yet untroubled by the question of value" (ibid.) was, for Freund, the most important pre-condition of Nadar's work. Monnier's book shop might seem an unlikely counterpart to the disinterested space of Nadar's atelier, yet "La Maison des amis des livres" as characterized by Monnier and Freund is a place of work and conversation, its ethos, as the name suggests, one of friendship and devotion to literature, not personal gain.

There is, however, a further significant material alignment, this time at the level of photographic practice. Freund argues that the relatively primitive state of photographic technology prevented the commodification of Nadar's portraits, thus ensuring a commercially "untroubled" relationship between photographer and subject, and, in turn, the aesthetic value of the photographs: disinterested, therefore art. But the relationship between Nadar and those he photographed was in another sense and of necessity a close collaboration, since the slow exposure of film at this time demanded that the subject hold their pose. Quoting (with some license) Walter Benjamin's "A Short History of Photography" (1931), Freund notes: "The synthesis of expression which was achieved through the long immobility of the model is the main reason why these images, which are luminous in their modesty, are works of a profound and lasting charm, like that of a well drawn or painted portrait, a charm which recent photographs do not possess" (42-3).

Freund's own use of color might be said to simulate the conditions which she saw as at least in part productive of Nadar's genius: color required longer exposure, the subject's pose had to be held for longer, and this is a point to which she frequently adverts in accounts of her work. But what seems to be more significant for Freund, and also more ambiguous, is her use of a medium which was in its infancy as black and white photography had been for Nadar. While the expense of color reproduction meant that Freund's own practice was almost exclusively non-commercial, the medium more generally was quickly appropriated by and associated with the world of advertising. Color situates her project of the literary portrait on the line between the disinterested and the interested, between art and commerce.

Freund's Nadar allows us to understand her mythmaking, that is the myth of a Golden Age of the photographic and, in particular, the literary portrait, by which she sought to define her own aesthetic and practice. By "mythmaking" I do not mean to suggest that Freund was not genuine. On the contrary, I think that she believed passionately in the aesthetic—the disinterested truth—of her literary portraits, but that others around her, writers *and* publishers, were aware at an earlier stage of the potential commercial interest of these photographs. This mythmaking also explains the absence of experimentation in her work, since her portraits are related to the vision of Nadar, a vision of the wholeness and integrity of the subject. Paradoxically, Freund wanted to capture this integrity in a generation of writers who most called it into question—reinventing the subject as multiple, fragmented, socially constructed, illusory. Freund's vision is, in its intention, equally foreign to the repetitive physiognomic readings which were to consolidate writers as stars on the cover of *Time*; yet it is this style of reading to which her work was and is particularly susceptible—it is also key to the dialogue that ensued between the photographer and Virginia Woolf.

The dialogues that determine images after the photographic act are many and various, particularly, as Brenda Silver's *Virginia Woolf Icon* has shown, when the image is that of Virginia Woolf. I want to conclude by focusing on the initial dialogue between photographer and subject as revealing for its anticipation of many later disputes and contests around representations of Woolf.

Ironically, Freund felt that her photograph of Woolf was the best she had ever taken; it was also her only literary portrait to be contested. The misunderstanding is characteristic of the uncertain status of Freund's photography—at the borderline between private and public, art and commerce, collection and dissemination—but in this particular case it also has to do with absence. Virginia Woolf never saw the photographs. The war prevented Freund from projecting the slides for the Woolfs, and shortly after her return to Paris the photographer—a German Jew who had also been a political activist—was forced into hiding. In 1941, with the help of Ocampo, she fled France for Argentina. In 1941 Woolf committed suicide.

Woolf's diary entry, written the day after her sitting to Freund (24 June 1939), is well known:

> Yes, London broke in fairly vigorously yesterday. Ocampo bringing Giselle Freund & all her apparatus, [. . .] & all the lit. gents & ladies shown on a sheet. [. . .] And the upshot is, a sitting—oh curse this petty vulgar photography-advertising stunt—at 3. No getting out of it, with Okampo on the sofa, & Freund there in the flesh. So my afternoon is gone in the way to me most detestable & upsetting of all. A life sized life coloured animated photograph–however L. is drawn in. (*D5* 220)

Woolf's hyphen emphatically conflates photography and advertising; while the description of the photograph as "life sized life coloured" and even "animated" is expressive of Woolf's anxiety that this image is too monstrously true and independent a replica.

Freund's aesthetic is, in this photo session, displaced from its context of justification and the environment in which it evolved, "La Maison des amis des livres." In Paris the nun-like Monnier is Freund's mentor, her monochrome costume representative of her role of serving the arts.[4] In London, however, the photographer is accompanied by the flamboyant Ocampo. As Woolf notes, suspiciously, Ocampo is "very ripe & rich; with pearls at her ears, as if a large moth had laid clusters of eggs; the colour of an apricot under glass; eyes I think brightened by some cosmetic" (26 Nov 1934: *D4* 263). The dispute which ensues over the photo-session is in part explicable in terms of this displacement (and, in addition, the gendered implications for reading color on faces, whether the color of photographic film or of cosmetics, are clear). But it originates too in the disparity between Freund's idealization of the writer's image and Woolf's sharper understanding of that image as a commodity, and her need to control its dissemination.

If this diary entry constitutes Woolf's caption to the unseen photographs, establishing the taking of them as an act of aggression, Freund counter-captions years later in an attempt to reclaim the truth of her image:

> Decades after having met her, I read her diary and letters. I was very much surprised to read her reactions to the memorable sitting that took place on June 24, 1939 [. . .] and the comments of the editors of her works. [. . .] Her exegetes accuse me of having "violated" Virginia Woolf by making her pose for me. [. . .] The truth is quite another story!
> (*Photographer* 96)

Ocampo had already told Freund of Woolf's reaction, but the publication of the diaries is significant for its public voicing of the accusations. Freund's response, published in a collection of her work, is careful to quote not the writer herself but the editorial apparatus. More than a public reclamation of her image of Woolf, Freund's caption is a defense in the trial of her own aesthetic and professional integrity.

From this failed dialogue a composite Woolf, a montage perhaps, emerges Janus-faced. But the image leaves unresolved the question of the second photo-session. Why, in the late 1960s, did Leonard Woolf allow Freund to take further photographs of himself and, for the first time, of Woolf's diary? The answer lies outside the intimate links between the two photo-sessions, beyond the cultural context of the 1930s to what has changed both in the medium (the rank proliferation of photography), and in the production and consumption of what is imaged here, the writer. In the mid 60s, by the time of Freund's second visit, both photographer and subject needed literary photographs. Publication of the first volumes of his autobiography meant that Leonard Woolf was becoming recognized as a writer in his own right, and this, of all genres, required photographs. Posthumous editions of Virginia's unpublished work, for which Leonard was the literary executor, would also benefit from images.[5] Freund, having just republished her Joyce reportage in book format as *James Joyce in Paris* (another sign of the changing literary and photographic marketplace), was herself looking for supplementary photographs with which to create a similar (unrealized) "tribute" to Woolf.

But even this elucidation, or caption, to the second series of Freund-Woolf photos has another—less pragmatic—face. Freund's 1939 portraits of the Woolfs are the only professional photographs to show the couple together. In the second series too, both are represented: the *memento mori* to Virginia, the photograph of the writing table in which the book stands for the body, partners the vanitas in which Leonard confronts the camera with his loss, while in the background a candle seems to gutter.

Notes

[1] For ease of access, all references to images are to *Gisèle Freund Photographer*.

[2] The study *Photographie et Société* is a revised and updated version of Freund's thesis. The revisions are for the most part stylistic and slight, such that, for ease of reference, I have quoted almost exclusively from this readily available edition, rather than from the thesis itself.

[3] Freund's precision–"first plates"–distinguishes between the two periods into which she divides Nadar's work: his early non-commercial photographs whose aesthetic value she defends, and his later, lesser, commercial photo-portraits (*Photographie et société* 47-8).

[4] "These clothes are my character. Gray is the color of cities and forms. It corresponds with activity and energy. Blue is the symbol of peace, and white of the mind's pure state of grace—and I shall always wear them" (Buchner 17).

[5] The photograph of Woolf's writing table was subsequently emulated in the cluttered work surfaces of the cover illustrations to the five volume Penguin *Diary of Virginia Woolf*.

Works cited

de Beauvoir, Simone. Introduction to Gisèle Freund, *James Joyce in Paris: His Final Years*. New York: Harcourt Brace, 1965. vii-ix.

Boscagli, Maurizia and Enda Duffy. "Joyce's Face." *Marketing Modernisms: Self-Promotion, Canonization, Rereading*. Eds. Kevin J. H. Dettmar and Stephen Watt. Ann Arbor: University of Michigan Press, 1996. 133-59.

Buchner, Carl H. "Adrienne Monnier. Eine Farbenlehre." In *Gisèle Freund, Gesichter der Sprache: Schriftsteller um Adrienne Monnier*. Hannover: Sprengel Museum, 1996. 15-29.

Freund, Gisèle. *La Photographie en France au dix-neuvième siècle. Essai de sociologie et d'esthétique*. Paris: La Maison des amis des livres / A. Monnier, 1936.

——. *Photographie et Société*. Paris: Seuil, 1974.

——. *Gisèle Freund Fotografien 1932-1977*. Cologne: Rheinland-Verlag, 1977.

——. *Gisèle Freund, Photographer*. Trans. J. Shepley. New York: Harry N. Abrams, 1985.

——. *Gisèle Freund. Die Frau mit der Kamera*. Munich: Schirmer Mosel, 1992.

Freund, Gisèle & Rauda Jamis. *Gisèle Freund Portrait: Entretiens avec Rauda Jamis*. Paris: des femmes, 1991.

Monnier, Adrienne. "In the Land of Faces". *Verve*. Vol. 2: Nos. 5 and 6. July-Oct 1939: 119.

Ray, Man. Letter of 1 June 1966. Unpublished. Monk's House Papers: University of Sussex Library.

Richardson, Elizabeth P. *A Bloomsbury Iconography*. Winchester: St Paul's Bibliographies, 1989.

Silver, Brenda. *Virginia Woolf Icon*. Chicago: University of Chicago Press, 1999.
Sontag, Susan. *On Photography*. London: Penguin, 1977.
Woolf, Virginia. *The Diary of Virginia Woolf*. Ed. Anne Olivier Bell, 5 vols. London: Penguin, 1987.

All translations are, unless otherwise noted, my own.

Maggie Humm
Matrixial Memories in Virginia Woolf's Photographs

"Your films came last night [...] Two beautiful packets of superfine celluloid. Films! A thousand thanks (as the French say) my dear Herbert for this munificent gift—I shall devote not a few to your remarkable face"
Virginia Woolf, age 15, letter to her brother Thoby, 1897.

From the age of fifteen, photographs framed Woolf's world. Virginia Woolf wrote about photography in her diaries, letters and essays, and used photographic terms descriptively in her fiction. Before her marriage, and then together with Leonard, Woolf took, developed and preserved photographs in albums.[1] Photography was a continuous part of the Woolfs' lives even if their photographic albums do not tell a coherent life story. The Frederick Koch collection in Harvard Theatre Library houses over one thousand photographs. Although Woolf states in her letters that "I keep a family album" (*L6* 169) in the singular, and many entries in the albums are in her hand, it is impossible to establish, either from their several diaries and autobiographies, or from internal evidence in the albums, who "authored" each album. The albums are formally constructed with many sequential and paired matching photographs of friends sitting in armchairs, in close up or medium shot, a striking example of the issue of finding or making "significant form" that so intrigued Bloomsbury art critics. In many ways Woolf's album making mirrors her aesthetics. In Woolf's fiction a visual image is frequently more truth telling than a linear narrative. The albums likewise are composed in visual patterns rather than chronologically. The albums are crucial artefacts, encapsulating and emblematising Woolf's responses to the arts and to her life and friendships.

Photographs preserve relationships. Any album's sequencing of photographs creates meaning out of random events. In this respect albums are memories constructed in the present but, unlike memories, photographs arranged in albums have a connectedness independent from present time. Album photographs are their own visual story. The representation of an isolated moment in time means nothing. Meaning depends on how we connect moments. As Henri Bergson the philosopher argues, a memory only becomes "actual" by "borrowing the body of some perception into which it slips"(Bergson 67). The principles of selection, montage and tableaux, are the skeleton of a story, a way of making aesthetic order out of our worlds, which becomes an aesthetic narrative of that world. Psychoanalytically speaking, albums are often a testimony to our unconscious pasts rather than the pasts we consciously choose to remember. In a classic and often cited essay "A Short History of Photography," Walter Benjamin argues that photography, "makes aware for the first time the optical unconscious"(Benjamin 5). Similarly the Monk's House albums are Woolf's unconscious testimony to her childhood past.

Memories or the "presence without representation," Jean-Francois Lyotard calls "the stranger in the house" (Lyotard 16). Where, for Freud, the stranger is the scene of seduction perpetrated on the child, to Lyotard the stranger represents a more general individual incapacity to "represent and bind a certain something," something which "can introduce itself there without being introduced, and would exceed its powers" (17). For me, it is the 1892 photograph of Woolf's seated mother and father with Woolf in the background mounted as a significant frontispiece in Monk's House album 3 which "exceeds its powers" and shapes Woolf's albums. It is precisely for these reasons, I feel, that the albums are so unusually anti-chronological since the albums focus on the unrepresentable, on the immemorial, as Lyotard argues, "the immemorial is always 'present'" (20).

Woolf's male artistic contemporaries thought photographs visually undistinguished. Clive Bell dismissed photographs because "we expect a work of plastic art to have more in common with a piece of music than a coloured photograph" (Bell 349). Indeed Simon Watney argues that, throughout this period, photography "served in England to define negatively what art was not" (Watney 20). Woolf herself frequently equates the "snapshot" with a limited eye. Writing to Vanessa Bell in Cassis, Woolf worries "What am I to say about you?" (Woolf eventually decided to refer to Bell and Fry's affair as "friendship"). "It's rather as if you had to paint a portrait using dozens of snapshots in the paint" (*L6* 285). Yet Woolf, as a photographer skilfully transformed friends and moments into artful tableaux and she was surrounded by female friends and family who were also energetic photographers. Lady Ottoline Morrell's photographs "come out so much better than the professionals"; Vita Sackville-West and Dora Carrington all exchanged photographs with Virginia (*L3* 46). Julian Bell's girlfriend Lettice Ramsey ran a professional photography agency, Ramsey and Muspratt.

The essence of photographs lies in the appeal of the experience or the event portrayed to a viewer. Woolf, like her sister and her great aunt the photographer Julia Margaret Cameron, frequently invited friends to share her reflections. The letters and diaries describe a constant exchange of photographs, in which photographs become a meeting-place, a conversation, *aide-mémoires*, and sometimes mechanisms of survival and enticement. At age 16, photographs were "the best present I can think of" (*L*1 497). Woolf invited friends to share their lives with her through photographs. She liked "very much" to have baby photographs—"he's an interesting little boy" [Katherine Arnold-Forster's son Mark] (*L*2 495). After their deaths, photographs of friends were important memento mori. After the death of Jacques Raverat, the French painter, in 1924, Woolf needed photographs to continue her mental conversations. From Gwen Raverat, Woolf desperately wanted "a snapshot or any photograph of him? I go on making things up to tell him" (*L*3 172).

Woolf's albums are more enduringly invitational. Monk's House 5 (45-6) contains one of the Woolf's favourite "comfy chair" paired sequences of Dorothy Bussy sitting framed by the sharply angled attic roof, together with her daughter Janie. Magnification revealed that Dorothy was laughing at the very album in which the Bussy's would themselves appear. It is as if the album's viewers share the album's narrative construction. Woolf's frequent use of invitational or rhetorical questions in her fiction is matched here by the albums' appeal to an active spectator. The album is being spectated in the act of memorializing, as if the Bussy's see themselves through the photographic gaze of another. Psychoanalytically speaking, one gains a sense of identity through recognition by another.

Perhaps for this reason Woolf believed that photographs could help her to survive those identity destroying moments of her own life—her incoherent illnesses. For example, writing to Margaret Llewelyn Davies in 1915, Woolf "wanted to say that all through that terrible time" [a week's attack of apparent insanity] "I thought of you, and wanted to look at a picture of you, but was afraid to ask!" (*L*2 60). Mutual image making would also create relationships. Woolf used photographs to entice Vita Sackville-West. Writing to "Mrs Nicolson" in 1923, Woolf asked Vita to visit in order "to look at my great aunt's photographs of Tennyson and other people" (*L*3 4). In short, photographs may be "only an eye" but one that enabled Woolf to see more clearly.

Still, for all her enthusiasm as an amateur photographer, in her letters Woolf consistently condemns professional photography. Cecil Beaton ["I was so furious at being in Beaton's Book—I was never asked—never sat—never saw the horrid worm"] chose baroque settings far removed from Woolf's seriality (*L*5 238). Even being photographed by a woman photographer, Giséle Freund, seemed to Woolf like "being hoisted about on top of a stick for everyone to stare at," yet Woolf happily changed her clothing for Freund as this composite reveals (*L*6 351).

The Woolfs' skilful intent is not constrained by the limitations of camera technology which it might be appropriate to consider. Until the acquisition, "with violent impetuosity," of a Zeiss camera costing £20 (or $600 at current prices) in July 1931, from the size of the album prints the

Woolfs probably relied on the popular 3A vest pocket Kodak which succeeded Virginia's Frena (*L4* 361). The inexpensive, light camera was particularly popular with women. The *Photographic News* reported, in September 1905, that "thousands of Birmingham girls are scattered about the holiday resorts of Britain this month, and a very large percentage of them are armed with cameras" (Coe and Gates 28). The modernity of the albums is striking and might owe much to Woolf's knowledge of modernism including Cézanne's painting series and Eisenstein and German cinema. The Woolfs' use of composite images, the recognition that the process of construction is part of the content of a constructed piece, synchronizes with other modernist developments in the 1920s and 1930s. Woolf's quadruple portraits of Ethel Smyth (Monk's House 3, 12) are a sequential series of 4 by 3 photographs probably taken with a 3A Vest Pocket Kodak from the size of the prints, in which overlapping eye lines and seated positions carry an emotional charge. The albums also synchronize with cinema's new range of effects in the 1920s and 1930s.

Virginia's first diary describes her 1915 birthday treat "at a Picture Palace" as well as the attraction of regular movie going over political meetings. "I went to my Picture Palace, and L. to his Fabians; and he thought, on the whole, that his mind and spirit and body would have profited more by the pictures than by the Webbs" (*D1* 28). The Woolfs acknowledged the importance of cinema by publishing in the Hogarth Press a film text—Eric White's *Parnassus to Let: An Essay About Rhythm in Film* (1928). As Lyotard claims, cinematography is the prime condition of all narration. Woolf's own writings about cinema, more than most, have a keen-eyed modernist vision. "The Cinema, Movies and Reality," first published in *Arts* in New York in 1926, explores new relationships between movement and repetition, emotions and spatial organizations (Humm 1997). Similarly the albums are not chronologically catalogued. The Woolfs do not construct ideal versions of their lives and friendships and both husband and wife are equally visible. There is no absent implied male photographer as in most albums since many photographs are evidently taken by Virginia.

The Woolfs photograph each other in similar poses in similar comfy chairs and similarly photograph friends in comfy chairs in multiple shots taken on different days, sometimes in different years, but grouped together in the album. Some album pages have a real gravitas and impact. For example, a powerful sequence are the photographs of William Plomer, Vita Nicolson [Sackville-West] and Charles Siepmann united across time by the chair motif (31). Of course Julia Margaret Cameron carefully posed sitters and utilised chiaroscuro, the play of light and shadow. Yet Woolf's devotion to sequential and associative poses differs from Cameron's singular portraits. In Lacanian terms, Woolf's continual photographic repetitions would suggest the "return" of a visual event which took place outside her contemporary frames. As Lacan suggests "the real is that which always comes back to the same place" (Lacan 42). Crucially Leslie Stephen explicitly memorializes the exact photograph which Virginia avidly highlights in the opening of Monk's House Album 3. "When I look at certain little photographs—at one in which I am reading by her side at St. Ives with Virginia [...] I see as with my bodily eyes the love, the holy and tender love" (Stephen 58). It is the visual language of this particular photograph, what we might call its trauma fragments, which determines Woolf's own photographic constructions. There are similar quiet connections and discontinuities between the sisters' albums. Both Vanessa and Virginia are drawn to the maternal. Pregnant, Vanessa fantasizes to Virginia that "I shall see you every day and gaze at the most beautiful of Aunt Julia's photographs [that of their mother] incessantly" (Marler 67). Both shared a Bloomsbury party visit to a film of a caesarean operation. "Really it is quite the oddest entertainment I've ever been to [. . .] Leonard felt very ill" (361-2).

Whereas the Monk's House albums, in some respects, reveal Woolf to be an enthusiastic modernist, in other respects they are too repetitious, too obsessive to be catalogued simply as modernist. The page compositions and repeated use of particular objects—the armchairs and vertical flowers and bookcases—seem shaped as much by the psychic as by the formally aesthetic. All photographs comprise a language and Woolf's language was maternal. "She has haunted me" (*L3* 374). Woolf wrote "through" the maternal. "Here I am experimenting with the parent of all pens—the black J, *the* pen, as I used to think it, along with other objects, as a child, because mother used it" (*D1* 208). Woolf frequently said about her mother "It is a psychological mystery why she should be: how a child could know about her; except that she has always haunted me" (*L3* 383). Julia Stephen's early death meant that, to Woolf, she became the fantasmatic mother, that is a mother who can exist only as an image, who can be seen or mirrored only in identifications and who might incite the visual imagination (of a photographer) into hallucinatory significations (Jacobus iii). In "Moments of Being" Woolf describes how it was her mother's death, which "made me suddenly develop perception"(103).

This creation of self-identity through maternal memories is the key theme of the work of Bracha Lichtenberg-Ettinger. In *The Matrixial Gaze* and her many essays in *Differences* and elsewhere, Lichtenberg-Ettinger challenges Freud's specular account of Oedipal identity in favor of a matrixial source of identity. The matrixial corresponds, she suggests, to a new feminine symbolic discourse of the co-existence of the maternal "I" and infant "Not-I." Artists, Lichtenberg-Ettinger claims, inscribe "traces of subjectivity" in cultural objects and by analyzing these "inscriptions" it might be possible, she hopes, to "elaborate traces of an-other Real" (Lichtenberg-Ettinger 196). The albums are matrixial encounters giving meaning "to a real which might otherwise pass by unthinkable, unnoticed and unrecognized" (Lichtenberg-Ettinger 45). Similarly in Barthes's *Camera Lucida,* memory and the mother are intimate in photography, and, as Bergson suggests, every perception is already memory. "There comes a moment when the recollection thus brought down is capable of blending so well with the present perception that we cannot say where perception ends or where memory begins" (Bergson 106).

It could be argued that the Woolfs' favorite sequences are a form of the matrixial, in a chain of perceptions. As I have described, Monk's House 3 opens with an enlarged 6 x $7^{1/2}$ photograph of Julia Stephen immediately followed by the photograph of Julia, Leslie Stephen and Virginia at St. Ives in 1892. The treasured 2 x $2^{2/8}$ photograph, protectively mounted on buff card before insertion in the album, is made larger by the 4 x 2 card. Monk's House 3 also contains the largest number of "comfy chair" photographs (40).

The details, or punctum, of this childhood photograph appear again and again in the Woolfs' photo sequences. The synchronic matching of the St. Ives and Monk's House furniture recalls Lichtenberg-Ettinger's idea that the language of the matrixial is a symbolization of the maternal, childhood home. That is, Woolf constantly repeats or mirrors this matrixial transitional object in photo sequences focusing attention on chairs, bookcases and flowers as well as on the face of each sitter. In a chapter "The Dead Mother" (which includes depressed and absent mothers) in *On Private Madness,* André Green suggests that the "mirror identification" with the mother "is almost obligatory" (Green 159). The child is always "recathecting the traces of the trauma" of loss in "artistic creations" (151). Green argues that "the fantasy of the primal scene is of capital importance" because "the subject will be confronted with memory traces in relation to the dead mother" (159). The 1892 photograph of Virginia with her parents at St Ives is like a primal scene as if Virginia and Vanessa collude, as Green suggests, in "erotic and intense destabilization of the primal scene to the advantage of intense intellectual activity" (160).

Obviously it is impossible to say how conscious Woolf was of any of these themes but all photographs are retrospective memories. It is hardly surprising that all of Woolf's work is obsessed with visual memories. As Lyotard suggests "the time of writing does not pass. Every writing" [and we could include art] "worthy of its name wrestles with the Angel and, at best, comes out limping" (Lyotard 34). Julia Stephen was Woolf's Angel in the house and becomes her "stranger in the house" in the album photographs. Woolf continually wrestled with a chain of reflecting memories in photographs which mirror a familial past. The photographs connected Woolf to the past, particularly to the matrixial. The photographs' repeated sequences, spatially organizing sitter, chair and flowers, are momentary memories of the past. Her sister's paintings taught Woolf that representations can resist death, and like Vanessa's paintings, Woolf's albums are a palimpsest. "This strange painters world, in which mortality does not enter and psychology is held at bay"(Woolf 'Vanessa Bell' 173).

Notes
[1] Essays on Woolf and photography include, among others, Duffy and Davis "Demythologizing Facts and Photographs in *Three Guineas*," Wussow "Virginia Woolf and the Problematic Nature of the Photographic Image" and "Travesties of Excellence," Flesher, "Picturing the Truth in Fiction," Gualtieri "Three Guineas and the Photograph," Knowles "A Community of Women Looking at Men," Schaffer, "Posing Orlando." Only Neverow "Thinking Back Through Our Mothers" and Gillespie's richly detailed "'Her Kodak Pointed at His Head': Virginia Woolf and Photography" to date, describe Woolf's photo albums but both focus on Woolf's utilisation of photographic referents in her writing.

Works Cited
Bell, Clive. *Art*. London: Chatto & Windus, 1914.

Benjamin, Walter "A Short History of Photography." *Screen* 13:1 (1972) 5-26.

Bergson, Henri. *Matter and Memory*. New York: Zone Books, 1991.

Coe, Brian and Paul Gates. *The Snapshot Photograph*. London: Ash and Grant, 1977.

Duffy, Julia and Lloyd Davis. "Demythologizing Facts and Photographs in *Three Guineas*" in *Photo-Textualities: Reading Photographs and Literature* ed. M. Bryant. Newark: University of Delaware Press, 1995.

Flesher, Erika. "Picturing the Truth in Fiction: Revisionary Biography and the Illustrative Portraits for Orlando" in V*irginia Woolf and the Arts: Selected Papers from the Sixth Annual Conference on Virginia Woolf* eds. D. F. Gillespie and L. Hankins. New York: Pace U P, 1997.

Gillespie, Diane F. "'Her Kodak Pointed at His Head': Virginia Woolf and Photography" in *The Multiple Muses of Virginia Woolf* ed. D. F. Gillespie. Columbia: U of Missouri P, 1993.

Green, André. *On Private Madness*. Madison, CT: International Universities, 1983.

Gualtieri, Elena. "*Three Guineas* and the Photograph: The Art of Propaganda," in *Women Writers of the 1930s* ed. M. Joannou. Edinburgh: Edinburgh U P, 1999, 165-78.

Humm, Maggie. *Feminism and Film*. Edinburgh: Edinburg U P, 1997.

Jacobus, Mary. *First Things: The Maternal Imaginary in Literature, Art and Psychoanalysis*. London: Routledge, 1995.

Knowles, Nancy. "A Community of Women: The Photographs in Virginia Woolf's *Three Guineas*" in *Virginia Woolf and Communities: Selected Papers from the Eighth Annual Conference on Virginia Woolf* eds. J. McVicker and L. Davis. New York: Pace U P, 1999, 91-6.

Lacan, Jacques. *The Four Fundamental Concepts of Psychoanalysis*. Ed. J. A. Miller. Trans. Alan Sheridan. New York: Norton, 1978.

Lichtenberg-Ettinger, Bracha. "Matrix and Metramorphosis." *Differences* 4:3 (1992) 176-208.

Lyotard, Jean-Francois. *Heidegger and "the Jews"*. Trans. A. Michel and M. S. Roberts. Minneapolis: U of Minnesota P, 1990.

Marler, Regina. Ed. *Selected Letters of Vanessa Bell*. London: Bloomsbury, 1993.

Neverow, Vara. "Thinking Back Through Our Mothers, Thinking in Common: Virginia Woolf's Photographic Imagination and the Community of Narrators in *Jacob's Room, A Room of One's Own*, and *Three Guineas*" in *Virginia Woolf and Communities: Selected Papers From the Eighth Annual Conference on Virginia Woolf* eds. J. McVicker and L. Davis. New York: Pace U P, 1999, 65-87.

Schaffer, Talia. "Posing Orlando," *Genders*, XIX, 1994, 26-63

Stephen, Leslie. *Mausoleum Book*. Oxford: Clarendon Press, 1977.

Watney, Simon. *English Post-Impressionism*. London: Studio Vista, 1980.

White, Eric. *Parnassus to Let: An Essay About Rhythm in Film*. London: Hogarth Press, 1928.

Woolf, Virginia. *The Diary of Virginia Woolf*. 5 vols. Ed. Anne Olivier Bell and Andrew McNeillie. New York: Harcourt Brace Jovanovich, 1977-1984.

——. *The Letters of Virginia Woolf*. 6 vols. Ed. Nigel Nicolson and Joanne Trautmann. New York: Harcourt Brace Jovanovich, 1976.

——. *Moments of Being: Unpublished Autobiographical Writings*. Ed. Jeanne Schulkind. New York: Harcourt Brace Jovanovich, 1976.

——. "Vanessa Bell." *The Bloomsbury Group*. Ed. S. P. Rosenbaum. London: Croom Helm, 1975.

Wussow, Helen. "Virginia Woolf and the Problematic Nature of the Photographic Image." *Twentieth Century Literature*, XLIL, 1994. 1-14.

——. "Traversties of Excellence: Julia Margaret Cameron, Lytton Strachey, Virginia Woolf, and the Photographic Image" in *Virginia Woolf and The Arts: Selected Papers from the Sixth Annual Conference on Virginia Woolf* eds. D. F. Gillespie and L. Hankins. New York: Pace U P, 1997. 48-56.

Mark Wollaeger
Woolf, Picture Postcards, Modernity

Virginia Woolf's imagination was marked by picture postcards. More specifically, her representation of the exotic other betrays the mediation of popular ethnography in the form of colonial postcards and imperial exhibitions. Some history will help introduce a discussion of Woolf's engagement with postcards as well as a brief reading of *The Voyage Out*.

Recognizable now as a symptom and bearer of modernity and modernism, at the turn of the twentieth century the picture postcard began as an amusing novelty and soon became an outright craze. First used in Great Britain in the 1890s, within a decade picture postcards had become highly prized objects for English collectors and the general public (Staff 56). An astonishing range of cards suffused all levels of culture: images of new technology, photos of actresses, Boer War battle commemorations, comic cards, and popular crazes from ping-pong to roller skating. Postcards soon provided the state, along with political groups of various stripes, with a new agent of propaganda, and topical postcards entered into debates about suffrage, tariff reform, and imperial policy. The advertising industry capitalized on the new form so effectively that by 1903 a man sending a South African postcard of an African woman washing a young child with the caption "O dirty boy!" to his sister on the Isle of Wight suggested it would be "a very good adv. for Pears Soap / you ought to send it to the firm."[1] Such postcards evince not only a deep link between advertising and postcards but also the degree to which both, spreading along paths cut by empire and the merchant marines, were mediating English views of the world.

The picture postcard spread so quickly owing in part to changes in British and international postal regulations. In 1899 England permitted the standard-sized card already used in Europe to circulate freely, and a special postal rate of one halfpenny for domestic delivery encouraged Edwardians to send postcards on the slightest pretext. "During the quarter of a century that preceded the Great War in 1914," according to one historian of the postcard, "it would have been hard to find anyone who did not buy postcards from genuine pleasure. People preserved them carefully in their albums, or they posted them to their friends or relations, in the expectation of receiving others in return" (Carline xv). Royalty was more cautious yet not immune: Queen Victoria asked a relative to compile an album for her.

Not everyone in England was pleased. The picture postcard soon became as inescapable as the cell phone is today, though not quite so annoying. "At the height of the industry's boom, postcards were virtually everywhere in the world"; in 1909 over 800 million were posted in Great Britain alone (Woody 43). As in contemporary fears about consumerism, women in particular were figured as both victims and carriers of a new cultural disease (Felski 66). An article in the *Standard* in 1899 observed drily that "The illustrated postcard craze, like the influenza, has spread to these islands from the Continent, where it has been raging with considerable severity. Sporadic cases have occurred in Britain. Young ladies who have escaped the philatelic infection . . . have been known to fill albums with missives of this kind from friends abroad" (qtd. in Staff 60). Woolf herself evidently caught the bug: "I was much amused by your post card of the two novelists," she wrote to Stephen Spender, "and have stuck it in my album" (*L6* 74). In 1903 the *Glasgow Evening News* worried that "In ten years Europe will be buried beneath picture postcards" (qtd. in Carline xv). Evidently Germany was to blame: "The traveling Teuton seems to regard it as a solemn duty to distribute [picture postcards] from each stage of his journey, as if he were a runner in a paper chase" (Staff 60). Pundits were right to single out Germany, for it was there that new methods for the mass reproduction of color photographic images made the modern picture postcard possible. The end of the craze was a more cosmopolitan affair: the decision of popular newspapers and magazines after 1910 to start publishing photographs gave commercial photographers, who previously relied chiefly on postcards, a new outlet for their work, the spread of the inexpensive Kodak Brownie, first produced in 1900 in America, increasingly made picture postcards less necessary, and World War I made the production of high quality cards unfeasible (Woody 14-21).

To a degree the postcard fad merely intensified processes of modernization already put in play by the emergence of print culture and the birth of the British postal service. But three new developments distinguish English epistolary culture at the turn of the twentieth century: the growing dominance of the image, the global circulation of information, and the increasingly formative influence of Empire. First, the picture postcard fused word and image, subordinating the former to the latter in such a way that Ezra Pound's contemporaneous definition of the "image" as "an intellectual and emotional complex in an instant of time" that produces "a sense of freedom from time limits and space limits" could apply just as well to England's newest mass cultural form (Pound 4). Second, picture postcards began to circumnavigate the globe along information routes pioneered by British maritime trade and rendered functional by the wide-spread adoption of the English postal system. An increasingly efficient system for mass distribution of mail in the eighteenth century had the effect of "abstracting distance into pure exchange" (Christensen 188); the circulation of colonial postcards in the twentieth century began to shrink not just England but the entire world. It is not surprising, then—and this is my third point—that many domestic English postcards disseminated complementary views of empire: cards showing scenes of cricket, for instance, betokened the expanding sphere of a sport used to train colonials how to be English, and cards featuring Kew Gardens evidenced the gravitational pull of a global collection of plants and seeds gathered from outposts of empire.

The pump driving colonial postcards through the world's far-flung circulatory system was the modern problem of authenticity. The thrill of the postcard, Susan Stewart has argued, derives from a hunger for a sense of authenticity attached to location (133-38). An unprecedentedly public form of communication, postcards paradoxically functioned as a guarantor of the authentically personal at a time when, as Michael North has recently demonstrated, people had become highly self-conscious about the inevitable mediation of experience (29). "Here I am," the postcard declares to the recipient, thus bringing into being the "I" as both familiar sender and exotic locale, the two temporarily equated through the metaphor of location. Insofar as the postcard's uncanny subject assumes a dual relation to the pictured site, one that restages (in a less threatening register) the precarious dynamics of colonial exchange, the colonial postcard contributes to the formation of imperial subjects: the tourist assumes the subject position of the colonizer by appropriating the exotic site and returning it to the metropole;

yet the familiar subject, with its articulation propped on the authenticity of "being there," also appears to have "gone native" by merging with the space of the exotic, a transformation typically triggered within the recipient as well, who gazes at the image as if through the sender's eyes.

By the turn of the century, English tourists were sending home many millions of colonial postcards. Far from mere exotic throwaways, these widely-collected cards contributed to imperial stereotyping by disseminating primitivist images of indigenous peoples during the most jingoistic period of England's global dominance. Images of the native other were also imprinted onto the English imagination by domestic postcards printed for imperial exhibitions. In fact, the first picture postcards apparently emanated from the Paris Exhibition of 1889, and many more were produced in England for such large-scale exhibitions as London's Imperial International Exhibition in 1909 and the British Empire Exhibition at Wembley in 1924. Woolf may well have attended the 1909 Exhibition, and she published an article about the 1924 Exhibition entitled "Thunder at Wembley" (*E3* 410-14). Beginning with Paris, reconstructed native villages—in effect human showcases—became more prominent than ever before (Greenhalgh 82), and many domestic postcards show not only villages but also English spectators lined up for a peek at "real natives." Such postcards "complemented efforts of exposition sponsors in England and France to construct national identities that would embrace specific national colonial projects as a central component of modernity" (Rydell 54). In this context, postcard collections can be said to epitomize the effort of imperial exhibitions to assemble a complete image of the emerging global system even as individual cards herald the fragmentation of the totality that such exhibitions sought to represent.

Viewed from the twenty-first century, then, the picture postcard begins to look like an emerging modernist form—displacing the formal conventions of epistolary style with now familiar vacation shorthand; eschewing the totalizing expansiveness of Victorian narrative in favor of fragmentary utterances and the primacy of the image; subordinating authorship to mechanical reproduction; and seeking authenticity beyond the artifice of civilization. Among contemporary commentators, James Douglas captured the peculiar modernity of postcards best in 1907 when he imagined thirtieth-century archeologists fastening on "the Picture Postcard as the best guide to the spirit of the Edwardian era": "Every pimple on the earth's skin has been photographed, and wherever the human eye roves or roams it detects the self-conscious air of the reproduced" (qtd. in Staff, 79). That last phrase, the "self-conscious air of the reproduced," nicely evokes a range of experiences of modernity, from Walter Benjamin's ambivalent eulogy for the auratic in an age of mechanical reproduction to the growing desire in late imperial romance for the authentic in the guise of the exotic.

Woolf undoubtedly was attuned to the increasingly inescapable influence of postcards. Like everyone else, she sent picture postcards, requested them from others, and complained about them as well, sometimes because she didn't receive enough from friends abroad, sometimes because she did and would have preferred a letter (*L2* 452, *L6* 244). Woolf mocked the older generation for their belief that postcards were killing the art of letter-writing, believing instead that the penny post was making letter-writing less studied and more sincere—which is to say more modern (*E2* 182). In 1930 Woolf even wrote a caption for a National Portrait Gallery postcard of George Eliot (Smith 8). *The Waves* (1931), published well after the craze for postcards subsided, registers their diminished visibility in Neville's thoughts about Percival: "He will forget me. . . . I shall send him poems and he will perhaps reply with a picture postcard" (*TW* 60). Bittersweet tokens of neglect, post-cards here seem to speak of their own evanescence.

However evanescent, postcards nevertheless helped Woolf fill in the blank spots on the map. To a friend in 1925 she wrote: "Send me a picture post-card so that I may imagine your house" (*L3* 188). In *Jacob's Room* (1922) Fanny Elmer also turns to postcards to compensate for absence: her stylized "idea of Jacob" while he is abroad for "two months" is "[s]ustained entirely upon picture post cards" (*JR* 170). But such ephemera are not always sufficient, as Woolf acknowledged while struggling with her biography of Roger Fry: "how can one make a life," she wrote to Vita, "out of Six cardboard boxes full of tailor's bills love letters and old picture postcards" (*L6* 373). How indeed? The problem of making a life out of postcards guides my closing discussion of *The Voyage Out*.

Written during the so-called golden age of the picture postcard, *The Voyage Out* follows Rachel Vinrace up the Amazon in search of a place "where none but natives had ever trod" (*VO* 237). What she discovers instead is the difficulty of disentangling herself from a characteristically modern form of expression. In the opening pages, Helen and Ridley jostle their way through London's narrow streets toward a ship bound for South America, and Ridley momentarily becomes "entangled . . . with a man selling picture postcards" (*VO* 11). When Rachel later attempts to recall London life while strolling through the imaginary town of Santa Marina, she begins by acknowledging the kind of entanglement Ridley tries to leave behind: "First there are men selling picture postcards" (*VO* 99). Only recently the process of globalization has made necessary the coinage "globality" to describe the economic integration of a wholly interconnected world; though the process was far less advanced in the early twentieth century, *The Voyage Out* registers an impression of impending globality by linking the crowded banks of the Thames to the exotic streets of Santa Marina through the ubiquity of the picture postcard: Ridley's literal entanglement becomes Rachel's imagined one, making the realization of Richard Dalloway's goal of global consolidation under the Union Jack—"Unity of aim, of dominion, of progress" (*VO* 64)—seem all the more imminent. Given, then, that Woolf never set foot in South America, it is not surprising that her description of village women up the Amazon is informed by the popular ethnography of colonial postcards and imperial exhibitions, nor is it surprising that the mossy path running alongside the river begins to resemble "a drive in an English forest" (*VO* 270).

Colonial postcards were instrumental, I have already suggested, to the modern construction of race, and *The Voyage Out* turns, for the first and last time in Woolf's career, on a cross-racial encounter. Sending Rachel deep into the jungle, Woolf chooses to bring her face to face not with a mirror image of her own forbidden desires, as in most imperial romances, but with an image of what *others* desire *for her* in a tableau of domesticated women. In what amounts to a scene of exhibition, the women Rachel encounters in the long descriptive passage in chapter 21 seem to exist in an endlessly repeated moment of nursing, weaving, and staring (*VO* 284-85). Related images of women dominate colonial postcards, and they resonate, by virtue of being split between the erotic and the domestic, with the conflicted energies underlying Rachel's response to Woolf's human showcase up the Amazon. A British East African card captioned "A Kikuyu Family," for instance, shows three adults and seven children casually grouped before a hut, but who is to say what brought them together in the frame? The ethnographic fascination with native mothers and families in such cards is driven by a cultural need to ease anxieties in a time when falling birthrates were thought to presage the decline of English power. Erotic postcards display their power to frame even more vividly by locking indigenous women into seductive poses. While some cards dispensed with an aesthetic or ethnographic alibi, a complex 1904 card from Natal (fig. 1) condenses the erotic-domestic split into a single image. The subordination of the body to an abstract design is heightened and complicated by the banjo, which both completes the triangular motif established by her right arm and operates, owing to its incorporation into minstrel shows, as a signifier of race. Virtually abstracted, she is a harbinger of the primitivism that would sweep across Europe in the next decade. Although her pose is dictated as much by the photographer's desire to have her breast lifted toward the camera as by the formal requirements of symmetry, the suggestiveness that would have been activated by any sexual innuendo in the message is mitigated here by the banality of the inscription—"I am feeling better again. Will write next week." Without fully erasing the erotic investment in the exotic other that motivated the production of the card, then, the image also takes on a clinical quality owing to a kind of aesthetic domestication, an effect consonant with the emergence of museum culture and reinforced by the ethnographic perspective solicited by the printed caption, "A native Musician."

A cognate tension between the erotic and the domestic finds narrative expression in *The Voyage Out* in the tightly linked events that lead to Rachel's encounter with the women "squatting on the ground in triangular shapes" (*VO* 284): in rapid succession she and Terence kiss in the jungle and find themselves engaged; Helen pulls Rachel to the ground in an ambigu-

Eros and Abstraction: "A Native Musician" (fig. 1)
Black and white postcard, bearing Natal stamp, postmarked June 24, 1904; photographer and printer unknown. The inscription reads: "I am feeling better again. Will write next week."

ously erotic embrace; the expedition enters the village. The anarchic erotic energies of Woolf's novel clearly exceed, as many have noted, a heterosexual paradigm, thus making the tension between untrammeled desire and domesticity all the more fraught: when Rachel sees a vision of her possible future in the native women—"So it would go on for ever and ever, she said, those women sitting under the trees, the trees and the river" (*VO* 285)—her sudden despondency is the first sign of her impending death.

Woolf's scene of exhibition is complicated by one more link to postcard images. In *Melymbrosia* the women look back "without hostility" (*MEL* 211); in revision Woolf decided to make the women look back "not without hostility" (*VO* 285, emphasis added). This change invokes a complex dynamic between photographers and their human subjects that tends to get lost in abstract treatments of "the gaze" as a mode of domination,[2] for in many postcards indigenous women assert their limited agency with a counter-stare that is indeed not without hostility, just as many "natives" in exhibition villages fought against inhumane living conditions and in their native language derided unwitting spectators (Rydell 51). The flicker of subjectivity in Woolf's native women, whose "eyes . . . never left their faces," makes the English feel like "tight-coated soldiers" (*VO* 285) and recalls the defiantly returned stare in many colonial postcards. Situating Woolf's first novel and colonial postcards as mutually illuminating texts in the Edwardian culture of exhibition throws into relief the uniqueness of this cross-racial encounter: typically unable to imagine non-white subjectivity, Woolf momentarily sees beyond her limitations into a potentially equivalent center of self that resents Rachel's stare.

To close, a glance at Rachel's death through the cultural optic of the picture postcard: while postcard sellers in Woolf's novel have not yet set up shop in the heart of darkness, one could say that by populating the blank spots in her own private South America with postcard images, Woolf infects Rachel with a fatal strain of the cultural disease the *Standard* saw spreading across the globe. Through Rachel, that is, Woolf inoculates herself against the emblems of modernity she invites into her imagination.

Notes

[1] This essay derives from a talk that featured eighteen images. The postcard reproduced later with the kind permission of the Yale Library (fig. 1) comes from the African Postcard Collection, Manuscripts and Archives, Yale University Library. For a related argument that includes more images and more readings of Woolf's texts, see Wollaeger.

[2] Woolf alludes to this dynamic in a description of a photograph of Rachel's mother (*VO* 84).

Works Cited

Carline, Richard. *Pictures in the Post*. Bedford, Eng.: Gordon Fraser, 1959.

Christensen, Jerome. *Practicing Enlightenment: Hume and the Formation of a Literary Career*. Madison, WI: U Wisconsin Press, 1987.

Felski, Rita. *The Gender of Modernity*. Cambridge, MA: Harvard U Press, 1995.

Geary, Christraud M. and Virginia-Lee Webb, ed. *Delivering Views: Distant Cultures in Early Postcards*. Washington and London: Smithsonian Institution Press, 1998.

Greenhalgh, Paul. *Ephemeral Vistas: The "Expositions Universelles," Great Exhibitions and World's Fairs, 1851-1939*. Manchester, Eng.: Manchester U Press, 1988.

North, Michael. *Reading 1922: A Return to the Scene of the Modern*. New York: Oxford U Press, 1999.

Pound, Ezra. *Literary Essays of Ezra Pound.* Ed. T. S. Eliot. New York: New Directions, 1968.

Robert W. Rydell, "Souvenirs of Imperialism: World's Fair Postcards." Geary and Webb 47-63.

Smith, Charles Saumarez. "A Question of Fame: Virginia Woolf and the National Portrait Gallery." *Charleston Magazine* 12 (1995): 5-9.

Staff, Frank. *The Picture Postcard & its Origins.* London: Lutterworth Press, 1966.

Stewart, Susan. *On Longing: Narratives of the Miniature, the Gigantic, the Souvenir, the Collection.* Baltimore, MD: John Hopkins U Press, 1984.

Wollaeger, Mark. "Woolf, Picture Postcards, and the Elision of Race: Colonizing Women in *The Voyage Out.*" *Modernism / Modernity* 8:1 (January 2001).

Woody, Howard. "International Postcards: Their History, Production, and Distribution (Circa 1895 to 1915)." Geary and Webb 13-45.

Woolf, Virginia. *The Essays of Virginia Woolf.* Ed. Andrew McNellie. New York and London: Harcourt, Brace, Jovanovich, 1988-.

——. *Jacob's Room.* New York: Harcourt, Brace, Jovanovich, 1960.

——. *The Letters of Virginia Woolf.* Ed. Nigel Nicolson and Joanne Trautmann. New York and London: Harcourt Brace Jovanovich, 1979. 6 vols.

——. *Melymbrosia: An Early Version of* The Voyage Out. Ed. Louise A. DeSalvo. New York: New York Public Library, 1982.

——. *The Voyage Out.* New York and London: Harcourt Brace Jovanovich, 1948.

——. *The Waves.* New York: Harcourt, Brace, 1931.

Jennifer Wicke
Frock Consciousness: Virginia Woolf's Dialectical Materialism

Virginia Woolf herself tells us that dress hovered over her transformation to modernity, one slightly stained dress in particular, worn by her sister Vanessa as she sat sewing in their Bloomsbury drawing room. Although Woolf is unclear about whether or not she may have made this up, or misremembered it, she recalls Lytton Strachey entering the room and asking "Is that semen on your skirt?" In her memoir *Moments of Being*, Woolf emphasizes the galvanizing shock effect of this remark: "with that one word . . . a flood of the sacred fluid seemed to overwhelm us"(*MOB* 26).[1] While they were awash in the seminal backsplash, a watershed moment for Bloomsbury and Woolf alike erupted, a human stain crystallizing a modernity unencumbered by sexual reticence, shame, or inequality of desire.

As salient as is the spermatic detail of the comment made either by Strachey or fantasized by her own admittance by Woolf, so too is the dress where it putatively came to rest. Vanessa's skirt that day bore the traces, if not of actual ejaculate in this instance, then of a sea-change in modernism

221

which Woolf's writing was to articulate. As posed by Strachey or whomever, the question doesn't give priority to the sperm, but to the skirt of the dress that bears its residue. It matters that even imaginary semen spatters an article of clothing, a frock, in what may be an imagined anecdote. The liberating sacred fluid she notes as overwhelming them was not imaginary in its effects—"so now there was nothing that one could not say, nothing that one could not do, at 46 Gordon Square" (*MOB* 27). Despite the metonymic parallel between semen and a sudden flood, I would like to argue that even in this parable of "Bloomsbury 2nd chapter," as Woolf calls it, the dress is the *sine qua non*, and the juxtaposition of fashion and fucking, if one can pardon the alliteration, marking a permeable border her writing crosses again and again.

My title puns on Marxist dialectical materialism, of course, the linchpin of Marx's interpretation of history and the lens for comprehending social relations in their entirety, including thought and art. I neither wish to annex Woolf's textual practice to a specifically Marxian mode of analysis, nor to insinuate that her texts offer a substitutive model of political economy. Far more modestly, I want to draw attention to the dialectics of Woolf's material images, images that in large part are conceived in material—i.e. cloth-related—terms. Dialectical materialism in this sense continues to reverberate with Marx's insistence that the materiality of human labor and its products fashions the world as each human being knows it, but adds also what Walter Benjamin brought to our attention in his phrase "dialectical images."[2] Such images—and they run the gamut from representations to events, from department stores to novels—are dialectical because they catch human subjectivity in historical nets, and oscillate between past and present, time and space, in a violent synthesis with no apparent thesis and antithesis. Benjamin refers in the lapidary prose mosaic of his vast and uncompleted *Arcades Project* to "dialectics at a standstill—this is the quintessence of the method" (865). A specific dialectical image is arrested and held poised in thought, the better to allow history in all its facets to reveal its truth.

Woolfian dialectical materialism emerges for me in passages seemingly innocent of political content, or masquerading as a reductive idea of the scope of the political. That is, in Woolf's tremendous literary concentration on fashion, clothes, and dress, and on the process of shopping for, gazing at, or identifying clothing. The fashion-tropism detectable throughout Woolf's work is not to be explained by her gender, in that any number of fellow modernists, all of them male, stud their pages with detailed fashion descriptions. None of them, however, whether Joyce or Proust or Lawrence, envision fashion or clothing as the material interface between individual subjects and the social world, except in the relatively trivial sense of fashion as a mark of status or conspicuous consumption.[3] In Woolf's literary language, though, language is written on the body in the form of clothes, and the clothes perform a material dialectic, a dialectic made of and shown through material as fabric.

222

Materiality in Woolf criticism is often shorthand for the materiality of language, and indeed Woolf's succulent language and its profusion of tropes do indeed "materialize" language as a substance, where mystical words can cavort in the sky in the form of sky-written smoke, or where words dissolve like hard candy, leaving but a trace behind. Most arguments for the materiality of language, however, stop there, fingering the texture of the written fabric as a weave with a visible language stripe consolidating its pattern. The etymological tie between "text" and "textile" yields a host of metaphors of text as fabric and texts weaving language, but this critical commonplace, useful as it is for metaphorizing texts, doesn't encompass the material thrust outside the text any description of fashion provides. Linguistic materiality stops short of explaining how language as a material thing intersects with subjectivity and history, preferring to see each of these as a phantom effect of language in the final analysis—language speaking the subject and the social world hailing that subject into history.

Virginia Woolf is known too for the philosophical shadings which dapple her works, those textual moments of the explication of consciousness, being, and indeed truth. In *To the Lighthouse* philosophy is foregrounded in the person of Mr. Ramsay and in the philosophical problematics that engage his circle; the novel circles around those problematics as it envisions alternative models of subjectivity; the Humean notion that a perception of a table is a kind of table in the mind inflects the image of a table hanging in a tree, just as William James's "blooming, buzzing confusion" definition for consciousness is altered into the piercing image of a net cast over a tree whose branches tremble with an exaltation of rooks.[4] Woolf is and should be credited with the imaging and elaboration of a philosophy of mind that extends throughout her disparate works; at the same time, her affinity for dialectical thinking, with its social and historical ramifications, has been seldom noted, unless it is to cite, as I and others have done, the richly political imbrications of her oeuvre, written under the sign of empire, patriarchy, and class warfare.

Nor is Woolf's self-professed love of fashion and nice clothes responsible for the dialectical role of clothing in her writing. Her polemical essay against realist fiction as exemplified by Arnold Bennett demonstrates that descriptions of clothing or fashion in her writing are anything but verisimilitudinous. She isn't describing the clothes, in other words, to describe the clothes, in the manner of a Judith Krantz or Barbara Cartland. Benjamin may again be able to draw the distinction, when he writes a telegraphic entry in the *Arcades Project* as follows: "Fashion. A sort of race for first place in the social creation. The running begins anew at every instant" (249). And: "Movement of the life of fashion: change *a little*" (651). The fashion details that litter each and every Woolf text, when you begin to look out for their presence, are meta-fashion, meta-material. They sew subjects into a garment incapable of containing their "social creation," wrapping the characters, who are characters "in pieces," in any event, without that "old stable ego" of realism, in a mesh that in part stitches them to history and in part enmeshes them in material relations that extend beyond the text in space and time. That dialectic is akin to a more original meaning of dialectic, the *dialegien* of Platonic philosophy, where language is a shuttle that weaves out of dialogue a partial fabric of truth, a truth never to be completely realized in the back-and-forth movements of the loom.

It is not clear from the story what degree of fashionability Vanessa's frock possessed on that momentous occasion when hierarchical barriers between the sexes and various sexualities were razed in a twinkling. On almost every other crucial occasion of memory Woolf has the frocks and accoutrements down cold. She begins the reminiscence of "Old Bloomsbury" with fashion and dress at the forefront, although in deshabille: "I was undressing at the top of that house when my last memoir ended, in my bedroom at the back. My white satin dress was on the floor. The faint smell of kid gloves was in the air. My necklace of seed pearls was tangled with hairpins on the dressing table" (*MOB* 126). The previous memoir had stopped just at the point of George Duckworth's entry into her bedroom at night, for the "cuddling and kissing and otherwise embracing me" (*MOB* 123) he insisted was meant to comfort her as her father lay dying. Woolf segues almost immediately from that morbidly riveting scene to set the stage for the passage from Victorian Bloomsbury to its Edwardian incarnation. She establishes the space of memory by a veritable strip-tease; it must be evident that I am in no way suggesting Woolf's prose here is the equivalent of a cheap come-on, just that it is crucial for her to embody the texture of that moment of being in and through a white satin gown and its complementary trappings, as these lie in disarray in her private room, ghostly mementoes of the person who has just stepped forth from their material embrace.

The essay "Am I a Snob?" which follows permits no such scenes, whether of Woolf shedding a gleaming white evening gown to wait silently in her bed for the unwanted sexual assaults of a half-brother, or of the blithe "spots of time" made manifest on the canvas of Vanessa's skirt. Nonetheless, clothing is the material basis for this effervescent confessional piece, wherein Woolf reveals to herself and her audience that she is not only "a coronet snob; but also a lit up drawing room snob; a social festivity snob. Any group of people if they are well dressed . . . sends up that fountain of gold and diamond dust which I suppose obscures the solid truth" (*MOB* 156). A summons to tea or dinner from a titled hostess alters the atmosphere; rushing despite herself to accept such invitations, Woolf spends these idyllic coroneted hours in an "air that seemed made of gold dust and champagne." Confessing shamefacedly to an enthrallment with "old coronets" such as Lady Asquith and Lady Colefax, she is forced too to face her "dress complex," although she can only allude to it shyly, as she says; these disavowals on the page of something that is nonetheless expressed or represented are a leitmotif of Woolf's work. The dress complex consists of a simple equation: "I hate being badly dressed; but I hate buying clothes." The ineluctable underpinning for the best clothes is underwear, or lingerie, as Woolf does not refer to it. She does admit that "In particular I hate buying suspenders." Her writing deliberately skirts the issue of undressing, or at least the word, since the manuscript reveals she took the words "you must undress" and replaced them in the margin with what nows stands in the quote: "It is partly, I think, that in order to buy suspenders you must visit the most private room in the heart of a shop; you must stand in your chemise." Standing in one's chemise one is subject to the prying eyes and sniggers of "shiny black satin women," lingerie saleswomen turned into articles of clothing by synecdoche. Her reluctance to run the shopping gauntlet forces her to stay at home, until finally she must face the dread challenge of a suspender run when asked to Argyll House to meet Arnold Bennett, since "in those days skirts were short; stockings had to be neat; my suspenders were old; and I could not face buying another pair—let alone hat and coat." But face it she does for the sake of Sibyl Colefax, "a bunch of red cherries on a hard black straw hat." The soirée was a social success for Woolf, in that Sibyl began to extend a certain intimacy to her—"can snobs be intimate?" Woolf asks of both herself and Lady Colefax—by dropping by for chats about the grievances of the great world of society counterpointed by Woolf's struggles with "English prose." The picture of Sibyl drawn in that exquisite prose is telling, since it touches on the intimacy of underwear; "she would sit on the floor, pull up her skirts, adjust her knickers—she only wears one undergarment, I may tell you; it is of silk. . ." One wonders whence derives the confident "I may tell you" of a woman who says of herself "I am very shy under the eyes of my own sex when in my chemise." Of further interest is the one-piece silken garment that replaces chemise and suspenders—perhaps this is what we now call a "teddy," perhaps not. The fusion of fashion with the ambience of aristocracy, the sheer snobbery inherent in these reciprocal transactions, turns on the materiality of material—fabric, "stuff," textiles, cloth. Even the "luster and illusion" of Bloomsbury before the war is captured by material transformations and transformations of material: "By this time we were far from drab . . . we made dresses of the printed cotton that is specially loved by Negroes; we dressed ourselves up as Gauguin pictures and careered around Crosby Hall. Mrs. Whitehead was scandalized. She said that Vanessa and I were practically naked" (*MOB* 29). In Auden's words, how naked go the oft-times nude.

Having attempted to short-circuit the gender explanation for fashion's profusion in Woolf, I now want to circle back to it, but with a difference. Instead of relying for its force on some innate female proclivity for clothes, a feature of modernist thought running through the work of Georg Simmel, Nietzsche, and Freud, among others, the propensity for fashion as a material substratum in Woolf's writing could derive from a material, historical feature inherent in cloth and clothing. The anthropologist Annette Weiner proffers this explanation in her groundbreaking treatment of fabric as a historically feminized exchange, *Inalienable Possessions: The Paradox of Keeping-While-Giving*. Writing to contradict and to complexify the still-prevalent thesis, advanced by Claude Lévi-Strauss and later attacked by Gail Rubin, that women in non-developed and developed societies alike are simply a form of currency, exchanged like language or money among men, Weiner demonstrates that in so-called "primitive" societies women wield social power deriving from their control over cloth and their social identification with it. It isn't a simple matter to "translate" this recognition into its social equivalent in modern industrial societies, where few women have any stake in weaving cloth, and those who manufacture clothing are among the most oppressed workers on earth. Still, what Weiner advances based on her ethnographic research is an enlarged understanding of consumption beyond commodification. Fabrics, she shows, in the form of such things as Samoan fiber mats or Polynesian batik, where woven by women are not only items of exchange, but also "political and even sacred repositories of wealth" (xii). Linking the production of cloth, and its possession, to Benjamin's notion of "aura," Weiner writes: "If I possess a sacred cloth, in Walter Benjamin's terms its "aura" extends to my other possessions as well, because my social identity, rank, or status is legitimated by my possession of one sacred object" (10).[5] Not that even sacred wealth is exempted from the exigencies of political hierarchy; Weiner posits a social politics lodged at the very heart of inalienable property, with cloth as the exemplary possession. The paradox Weiner cites is apposite in the extreme for Woolf's materialism: that is, the more a totem or fetish or auratic, sacred object is given away, the more it (or its powers) are *kept*. The transactions of exchange are suspended, and the invisible properties of the sacral and the powerful, of "glamour" in the original Irish meaning of the word, override commercial exchange, in favor of women's inalienable powers. Woolf's fashion discourse exceeds the parameters of the fashion system *per se* by installing fashion at the very heart of darkness, a darkness or "black box" in Wittgenstein's phrase, wherein the transactions of social commerce take place out of sight, out of mind. [6]

The dialectical material of fashion emerges powerfully in unforgettable textual garments which sparkle and accumulate across Woolf's written arc, mythic or totemic fashion garments on the order of Mrs. Ramsay's shawl, wafting through *To the Lighthouse* and once apotropaically wrapping the frightening cow's skull on the wall in the children's room. Or the dresses evoked in the evanescent moment in *Mrs. Dalloway* when Clarissa glides down the staircase at Bourton "feeling as she crossed the hall 'if it were now to die 'twere now to be most happy,' [. . .] all because she was coming down in a white frock to meet Sally Seton! *She* was wearing pink gauze—was that possible? She *seemed*, anyhow, all light, glowing, like some bird or air ball that has flown in [. . .]" (*MD* 51). The diaphanous fabric of Sally's frock introduces a diaphanous surface between memory and desire; it is tempting to think of this veil as language, with its porous borders, but I would prefer to see it as the intrusion of material reality writ as material, in this case pink gauze, tautly yet transparently encasing the past. Clarissa's dress at the party the novel is threshold to is a crucial material site, if you will, a place where language receives material momentum from the clothing, and where the clothing materializes a magical tear in the otherwise constraining social fabric: "And now Clarissa escorted her Prime Minister down the room, prancing, sparkling . . . . She wore ear-rings, and a silver-green mermaid's dress. Lolloping on the waves and braiding her tresses she seemed, having that gift still; to be; to exist; to sum it all up in the moment as she passed [. . .]"(*MD* 264). Clarissa encounters guests like Lady Bruton, "a spectral grenadier draped in black," and Lady Bradshaw, garbed in "grey and silver." Ellie Henderson, the very poor relation, muses on the lovely frocks as she stands in the corner in her old and only black dress with a shawl thrown over it; Sally Seton later remembers Ellie's mortification "cutting up underclothes at the large table by the window" at Bourton. The humiliation implied by cutting up underwear—presumably old garments cut up to make rags, rather than the cutting of new garments from a pattern—stems in part from its place on the fashion spectrum, when a piece of clothing has fallen out of time and is now totally deconstructed, torn into ribbons of cloth without fashion meaning. The memory prompts Sally to label Clarissa a "terrible snob" for inviting Ellie to the party as Sally desultorily reminiscences with Peter Walsh. Clarissa's imputed snobbery no doubt has a basis in fact, if even Woolf ironically placed herself in the camp of snobs. Yet in dialectical terms, assuming that fashion operates as a material dialectic in Woolf's writing, it isn't sufficient to see Clarissa as "classist," nor Woolf, for that matter. Ellie's unfortunate place on the fashion continuum is dialectically ordained—dialectics at a standstill. And such subjugation, envisioned clearly by Woolf, does not sever Ellie from the temporal beauty of fashion, nor from its ruthless race for first place. Both Ellie and later Richard Dalloway, with different inflections, are seized by the vision of Elizabeth Dalloway in "her lovely pink frock," that very Elizabeth who has narrowly escaped the anti-fashion confines of the Army-Navy Stores under Miss Kilman's fashion-negating tutelage. And it is Ellie who admonishes her silently by thinking, "But girls when they first came out didn't seem to wear white as they used. (She must remember everything to tell Edith.) Girls wore straight frocks, perfectly tight, with skirts well above the ankles. It was not becoming, she thought" (*MD* 257).

When Clarissa is first told by Sir William Bradshaw that "an accident" has detained the couple, "Always her body went through it first, when she was told, suddenly, of an accident; her dress flamed, her body burnt" (*MD* 280). Not a literal stage direction, this dialectical image of Clarissa with a burning dress like a character from Greek tragedy infuses the present mundane moment between the wars with the violent intensity tragedy could represent. A material image drawn from ancient times may not seem to be all that is required for the dialectical turn of the screw. Yet ruminating on Septimus's anonymous suicide, Clarissa feels that "it was her punishment to see sink and disappear here a man, there a woman, in this profound darkness, and she forced to stand here in her evening dress." I hope it is not too much to read this as fashion's witness to the ravages of the very time it is fueled by, a fashion that, in dialectical fashion, holds time at bay by transfiguring it, even while it submits to time's yoke.

Woolf's famous "wedge-shaped core of darkness," the dark heart of Lily Briscoe's painterly representation of Mrs. Ramsay, and, earlier in *To the Lighthouse*, the phrase for Mrs. Ramsay's absent presence, intersects with the heart of darkness upon which Woolf embroiders in *Mrs. Dalloway*. Borrowing the materiality of Conrad's phrase "heart of darkness," which in his eponymous novel is a densely material absence, comprised of history and language and violence and subjectivity and unconsciousness, and making that materiality dialectical with the preceding list, just as does Conrad, Woolf strikes out anew by privileging the dark core, weaving dialectically to show the dark side of the moon of being. Woolf's work creates a fabric, then, but not in the mode of Joyce's dense encyclopedia, nor Eliot's assemblage of shards, nor Lawrence's loom of oscillating natural cycles. Text as "tissue," women as weavers: her dialectical modernist style would seem to be over-determinately gendered. The textual skeins of her work are not, however, best read as the cultural norms in circulation from Penelope in the *Odyssey* on to the twentieth century would have us do. Freud suggested, in his off-hand comment in *Civilization and its Discontents*, that women began to weave by analogy to their own pubic hair, which covers over a regrettable nothingness with interwoven and compensatory strands. Women's weaving can only be a disavowal of their lack, which happens to be productive in this instance, or a culture-wide substitute for male power (81-83). Despite its evocative power, there are similar problems in conceiving Woolfian style as a matter of weaving her texts as a spider its web, tracing filaments that hang suspended in a nothingness without gender, without language, without value, without fashion. For Woolf, though, the dark core of nothing at the heart of her texts is itself woven and whole, a dialectical paradox. Virginia Woolf creates out of whole cloth.

Notes

[1] The essays which comprise *Moments of Being* are the locus for most of Woolf's explicit remarks on fashion and her experiences with clothing, shopping for clothes, and gendered dress in this article.

[2] Walter Benjamin's majestic, incomplete and essentially uncompletable work has been translated and published by Harvard University Press in 1999.

[3] The best single source for twentieth century fashion theory is still Elizabeth

Wilson's *Adorned in Dreams: Fashion and Modernity* (Berkeley, University of California Press, 1985). See chapter three especially in relation to Woolf and the necessity to theorize fashion beyond the market alone.

4 William James' memorable phrase crops up in his *Essays in Psychology*, "Consciousness."

5 The reference to Benjamin and his concept of "aura" derives from his essay, "The Work of Art in an Age of Mechanical Reproduction," collected in Illuminations, trans. H. Zohn [New York, Schocken, 1969], pgs. 142-157.

6 Wittgenstein's discussion of the "black box" takes place in his *Philosophical Investigations* [Oxford, Blackwell, 1958], para. 304-306, p. 102, in a series of passages that ask the reader to imagine both pain and also language secreted within a box, and thus seemingly "private," which he refutes.

Works Cited

Benjamin, Walter. *The Arcades Project*. Trans. Howard Eilander and Kevin McLaughlin. Cambridge: The Belknap Press of Harvard U P, 1999.

Freud, Sigmund. *Civilization and its Discontents*. Trans. James Strachey. New York: W. W. Norton, 1961.

James, William. *Essays in Psychology*. Boston: Holt & Co., 1927.

Weiner, Annette. *Inalienable Possessions: The Paradox of Keeping-while-Giving*. Berkeley: U of California P, 1992.

Wittgenstein, Ludwig. *Philosophical Investigations*. Oxford: Blackwell, 1958.

Woolf, Virginia. *Moments of Being*: unpublished autobiographical writings. Ed. Jeanne Schulkind. New York: Harcourt Brace Jovanovich, 1976.

——. *Mrs. Dalloway*. San Diego: Harcourt Brace Jovanovich, 1990.

——. *To the Lighthouse*.

Elizabeth Outka
"The Shop Windows Were Full of Sparkling Chains": Consumer Desire and Woolf's *Night and Day*

"You know the horror of buying clothes" (*L2* 232), wrote Virginia Woolf to her sister in 1918. This statement takes us to the heart of early critical assumptions about Woolf and consumerism. Following good modernist principles, the argument ran, Woolf's art was naturally above shopping, distinct from and even a reaction against consumer culture. More recently, critics such as Jennifer Wicke, Rachel Bowlby, and Reginald Abbott have unsettled this separation and have started to consider the complex relations among consumption, the market, and Woolf's writing. Most of this attention, however, has focused either on selected essays or on *Mrs. Dalloway*, with its diverse scenes of stores and shopping. This paper addresses an earlier work,

Woolf's *Night and Day*, published in 1919. *Night and Day* is surprisingly connected to consumer culture, connected in ways that can deepen our understanding of consumerism in Woolf's later works. Woolf suggests in this early novel a critical two-part illusion: first, as a smart shopper, one might reach the tantalizing vision behind the glittering shop windows; second, one might reach this elusive vision without actually engaging in a material transaction. *Buying* clothes may be a horror, but what those clothes might deliver—the promise they promise—is another matter. This desire to purchase the illusions while hiding the material transaction actually paralleled emerging selling techniques and new modes of window display in London's department stores, most notably at Selfridges, which opened in 1909. I will put a central scene of window shopping in *Night and Day* into dialogue with these emerging techniques, and suggest that such a dialogue reveals the surprising, often paradoxical nature of shopping within Woolf's novels.

Early in *Night and Day*, Ralph Denham is walking through the streets of London, gazing in at shop windows on his way to an appointment. As he wanders and gazes, his surroundings become almost dreamlike: "on both sides of the road the shop windows were full of sparkling chains and highly polished leather cases, which stood upon shelves made of thick plate-glass. None of these different objects was seen separately by Denham, but from all of them he drew an impression of stir and cheerfulness" (130). The atmosphere here seems almost artificially enchanted. The natural light is fading, replaced by green and yellow streams. The objects in the shop windows hold qualities designed to dazzle and hypnotize the gazer—the chains sparkle, the cases are highly polished, the items stand on "thick plate-glass," suggesting a hazy visibility. Ralph absorbs the hypnotic atmosphere of the objects behind glass, not seeing them distinctly, but taking "an impression of stir and cheerfulness." The glittering atmosphere emanating from the shop windows produces in Ralph a dreamy and receptive mood.

Katharine seems to emerge directly from this window shopping. After Ralph has drawn his impressions from the store windows, Woolf writes "*Thus* it came about that he saw Katharine" (130, emphasis added) as if the reverie itself, inspired by the sparkling commodities, has conjured Katharine's presence. Katharine seems to Ralph "only an illustration of the argument that was going forward in his mind" (130), an extension, as it were, of his own internal thoughts. Yet at the same time, she seems absolutely distinct. Separated by "her height and the distinction of her dress" (130), Katharine appears both literally and figuratively above the crowd. Much like the objects set behind glass, she stands apart from the gazers. It is as if Ralph's Pygmalion-like gaze animates a store mannequin, allowing it to step out of the display to become a mobile commodity, a product of the store windows' glittering promise and Ralph's own imaginings. She materializes, in the most literal sense.

Katherine's appearance has an extraordinary effect on Ralph and his perceptions of his surroundings. As she passes by, "immediately the whole scene in the Strand wore that curious look of order and purpose which is imparted to the most heterogeneous things when music sounds" (130). Ralph is captivated, and the first thing he can think to do, after she walks past, is to keep looking. He wants simply "To walk though the streets of London until he came to Katharine's house, to look up at the windows and fancy her within" (130). Ralph wants to continue his window shopping. He has no desire to actually talk to Katharine; he instinctively knows that the allure depends on distance. He wants to remain in his position as gazer, staring up at an imagined image behind glass.

This scene is representative of many that appear throughout *Night and Day*, moments of intense and rhapsodic desire, when a character imagines that all light, all beauty, lies through a window, a vision usually inspired by the glamorous and idealized figure of Katharine Hilbery. Even Katharine has related moments of complex longing, such as when she stands outside Ralph's office or when she gazes up at the light from Mary Datchet's window. Most of these scenes, though, involve Ralph looking through windows at Katharine, in ways similar to the scene I have described in detail. These scenes reach a climax near the end of the novel, when Ralph at his most rhapsodic imagines that "all dryness, all safety, all that stood above the surge" (395) lies just through the window, with Katharine as "a shape of light" (395) within.

Such scenes seem a strange hybrid of commercialism and romantic fantasy. On the one hand, the glittering store windows produce the appropriate atmosphere for Ralph's distracted, *flaneur*-like window gazing. On the other hand, the scene seems less commercial than romantic fantasy. Ralph does not buy anything, or even enter a store; Katharine is not (at least technically) for sale, and her very distinction and promise seem the antithesis of reproducible commodities. Yet the very hybrid nature of these scenes actually connects them in complicated ways to commercialism in London as it was emerging at the time. The dreamy, enchanted quality of this scene, the lack of any actual purchase, and Katharine's seeming distinction, all suggest new modes of window displays and selling techniques in London department stores. Let me highlight a few central shifts in the commercial landscape of London, and then suggest why they matter to our reading of *Night and Day*.

In 1909, Gordon Selfridge, an American entrepreneur, opened an enormous new department store in London, and in the next ten years revolutionized the way commodities were presented and sold to the British public. Selfridge's central aim was to dignify commerce (Pound 3). He continually emphasized the elegance and beauty of the store, and wherever possible he hid the commercial nature of the enterprise (Honeycombe 9). Shoppers were invited to come and spend the day, without buying anything.

The interior of the store was designed to produce a distracted reverie in the guests: hidden string quartets played music, and lighting was arranged to highlight different commodities and to make the store seem enchanted (Pound 67).

Selfridge likewise revolutionized window displays. Formerly, stores had tended to pile up their goods in the window, with prices displayed prominently. Selfridge changed all this, forming special design teams to create carefully crafted artistic displays. Special lighting gave the windows a fairy tale atmosphere, designed to mesmerize the outside gazer. Window designers were instructed to visit art galleries, museums, and libraries to obtain ideas. While commodities were sometimes massed for effect, the trend was to set objects apart under special lights. In the store windows, the designers emphasized fantasy, beauty, and distinction, never the commercial exchange. In fact, price tickets were nowhere to be found (Honeycombe 10, Pound 71). Such window displays often inspired gushing description; as one literary magazine commented during the war, the "'beautifully arranged'" windows seemed to exude the promise of "'beauty and order'" within (qtd. in Honeycombe 45), offering a welcome oasis from the violent atmosphere outside.

We can see these new modes of selling at work in Woolf's scene of window watching.[1] The atmosphere, created by artificial lights and glittering objects, places Ralph in the kind of dreamy, distracted mood that Selfridge desired to produce in his shoppers. Katharine, separated from the crowd around her, takes the form of a distinct commodity. Like the string quartets hidden behind the palm trees at Selfridges, the effect of all this on Ralph is to bring a sense of order and beauty to heterogeneous things, as if music suddenly played in the background. And like a good shopper, Ralph can only wish to stay distracted, to continue to gaze and desire.

What should we make of these links between Woolf's scene of window shopping and Selfridge's new techniques? Woolf encapsulates an underlying promise of commodity culture, a tantalizing vision of the possibilities available behind the glass. She presents Ralph, the dazed consumer, staring in a dream-like reverie inspired by the dream-like displays, along with the appealing, just-out-of-reach commodity, surrounded by the promise of distinction and glamorous style. She leaves out, of course, what the store windows leave out: the actual commercial exchange. The horror of shopping is nowhere to be found, which is in fact part of what the store windows promise.

Arguments on consumerism often seek to expose such window shopping, whisking away the glittering façade to reveal the sordid but actual truth behind the curtain. We might, for example, discuss the false nature of marketing and store display, and consider how idealized images were designed to trick the consumer. In a similar vein, we might expose Ralph's idealization of Katharine as inaccurate and trace it to a whole line of familiar romantic delusions involving women as objects. Exposing these promises is important, but exposure is not my aim here. Instead, I want to take seriously the gazer's overwhelming desire that the vision behind the window might be obtained without any actual purchase.

Let me clarify this fantasy of possessing the promise without the purchase by turning to the letter with which I opened this paper, a letter Woolf wrote to her sister in 1918, the same year she was finishing *Night and Day*. The letter reveals a fascinating juxtaposition between actual shopping and Woolf's own idealized vision of the promised "result," in this case embodied by her sister Vanessa. In the first part of the letter, Woolf dramatically tells her sister of a terrible shopping excursion:

> I can't describe to you what an agony this afternoon was to me. You know the horror of buying clothes, especially for one forced as I am to keep my underclothes pinned together by brooches. [. . .] I flung myself into a shop in Holborn. [. . .] The impropriety seemed to me beyond anything we know. So it went on: I tried shop after shop; and then in a perfectly random way went and bought a wine-coloured black striped coat or dress [. . .]. (*L*2 232)

The language seems intentionally over-blown. Buying clothes is an agony, a horror, even improper. Here we have not the promised vision, the suspended moment of looking that we see with Ralph, but the tiresome process of going from store to store and actually engaging in a material transaction. Like "underclothes pinned together by brooches," it is the disorderly, unglamorous underside of shopping.

Immediately after the above description, however, Woolf makes a telling shift. She relates how she has been writing her novel about Vanessa that morning—her sister was the explicit model for Katharine in *Night and Day*.

> I've been writing about you all the morning, and have made you wear a blue dress; you've got to be immensely mysterious and romantic, which of course you are; yes, but its the combination that's so enthralling; to crack through the paving stone and be enveloped in the mist. (*L*2 232)

Woolf leaps from the sordid scene of shopping and actual purchase to the glittering promise of the store window. In Woolf's vision, Vanessa need not buy a dress, she already wears one, taking on the mysterious and romantic quality so seductive to Ralph. Like a dreamy window shopper who is magically whisked from the sidewalk to the enchanted vision before her, Woolf's fantasy is to crack through the material hardness of the paving stone and be enveloped in the ethereal mist. Woolf imagines in Vanessa, and by extension in Katharine, a deliberate exclusion of any act of consumption, presenting only the oasis promised by the finished product.[2]

Woolf captures in this letter the very leap we see in Ralph and the very leap promised to Selfridge's shoppers: that one could skip over any material transaction and simply obtain the tantalizing vision. It is important to stay alert to the problems inherent in this vision: to the dangers of Ralph's idealization, to insidious marketing techniques, and to Woolf's overly romantic notions of her sister. It is also important, however, to understand that part of the romanticized promise is not having to do this, not having to leave the mist to be deposited on the material truth of the paving stone. Attentive to the dangers, we might nonetheless stand for a moment with Ralph, hoping that just through the lighted window lies the answer to everything, or that a store window might give off such order and beauty as to hide the ugliness of a war, or that a lovely and mysterious sister might make up for a terrible morning of shopping.

I have linked Ralph's window gazing, Selfridge's new displays, and Woolf's note to her sister because, read together, they alert us to an important way to approach Woolf and material culture, one we might miss if we hurry too quickly to expose them. Woolf imagines a consumerism without the consumption, a purified shopping, a shopping made aesthetic. Yet at the same time she is writing, London department stores are creating a similar fantasy, imagining an aesthetic mode of shopping, one appealing *because* it hides its commercial nature. It is a desire akin to many modernist endeavors: to hold an aesthetic vision without the seeming taint of commercialism.[3] The lines among shopping, consumption, fantasy, and pure aesthetics become increasingly blurred, and I would urge us to keep these competing impulses in mind when considering Woolf and material culture. Woolf's works are neither above consumerism, nor do they simply embrace it. Scenes such as the one I have discussed in *Night and Day* hold contradictions, hold the desire both to be above consumer society and of it, a desire which itself reflected new trends in the commercial landscape of London.

Notes

[1] Ralph, of course, is walking near the Strand, not on Oxford Street, where Selfridges was located. Woolf does write specifically of Oxford Street and its atmosphere in "Oxford Street Tide," where she contrasts the "sublime rites" (16) of shopping on Bond Street with the "too blatant and raucous" (16) buying and selling on Oxford Street. By 1932, when Woolf published her article, Selfridges was much less focused on hiding the commercial exchange, and more content to highlight prices and bargains.

[2] See also the "blue dress" scene in *Night and Day*, where Cassandra as the dazzled gazer watches Katharine's reflection in the looking-glass (*ND* 343-344).

[3] For a summary of the modernism/marketing debate, and essays on the interaction of modernism and the market, see Dettmar's collection of essays.

Works Cited

Abbott, Reginald. "What Miss Kilman's Petticoat Means: Virginia Woolf, Shopping, and Spectacle." *Modern Fiction Studies*. 38.1 (1992): 193-216.

Bowlby, Rachel. "Meet Me in St. Louis: Virginia Woolf and Community." *Virginia Woolf and Communities: Selected Papers from the Eighth Annual Conference on Virginia Woolf.* Ed. Jeanette McVicker and Laura Davis. New York: Pace UP, 1999. 147-60.

——. "Walking, Women and Writing: Virginia Woolf as Flaneuse." *New Feminist Discourses: Critical Essays on Theories and Texts.* Ed. Isobel Armstrong. London: Routledge, 1992. 26-47.

Dettmar, Kevin J. H. and Stephen Watt, Ed. *Marketing Modernisms: Self-Promotion, Canonization, Rereading.* Ann Arbor: U of Michigan P, 1996.

Honeycombe, Gordon. *Selfridges: Seventy-Five Years, The Story of the Store 1909-1984.* London: Park Lane Press, 1984.

Pound, Reginald. *Selfridge: A Biography.* London: Heinemann, 1960.

Wicke, Jennifer. "Côterie Consumption: Bloomsbury, Keynes, and Modernism as Marketing." In Dettmar and Watt. 109-32.

Woolf, Virginia. *The Letters of Virginia Woolf.* Ed. Nigel Nicolson and Joanne Trautmann. Vol. 2. New York: Harvest/HBJ, 1978.

——. *Night and Day.* 1919. San Diego: Harvest/HBJ, 1948.

——. "Oxford Street Tide." *The London Scene.* 1975. London: Hogarth, 1982.

Intertexts and Contexts

Vanessa Manhire

"The Lady's Gone A-Roving": Woolf and the English Folk Revival

As many critics have noted, Virginia Woolf's reworking of the ballad of the Queen's Marys in *A Room of One's Own* functions to make a point about the suppression of women's voices. The timing of this speech—at the height of the English Folk Revival—suggests that the submerged ballad might also serve as a critique of the revival's ideology and its implications for women's voices. The folk revival's stress on authentic Englishness, tradition, and collective amateur anonymity, for example, gives added relevance to Woolf's suspicion that "Anon [. . .] was often a woman" (*AROO* 45). This paper considers representations of folk music in Woolf's work alongside texts by contemporary folk revivalists. First, I briefly outline the English folk revival's attempts to preserve—even construct—a communal national identity in response to the growing cosmopolitanism of the late nineteenth and early twentieth centuries. Next I discuss the gender and class implications of the revival's ideology in conjunction with two of Woolf's recurring representations of song. Finally I turn to the relationship between tradition, history, and the folk in her writings from the late 1930s. Woolf shares the revivalists' interest in the past but not the ideology which accompanies their stress on authenticity. Where the rhetoric of the folk revival advocated the return to a simple and "natural" tradition, Woolf's deployment of folk music traces a more complicated sense of historical change. Rejecting the revival's concept of purity, Woolf offers instead the figure of the lady "gone a-roving" to explore the varying associations of historical and cultural change.

In *Noise: The Political Economy of Music*, Jacques Attali argues that music is a crucial signal of social and cultural change. "Listening to music," he argues, "is listening to all noise, realizing that its appropriation and control is a reflection of power, that it is essentially political" (6). We can see struggles for such auditory appropriation and control in early twentieth-century England, which was marked by rapid changes both in the institutions of music and in their cultural associations. In the late nineteenth century, large concerts and recitals became more and more popular, while music's role in the theater diminished as melodrama's operatic focus on tableaux, sound and gesture began to give way to dialogue-based realism and society drama.

Meanwhile, the predominantly European repertory of the opera house at Covent Garden drew crowds from a range of social backgrounds, as did the music halls (which underwent rapid expansion towards the end of the nineteenth century). Gilbert and Sullivan's comic operettas drew on a combination of musical registers and sources, all the while exploiting their materials for parody. Henry Wood's establishment of the Promenade concerts at the turn of the century sought to counter the conception of England as "Das Land ohne Musik" ("the land without music") by promoting the works of English composers such as Parry, Stanford, and Elgar; the nationalist impulses behind this so-called "English Renaissance" are also apparent in the English Folk Revival movement.

The English folk revival stressed the importance of traditional English music and sought to record and recreate folk culture more generally. As Georgina Boyes explains in *The Imagined Village: Culture, Ideology, and the English Folk Revival*, the revival worked in response to perceived threats to English racial and cultural superiority: she points out that "the prevalence of German music in the concert hall [and, I'd add, international influences on the music hall] was as insidious a symptom of national decline as the reported refusal of middle-class women to undertake their allotted role in the maintenance of empire by producing large families" (24). Cecil Sharp, the leading figure in the folk revival, saw international influences as a threat to the integrity of English national character. "Our system of education," he argued, "is, at present, too cosmopolitan; it is calculated to produce citizens of the world rather than Englishmen" (Sharp 135-36). Foreign music assaulted English ears with its "alien sounds, or sounds fugitive and flashy, or pretty and insincere, or ugly and downright harmful" (139). And traditional folksong was thought to contain values which would work to rebuild English cultural identity. Sharp saw folk music as a potential "purifying and refining influence" for the nation (xxi), claiming for it a unique status as "not the composition of the individual and, as such, limited in outlook and appeal, but a communal and racial product, the expression, in musical idiom, of aims and ideals that are primarily national in character" (xx).

The 1898 founding of the Folk Song Society by Cecil Sharp emphasized the "purity" of folk music in contrast with the "tawdriness" of contemporary urban music. In his inaugural address to the society, the composer Sir Hubert Parry took up this subject directly: "the modern popular music [. . .] is made with a commercial intention out of snippets of musical slang. And this product it is which will drive out folk-music if we do not save it [. . .] old folk-music is amongst the purest products of the human mind. It grew in the hearts of the people before they devoted themselves so assiduously to the making of quick returns" (Boyes 25). Parry's definition of "true" folksong, containing "no sham, no got up glitter, and no vulgarity," nothing "common or unclean" (24), sets in place a new ideal of English music—and by extension an ideal of English character. The folk movement aimed to educate according to such an ideal, and its programs are described in explicit contrast to the songs of the music hall. Sharp's outline of a program of education builds those contrasts into direct competition: "[f]lood the streets [. . .] with folk-tunes, and those, who now vulgarize themselves and others by singing coarse music-hall songs, will soon drop them in favour of the equally attractive but far better tunes of the folk. This will make the streets a pleasanter place for those who have sensitive ears, and will do incalculable good in civilizing the masses" (137).

Ralph Vaughan Williams, writing in 1934, highlights the folk revival's evolutionary and evangelical zeal, telling us that "Parry had applied the Darwinian theory of evolution to music, and had proved the necessity of folk song" (Sharp v). The evolutionary mode of Sharp's thinking can be seen in his description of rural music as the survival of the fittest: he claims that "town songs have never taken root in the country; they have been ousted in the struggle for existence by the superior and more permanent attributes of the peasant song" (111). But song-recorders tended to erase any interactions between traditional and new musics: Vaughan Williams, for example, excised from his collections those songs which displayed the influence of popular urban music. In *Music Ho! Modern Music in Decline* (1934), Constant Lambert describes English folk music as "both unbearably precious and unbearably hearty," conjuring up "the hideous faux bonhomie of the hiker, noisily wading his way through the petrol pumps of Metroland, singing obsolete sea chanties with the aid of the Week-End Book" (154). As his parody illustrates, the folk revival was a constructed culture industry: the imaginary Englishness of its pastoral peasant classes was largely for the benefit of nostalgic city-dwellers.

The invented traditions of the folk revival, then, tended to ignore working-class traditional music as it actually existed. Moreover, as Edward Lee has pointed out, some urban merchants preserved old folksongs for selling—and ironically it was these merchants that the folk revivalists most deplored, seeing their own idea of the authentic folk as an antidote to such corrupt commercialism. Sharp's idea of the common people, of course, was nothing if not selective: "they form an exceedingly small class—if, indeed they are to be called a class at all—and are to be found only in those country districts which, by reason of their remoteness, have escaped the infection of modern ideas" (4). Work songs, such as street sellers' cries, were not always included in definitions of folk music, which were most often created by establishment figures and academic collectors. The largely imagined rural folk culture, those paradoxically rare "common people," could not be seen as coexisting with the urban squalor and commercialism against which the folk movement was established.

Where proponents of the Folk Revival advocated for the reconstruction (if not invention) of English national traditions—what Georgina Boyes has called the "imaginary village" of pastoral ritual and morris dancing on the green—Woolf, by contrast, pays more attention to a wider range of contemporary musical registers. Peter Jacobs has described Woolf as a "common listener" (239), and scenes of urban music recur throughout her work, from the 1905 essay "Street Music" to the violet sellers and barrel organ players in *The Years*. Here I want to look briefly at two singing figures.

A challenge to intelligibility faces characters, the narrator, and the reader of *Mrs Dalloway*, in the form of the beggar woman singing to herself: she is identified with a communal natural sound but her song is not immediately comprehensible, creating what is described as "a frail, quivering sound, a voice bubbling up without direction, vigour, beginning or end, running weakly and shrilly and with an absence of all human meaning [. . .] the voice of no age or sex" sings "ee um fah um so/ foo swee foo eem oo" (*MD* 74). Woolf takes the revival's idealized pastoral scene and recasts it within contemporary, dirty, commercialized London. It is this voice, described without nostalgia, that Woolf invokes to speak more genuinely for a mass of people, rather than a rarefied version of bygone days.

And in the central section of *To the Lighthouse*, "Time Passes," Mrs McNab, the charwoman, sings as she cleans the house to prepare for the family's summer arrival. We hear only fragments of her song, one which comes from music-hall repertory. It is "something that had been gay twenty years before on the stage perhaps, had been hummed and danced to, but now, coming from the toothless, bonneted, care-taking woman, was robbed of meaning, was like the voice of witlessness, humour, persistency itself, trodden down but springing up again" (*TTL* 149). Here the music hall is neither the liberatory space it promised to be in *Night and Day* nor the cheerfully mundane men's club Dr. Holmes believed it to be in *Mrs Dalloway*; rather, its song is transmitted from performative public space into a domestic setting overrun by the natural world, via the distorted crooning of an old woman, whose singing identifies her with the physical forces gradually overtaking the house.

These singers are old working-class women; they are solitary figures but in public contexts—paid domestic work and the street. One is singing a seemingly private song for commercial purposes, and the other sings contemporary urban music; yet their unreadable and almost disembodied voices are given some kind of organic Romantic connection to the land, approaching the state of Wordsworth's "Solitary Reaper." Here Woolf, like the revivalists, turns to song to represent lower-class figures: music provides a means by which she can ventriloquize other voices and languages. She gives us a more real idea of mass popular music and the "common people" than that of the folk revival, which stressed that traditional English music was performed only by men: these singing figures complicate its clear-cut divisions between urban and rural, folk music and the music hall, and individual and communal voices. And in Woolf's late works, she further undercuts the revival's ideas of a knowable or pure folk music tradition.

In Woolf's only recorded radio broadcast, the 1937 address "Craftsmanship," she takes up the question of historical and linguistic change, arguing that words need not retain the "purity" of their original meaning, but rather gain associations and texture as a result of varying usage. Her discussion of the dynamism and agency of words takes aim at purists like the folk revivalists, refuting their rhetoric by parodying their very language: "[t]he less we inquire into the past of our dear Mother England the better it will be for that lady's reputation—for she has gone a-roving, a-roving fair maid" (*DM* 205). This idea of linguistic movement emphatically rejects the static authenticity upheld by Parry and Sharp. Woolf dismisses such notions of purity as restrictive, and their institutionalization as ultimately ludicrous: "[words] do not like to have their purity or their impurity discussed. If you start a Society for Pure English, they will show their resentment by starting another for impure English" (204-05).

In *The Years* (also 1937), Woolf uses music and song to register historical change. Each of the novel's time periods opens with a street scene involving music, and the barrel organ, street merchants' cries, and songs of Pippy the nursemaid serve as taglines which both draw together and differentiate the historical settings. The cockney children's "discordant" and "unintelligible" song at the end of the novel shows the kind of linguistic play and productive impurity of sound which Woolf evokes in "Craftsmanship" (*TY* 314). Sung in the small hours of the morning, at the threshold of the house where a family gathering is taking place, it functions as an anti-lullaby: rather than being sung by parents in order to placate (or in Sharp's scheme, to educate), it is sung *to* adults, and its unfamiliarity disturbs them. But this discord is not ultimately threatening: rather, its nonsense words suggest a kind of ugly beauty, negating the soporific effects of musical convention and highlighting the potential for new kinds of meaning.

While writing *Between the Acts*, Woolf was also working on an early draft of a history of English literature, the first part of which is the essay "Anon." In an argument with marked parallels to Walter Benjamin's "The Storyteller," Woolf starts to historicize the development of English fiction, focusing on its origins in oral and aural traditions, and on its affinities with music, the visual arts, and the stage.[1] As Woolf told Ethel Smyth in a 1940 letter, she wanted "to investigate the influence of music on literature" (*L6* 450). "Anon" displays her interest in the relation of print media to oral traditions and the interplay of words and music, sounds and meaning. The anonymous and androgynous voice she discusses here is, as Brenda Silver describes it, "an outsider capable of cutting through the layers of social convention in order to tap the reservoir of shared emotions hidden beneath" (26). Woolf's impulse in "Anon" is not unlike that of the folk revivalists in its desire to look to the past and to the origins of artistic, musical and literary forms, and in its stress on a kind of community out of which the anonymous voice speaks without individuation. But what she doesn't share

240

with the revivalists is the ideological baggage—what she calls the "padding" of Parry's writings on music (*L6* 450). Woolf doesn't advocate the erasure of the contemporary and the cosmopolitan which the revival attempted in its bid to reimagine traditional forms and rituals.

In her final novel *Between the Acts* Woolf uses ideas of music and of folk culture to trace lines of tension between interiority and exteriority, concord and discord, and the organic and the mechanical. The questions of generic disruption and continuity raised in "Anon" are played out here in the interactions between LaTrobe, her audience, and the history of Pointz Hall. The novel works primarily through the alternation of different voices, whether they be human, non-human, or quotations from literary texts, to create what Patricia Laurence has called "the anxious counterpoint of a modern musical composition" (180). While the village pageant was a key component of the folk revival, with its process through English national history, it also works here as a reversal of the revival's aim of restoring pastoral ideals. Instead of driving out corrupting urban influences, LaTrobe's rural pageant consists almost solely of city scenes and sounds, its gramophone record entitled "London Street Cries—a potpourri" exemplifying its mixing of genres and registers. Music and sounds, from traditional rhymes to jazz to God Save the King to the "music" of a plane flying overhead, forge connections between the listeners while also pointing to the fragile nature of community, as the broken gramophone reminds us: "[t]he gramophone gurgled Unity—Dispersity. It gurgled Un . . . dis . . . And ceased" (*BTA* 201). Woolf explores mechanization's impact both on communication and on community, using music to examine what happens to voices when they are preserved through different spaces and times.

The folk revival's emphasis on preservation emphasized recording as crucial; it was for Sharp and others "a matter of the highest importance that not only the songs, but that all things that relate to the art of folk-singing, should be accurately recorded while there is yet the time and opportunity. They, one and all, form part and parcel of a great tradition that stretches back into the mists of the past in one long, unbroken chain, of which the last link is now, alas, being forged" (xviii). Woolf's sense of historical change, however, is more vexed. Sharp's unbroken chain is hinted at in the pageant audience's responses to music—it makes them "see the hidden, join the broken"—but is replaced by the "scraps, orts and fragments" of the present moment, which reflect a more complicated and dynamic sense of history, the "echoes, memories, associations" discussed in "Craftsmanship." Woolf does not attempt to reproduce the anonymous communal voice suggested by the revival. In place of the specter of "pure Mother England" which stands in for the dubious authenticity of invented traditions, Woolf invokes an enabling and productive figure of contamination and movement in the lady who has "gone a-roving."

Notes

[1] For discussions of *Between the Acts* which take up the novel's treatment of English tradition in terms of voice, language, and community, see Beer; Bowlby 146-59; Briggs; Hussey; Lawrence 170-213; Leaska.

Works Cited

Attali, Jacques. *Noise: The Political Economy of Music*. 1977. Minneapolis and London: Minnesota UP, 1985.

Beer, Gillian. "The Island and the Aeroplane: The Case of Virginia Woolf." *Nation and Narration*, ed. Homi Bhabha. London: Routledge, 1990. 265-90.

Bowlby, Rachel. *Virginia Woolf: Feminist Destinations*. Oxford: Basil Blackwell, 1988.

Boyes, Georgina. *The Imagined Village: Culture, Ideology, and the English Folk Revival*. Manchester: Manchester UP, 1993.

Briggs, Julia. "The Novels of the 1930s." *The Cambridge Companion to Virginia Woolf*, eds. Sue Roe and Susan Sellers. Cambridge: Cambridge UP, 2000.

Hussey, Mark. " 'I' Rejected; 'We' Substituted: Self and Society in *Between the Acts*." *Reading and Writing Women's Lives: A Study of the Novel of Manners*, eds. Bege K. Bowers and Barbara Brothers. Ann Arbor: UMI Research P, 1990. 141-52.

Jacobs, Peter. " 'The Second Violin Tuning in the Ante-Room': Virginia Woolf and Music." *The Multiple Muses of Virginia Woolf*, ed. Diane Gillespie. Columbia and London: U of Missouri P, 1993. 227-60.

Lambert, Constant. *Music Ho! Modern Music in Decline*. London: Faber, 1934.

Laurence, Patricia Ondek. *The Reading of Silence: Virginia Woolf in the English Tradition*. Stanford: Stanford UP, 1991.

Leaska, Mitchell. *Virginia Woolf, Pointz Hall: The Earlier and Later Typescripts of Between the Acts*. New York: University Publications, 1983.

Lee, Edward. *Music of the People: A Study of Popular Music in Great Britain*. London: Barrie and Jenkins, 1970.

Sharp, Cecil. *English Folk Song: Some Conclusions*. 1907. 3rd ed. London: Faber, 1954.

Silver, Brenda. *Virginia Woolf's Reading Notebooks*. Princeton: Princeton UP, 1983.

Woolf, Virginia. "Anon." Ed. Brenda R. Silver. *The Gender of Modernism*, ed. Bonnie Kime Scott. Bloomington, IN: Indiana UP, 1990. 679-96.

———. *Between the Acts*. New York: Harcourt Brace, 1970.

———. "Craftsmanship." *The Death of the Moth and Other Essays*. London and New York: Harcourt Brace, 1970. 198-207.

———. *The Letters of Virginia Woolf*. Ed. Nigel Nicolson and Joanne Trautmann. 6 vols. London: Hogarth P, 1975-80.

———. *Mrs Dalloway*. San Diego: Harcourt Brace, 1990.

———. *A Room of One's Own*. Ed. Michele Barrett. Harmondsworth: Penguin, 1993.

———. *To the Lighthouse*. New York: Harcourt Brace, 1990.

Caroline Webb
"All was dark; all was doubt; all was confusion": Nature, Culture, and *Orlando*'s Ruskinian Storm-Cloud

In this paper I am going to be talking about a very small passage in *Orlando* and considering its implications—only a very small part of which, I am afraid, has to do with Romanticism.

At the end of Chapter Four of Virginia Woolf's novel *Orlando: A Biography*, a great black cloud gathers over all of London. At sight of this cloud, the narrator declares "All was dark; all was doubt; all was confusion. The Eighteenth century was over; the Nineteenth century had begun" (*O* 226). Clearly, the reader says, this is an allegorical cloud: it represents the transition from the Age of Enlightenment, when Orlando listened to the witticisms of Pope, to the period of doubt, of loss of faith, of confusion over the nature of God and of the earth, initiated by the discoveries of Darwin and the geologists. But Woolf doesn't leave this rather amusing image there. In the following pages the narrator analyses the effects of the accumulated humidity on Victorian England (*O* 228-30). This passage is of course highly comic: it takes the more amusing, and/or, to Woolf and her contemporaries, objectionable features of Victorian fashions in domestic and artistic culture and attributes them all to a change in the weather. Such a move is typical of Orlando's biographer, who has already commented solemnly on how much more lurid the skies of the early seventeenth century were than those of the early twentieth. This narrator is very ready to perceive the natural world in terms of how it has been portrayed, following Oscar Wilde's remarks on how nature imitates art in "The Decay of Lying": "At present, people see fogs, not because there are fogs, but because poets and painters have taught them the mysterious loveliness of such effects. There may have been fogs for centuries in London. I daresay there were. But no one saw them, and so we don't know anything about them. They did not exist until Art had invented them" (Wilde 34). When we read in Chapter Five of *Orlando* that "purples, oranges, and reds of a dull sort took the place of the more positive landscapes of the eighteenth century" (227) we might well wonder whether Woolf is writing of actual skies or of painted landscapes.

But the lengthy passage on the relationship between the weather and Victorian culture is not only about perceptions of the weather: the narrator is here apparently inventing a delightfully symbolic climatic change to account for *cultural* symptoms that might seem less direct than the poetry describing the sun in the Renaissance. It is worth remembering that Woolf's narrator frequently adopts the biographical approaches or even the literary styles corresponding to the period of Orlando's life—which is to say, the period of English literary history—that he or she is then describing. What is it, then, about the nineteenth century that makes a parodic turn to the natural world as an explanation for cultural phenomena peculiarly apposite in Woolf's eyes?

Clearly she identifies the early nineteenth century with a sentimental passion for the natural: this is, after all, the period of Romanticism, and within a few pages Orlando will go out onto the moor proclaiming herself to be "nature's bride," sprain her ankle, and fall in love, like a good Romantic heroine, a relative of Austen's romantically minded Marianne Dashwood and of Emily Brontë's Catherine Earnshaw (though not of course of Charlotte Brontë's Jane Eyre, who rescues Rochester when he sprains *his* ankle instead). Woolf seems to be mocking this sudden discovery of Nature as the basis for human life and poetry: early in the chapter, Eusebius Chubb's melancholy identification of Nature as a vast feather bed of "undistinguished fecundity" leads him, in fact, to suicide (*O* 231).

But as Woolf traces the step-by-step development from the adoption of coffee as after-dinner drink—"coffee led to a drawing-room in which to drink it, and a drawing-room to glass cases, and [. . .] (skipping a stage or two) to innumerable little dogs, mats, and antimacassars" [*O* 228])—she seems also to be mocking the later scientific endeavor that traced the evolution of human life from a different kind of nature, Tennyson's "Nature, red in tooth and claw" (56.15). The inexorable repetitions in the passage insist on a logic more mathematical than intuitive, in form at least, and therefore quite different from the associative patterns that characterize Woolf's own style and the mental processes of her characters. It is also both dull, because of the repetitions, and absurd: the idea that coffee leads to a drawing room in which to drink it may almost seem plausible, but that the drawing-room leads to glass cases and that mantelpieces lead to pianofortes seems merely comic, a jest both at the Victorian taste for elaboration Woolf and her Bloomsbury artist colleagues found distasteful and at the stolid logic that she associates with Victorian masculinity.

There is a further twist to Woolf's story of the cloud that produced Victorian England. In 1884 John Ruskin had delivered what became a famous pair of lectures entitled "The Storm-Cloud of the Nineteenth Century," in which he spoke of his own recorded observations of a persistent storm-cloud, or "plague-cloud" (28), which he described as having appeared around 1871 or earlier and being associated with no particular direction of wind. (Note that in Chapter Four of *Orlando* the cloud comes from all directions at once.) Ruskin points out that to "the men of old time" such a cloud would have been a warning that the state was in "moral gloom," "Blanched Sun,—blighted grass,—blinded man" (30); he had earlier remarked of the ages before this plague-cloud came, "In the entire system of the Firmament, thus seen and understood, there appeared to be, to all the thinkers of those ages, the incontrovertible and unmistakable evidence of a Divine Power in creation, which had fitted, as the air for human breath, so the clouds for human sight and nourishment" (2). The implication here seems to be that such an inference could not be drawn from the contemporary heavens; that the storm-cloud of the nineteenth century is, as Woolf puts it at the end of Chapter Four, a cloud inducing darkness, doubt, and confusion. Indeed, in Ruskin's second lecture on the subject, he admitted that

> had the weather when I was young been such as it is now, no book such
> as [his] 'Modern Painters' [sic] ever would or *could* have been written;
> for every argument, and every sentiment in that book, was founded on
> the personal experience of the beauty and blessing of nature [. . .] and on
> the then demonstrable fact that over a great portion of the world's sur-
> face the air and the earth were fitted to the education of the spirit of man
> as closely as a schoolboy's primer is to his labour, and as gloriously as
> a lover's mistress to his eyes. (65)

Nevertheless, the conclusion Ruskin offers at the end of the first lecture is a conclusion based on such a belief in the morality he derives from God, one like what "the men of old times" (30)—like Gloucester in *King Lear*—would have concluded. "Whether you can affect the signs of the sky or not, you *can* the signs of the times. Whether you can bring the *sun* back or not, you can bring back your own cheerfulness, and your own honesty" (Ruskin 30). We might compare with this the polyprogenitive Eusebius Chubb's rhetorical question "Did not heaven itself, or that great frontispiece of heaven, which is the sky, indicate the assent, indeed, the instigation of the heavenly hierarchy?" (*O* 230)—an assumption that leads him, ironically, to deadly despair.

That Woolf has Ruskin's storm-cloud in mind is clear not only in the use of moralizing, the assumed connection both make between the sky and human experience, but even in the physical descriptions of their effects. Ruskin quotes a passage from his own diary as evidence that his observation of the cloud has been scientifically recorded, not vaguely felt:

> Sunday, 17th August, 1879. Raining in foul drizzle, slow and steady; sky
> pitch-dark, and I just get a little light by sitting in the bow-window; dia-
> bolic clouds over everything: and looking over my kitchen garden
> yesterday I found it one miserable mass of weeds gone to seed, the roses
> in the higher garden putrefied into brown sponges, feeling like dead
> snails; and the half-ripe strawberries all rotten at the stalks. (Ruskin 28)

Compare with this Woolf's account of Chubb wandering in his garden ("Soon he found himself involved in the shrubbery. [. . .] vegetation was rampant" [*O* 230]).

Of course, there is a difference here. Ruskin sees decay and is depressed, we infer, by its suggestion of a moral parallel, Hamlet's "unweeded garden / That grows to seed" (*Ham.* 1.2.135-36). Woolf, on the other hand, records growth ("things rank and gross in nature / Possess it merely" [*Ham.* 1.2.136-37]). She identifies the storm-cloud with a damp that engenders a horrifying fertility, whether in ivy and mould, Chubb's "scrolloping" cucumbers and giant cauliflowers (*O* 230), or the "fifteen or eighteen children" the average woman had "by the time she was thirty" (*O* 229). Where Ruskin sees rot, Woolf sees an appalling excess that is in its own way fatal.

Harold Bloom has recently argued that Woolf's passion is for literature, not for politics, chiding those many recent scholars (including many at this conference!) who have been paying attention to the political implications of the fiction or even of *A Room of One's Own*. But it seems to me that this whole section of *Orlando* affords an excellent demonstration of the extent to which the literary and the social are inextricably linked in Woolf's œuvre. In a move characteristic in particular of *Orlando: A Biography*, she links them within a sentence: the fecundity of women is associated with the swelling of ink, and the British Empire and the growth of "essays a column long" into "encyclopaedias in ten or twenty volumes" are ascribed to the same cause with parallel "thus"es (*O* 229).

We are left to infer that the British Empire derives from the sudden rise in fertility, itself implying a less noble motive for the excursion into foreign territories than the Victorian claims—which Woolf omits—about bringing light into the darkness of savage lands, etc., etc.. On the contrary, the British Empire appears to derive from the darkness of the storm-cloud, which has blotted out the Age of Enlightenment and produced such paradoxes as increased separation between the sexes accompanying an increase in the birthrate.

> Men felt the chill in their hearts; the damp in their minds. In a desperate attempt to snuggle their feelings into some sort of warmth one subterfuge was tried after another. Love, birth, and death were all swaddled in fine phrases. The sexes drew further and further apart. No open conversation was tolerated. Evasions and concealments were sedulously practised on both sides. And just as the ivy and the evergreen rioted in the damp earth outside, so did the same fertility show itself within. The life of the average woman was a succession of childbirths. [. . .] Thus the British Empire came into existence [. . .] (*O* 229)

As you see, the British Empire might as easily derive from the "swaddling" of fundamentals in fine phrases (remember Jacob Flanders arguing with Bonamy over terms like "good" and "justice" [*JR* 102]), and from evasions and concealments, as from the actual rise in the population. The confusion Woolf indicts here is the pouring together of ill-thought-out ideas that produces the British Empire as well as the voluminous phrases of the encyclopaedias that have replaced the essay, Woolf's own preferred form (and, incidentally, that swell this whole opening section of Chapter Five). I have written elsewhere of the subversive effect of Woolf's deployment of lists, notably in the Preface to *Orlando* (Webb, "Listing"): she uses such lists to parodic effect throughout the text, but nowhere to more ludicrous effect than in the *gradatio* leading from coffee to antimacassars. The humor here seems more jeering, less generous, I think, than anywhere else in the text—which may be due to Woolf's hostility to Victorian fashion, to encyclopaedic writing, to the British Empire, or to the sedulous practice of evasions and concealments that underlies them all.

This is of course not the only occasion in the novel where nature and human experience have been connected. In Chapter Two, for instance, nature was alleged to "delight in muddle and mystery, so that even now (the first of November, 1927) we know not why we go upstairs, or why we come down again" (*O* 78). The date in this passage links Orlando's seventeenth-century experience with contemporary perceptions, and the subsequent discussion of Memory, the capricious seamstress, indeed seems as apt to Woolf's habitual representation of mental process as it does to the age of Locke. (By contrast, the nineteenth century will be the first time Orlando feels herself alien to the spirit of the *times*.)

Ruskin's lectures provide an insight into the nature, as it were, of Woolf's animus against Romantic and Victorian ideas about Nature. Wordsworth, rather medievally, saw the natural world as the medium through which the human soul experienced (or rather regained) the divine. The Romantics sought sermons in stones, and their literal-minded Victorian successors set out to be geologists, naturalists, to understand the logic of the natural world (as Woolf mocks with the chain from coffee to antimacassars) and so to put this Romantically overwhelming force back in its place. In so doing they affirmed what one might call the British Empire attitude to the environment, "Dominion over palm and pine" (Kipling 4). Ruskin himself chose to moralize over possible parallels between the signs of the sky and the signs of the times, but explicitly declined to speculate on whether his audience could influence the former as well as the latter. But his contemporaries recognized the facts behind his observations: there was a close correspondence between the dates he gave for the growth of his storm-cloud and the rise in the industrial consumption of coal. Ruskin himself refers briefly to the "Manchester devil's darkness" (27), but does not directly address the fact that his cloud is what we would call industrial pollution.

I am not suggesting that Woolf was a proto-environmentalist. Rather, I am interested in the mere fact that this grand Ruskinian vision of the admonitory Firmament demonstrates the effect of the human on the natural (or, if you like, the rest of the natural) world, something Woolf certainly knew. (*Orlando*'s pastoral is not of course marred by any reference to industry, although by Chapter Six the protagonist is driving a car and taking trains to stores rather than a carriage to court.) The Romantics assumed that Nature is provided for our spiritual benefit—an idea mocked in the vision of the sky as feather bed (*O* 231). The Victorians assumed that nature and the world in general is provided for our practical economic benefit—an idea mocked in the monstrous pile of kitsch Orlando discovers soon after, a pile whose accretions themselves demonstrate the contradictions between

Wordsworthian ideas of the dangerous thickening of social experience around the glorious soul and the Victorian practice of materialism. Both ideas of nature are represented in nineteenth-century literature by the abundant deployment of the Pathetic Fallacy—a concept identified, ironically, by Ruskin, and exemplified in the behavior of his double Eusebius Chubb.

But what Ruskin's lectures actually demonstrate is the extent to which the natural is crucially affected by the cultural, something late eighteenth-century writers like Goldsmith had noted. At the end of the twentieth century we are as a society starting to take account of this relationship, and it is—belatedly, you might think—becoming a hot topic in philosophy of science. How can there be such a thing as "the natural," out there and separate, when nature can be transformed completely by the effects of human cultural change? How separable are nature and culture anyway? I have argued elsewhere that Woolf was aware of modern, Heisenbergian notions that the scientist is crucially a part of what he (or she) observes (Webb, "Room"). This is even dizzyingly visible at this moment in *Orlando*. The fact that the cloud alludes to Ruskin's "Storm-Cloud of the Nineteenth Century" further complicates the relationship between nature and culture established, or undone by satire, at this point in the novel. Instead of being an invention—an original, spontaneously developed and directly appropriate fiction—Woolf's cloud alludes to a "real" phenomenon: nature has indeed informed her art. But the cloud, and the association with doubt, also derive from Victorian culture by way of that grand old man, the much-respected Ruskin. Once again, the natural arrives in *Orlando* by way of the cultural, and is always dependent on it. Even what appear to be Woolf's own *naturally* created images turn out to be borrowed: however revolutionary the theoretical insights of *Orlando*, its language and images lead inexorably to, and from, other literatures.

Such a recognition of course returns to the literary and the political in the same moment. Suzanne Young has persuasively argued that the very prevalence of artifice in *Orlando* acts as a code for lesbianism in early twentieth-century English culture. The idea of writing as a lesbian (a phrase Young avoids) may imply an essentialist notion of biological identity. But the insistence on the literariness or culturalness of things exemplified by Woolf's use of Ruskin's storm-cloud is itself an insistence that there is no such thing as the natural, in anything, that is separable from the cultural. The cloud is real and literary, natural and man-made, at the same time. Woolf's novel examines the whole question of gender identity, offering at various times various answers to the question of whether such identity is naturally or culturally determined—whether the apparently transgendered Orlando has always been female, or is now male, or is made female by the adoption of clothing or ways of thought; and the answers the narrator gives are always appropriate to the literary historical moment. The vexed question "What sex is Orlando?", or even "What sexuality is Orlando?", is answered for us from the moment we recognize that the world of the novel is a world shaped entirely by the lens of cultural history through which Woolf observes it. The answers to such questions, whatever "The Truth and nothing but the Truth" of the matter (*O* 136), can only ever be culturally determined ones.

Works Cited

Bloom, Harold. "Feminism as the Love of Reading." *Raritan: A Quarterly Review* 14 (Fall 1994): 29-42.

Kipling, Rudyard. "Recessional." 1897. *The Complete Verse*. London: Kyle Cathie, 1990. 266.

Ruskin, John. *The Storm-Cloud of the Nineteenth Century: Two Lectures Delivered at the London Institution February 4th and 11th, 1884. The Complete Works of John Ruskin*. New York: Crowell, n.d. Vol. 23-24. 24: [2]: 1-68.

Shakespeare, William. *Hamlet*. Ed. Harold Jenkins. The Arden Shakespeare. London and New York: Methuen, 1982.

Tennyson, Alfred. *In Memoriam A.H.H. The Poems of Tennyson*. Ed. Christopher Ricks. 2nd ed. Vol. 2. Harlow: Longmans, 1987. 304-459.

Webb, Caroline. "Listing to the Right: Authority and Inheritance in *Orlando* and *Ulysses*." *Twentieth Century Literature* 40 (1994): 190-204.

——. "The Room as Laboratory: The Gender of Science and Literature in Modernist Polemics." *Modernism, Gender, and Culture: A Cultural Studies Approach*. Ed. Lisa Rado. New York: Garland, 1997. 337-52.

Wilde, Oscar. "The Decay of Lying." *Intentions and Other Writings*. 1891. Garden City, NY: Doubleday, n.d. 13-42.

Woolf, Virginia. *Jacob's Room*. 1922. New York and London: Harcourt, 1950. *Virginia Woolf*. CD-ROM. Major Authors on CD-ROM. Woodbridge, CT: Primary Source Media, c1997.

——. *Orlando: A Biography*. 1928. New York and London: Harcourt, 1956. *Virginia Woolf*. CD-ROM. Major Authors on CD-ROM. Woodbridge, CT: Primary Source Media, c1997.

Young, Suzanne. "The Unnatural Object of Modernist Aesthetics: Artifice in Woolf's *Orlando*." *Unmanning Modernism: Gendered Re-Readings*. Ed. Elizabeth Jane Harrison and Shirley Peterson. Knoxville, TN: U of Tennessee P, 1997. 168-87.

David Vallins
"Whose shape is that within the car? & why?": *Mrs Dalloway* and "The Triumph of Life"

The episode of *Mrs. Dalloway* describing the journey through London of a car concealing an (unidentified) "face of the very greatest importance" and the reactions of the crowd surrrounding it is one of the most enigmatic and intriguing in the novel (see *MD* 13-20). Its primary effect, I will suggest, is to satirize the reverence for power and authority manifested in the crowd's fascination with the identity of the car's occupant (which is never revealed to them or to the reader). This satirical image, moreover, highlights the oppressive conventionality of a society "in denial" of its disastrous losses in the First World War, as well as of its own continuing divisions—a denial whose effects are most prominent in the mistreatment and death of Septimus Warren Smith (see Zwerdling 71). In addition to these more obvious meanings, however, the fact that Woolf never identifies the figure in the car, yet enigmatically states that "The face in the motor car will [. . .] be known" at a remote future time "when London is a grass-grown path" and its residents are "but bones with a few wedding rings mixed up in their dust and the gold stoppings of innumerable decayed teeth" (*MD* 16) seems riddlingly to hint at some further, as yet unexplained meaning. One of the questions raised by this passage concerns the relationship of the figure in the car to the Prime Minister who appears at Clarissa's party at the end of the novel—prompting similarly reverential reactions in his fellow-guests, as well as in Clarissa herself—and who is among those whom members of the crowd believe may be within the car in Bond Street (*MD* 14-17, 187-90). Woolf's early drafts of the novel involve no ambiguity on this point: the opening chapter, indeed, was originally called "The Prime Minister," and describes the premier's appearance in sufficient detail for his identity to be unambiguous. The figure "with his cigar between his lips [as the Daily Mirror shows him] [. . .] democratically beaming good fellowship," that is, recalls many popular images of Lloyd George,[1] albeit that another early draft for the novel refers rather to his predecessor, H. H. Asquith, as the intended recipient of Septimus's discovery that "Trees are alive" and "There is no crime."[2] In contrast, the published text of *Mrs. Dalloway* resists any such identification either of the Prime Minister, or of the figure within the car, though the specificity with which it situates the events in June, 1923 implies that the Prime Minister is neither Asquith nor Lloyd George, but rather the Conservative, Baldwin, who succeeded to the premiership in May that year (see *MD* 77 and Butler 9).

Woolf's riddling statement as to the eventual discovery of "the face in the motor car" thus remains perplexing. Yet the opening scene of the novel is notably anticipated by several earlier passages both in Woolf's own writing and in contemporary and earlier authors with whose works she was undoubtedly familiar. Among the most interesting of these is a passage in her diary describing her own observation of Asquith's triumphal return to parliament following his re-election as an M.P. in 1920, many aspects of which are echoed in the well-known scene of *Mrs. Dalloway* (*D2* 22). This passage, moreover, not only anticipates her original identification of the figure in the car with one of the Liberal leaders of the wartime period, but also highlights Woolf's own very mixed feelings towards the once-radical premier who led Britain into the First World War, and who—together with his successor, Lloyd George—thus held substantial responsibility for the sufferings highlighted by her portrayal of Septimus, and which form a central part of the context of the novel (see Levenback 45, *D2* 51, *L2* 97-101, *L2* 57, *L2* 71, and Morgan 109-10, 114-5)

At the same time, however, the opening passage echoes, and seems to parody, several earlier evocations of triumphal processions or pageants, one of which is Joyce's description of the progress of the viceregal cavalcade through the streets of Dublin in the "Wandering Rocks" episode of *Ulysses*, which similarly focuses on the reactions of the diverse population which observes it, as well as the "obsequious" salutes which it receives from policemen and others (see Jenkins 516, Snaith 139, Joyce 242-4). Woolf's reading of *Ulysses* during her composition of *Mrs. Dalloway* increases the likelihood of a connection; yet as Anna Snaith comments, the most significant difference between the two passages is the fact that Woolf leaves "the identity of the figure in the car unknown" (Snaith 139). According to Snaith, Woolf uses this device to "subvert" the authority figure in the car by shifting the focus of her narrative to the "community of characters" observing it (Snaith 139-40). Yet though this passage undoubtedly mocks the image of authority, it also places so much emphasis on the habitual or automatic nature of the crowd's reverence for power and tradition as implicitly to satirize the society as a whole, and especially its ritualistic fascination with what Woolf ironically calls "the majesty of England."

In addition to this contemporary parallel, however, Woolf's enigmatic description of the passing car bears striking resemblances to what is probably the most celebrated (if also the most ironic) version of such a triumphal procession in 19th-century literature—namely Shelley's description, in "The Triumph of Life," of a "chariot" or "car" bearing a veiled and mysterious presence with which the surrounding crowd expresses an automatic and ultimately maniacal fascination ("The Triumph of Life" ll. 79-180, Shelley 457-60). Shelley's vehicle, and the ironically-depicted pageantry that surrounds it, form the central image of "The Triumph of Life," while the ignorance of the crowd as to the identity of the vehicle's occupant is central to the message of his poem. What this image signifies in Shelley is not only the mindless obedience to power and authority which has dissolved or suppressed the optimism of the earlier Romantics, but also the passage of time itself, which—he suggests—inevitably lays waste to youthful optimism and idealism. Woolf's parallel image, I will suggest, not only highlights the destructive authoritarianism and conformity of post-war British society, but also the fading of youthful radicalism exemplified by those who—like Clarissa and Sally Seton (now boasting of her "ten thousand a year" and sons at Eton)—once dreamed of "reforming the world," even of founding "a society to abolish private property" (*MD* 205, 206, 35).

To connect Woolf with Shelley, moreover, is by no means so surprising as the conventions of scholarship might suggest. Gillian Beer, indeed, suggests that "The Triumph of Life" may well have provided the model for Woolf's evocation of dawn in *The Waves* (Beer 86), while her references to Shelley's *Adonais* in *The Voyage Out* and the short story "Mrs Dalloway in Bond Street" have been discussed by several critics (see *VO* 55, *CSF* 148, 149, 152, "Adonais" ll. 356-7, Shelley 402, Saunders 139-40, and Schlack 74-6). Clarissa Dalloway and Sally Seton, moreover, are described as having—at the time of their youthful infatuation—"read Shelley [together with Plato and Morris] by the hour"—a description interestingly echoed by Woolf's statement, in a diary-entry which also discusses the progress of *Mrs Dalloway*—that "When I was 20 [. . .] I read masses of Carlyle. . . Gibbon . . . & Shelley" (*MD* 35 *D2* 310). That Shelley's works should have been of particular interest to her, moreover, may well be due not only to the "sexless" or androgynous quality which she attributes to him in *A Room of One's Own* (*AROO* 128-9, 135), but also to his persistent criticisms of the oppressive nationalism of Britain in his own period (see, for example, "The Mask of Anarchy," Shelley 301-10)—an attitude echoed in Woolf's response to British politics in the First World War. Her statement, in a letter of August 1914, that "It is rather like Napoleonic times I daresay" highlights her sense of the parallels between the two eras, while Clarissa's reading of Baron Marbot's memoirs—and particularly his descriptions of Napoleon's Russian campaign (in which more than half a million French and allied troops were killed)—seems to represent a half-submerged (and thus mimetic) allusion to the wartime losses which Clarissa and others have suppressed (see *L2* 50, *MD* 32, Schlack 62, Marbot 2:283-4, Nafziger 333).

As in "The Triumph of Life," moreover, the view of Romantic optimism and idealism implied in Woolf's depiction of the aftermath of war is a highly ambivalent one. Clarissa's Wordsworthian sense—significantly presented immediately after Septimus's death—that the "unseen" spiritual essence of each individual "might survive, be recovered somehow attached to this person or that, or even haunting certain places after death" (*MD* 166), indeed, as much suggests an idealist compensation for the fragmentariness and isolation of present experience, as any authorial endorsement of Wordsworth's or Coleridge's position. And just as Shelley repeatedly questions the transcendent unity of being evoked by Coleridge or Wordsworth, so the seemingly random juxtaposition of voices and visions in *Mrs Dalloway* evokes the isolation of individual consciousness in ways which inevitably challenge Clarissa's Romantic speculations.

In addition to these larger themes, however, there are several striking parallels between the settings and structures of Woolf's and Shelley's texts. In both cases, the events described take place on a single day in June in a crowded city, and both texts begin by evoking the splendour of a summer morning, and later describe a figure of authority (in Shelley's case,

Napoleon, in Woolf's the unnamed Prime Minister) who is strangely bereft of his customary grandeur or impressiveness ("The Triumph of Life" ll. 217-34, Shelley 461, and *MD* 187-8). Just as Woolf's evocation of summer mornings at Bourton is immediately followed by her description of Clarissa's journey through London (*MD* 1-2), moreover, so the "vision" following the evocation of dawn in Shelley's prologue begins as follows:

Methought I sate beside a public way

Thick strewn with summer dust, and a great stream
Of people there was hurrying to and fro
Numerous as gnats upon the evening gleam,

All hastening onward, yet none seemed to know
Whither he went, or whence he came, or why
He made one of the multitude [. . .]

Old age and youth, manhood and infancy,

Mixed in one mighty torrent did appear,
Some flying from the thing they feared and some
Seeking the object of another's fear

[. . .]
And others mournfully within the gloom

Of their own shadow walked, and called it death
And some fled from it as it were a ghost,
Half fainting in the affliction of vain breath.
("The Triumph of Life" ll. 43-61, Shelley 456-7)

Despite the Dantesque quality of Shelley's images, the fact that these portentous states of being occur "beside a public way,/Thick strewn with summer dust," among "a great stream/Of people [. . .] hurrying to and fro," none of whom "seemed to know/Whither he went, or whence he came, or why/He made one of the multitude," seems strikingly appropriate to the setting of Clarissa's journey and of Septimus's first appearance, among the populace so fascinatedly demonstrating their obeisance to the unseen, majestic presence in the "motor-car [. . .] opposite Mulberry's shop-window" (*MD* 13-14). When compared with Shelley's text, indeed, the automatism with which not only Woolf's working-class characters, but also Clarissa Dalloway thrill to what she calls "the pale light of the immortal presence" (*MD* 18), suggests a metaphor for Clarissa's more important habit of accepting or adapting to the losses of her youth, as well as the divisions of society (see *MD* 33, 63-44, and Zwerdling 78). Both of these forms of acceptance or obeisance, moreover, are central to Shelley's vision of the failure of the Enlightenment and the triumph of an automatism which—despite the very different tone and context in which he presents it—closely parallels that of Woolf's enthralled Londoners.

The details of Shelley's and Woolf's descriptions of the car and its occupant, moreover, make the analogy still more suggestive. "So came a chariot on the silent storm/Of its own rushing splendour," Shelley writes:

> and a Shape
> So sate within as one whom years deform
>
> Beneath a dusky hood and double cape
> Crouching within the shadow of a tomb,
> And o'er what seemed the head a cloud like crape
>
> Was bent, a dun and faint ethereal gloom,
> Tempering the light [. . .]
>
> ("The Triumph of Life" ll. 86-93, Shelley 457)

Even the first appearance, in *Mrs. Dalloway*, of the car containing "a face of the very greatest importance" (*MD* 13) includes several striking parallels to Shelley's introduction of the chariot bearing this mysterious presence. Perhaps the most important of these is the resemblance between Shelley's figure, crouching "Beneath a dusky hood and double cape," and the appearance of whose head is barely distinguishable beneath "a cloud like crape" or "dun and faint ethereal gloom/Tempering the light," and the "face" described by Woolf, appearing only momentarily "against the dove-grey upholstery, before a male hand drew the blind and there was nothing to be seen except a square of dove-grey" (*MD* 13). The analogy between Shelley's and Woolf's reduction of the presence in the car to little more than "a cloud like crape" or "a square of dove-grey" is far more than merely visual. In both cases, indeed, it is precisely the invisibility or characterlessness of this presence that enables the crowd's subsequent fascination with it to become so powerful a symbol of unthinking obedience to conventional values—and, in a broader sense, to the nullifying force of habit and experience which Woolf contrasts with the ill-fated radicalism of Clarissa's youth (see *MD* 35 and Fleishman 74), and Shelley with the similarly disappointed optimism of Enlightenment thinkers from Voltaire to Rousseau.

The parallels between Woolf's and Shelley's texts are, however, still more prominent in the detailed evocation of the adoring crowd which follows in both authors. "The crowd gave way," Shelley continues,

> and I arose aghast,
> [. . .]
> And saw like clouds upon the thunder blast
>
> The million with fierce cry and maniac dance
> Raging around; such seemed the jubilee

As when to greet some conqueror's advance

Imperial Rome poured forth her living sea
From senatehouse and prison and theatre
[. . .]

Nor wanted here the just similitude
Of a triumphal pageant, for where'er

The chariot rolled a captive multitude
Was driven; all those who had grown old in power
Or misery,—all who have their age subdued,,

By action or by suffering, and whose hour
Was drained to its last sand in weal or woe,
So that the trunk survived both fruit and flower [. . .]
("The Triumph of Life" ll. 107-24, Shelley 458)

Woolf's continuing description of the effects produced by the car in Bond
Street suggest both general and specific analogies to Shelley's imagery. As
in many passages of Joyce's *Ulysses*, indeed, her narrative repeatedly seems
to involve a parodic comparison of contemporary reality with a myth which
highlights its mundanity, yet at the same time gives shape and meaning to
her portrayal of the contemporary. "The motor car with its blinds drawn and
an air of inscrutable reserve," she writes, "proceeded towards Piccadilly"
(*MD* 16), just as—after its first appearance—Shelley's "car [. . .] past/With
solemn speed majestically on." That the "greatness" concealed within the
car is that of what Woolf—with gentle mockery of a traditional British cult
—calls "the majesty of England," moreover, not only parallels Shelley's
description of the "majestic" movement of the "car" itself, but also highlights the importance, in both texts, of the connection between habitual
veneration for conquerors or rulers, and the larger theme of the voluntary,
yet almost automatic, sacrificing of moral and political idealism to the false
gods of conformity and acceptance, or—as both authors also emphasize—to
the passage of time and of "Life" itself. Shelley's ironic—if also despairing
—description of this "triumphal pageant," comprising "all [. . .] who had
grown old in power/Or misery," indeed, strikingly prefigures Woolf's
panoramic emphasis on the diversity of classes involved in such willing ado-
ration of their traditional "conqueror"—be it the arbitrary forms of authority
evoked by their blindness to the car's occupant, or the increasing acceptance
of social division illustrated, for example, by Clarissa's ultimate indifference
to those outside the elite attending her party (see Wyatt 443-4 and Beer 55).
And just as this decay, in Shelley, draws the life of the multitude "to its last
sand in weal or woe/So that the trunk survived both fruit and flower," so
Clarissa's repeated recollections of the youth in which, with the radical Sally
Seton, she "read Plato [. . .] read Morris; read Shelley by the hour" (*MD* 35)

are gradually replaced by the fascination with royalty and power with which Woolf also characterizes the "crowd" surrounding her (*MD* 16-18).

Perhaps the most striking aspect of the relationship between the two texts, however, is the irony with which Woolf seems to convert Shelley's image of the "great winter" at the end of life, or time ("The Triumph of Life" ll. 126-7, Shelley 458), into an evocation of a future period in which "curious antiquaries, sifting the ruins of time" will finally discover the full significance of an earlier age's crazed fascination with "majesty" or "the enduring symbol of the state" (*MD* 16). By stating, in her next sentence, that in this period after the destruction of London, "the face in the motor car will [. . .] be known" (*MD* 16), indeed, Woolf enlarges the significance of her archeological analogy to include an apparent reference to the way in which her text itself conceals—yet at the same time half reveals—its repeated echoes of Shelley's "Triumph of Life." What the face in her motor-car represents, that is, will—it seems—only be "known" when literary archeologists have unveiled her allusions to the destructive cycle of human existence to which Shelley, with a last and bitter irony, gives the name "Life." And just as Woolf, with strange portentousness, says "The face in the car will then be known," so Shelley writes—with similarly mythic yet perplexing force—

> Struck to the heart by this sad pageantry,
> Half to myself I said, "And what is this?
> Whose shape is that within the car? & why"—
>
> I would have added—"is all here amiss?"
> But a voice answered . . "Life" . . .
> ("The Triumph of Life" ll. 176-80, Shelley 460)

The absurd yet tragic "pageant" which Woolf, like Shelley, associates with the unknown "face"—the face which, in both texts, dissolves into nothing more than its physical frame, symbolizing the mind's automatic creation of imprisoning "idols"—is thus explicitly identified by Shelley with the process and effects of experience which Woolf depicts in a practical and quasi-factual manner through the combination of Clarissa's and other characters' carelessly-flowing consciousnesses with the recollection of their earlier—and far more promising—selves.[2] That the question of Shelley's narrator as to the identity of the shape within the car is spoken "half to myself," moreover, may perhaps help to explain the riddling indirectness of Woolf's reference to the occupant of her own mythic vehicle.

Notes

[1] See *The Virginia Woolf Manuscripts* Reel 6 M119, 2^r (the square brackets are Woolf's); also Morgan, 150.

[2] See British Library MS Add. 51044, 58^r.

Works Cited

Beer, Gillian. *Virginia Woolf: The Common Ground.* Edinburgh: Edinburgh U P, 1996.

Butler, David, and Butler, Gareth. *British Political Facts 1900-1994.* Basingstoke: Macmillan, 1994.

Fleishman, Avrom. *Virginia Woolf: A Critical Reading.* Baltimore: Johns Hopkins U P, 1975.

Jenkins, William D. "Virginia Woolf and the Belittling of *Ulysses.*" *James Joyce Quarterly* 25 (1988): 513-519.

Joyce, James. *Ulysses.* Ed. Jeri Johnson. Oxford: Oxford U P, 1993.

Levenback, Karen. "Virginia Woolf's 'War in the Village' and 'The War from the Street': An Illusion of Immunity." In *Virginia Woolf and War: Fiction, Reality, and Myth.* Ed. Mark Hussey. Syracuse, NY: Syracuse U P, 1992. 40-57.

Marbot, Jean Baptiste Antoine Marcellin de. *The Memoirs of Baron de Marbot.* Trans. A. J. Butler, 2 vols. London: Longman's, 1892.

Morgan, Kenneth O. *Lloyd George.* London: Weidenfeld and Nicolson, 1974.

Nafziger, George. *Napoleon's Invasion of Russia.* Novato, CA: Presidio Press, 1988.

Saunders, Julia. "Mortal Stain: Literary Allusion and Female Sexuality in 'Mrs Dalloway in Bond Street.'" *Studies in Short Fiction* 15:2 (1978): 139-144.

Schlack, Beverly Anne. *Continuing Presences: Virginia Woolf's Use of Literary Allusion.* University Park, PA: Pennsylvania State U P, 1979.

Shelley, P. B. *Shelley's Poetry and Prose*, ed. Donald H. Reiman and Sharon B. Powers. New York: Norton, 1977.

Snaith, Anna. "Virginia Woolf's Narrative Strategies: Negotiating Between Public and Private Voices." *Journal of Modern Literature* 20 (1996): 133-148.

Woolf, Virginia. *A Room of One's Own* and *Three Guineas.* Ed. Morag Shiach. Oxford: Oxford U P, 1992.

——. *The Complete Shorter Fiction of Virginia Woolf.* Ed. Susan Dick. London: Hogarth Press, 1985.

——. *The Diary of Virginia Woolf.* Ed. Anne Olivier Bell. 5 vols. London: Hogarth Press, 1977-84.

——. *Letters of Virginia Woolf.* Ed. Nigel Nicolson. 6 vols. London: Hogarth Press, 1975-80.

——. *Mrs Dalloway.* San Diego: Harcourt, Brace, Jovanovich, 1990.

——. *The Virginia Woolf Manuscripts*: From the Henry W. and Albert A. Berg Collection at the New York Public Library. Woodbridge, CT: Research Publications, 1993.

——. *The Voyage Out.* London: Collins, 1978.

Wyatt, Jean M. "*Mrs Dalloway*: Literary Allusion as Structural Metaphor." *PMLA* 88 (1973): 440-451.

Zwerdling, Alex. "*Mrs Dalloway* and the Social System." *PMLA* 92 (1977): 69-82.

Donald T. Blume

"Because It Is There": George Mallory's Presence in Virginia Woolf's *To the Lighthouse*

The story of George Mallory and *To the Lighthouse* does not lend itself to a fifteen minute telling, but that said, I have fifteen minutes to tell you who George Mallory was, what his connections to Virginia Woolf were, and, very briefly, how his story informed Woolf's writing of *To the Lighthouse*.

Who was George Mallory?

On 8 June 1924 George Leigh Mallory, known to his many friends as "Sir Galahad," died while trying to reach the summit of Mount Everest, or Chomolungma, the "Goddess Mother." In a word, everything about Mallory's last climb was epic; thus, whether viewed from below, or from thousands of miles away and weeks and months later in England, when George Mallory led his young climbing partner Andrew Irvine up the mountain and into the deadly thin air near the summit only to disappear forever into the enshrouding mists, it was as if modern twentieth century reality briefly receded and the old gods and heroes met in one last epic battle. When news of the tragic outcome of that battle finally reached England on 21 June, thousands—perhaps tens of thousands—of climbers and non-climbers alike became obsessed with trying to solve the mystery of Mallory's last climb. Aided by detailed coverage in the London *Times* and other publications, widespread public interest in Mallory and his fate lasted many months.

Of course, Mallory was more than a news story. He was certainly much more than the preeminent mountaineer of his day who reportedly once uttered the phrase that opens this essay when asked to explain his desire to climb the highest mountain in the world. He was also much more than the breathtakingly handsome unrequited love-interest of Lytton Strachey. When he began his last climb at the age of 37, George Mallory was a husband and father of three young children, a Cambridge graduate, a war veteran, a respected writer and lecturer, and a recently appointed "assistant secretary and lecturer" in Cambridge University's groundbreaking Extra-Mural Studies program. Indeed, had Mallory succeeded in his attempt to climb Mount Everest, he would quite literally have returned to a still war-scarred England as an explorer and conquering hero very much in the mold of Sir Walter Raleigh, Captain James Cook, Sir Richard Francis Burton, Sir Henry Morton Stanley, Robert Falcon Scott, and Sir Ernest Henry Shackleton. Successfully conquering Mount Everest would have secured Mallory both the inside track to the authorship of a guaranteed classic mountaineering expedition narrative, and a knighthood (in 1953, Sir Edmund Hillary, a New Zealander, received this honor). But more importantly, it is clear that Mallory, a man who had strong progressive and liberal political views, who had taken active personal interests in woman's suffrage, Irish Home Rule, and the League of Nations' education program, considered the fame he would inevitably gain from the conquest of Everest as capital upon which he could build a meaningful career. In short, as Mallory's friend and climbing mentor Geoffrey Winthrop Young wrote in his powerful and moving tribute in the 5 July 1924 issue of *The Nation and Athenæum*, George Mallory knew that if he returned alive from the summit of Everest he could go on to have a "career of public usefulness" (438).

George Mallory's Connections to Virginia Woolf

A year after Mallory's death, in June of 1925, Virginia Woolf began seriously planning *To the Lighthouse*. At this same time, she pointedly called her proposed book an "Elegy." Shortly after energetically beginning the first draft of her book in August of 1925, Woolf became ill and did not resume work on the book until January of 1926 (Lee 470-1). Perhaps coincidentally, on 9 January *The Nation and Athenæum*, in all but title the official newspaper of Bloomsbury, published a lengthy and positive review of *The Fight for Everest, 1924*, the official book of the Everest Expedition. Noting that the book, like the expedition itself, was the product of "team work," the reviewer, Edmund Candler, wrote "if the separate parts could have been assimilated and given the unity of a single continuous narrative by one of the writers, it would have been all to the good." Candler went on to write that "Mallory, if he had survived, would have been the very man for the work" (528).

On 3 September 1927, two months and a day after *To the Lighthouse* was reviewed in its pages by Edwin Muir in some five hundred cryptic words, *The Nation and Athenæum* published Robert Graves' emotionally charged and much lengthier positive review of David Pye's *George Leigh Mallory: a Memoir*. Graves' review of Pye's book was decidedly biased: Mallory, in Graves' words "an outstanding beautiful character," had been Graves' teacher before the war and "best man" at Graves' 1918 wedding (723).

My use of the word "cryptic" in describing Edwin Muir's 2 July review of *To the Lighthouse* requires clarification. In part, Muir wrote that

> "To the Lighthouse" is a novel difficult to judge. Like the last volume on this list, it stands at the summit of the development of a remarkable writer. Its aim is high and serious, its technique brilliant; there are more beautiful pages in it than Mrs. Woolf has written before; a unique intuition and intelligence are at work in it almost continuously, and at high pressure. The difficulties which the author surmounts in it are such as few contemporary novelists would even attempt. Its positive merits are thus very high. [. . .] The symbolism is plain enough; but in the novel, so entangled is it with other matters, interesting enough in themselves, that it becomes obscured. [. . .] (450)

I believe that both Edwin Muir and Virginia Woolf knew that the entangling and obscuring "other matters" in *To the Lighthouse* concerned George Mallory and Mount Everest. The explanation for Muir's failure to reveal more clearly what was so plain to him may be on display in Woolf's 27 May 1927 letter to Roger Fry wherein she wrote that "Whether its right or wrong I don't know, but directly I'm told what a thing means, it becomes hateful to me" (Lee 472). Given Virginia Woolf's express aversion to such revelations of hidden meaning, I suspect Muir had been asked—quite possibly by Roger Fry or Leonard Woolf—to avoid any direct revelations of symbolic meanings in his review. Actually, Muir tipped his knowing hand quite creatively in the second sentence of his review: the last volume on the list of fiction he was reviewing along with Woolf's book was Thomas Mann's *The Magic Mountain*. Similarly, Muir pointed out that like George Mallory's desire to climb Mount Everest, the aim of Woolf's book was "high and serious," and like Mallory's climbing technique, so too was her writing "technique brilliant." Muir also coyly noted that writing *To the Lighthouse* apparently required Woolf to employ the literary equivalent of the supplementary "high pressure" oxygen Mallory employed on his final climb and that the difficulties Woolf surmounted were, like the mountaineering challenges Mallory was already famous for overcoming, so difficult that most other writers would not "attempt" them. Symbolically, the meaning inherent in Muir's cryptic use of mountaineering vocabulary to describe Woolf's book is, I feel, also "plain enough."

"But," I suspect some of you are thinking, "who was George Mallory to Virginia Woolf?"

On one level, Virginia Woolf was uniquely well-qualified to translate George Mallory's story into a work of fiction because so many of her friends were also Mallory's. My working list of the people Mallory considered his friends includes James Strachey, Geoffrey Keynes, Jacques Raverat, Lytton Strachey, Rupert Brooke, Duncan Grant, and Will Arnold Forster. Moreover, Mallory's interest in adult education eventually brought him into the orbit if not the direct line of sight of Leonard Woolf, the man who had quite literally written the official book on adult education. In addition, because he was a mountaineer, Mallory would have inevitably been known by many of the other recreational climbers who moved in Woolf's circle, including for example Woolf's friend Katharine Cox, who married Will Arnold-Forster who himself would eventually marry Ruth Mallory, George's widow, after Katharine's death in 1938. Thus, as a mountaineer, Mallory had many contemporary connections to Virginia Woolf and Bloomsbury. Even more significantly, Mallory's closest connection to Woolf was arguably through her own father, Sir Leslie Stephen—the crucial sub rosa reason Virginia Woolf was so well-placed to make use of George Mallory's epic story. In addition to having been a past President of the Alpine Club—one of the chief sponsors of the Everest Expeditions of the early 1920s, Leslie Stephen was the author of *The Playground of Europe*, a mountaineering classic that George Mallory would inevitably have read and reread during his formative climbing days. In turn, by the time of his last climb, Mallory had become the exemplar of the kind of man Leslie Stephen admired and envied, a fact which Woolf belatedly and still indirectly revealed in her 1932 essay "Leslie Stephen." In that essay, Woolf observed of her father that, "to the end of his days he would speak of great climbers and explorers with a peculiar mixture of admiration and envy," and then Woolf went on to write that "The Sunset on Mont Blanc," an essay her father had added to the revised version of his classic book, was "in his opinion the best thing he ever wrote" (76).

I can assure you, as sure as I am standing here before you today, that Virginia Woolf's journey to the lighthouse goes directly through "The Sunset on Mont Blanc" and the two chapters of *The Playground of Europe* that follow that essay—"The Alps in Winter" and "Regrets of a Mountaineer"—even as does George Mallory's journey to the heights of Everest. Both Virginia Woolf and George Mallory were intimately familiar with these three essays.

For her part, Woolf found inspiration for the physical setting of *To the Lighthouse* in "The Sunset on Mont Blanc" and "Regrets of a Mountaineer." In the first essay Leslie Stephen described the surrounding mountain ranges seen from the summit of Mont Blanc as being "drawn up in parallel ranks like the sea waves heaved in calm weather by a monotonous ground-swell," and he likened the effect of Mont Blanc's lengthening shadow on the surrounding sea of lesser mountains to the darkness cast by "the gnomon of a gigantic sundial" (273). Later in this same paragraph, Stephen noted that, "by some singular effect of perspective, rays of darkness seemed to be converging from above our heads to a point immediately above the apex of the shadowy cone," a kind of "anti-sun in the east, pouring out not light, but deep shadow as it rose" (274). Again, in "Regrets of a Mountaineer" Stephen described the experience of looking out from some summits as "far less striking when other mountains obviously look down upon you; when, as it were, you are looking at the waves of the great ocean of hills merely from the crest of one of the waves themselves, and not from some lighthouse that rises far over their heads" (336). Stephen could not know it, but in these images he was describing the original metaphors his daughter adapted for use in *To the Lighthouse*. Finally, in her father's essay "The Alps in Winter" Woolf found the model for Lily Briscoe's artistic quest for a vision: "The Alps in Winter" is Leslie Stephen's deliberate documentation of a personal and successful vision quest.

But before Woolf could write *To the Lighthouse* and thus have her own vision, George Mallory had to die on Everest. Beyond the fact that both Mallory's nickname of "Sir Galahad," and his audacious 1914 mountaineering essay, "The Mountaineer as Artist," can be traced back to Leslie Stephen's "Sunset on Mont Blanc," there are many rather eerie similarities between Mallory and Woolf's father. On the other hand, one pronounced difference between the two men is that while Leslie Stephen gave up the dangers of mountaineering when he became a husband and father—the unvoiced reason informing his "Regrets of a Mountaineer"—Mallory did not.

The combined importance of these observations should be obvious: Virginia Woolf had ample reason to be interested in George Mallory.

George Mallory in *To the Lighthouse*

George Mallory does not appear by name in *To the Lighthouse*, but his presence is never far beneath the book's surface. As I read it, the central expedition narrative of *To the Lighthouse* is the story of two conflicting wills—the masculine and the feminine—represented by Mr. and Mrs. Ramsay. Mr. Ramsay conceives of the journey to the lighthouse as an expedition or quest to be completed. Mrs. Ramsay sees the journey to the lighthouse in human terms and conceives it as a mission of mercy to be achieved by delivering "stockings" to the little boy with the "tuberculous hip," and whatever else she can find that might prove useful to the "poor fellows" at the lighthouse (5). Ultimately, Mr. Ramsay's expedition succeeds only because he has adopted Mrs. Ramsay's point of view. In short, when Mr. Ramsay makes the long-delayed expedition to the lighthouse he has taken up Mrs. Ramsay's feminine will and desire to "[b]ring those parcels" to the men at the lighthouse (207). Recognizing that Woolf was well aware of George Mallory's epic story, it should be obvious at this point that Mr. Ramsay's original "male" quest to go to the lighthouse reflects Woolf's translation of Mallory's quest to climb Mount Everest to the seaside geography of St. Ives. Less obvious is the fact that George Mallory's quest also has a central role in informing the novel's other great quest narrative: Lily Briscoe's struggle to realize her vision, a struggle which has long been recognized as a metaphor for Woolf's own attempt to complete her novel.

George Mallory's role in informing Mr. Ramsay's character is, as I have said, quite obvious. Chapter VI of "The Window," the first section of Woolf's book, is a particularly apt example. This chapter, from its opening question and answering tag from Tennyson's "Charge of the Light Brigade," to its description of Mr. Ramsay's Alphabet Campaign, and on through its closing paragraphs, is filled with material derived from Mallory's epic struggle on Everest as it was reported in the *Times*. Woolf's opening question—"But what had happened?"—was quite familiar to anyone and everyone interested in understanding George Mallory's fate, and Tennyson's line—"Someone had blundered"—was effectively the only logical answer people could give for the Everest tragedy. Mr. Ramsay's Alphabet Campaign to reach R, while it may seem to subtly allude to Leslie Stephen's work on the *Dictionary of National Biography*, similarly and quite blatantly echoes the mountaineering language used to describe the gradual, step-by-step advance toward Everest's summit. While Woolf in the final paragraph of this

chapter strategically causes Mr. Ramsay to retreat from the heights of
Everest to the presence of his wife, this retreat follows two paragraphs that
are rich in what were then widely known details bearing on Mallory's last
climb. The first of these two paragraphs is particularly interesting in light of
Mallory's story:

> Feelings that would not have disgraced a leader who, now that the snow
> has begun to fall and the mountain top is covered in mist, knows that he
> must lay himself down and die before morning comes, stole upon him,
> paling the colour of his eyes, giving him, even in the two minutes of his
> turn on the terrace, the bleached look of withered old age. Yet he would
> not die lying down; he would find some crag of rock, and there, his eyes
> fixed on the storm, trying to the end to pierce the darkness, he would die
> standing. He would never reach R. (35)

In this paragraph, Woolf conflates several perspectives: first, Mr. Ramsay's
story gives substance to the whole and is realized "in the two minutes of his
turn on the terrace;" second, George Mallory's tantalizing appearance and
disappearance into mists obscuring the summit of Everest informs the entirety of the paragraph; and third, and most crucially, Noel Odell's role as
observer is adapted by Woolf to Mr. Ramsay's imagined actions, for it was
Odell who, in the excitement of his own discovery, had climbed "a little
crag" on the slope of Everest (*Times* 18 Oct. 1924), and from it had his "fascinating vision" of Mallory and Irvine before they were swallowed up in the
obscuring mists:

> At 12.50, just after I had emerged in a state of jubilation at finding the
> first definite fossils on Everest, there was a sudden clearing of the
> atmosphere, and the entire summit, ridge, and final peak of Everest were
> unveiled. My eyes became fixed on one tiny black spot silhouetted on a
> small snowcrest beneath a rock-step in the ridge, and the black spot
> moved. Another black spot became apparent and moved up the snow to
> join the other on the crest. The first then approached the great rock-step
> and shortly emerged at the top; the second did likewise. Then the whole
> fascinating vision vanished, enveloped in cloud once more. (*Times* 5
> July 1924)

Of course, in its deliberate retreat from the heights, Woolf's subsequent portrayal of Mr. Ramsay paying "homage to the beauty of the world" at the end
of Chapter VI foreshadows one of the core themes of the book: the idea that
the expedition to the lighthouse must be humanized or seen through Mrs.
Ramsay's point of view by Mr. Ramsay before he can successfully complete
it (36).

While I feel Mr. Ramsay's connections to George Mallory are especially apparent, I also believe Lily Briscoe's quest to complete her painting or
vision and hence Virginia Woolf's book also draws heavily and draws in a
sense much more personally on Mallory's story. Thus, in Chapter IX of the

first section of *To the Lighthouse* Woolf describes the "awful trial" Lily Briscoe experiences upon realizing that Mr. Bankes is "looking at her picture" (52). At this point, Mr. Bankes notices a vague "triangular purple shape" that Lily Briscoe tells him represents "Mrs. Ramsay reading to James." Mr. Bankes immediately reinterprets this specific meaning as "Mother and child then—objects of universal veneration" which "might be reduced [. . .] to a purple shadow without irreverence" (52). The scene described in these lines seems to reflect a fairly pedestrian conflict between the traditional and impressionist schools of art, but I believe much more is going on here than apparently meets Mr. Bankes' critical eye. Chomolungma, Mount Everest's Tibetan name, would have been quite familiar to those who closely followed Mallory's story, including Virginia Woolf and Lytton Strachey, the two individuals who most prominently inform Lily Briscoe and Mr. Bankes. Chomolungma had and has several translations, all of which contain the opening phrase "Mother Goddess." And hence Chomolungma is what I believe Lily Briscoe means her picture was "of," albeit without being entirely the author of her own expression, when Woolf writes, "But the picture was not of them, she said. Or not in his sense" (52). In my sense of this exchange, Mr. Bankes and Lily Briscoe appear to be reprising a real conversation Lytton Strachey and Virginia Woolf must have had about the hidden subject matter of *To the Lighthouse*.

In the final chapter of *To the Lighthouse*, when Lily Briscoe finally does complete her painting, Woolf again appears to me to be thinking of a scene that may have taken place on the highest mountain in the world when she has Lily Briscoe first conclude that "He must have reached it" and then exclaim "He has landed," before she turns her attention to the still unfinished canvas and the steps: "She looked at the steps; they were empty; she looked at her canvas; it was blurred. With a sudden intensity, as if she saw it clear for a second, she drew a line there, in the centre. It was done; it was finished. Yes, she thought, laying down her brush in extreme fatigue, I have had my vision" (208-9). In other words, Virginia Woolf, gazing with the same intensity of desire that motivated Noel Odell, looked from the empty steps to Lily Briscoe's painting, and when the obscuring mists briefly cleared she saw George Mallory standing atop his mountain.

Works Cited

Candler, Edmund. "The Everest Team." Review. *Nation and Athenæum*. 9 Jan. 1926: 528.

Graves, Robert. "Mallory of Everest." Review. *Nation and Athenæum*. 3 Sept. 1927: 723.

Lee, Hermione. *Virginia Woolf*. New York: Knopf, 1997.

Muir, Edwin. Review of *To the Lighthouse*. *Nation and Athenæum*. 2 July 1927: 450.

Odell, Noel E. "The Last Climb," appearing in E. F. Norton's "Everest: The Last Climb." *Times*. 5 July 1924: 16.

——. "The Last Climb," appearing in "Mt. Everest: Explorers' Full Story." *Times*.
  18 Oct. 1924: 13-14.
Stephen, Leslie. "The Sunset on Mont Blanc," "The Alps in Winter," and "Regrets
  of a Mountaineer." *The Playground of Europe*. London: Longmans, 1907.
Woolf, Virginia. "Leslie Stephen." *Collected Essays by Virginia Woolf*. Vol. 4.
  London: Hogarth, 1967, 76-80.
——. *To the Lighthouse*. New York: Harcourt, 1955.
Young, Geoffrey Winthrop. "George Leigh Mallory." *Nation and Athenæum*. 5 July
  1924: 438.

Marilyn Schwinn Smith
Woolf's Russia: Out of Bounds

The romance of youthful Orlando with the Russian Princess struck my
imagination as the most memorable sequence in this novel of adventure and
fantasy. It first seemed extraordinary that Woolf should import the Russians
just here, at the beginning of her novel, a "biography beginning in the year
1500 and continuing to the present day"(*D3* 161); just here, at the beginning
of Woolf's "biography" of English literary culture. One first suspects its
source to be the contemporary "Russian fever" in England, which Gilbert
Phelps dates to the 1912 publication of Constance Garnett's translation of
The Brothers Karamazov (418). An early commentator on *Orlando* and its
Russian theme notes: "Orlando's fling with Sasha [. . .] might be construed
as a very loose analogy of the courtship of English readers—including
Virginia Woolf—with Russian literature" (Rubenstein 169).

Roberta Rubenstein establishes Woolf's critical writing on contemporary Russian literature as the context for reading *Orlando*'s Russian theme,
yet makes a significant observation. The "aura of intrigue" surrounding the
Princess is representative of the mystique which Russia and her literature
held for the English not only "in the fresh translations appearing in Virginia
Woolf's own time," but "in the early tales brought back by travellers in
Elizabethan times" (167). This time span, from the Elizabethans to the present day, matches that of the biography itself and invites us to inquire further
into the Russian theme in *Orlando*.

Woolf held definite views about the fundamental unknowability of
other times and places, speaking more than once of "the 'vast and devour-
ing space' of the centuries" ("Sir Walter Raleigh 92). In *The Common
Reader* she insists that we cannot know earlier generations (39). Yet *The
Common Reader*, covering the same cultural span as *Orlando*, seeks to undo
the devastation of time. Both works share a reconstructed chronology,
paving a road through time, to borrow an image Juliet Dusinberre uses
throughout her book to describe Woolf's willful creation of an alternative

tradition. Woolf's effort to know what was is prerequisite to what J. Hillis Miller calls her "raising of the dead" (170, 181, 190). In *The Common Reader*'s opening essay, "The Pastons and Chaucer," Woolf employs a technique to circumvent the unknowability wrought by time, which in another fashion she employs in *Orlando* to circumvent cultural difference. Woolf manipulates the reader's imagination, conjuring first a knowable bit of the present, then casting the reader—thus fully imbued with the present—into an otherwise unknown past (*CR*1 14-15). The imagination is the faculty which must come into play where knowledge fails. But it must be a knowledgeable imagination and must recognize the boundary to the known. It is to this end that Woolf employs satire in Orlando's encounter with the Russian Princess: to expose the gap attendant on not knowing.

The Russian scene in *Orlando* is an occasion for Woolf to focus on gender and cultural issues of difference. Not just contemporary, but Elizabethan notions regarding the barbarous state of Russia are effectively satirized when the tables are turned, and we are witness to the Princess's views of the English. Together with misinformation and prejudice, we should note what knowledge of Russia existed in Elizabethan times. There is a considerable body of literature on Russia published in England, pursuant to Chancellor's 1553 "discovery of Russia" and the creation of the Muscovy Company. The flourishing trade and diplomatic relations between the two countries "had created in England by the end of the 16th century a degree of knowledge of Russia and the Russian people which, with all its many limitations, was superior to that existing in any other European country" (Anderson 140).

Rubenstein's essay focuses on references in *Orlando* to Woolf's reviews of Chekhov. However, the Chekhovian references are adulterated by something quite foreign to Chekhov—notions of Russia directly traceable to Elizabethan sources. Elizabethan references to Russia are predominately to the northern latitudes, for the English entered the country through the north, through Lapland and the port founded by Elizabethan seamen, Archangel. Anthony Cross comments that "allusions to things Russian abound" in Elizabethan theatre, noting that Shakespeare's references are "mainly of a climatic or sartorial nature" (4). J. W. Draper cites the Russian reference in *Measure for Measure* (*MfM*, II, i, 128) as indicative of the degree to which Shakespeare "seems to have been impressed by the Arctic north" (218). The passages Rubenstein cites from *Orlando* paint not a Chekhovian landscape, but rather one of the Arctic north.

Rubenstein comments that "the loose tunic and trousers of the Russian fashion" (*O* 37), which initially deceive Orlando as to the Princess's gender serve as pretext for Woolf's later meditations on androgyny (167). The distinctive Russian attire gave rise also to Elizabethan comments on Russian gender relations. George Turberville, secretary to Sir Thomas Randolph on a diplomatic mission to Muscovy in 1568-9, employs the phrase "against our use" in noting a relative lack of differentiation between men and women. In the first of his widely published verse epistles, "To his especiall friend Master Edward Dancie," Turberville writes: "Almost the meanest man in all the countrey rides,/The woman eke, against our use, her trotting horse bestrides./In sundry colours they both men and women goe,/In buskins all, that money have on buskins to bestoe" (125). What is often overlooked, when apologizing for the text's blatant prejudices, is the clear intention of the author to convey in the surprisingly engaging mode of light verse, copious detail regarding the ordinary mores of Russian life, including that now much noted Russian attire. "Their shirts in Russie long, they worke them downe before,/ [. . .] That reacheth downe beneath the calfe, and that Armacha hight:/These are the Russies robes" (132).

Among the relatively objective items "of a climatic or sartorial nature," Elizabethan writing on Russia abounds in commonplaces of prejudice which mark the bounds of knowledge. Geographical knowledge newly acquired by the voyages of Spain and Portugal was late in being disseminated in England. Old notions were supplanted slowly (Parks 1-24). The old Ptolemaic geography had set the bounds of Europe at the River Don, beyond which lay Asia. "[T]his made the Russian an Asiatic people and Moscow an Asiatic city [. . .] Russia seemed [. . .] as remote [. . .] as the East Indies and was [. . .] regarded [. . .] as an oriental country" (Anderson 147). That Sasha's eyes should be slanted is in keeping with the level of Elizabethan knowledge.

There is a strong degree of correspondence between what appears in Elizabethan writing and what Woolf exaggerates for comic effect. The particular shape Woolf gives to her parody is notable. On one hand, she simply turns the tables, seeing the English through Sasha's eyes as the English see the Russians, or she reveals blindness to possessing a quality oneself. Cross asserts that the picture drawn by Turberville, "of 'A people passing rude to vices vile incline'd'" was "more than enough to convince Elizabethan England [. . .] that it indeed had dealings with a 'rude and barbarous kingdom', an impression [. . .] not dispelled by the visits to London of Russian embassies [. . .]" (3-4). I am reminded of the children's taunt: "I'm rubber and you're glue; what you say bounces off me and sticks to you." Compare accounts by English ambassadors and the agents of the Muscovy company attendant on the Tsar regarding their confinement to a single dwelling, forbidden to visit the town or converse with its inhabitants, with the scene when, no longer able to bear her confinement, the Princess complains the Court is like a cage. Slipping with Orlando under "the silken rope, which railed off the Royal enclosure from the public part of the river" she is off to see the ordinary sights of London (43). The Princess's plaint that one can travel the rivers in Russia (understand: unlike in England) "all day long without meeting a soul!" is intended as a comment on difference. Yet what is the difference? When she and Orlando head up the Thames: "not a living soul ever came their way" (44). The difference lies only in perspective. The narrator, knowing her own country, can readily explain the absence of people along the Thames. Indeed, the Russian fashion which "served to disguise the sex" (37) is not notably dissimilar to the English: "He—for there could be no doubt of his sex, though the fashion of the time did something to disguise it" (13).

Pondering the Princess's reluctance to divulge her pedigree, Orlando mentally runs through the fantastic tales he has heard of her people's "savage ways." But in comparing these tales with his actual experience, he must conclude that "her manners were certainly not those of a woman bred in a cattle shed" (48). Doubt re-asserts itself after their encounter with the Russian sailor. Orlando thought: "Was there not [. . .] something rank in her, something coarse flavoured, something peasant-born?" (52). It is but a short while, when the Princess has departed, her memory displaced by the image of the poet, before: "stranger still, [Orlando] bethought him with pride—for the thought was generally distasteful—of that great grandmother Moll who had milked cows" (86).

Much of the Elizabethan literature on Russia verges on a dehumanized portrayal of the ordinary person. A common theme is Russian cohabitation with animals. The following account appears in Turberville: "In coms the cattell then, the sheepe, the colt, the cowe,/Fast by his bed the Mowsike then a lodging doth allowe,/Whom he with fodder feeds, and holds as deere as life:/And thus they weare the winter with the Mowsike and his wife" (127). Relations with animals is a repeated topic of conversation between the Princess and Orlando. Reconciling after the incident on the ship, "she told him how, in winter in Russia, she would listen to the wolves howling across the steppes, and thrice, to show him, she barked like a wolf." Demonstrating that English practice is not so different from that recorded by Turberville and others, Orlando responded with a tale "of the stags in the snow at home, and how they would stray into the great hall for warmth and be fed by an old man with porridge from a bucket. And then she praised him, for his love of beasts" (54).

Orlando's association of the Princess with a fox is a prime example of the mingling of present and past, personal allusion and public knowledge in the novel. The fur trade was a major component of Russo-English commerce, and travellers' tales abounded in descriptions of the Russian fur-bearing fauna—the bear, the wolf, the fox. There is also a local source. Woolf's acquaintance, David Garnett, was, not surprisingly, much taken with Russia, having as a child accompanied his mother, Constance, on her Russian travels. He was fascinated by the boundaries of nationality, gender, race *and* species, which he explores in several of his novels. Inspired by his first wife, the Russophile illustrator, Ray Garnett, his first and most famous novel was published in 1922 and awarded the James Tait Black Memorial Prize and the Hawthornden Prize in 1923. The scenes of the Princess furtively gnawing on candle ends would have struck any Bloomsbury reader for its reference to the poignant scenes of Silvia's return to the wild in *Lady into Fox*.

Orlando's entire conception of the Princess is intimately bound up with notions of bestiality. "Sasha" is neither the Princess's name nor its diminutive. "Sasha" is Orlando's private nickname; for the Princess reminds Orlando of his childhood pet, a white Russian fox named Sasha. Sasha, the fox, had been "soft as snow," but certainly not cuddly. A creature of the wild whose propensity to use its "teeth of steel" on Orlando, the fox was killed for what may be interpreted as the nobleman's ignorance on coexistence with the Other.

Knowing, as we do, the consequences of English notions regarding the humanness of the native Americans or even of their neighbors, the Irish, it is worth noting Turberville's dilemma: "Wilde Irish are as civill as the Russies in their kinde, Hard choice which is the best of both, ech bloody, rude and blinde" (Turberville 131). Woolf's portrayal of the cultural divide which Orlando encounters in his relationship with Sasha nudges the commonplaces of ordinary prejudice down a slippery slope toward bigotry of nationality, of race, of class, of gender, to press against the boundary of human-animal, which Marc Shell perceives to lie barely concealed beneath the surface of all encounters with the Other—a boundary read as license to kill.

One further example—located, as most of the Russian episode, outside the bounds of James's court—brings together the images which tie the Russian romance to the novel's opening scene. They have survived that crisis, when Orlando might have killed the sailor had he not fallen in a faint, and they now while the hours between lovemaking in conversation. Orlando and Sasha "would talk of Moor and Pagan: [. . .] of a rat that fed from her hand at table; of the arras that moved always in the hall at home" (45). Casting Moor and Pagan as Other against their collective we, Orlando and Sasha elide their own brush with Otherness. Though Orlando will not, like his grandsires, bring home heads as trophies, nor will Sasha revert to that fellowship of animals, from which the human has divorced itself, the references to "a rat" and to "the arras" of the novel's opening passage bring into the reader's consciousness the difference that notions of civilization cast between Sasha and Orlando.

The Moor and Pagan of their conversation remind the reader of the grinning skull at the novel's opening. Modeled on the linkage of Clarissa and Septimus in the sound of a pistol shot, we have linked here, in one sentence, the noblemen's prey set swinging to and fro by the same wind which sets into perpetual motion the arras depicting noble hunters (13-14). The mention of Moor and Pagan gestures not only backwards, but foreshadows the Moor yet to be encountered, just before Orlando and Sasha slip back within the Court's bounds. The danger of Orlando's flirtation with the animal Other is mirrored in Othello's fatal marriage with the racial Other. "The frenzy of the

269

Moor seemed to him his own frenzy, and when the Moor suffocated the woman in her bed it was Sasha he killed with his own hands" (57). It is fair to say, with Orlando's biographer, that, from appearances, Orlando had been destined "precisely for some such [murderous] career." And so it should have been, he going "from deed to deed, from glory to glory" (15), perhaps bringing home, if not actual skulls, trophies of another kind, but for his encounter with Sasha. Woolf employs the Proustian moment to introduce, as the agent of change, Sasha: "He had indeed just brought his feet together about six in the evening of the seventh of January at the finish of some such quadrille or minuet when he beheld [. . .]" (22). Orlando will not kill, willy-nilly, as did his forebears. He has encountered, through the agency of an unknowable Other, the dark places of his own psyche which he shares all around.

Works Cited

Anderson, M. S. "English Views of Russia in the 17th Century." *The Slavonic and East European Review* 33 (1954): 140-60.

Bowen, Elizabeth. Afterword. *Orlando*. By Virginia Woolf. New York: Signet, 1960. 216-   222.

Cross, Anthony G. Introduction. *The Russian Theme in English Literature. From the Sixteenth Century to 1980. An Introductory Survey and Bibliography*. Oxford: Meeuws, 1985. 1-94.

Draper, J. W. "Shakespeare and Muscovy." *The Slavonic and East European Review* 33 (1954): 217-221.

Dusinberre, Juliet. *Virginia Woolf's Renaissance. Woman Reader or Common Reader*. Iowa City: U of Iowa P, 1997.

Garnett, David. *Lady into Fox* (1922) Illustrated with wood engravings by R. A. Garnett. London: Chatto, 1928.

Harbage, Alfred. Introduction. *Love's Labor's Lost*. By William Shakespeare. Baltimore, MD: Penguin, 1973. 14-23.

Miller, J. Hillis. "'Mrs. Dalloway': Repetition as the Raising of the Dead." 1982. *Virginia Woolf*. Ed. Harold Bloom. New York: Chelsea, 1986. 169-190.

Parks, George Bruner. *Richard Hakluyt and the English Voyages*. New York: American Geographical Society, 1928.

Phelps, Gilbert. "The Early Phases of British Interest in Russian Literature." *The Slavonic and East European Review* 36 (1958): 418-36.

Rubenstein, Roberta. "*Orlando*: Virginia Woolf's Improvisations on a Russian Theme." *Forum for Modern Language Studies* 9 (1973): 166-69.

Shell, Marc. "The Family Pet." *Representations* 15 (1986): 121-53.

Turberville, George. "Certaine letters in verse, written by Master George Turbervile out of Moscovia, which went as Secretarie thither with Master Tho. Randolph, her Majesties Ambassadour to the Emperour 1568, to certeine friends of his in London, describing the maners of the Countrey and people." 1587. *Principal Navigations Voyages Traffiques & Discoveries of the English Nation*. Comp. Richard Hakluyt. Vol. 3. New York: AMS, 1965. 124-35.

Woolf, Virginia. *The Common Reader*. New York: Harcourt, 1925.

——. *The Diary of Virginia Woolf*. Ed. Anne Olivier Bell and Andrew McNeillie. Vol. 3. New York: Harcourt, 1980.

——. *Orlando*. New York: Harcourt, 1928.

——. "Sir Walter Raleigh." Rev. of *Sir Walter Raleigh [1552?-1618]. Selections from his Historie of the World, his Letters etc.*, ed. G. E. Hadow. *Times Literary Supplement* 15 March 1917. Rpt. in *The Essays of Virginia Woolf*. Ed. Andrew McNeillie. Vol. 2. San Diego: Harcourt, 1987. 91-96

Diane F. Gillespie
"The Rain in Spain": Woolf, Cervantes, Andalusia, and *The Waves*

"The rain in Spain stays mainly in the plain," repeats Eliza Doolittle in *My Fair Lady*, Lerner and Loewe's fifties musical adaptation of Shaw's *Pygmalion* (1913). Instructed by Professor Higgins, Eliza alters her pronunciation of the vowels that mark her as lower class. Already in 1905 Virginia Stephen had linked "rain" and "Spain" with equally comic and serious results. Like Eliza Doolittle, she is engaged in crossing boundaries from one world to another. She grapples, however, not with the class hierarchy in England, but with the geographical, historical, cultural, and linguistic boundaries between nations. She makes mock-heroic jokes. "Woke this morning," she writes in her journal in Seville, "under my mosquito curtains—which the beasts merely laugh at—to find [. . .] a rain of pure English blood pouring outside. (That sentence [. . .] may be read 2 ways—but we do not live in the time of the Inquisition)" (*PA* 263). In place of the fifteenth-century Catholic Inquisitors, incited by Ferdinand and Isabella to rid Spain of heretics and unbelievers by trial and torture, we have twentieth-century Spanish mosquitoes selecting heretical English tourists as their prey. Indeed the one item of interest Virginia finds amidst the "dull florid" and "very ornate" architecture of the cathedral at Granada is "the tomb of Ferdinand & Isabella" (*PA* 264). "Rain in Spain" thus modulates, in her submerged metaphor, to the "reign in Spain" of a man and a woman who precipitate a reign of terror, who serve as early examples, in her reading and traveling, of hegemonic political power, empire-building, and intolerance.

Although Woolf and many of her friends traveled at one time or another to Spain, knew something about its art, and even tried to capture its architecture and landscapes in sketches, paintings, and prose,[1] it remains the neglected geographical sister in Bloomsbury and Woolf studies. When Spain figures at all in discussions of Woolf and her work, it does so primarily in connection with her responses in *Three Guineas* (1938) to the Spanish Civil War and to the rise of dictators in the 1930s. Her earlier visits to Spain, how-

271

ever, provide a context for *Three Guineas* and underscore her strong sense of having entered a geographical space with a history, culture, and language that both fascinate and alienate her. Her journeys there also mark turning-points: a new life after her father's death; the beginnings of her married life with Leonard Woolf and, having turned forty, a mature assessment of the human condition in general. Although the trips to Spain color her diaries and letters, they are also the impetus for two excellent travel essays, "An Andalusian Inn" (published in 1905 after her first trip) and "To Spain" (published in 1923 after her third).[2] Combined with her reading of Cervantes' *Don Quixote* in the years following her second trip, the third Spanish journey and "To Spain" also provide a context for Woolf's characterizations of Bernard and especially of Rhoda in *The Waves*.

Virginia Stephen first went to Spain with her younger brother Adrian in 1905. Not only did she leave England but, she wrote from the ship on the way to Portugal, she also felt she "had been cut adrift from the world altogether" (*L*1 184).[3] On shore again, though, her journal entries reveal a writer's fascination with foreign words and sounds, "splendid names" like "Estremadura, & Andalusia." The cities are equally strange to her. She prefers the narrow streets of Seville and the natural beauty of the gardens they visit to the "elephantine beauty" of the cathedral or the "splendid gilt & mosaic" of the Moorish Alcazar (*PA* 262-3). Feeling like an outsider, she watches the preparations for a festival: "They have stood huge wax figures in the Cathedral—I cant conceive why—and they are building stands," she reports. "Placards about the bull fight are up everywhere. I am glad we just miss it" (*L*1 185-6). When the rain of Seville becomes the snow beneath a "southern sun" on the mountains above Granada, however, more of the sights please her. The gardens of the Generalife "are very hot & fragrant, all in little inlaid terraces." She also unequivocally likes the Alhambra, the "gorgeous Moorish palace [. . .] within battered yellow walls" (*PA* 264). In retrospect, she declares Granada "far and away the best place we saw" (*L*1 187).

This first exposure to Spain immediately yielded two articles. One, a review essay essentially about guidebooks, explains her attempt in the other. On her trip, Virginia had carried several novels, two nineteenth-century accounts of experiences in Spain by George Henry Borrow, and a Baedeker guidebook (*PA* 257). In "Journeys in Spain" (1905), she notes that Baedeker provides information but little pleasure. The "more ambitious" guidebook, like Borrow's, requires the literary ability to balance description with describer, factual with personal, and is as pleasurable to read at home as it is helpful abroad (*E*1 44). Virginia Stephen tries her own balancing act in "An Andalusian Inn."[4] This essay describes the high expectations a hotel-keeper in Granada raises about the good, second-class inn available at a village in Andalusia during a weary train ride towards the coast. In her journal descriptions of cities, it is true, Virginia pays little attention either to the Spanish people or to how they may perceive her. Unable to understand their speech or identify with their traditions, she primarily records her impressions of foreign sights. In a village, however, the travelers themselves become foreigners, observed as well as observing. A crowd gathers as they struggle to communicate their desire for a hotel—using English, French, "three different kinds of Spanish," a Spanish dictionary, and gestures involving an umbrella (*E*1 50-1). Finally, they find themselves in a cottage that is also a public house. To Violet Dickinson, Virginia had written, with melodramatic effect, that "the company of Spanish peasants sat round and drank and stared at us, and we expected to have knives in our throats every moment" (*L*1 187). In the published essay, she recounts more moderately how their entrance created "a pause, in which several eyes inspected us at their leisure."[5] Ignorant of local customs, the travelers wonder why these supposedly honest country people stay up so late into the night, why the behavior of the innkeeper seems so "sinister" and "ominous," and why the Spanish seems so "vehement," "fierce and bloodthirsty." After a tense night spent lying fully dressed and conjuring up violent attacks, they are assaulted only by a "peasant woman with a basin of goat's milk in her hands" (*E*1 51-2). On the factual side, this early essay serves as a warning about the veracity of hotel-keepers' recommendations, about the problems that result when one does not speak the language, and about the standards of accommodation in small Spanish villages. On the more personal side, although there is certainly stereotyping of the Andalusian peasants, there is also self-mockery—of ignorance, unrealistic expectations, and overly vivid imaginations.

Virginia Woolf traveled to Spain a second time in 1912 as part of a six-week honeymoon trip to the continent. In spite of the ubiquitous mosquitoes, she concludes that "Spain is far the most magnificent country I have ever seen" (*L*2 8). On this trip, Woolf reads Russian, French, and English novels. Her most important *literary* encounter with Spain came a few years later, and only after she was shamed into reading Cervantes' *Don Quixote* (1605; part 2, 1615).[6] In 1918, she writes in her diary: "My intellectual snobbishness was chastened this morning by hearing from Janet [Vaughan] that she reads *Don Quixote* [. . .] in the evenings" (*D*1 192). Woolf subsequently records her responses to *Don Quixote* both in her diary (*D*2 55-6) and in "Reading," an essay written at about the same time. She considers the differences between the perceptions of Cervantes' original communal audience and the more educated, individualistic readers of the present who cannot help but wonder how conscious the author was of "the tragedy and the satire" in his tales. These concerns, however, do not obviate Woolf's pleasure in "the jolly, delightful, plain-spoken book," in Cervantes' "unassailable statement of man and the world" (*E*3 157-8).

The image of Don Quixote had long been a part of English culture. In 1915, Kenneth Clark even describes Roger Fry in Sickert's etching as a loveable, "quixotic character [. . .] looking like a bespectacled Knight of La

Mancha" (qtd. In Richardson, 99). In 1920 Woolf herself recalls Shaw, in connection with a portrait by Edmond X. Kapp, as "a knight-errant, candid, indeed innocent of aspect; a Don Quixote born in the Northern mists— shrewd [. . .] rather than romantic" (*E3* 165). Cervantes' character also recurs in *The Waves*. Bernard has thought of learning Spanish "by tying a string to the right toe and waking early" (*TW* 255). In draft 2, he realizes all the places he will not travel, everything he will not learn, among them to read "*Don Quixote* in Spanish" (Graham 610). In the published version, the reference is dropped, and when Bernard travels, it is to Rome. Yet Cervantes' knight of La Mancha re-emerges, along with the Arthurian and Wagnerian allusions that accrue to Percival, in the clash between the idealistic rhetoric of imperialism and the realistic futility embodied in his death. Similarly, Bernard's image of himself "with my spear couched and my hair flying back like a young man's, like Percival's, when he galloped in India" as he flings himself "unvanquished and unyielding" at Death (*TW* 297) is, in his defiant and loveable futility, as much like Don Quixote as he is like Percival.

Woolf's third trip to Spain occurred in 1923. Traveling by train, she and Leonard journeyed through France, then to Madrid, south to Granada, and from there to Gerald Brenan's house at Yegen, high in the Sierra Nevadas. Lytton Strachey, Ralph Partridge, and Carrington had preceded the Woolfs there. Carrington's attraction to the place is evident in her paintings, "Hill Town in Andalusia" (c. 1920) and the very sensual and partly imaginary landscape, "Mountain Ranges from Yegen, Andalusia" (c. 1924) (Carrington, plates 13 and 12). When the Woolfs planned to visit Brenan themselves, Strachey, who had proved dramatically ill-suited to Spanish food and travel by mule, tried to talk them out of it, "declaring in his high-pitched voice that 'it was death'" (Brenan 37). The Woolfs went anyway.

Brenan provides his own account of their visit. He describes Yegen as "a poor village, one of the poorest of the eighty or so that stud the Alpujarra, as this fertile region is called [. . .] high above the sea" (Brenan, xi). Leonard describes their slow ascent in a letter. Once there, he pronounces it "a superb country. We are about 4 to 5 thousand feet up, above on the tops of the mountains is perpetural [sic] snow & one can see the Mediterranean" (Woolf, L., 225-6). Virginia Woolf's own description of the ascent to Yegen appears in "To Spain" (1923).[7] She describes moving not just horizontally across European geographical space, but vertically and diagonally to a high vantage-point. Traveling "upon foot and mule-back," she notes repeatedly and hypnotically "stones, olive trees, goats, asphodels, irises, bushes, ridges, shelves, clumps, tufts, and hollows innumerable, indescribable, unthinkable. The mind's contents break into short sentences," she writes, and provides what sounds like a parody of Hemingway: "It is hot; the old man; the frying pan; it is hot; the image of the Virgin; the bottle of wine; it is time for lunch; it is only half-past twelve; it is hot."[8] As they struggle upward, dreamily trusting to the mules' knowledge of the route in the mist, they seem to be virtually "riding out of life towards some very enticing prospect" (*E3* 363-4). Again, as on board ship in 1905, travel has "cut [her] adrift from the world altogether" (*L1* 184). She experiences a total transcendence not just of space but also of time as she hears the sounds from "the heart of a village which has faced the African coast with a timeless and aristocratic endurance for a thousand years" (*E3* 364).

The trip on mule-back to Yegen re-emerges in *The Waves* in Rhoda's final speech in the seventh section. A trip to southern Spain has taken her to the very edge of Europe. Although Rhoda shares many of Woolf's characteristics and experiences, some of them—the discomfort with her female body and the intense responses to her surroundings—are also Carrington's, whom Woolf would associate with Brenan's part of Spain. In moving Rhoda south, therefore, Woolf underscores Rhoda's ambiguous relationship with British cultural norms. Woolf taps into the literary tradition in which the inclement weather, work ethic, rationality, and conventional heterosexuality of northern Europe oppose the warm climate, leisurely lifestyle, emotional vitality, and alternate sexual preferences associated with the south. I would like to add, therefore, a Spanish context to Annette Oxindine's discussion of what she calls Rhoda's "lesbian suicide."[9] Rhoda has moved horizontally south from England. Now she moves vertically to a point from which she can see even farther south: "Now [. . .] I climb this mountain, from the top of which I shall see Africa" (*TW* 203). Woolf transforms the passive feelings of "riding out of life towards some very enticing prospect" and of transcending time described in "To Spain" into the poetry of Rhoda's solitude and her combined desires for dissolution and for another world:

> "Now I climb this Spanish hill; and I will suppose that this mule back is my bed and that I lie dying [. . .]. We stumble up—we stumble on. My path has been up and up, towards some solitary tree with a pool beside it on the very top [. . .]. The ridge of the hill rises like mist, but from the top I shall see Africa." (*TW* 205-6).

Kathy Phillips assumes that Rhoda's climb is imaginary and, further, that she is just another proto-imperialist who, admitting her own corruption, would only "corrupt Africa" as well (169). Like other modernist writers, however, Woolf responds to Africa in multiple ways. Here it suggests escape. Rhoda has the sensation of falling through her mule-back bed and launching "out now over the precipice," over the "rippling grey, innumerable waves." As a child she has played with Armadas of white petals (*TW* 18-19, 27-8), recalling the famous Spanish naval fleet sent against England and defeated during the reign of Elizabeth I (1588). Now, climbing the Spanish hill, Rhoda imagines her Armada sinking: "Rolling me over the waves will shoulder me under. Everything falls in a tremendous shower, dissolving me" (*TW* 206). Her blurring of boundaries between cliffs and waves, ground and mule-back, life and death, as she feels herself launching out "over the precipice" forecast Bernard's later report of her suicide. In his imagination he can "feel the rush of the wind of her flight when she leapt" (*TW* 289). For a moment, she transcends what Susan Friedman calls "questions of power as they manifest themselves in relation to space on planet Earth" (109). Rhoda's Spanish Armada is not so much defeated by England as it is swamped by the waves of the seas that encircle continents. Britannia does not rule the waves. No one rules the natural world with its endless, repetitive, and infinitely various cycles of life and death, creation and destruction.

Rhoda, after her climb, is brought back physically to the Spanish earth: "Putting my foot to the ground I step gingerly and press my hand against the hard door of a Spanish inn" (*TW* 206). Similarly, Woolf came down to earth again after the "playpoem" (*D3* 203) in which she backed off to observe not just "the detail" of the human experience, but also "the outline" of larger spatial and temporal patterns within which individuals live and die (*E4* 435). Woolf's experiences of Spanish history and culture contributed to her ability to put reigns of terror, past or present, in Spain or elsewhere, into a larger perspective. In *Three Guineas* she takes on the power structures of her society with some of the shrewd, quixotic energies of Fry and Shaw. Using her own experiences as an educated man's daughter, including travel, she seeks new perspectives on English culture from different vantage points. In "A Born Writer" (1920), she had distinguished between English and Spanish cultures. "For when Mr Moore calls *Esther Waters* 'as characteristically English as *Don Quixote* is Spanish,'" she writes, "he means perhaps that in the person of Esther he has laid bare honesty, fidelity, courage, and has made these, the Saxon virtues, rather than the charms and subtleties of the Latins, the leading qualities in the drama" (*E3* 251). In this sense—"honesty, fidelity, courage"—Woolf herself identified, not so much with Joan of Arc, the martyred icon of the suffrage movement, as with a northern and feminist version of Spain's Don Quixote.

Notes

[1] An example is Fry's *A Sampler of Castille*.

[2] Morris does not consider Woolf a noted travel writer (1). Friedman observes that Woolf did not have the "zest or restlessness for travel" of many other modernist writers (263 n. 19), associating, in fact, travel with illness, her own, Thoby's and Vanessa's (117).

[3] As several have noted (e.g. King, 151), the South American experiences in Woolf's first novel, *The Voyage Out*, combine Woolf's ship voyage of 1905 with her journeys in Italy, Portugal, and Spain.

[4] The essay elaborates upon a brief description in her journal (*PA* 265) and a longer one in a letter to Violet Dickinson (*L1* 187). Although she considered sending the article to *The National Review*, it was published in the *Guardian* (19 July 1905).

⁵ This passage anticipates the one in *The Voyage Out* in which the English travelers who have hiked to a native village are aware of the gaze of the village women (*VO* 384-5).

⁶ Thomas Shelton translated *Don Quixote* into English as early as 1611. Woolf's library in the Washington State University archives contains two English translations, one of them (Smith Elder, 1885) inherited from her father, Leslie Stephen.

⁷ Another possible result of this trip is, as Lee notes, Woolf's idea of using some of Brenan's characteristics, along with those of Ralph Partridge and herself, in creating Septimus Smith and "the post-war trauma of a whole generation" (459).

⁸ Woolf, however, did not review Hemingway's novels and stories until 1927. Hemingway lost his temper when he read "An Essay in Criticism" (*E4* 456 n. 1).

⁹ Oxindine considers Woolf's deletion of Greece, but not Rhoda's emergence in Spain. As Fassler indicates, Spain as well as Greece was among the "southern or oriental peoples [. . .] more strongly disposed to homosexuality than inhabitants of more northerly and westerly lands" (244-5). Colburn makes a parallel argument about Woolf's fascination with Istanbul.

Works Cited

Brenan, Gerald. *South From Granada*. New York: Farrar, Straus and Cudahy, 1957.

Carrington, Noel. *Carrington: Paintings, Drawings and Decorations*. London: Thames and Hudson, 1980.

Colburn, Krystyna. "Spires of London: Domes of Istanbul." In *Virginia Woolf: Texts and Contexts: Selected Papers from the Fifth Annual Conference on Virginia Woolf*. Ed. Beth Rigel Daugherty and Eileen Barrett. New York: Pace U P, 1996. 250-54.

Fassler, Barbara. "Theories of Homosexuality as Sources of Bloomsbury's Androgyny." *Signs: Journal of Women in Culture and Society*. 5.2. (Winter 1979). 237-51.

Friedman, Susan Stanford. *Mappings: Feminism and the Cultural Geographies of Encounter*. Princeton: Princeton U P, 1998.

Fry, Roger. *A Sampler of Castille*. London: Hogarth, 1923.

Graham, J. W., ed. *Virginia Woolf: The Waves: The Two Holograph Drafts*. Toronto: U of Toronto P, 1976.

King, James. *Virginia Woolf*. London: Penguin, 1995.

Lee, Hermione. *Virginia Woolf*. New York: Knopf, 1997.

Morris, Jan. *Travels with Virginia Woolf*. London: Hogarth, 1993.

Oxindine, Annette. "Rhoda Submerged: Lesbian Suicide in *The Waves*." In *Virginia Woolf: Lesbian Readings*. Ed. Eileen Barrett and Patricia Cramer. New York: New York U P, 1997.

Phillips, Kathy. *Virginia Woolf Against Empire*. Knoxville: U of Tennessee P, 1994.

Richardson, Elizabeth P. *A Bloomsbury Iconography*. Winchester: St. Paul's Bibliographies, 1989.

Woolf, Leonard. *Letters of Leonard Woolf*. Ed. Frederic Spotts. San Diego: Harcourt Brace Jovanovich, 1989.

Woolf, Virginia. *A Passionate Apprentice: The Early Journals of Virginia Woolf.* Ed. Mitchell A. Leaska. San Diego: Harcourt Brace Jovanovich, 1990.

——. *The Diary of Virginia Woolf.* 5 vols. Ed. Anne Olivier Bell. San Diego: Harcourt Brace Jovanovich, 1977-84.

——. *The Essays of Virginia Woolf.* Ed. Andrew McNeillie. 3 vols. San Diego: Harcourt Brace Jovanovich, 1986-88; vol. 4. London: Hogarth, 1994.

——. *The Letters of Virginia Woolf.* 6 vols. Ed. Nigel Nicolson and Joanne Trautmann. New York: Harcourt Brace Jovanovich, 1975-80.

——. *The Voyage Out.* New York: Harcourt, Brace and World, 1948.

——. *The Waves.* San Diego: Harcourt Brace, 1959.

Notes on Contributors

GENEVIEVE ABRAVANEL (113) is a PhD candidate in English at Duke University.

TODD AVERY (145) received his PhD in English and Cultural Studies from Indiana University. He has published on Victorian ethics and aestheticism, and Bloomsbury. An essay, "Reading Modernism," co-authored with Patrick Brantlinger, is forthcoming in the *Modernism* volume of Blackwell's *New Perspectives on Literature and Theory* series.

MICHÈLE BARRETT (120) is Professor of Modern Literary and Cultural Theory in the School of English and Drama at Queen Mary, University of London. Her works include an edition of Woolf's essays, *Women and Writing* (The Women's Press, London, 1980) and a combined edition of *A Room of One's Own* and *Three Guineas* (Penguin 1993). Her other publications include *Imagination in Theory* (1999), *The Politics of Truth* (1991), *Women's Oppression Today* (1980). Her most recent book is *Star Trek: The Human Frontier* (with Duncan Barrett).

SUZANNE BELLAMY (186), an Australian artist and writer, has been developing a research project called the Visual Essay, focusing currently on the intersections between Virginia Woolf and Gertrude Stein as interpreters of visual fields and perceptual shifts in early modernism. Her collaborative painting project with Isota Tucker Epes also continues. They will be completing the third part of their trilogy on Woolf's works with *A Room of One's Own*, and will hold a major retrospective, planned for the 2002 Woolf Conference in California. Suzanne Bellamy runs a print and sculpture studio in southern New South Wales, Australia, and exhibits internationally.

JESSICA BERMAN (1) teaches English and Women's Studies at the University of Maryland, Baltimore County and was the director of the Tenth Annual Conference on Virginia Woolf. She has published on Woolf and on Henry James. Her book, *Modernist Fiction, Cosmopolitanism and the Politics of Community* is forthcoming from Cambridge University Press in 2001.

EDWARD L. BISHOP (52) (not to be confused with Edward Bishop, the war historian who writes on the Battle of Britain) has published *Virginia Woolf's JACOB'S ROOM: The Holograph Draft* (Pace UP, 1998), as well as articles on the paratexts of Woolf, Joyce, and Modernist magazines.

EMILY BLAIR (13) is a graduate student at the University of California, Davis. She is currently writing her dissertation on Virginia Woolf and her connections to popular nineteenth-century women writers and the literary domestic.

DONALD T. BLUME (258) As a young boy in the early 1970s, I read *Mallory of Everest* by Showell Styles and found the story of Mallory's last climb both fascinating and unforgettable. Some twenty years later, I read *To the Lighthouse* for the first time and realized Virginia Woolf had had a similar reaction.

JAMIE CARR (19) is currently in the PhD program in English at the University of Rhode Island. Her interests include British and European Modernism, theories of modernism and fascism, and critical theory.

LISA CARSTENS (39) is an Assistant Professor of English at Virginia Wesleyan College. She has an article on confessional testimony in *Sophie's Choice* forthcoming in *Twentieth Century Literature* and is completing a book-length project concerned with the trope of sex change in modern British narratives of cultural authority.

MELBA CUDDY-KEANE (58) is Associate Professor of English and a Northrop Frye Scholar at the University of Toronto, and a former President of the International Virginia Woolf Society. Having written on Woolf, money, cars, comedy, history, rhetoric, China, value theory, and sound technology, she is now completing a book on Woolf's democratic highbrowism.

JANE DE GAY (31) is Lecturer in English at Trinity and All Saints, University of Leeds. She has published articles on Woolf in *Woolf Studies Annual, English Review* and *Critical Survey*, and is currently writing a book on Woolf's responses to the literary past. She is also the co-editor of two Routledge Readers in performance studies.

LAURA DOYLE (129) is Associate Professor of English at the University of Massachusetts-Amherst. She is author of *Bordering on the Body: The Racial Matrix of Modern Fiction and Culture* (Oxford 1994) and editor of *Bodies of Resistance: New Phenomenologies of Politics, Agency, and Culture* (Northwestern 2001).

JUSTINE DYMOND (140) is a PhD candidate in English at the University of Massachusetts at Amherst where she received her MFA. in creative writing. Her specialties include modernist studies and twentieth-century American literature. Her essay is part of a longer project on intercorporeality in the work of Virginia Woolf and Gertrude Stein.

ISOTA TUCKER EPES (192), a longtime Virginia Woolf reader, has worked most of her life as an editor, writer, or teacher of English Literature. At 67, she retired from the classroom to study studio art. Now, fifteen years later, she still paints with pleasure and regularly enters her work in juried solo and group exhibits.

DIANE F. GILLESPIE (271), Professor of English at Washington State University, is author of *The Sisters' Arts: The Writing and Painting of Virginia Woolf and Vanessa Bell* (1988). Among her more recent books are an essay collection entitled *The Multiple Muses of Virginia Woolf* (1993) containing her essay on Woolf and photography, and an edition of *Roger Fry: A Biography* for the Shakespeare Head Edition of Woolf's works (1996).

LOIS J. GILMORE (165) has a PhD in English from Temple University and an MA from the University of California, Riverside. She is Professor of English at Bucks County Community College, Newtown, PA, where she teaches British literature, composition, and Women's Studies and is Writing Program Administrator.

JANE GOLDMAN (1) lectures in English and American literature at the University of Dundee and is author of *The Feminist Aesthetics of Virginia Woolf: Modernism, Post-Impressionism and the Politics of the Visual* (CUP, 1998).

CHENE HEADY (97) is a PhD candidate in Victorian and Edwardian literatures at Ohio State University. He is the author of "Heraldry and Red Hats: Linguistic Skepticism in Chesterton's Revision of Ruskinian Medievalism," forthcoming in *Prose Studies*. He is working on a dissertation on the autobiographies of Victorian and Edwardian sages.

MAGGIE HUMM (206) teaches in the Department of Cultural Studies, University of East London. Her writing on Woolf is in her books *Feminist Criticism* (1986), *Border Traffic* (1991), *Practising Feminist Criticism* (1995) and *Feminism and Film* (1997) and chapters in *Writing a Woman's Business* eds. K. Fullbrook and J. Simons (1998), *Virginia Woolf in the Age of Mechanical Reproduction* ed. P. Caughie (2000), *Transformations* eds. S. Ahmed et al (2000). She is researching the photography and visual aesthetics of Woolf, Bell and other modernists for her book *Borderline*, Edinburgh University Press.

NANCY KNOWLES (67), Assistant Professor of English/Writing at Eastern Oregon University, has published papers on Virginia Woolf in *Woolf Studies Annual* and in a previous *Selected Papers*. Currently, she is co-editing a volume of essays on Woolf and the real. She is a fellow of the Redwood Writing Project.

KATHRYN LAING (86) is a research fellow at the National University of Ireland, Galway. She has published articles on Woolf, West and Marcel Proust and is currently editing an edition of an early novel by Rebecca West.

KAREN L. LEVENBACK (170) taught at George Washington University and is a former president and secretary-treasurer of the International Virginia Woolf Society. Her book, *Virginia Woolf and the Great War*, was published by Syracuse U P in 1999 and she is currently book review editor of the *Virginia Woolf Miscellany*.

JANE LILIENFELD (92) is an Associate Professor of English at Lincoln University, an historically Black college. She is the author of *Reading Alcoholisms: Theorizing Character and Narrative in Selected Novels of Hardy, Joyce, and Woolf*, and co-editor of *The Languages of Addiction*. This essay is from her book-in-progress, *Circumventing Circumstance*.

NICOLA LUCKHURST (197) is a British Academy research fellow at Somerville College, Oxford. She has published on Proust (*Science and Structure*), Woolf and Montaigne; co-edited a collection of Mallarmé's letters and, with Mary Ann Caws, *The Reception of Virginia Woolf in Europe.* She is currently translating Freud's *Studies in Hysteria* and writing a study of Gisèle Freund.

VANESSA MANHIRE (236) is a graduate student in English at Rutgers University in New Brunswick, NJ. She has an MA from Otago University in Dunedin, New Zealand.

KATIE MARTS (176) is a sophomore at George Washington University, Washington, D.C., majoring in International Affairs and minoring in English Literature.

ANN MARTIN (25) is a doctoral candidate at the University of Toronto. Her dissertation, "'Red Riding Hood and the Wolf in Bed': Modernism's Fairy Tales," explores the relationship between fairy tales, gender performance, and commodity culture in the novels of James Joyce, Djuna Barnes, and Virginia Woolf.

PATRICIA MORAN (6) is Associate Professor of English at the University of California, Davis. She is the author of *Word of Mouth: Body Language in Katherine Mansfield and Virginia Woolf* as well as articles on modernist women writers and psychoanalytic theory. She is currently completing a study of Woolf and corporeality.

ELIZABETH OUTKA (229) is a doctoral student at the University of Virginia, where she is completing a dissertation entitled "Consuming Tradition: Nostalgia, Consumerism, and the British Novel, 1909-1919."

STEVEN PUTZEL (105) is Associate Professor of English at Penn State University, Wilkes-Barre. He is author of *Reconstructing Yeats*, and has published articles on Yeats, Sam Shepard, James Stephens, James Joyce, Sheila Watson, and on other issues in modern American, Irish and British poetry and drama. His most recent essays, including "Virginia Woolf and 'The Distance of the Stage'" in *Women's Studies* (1999), are parts of a work in progress, *Virginia Woolf and the Theatre*.

DEBRAH RASCHKE (79) is an Assistant Professor of English and Director of Graduate Studies at Southeast Missouri State University. She has published on modern and contemporary literature, as well as on contemporary theory and film.

MARILYN SCHWINN SMITH (265) has published essays on Woolf and her contemporary, the Russian poet Marina Tsvetaeva. An independent scholar, she finds employment as coordinator for the Northampton Silk Project, located at Smith College.

NANCY SHAY (180) teaches English at Richard Montgomery High School in Rockville, Maryland. She has an MEd in English Education from the University of Virginia and an MA in English from the University of Maryland. She lives in Gaithersburg with her husband Jeff Coster.

BRENDA R. SILVER (157), Professor of English, Dartmouth College, has published *Virginia Woolf Icon*, *Virginia Woolf's Reading Notebooks*, and *Rape and Representation*. She is currently at work on a study of the rhetorical intersections among hypertext, iconicity, narrative strategies, and social spaces that uses Virginia Woolf icon as its starting point.

DIANA L. SWANSON (46) is Associate Professor of Women's Studies and English at Northern Illinois University. Her publications on Woolf include articles in *Woolf Studies Annual, Twentieth Century Literature,* previous *Selected Papers,* and *Creating Safe Space: Violence and Women's Writing* (Tharp and Kuribayashi, editors).

DAVID VALLINS (249) is a Lecturer in English at the University of Hiroshima, Japan, and previously taught at universities in Britain and Hong Kong. His publications include *Coleridge and the Psychology of Romanticism* (Macmillan, 1999), and articles on Akenside, Coleridge, Mary Shelley, and R.W. Emerson.

CAROLINE WEBB (243) teaches English at the University of Newcastle, Central Coast Campus, Australia, specializing in twentieth-century fiction by women. She has published essays on Woolf and others in Modern Fiction Studies and elsewhere, and is working on a book about twentieth-century women writers' use of earlier narratives about female lives.

KARIN E. WESTMAN (73) is a Visiting Assistant Professor of English at Kansas State University, where she teaches courses in contemporary British literature and women's literature. She has published on Virginia Woolf, Pat Barker, and J. K. Rowling, and she is currently working on a book-length study of twentieth-century British women writers.

MICHAEL WHITWORTH (151) works at the University of Wales, Bangor, where he teaches modules on Woolf, Literary Theory, Victorian Literature, and Hypertext. He has recently completed the manuscript of a book titled *Einstein's Wake: Relativity, Metaphor, and Modernist Literature.*

JENNIFER WICKE (221) is Professor of English at the University of Virginia. She has written widely on modernist literature and culture.

MARK WOLLAEGER (213), author of *Joseph Conrad and the Fictions of Skepticism* (Stanford, 1990) and co-editor of *Joyce and the Subject of History* (Michigan, 1996), teaches modern British literature at Vanderbilt University. He is currently writing a book on new media and the emergence of British modernism.

Virginia Woolf Out of Bounds

Tenth Annual Virginia Woolf Conference
The University of Maryland, Baltimore County
Jessica Berman, Conference Director

Wednesday, June 7: Conference attendees are encouraged to join us Wednesday evening for an informal reception, 7-9, in the atrium of the UMBC Physics Building. Dorms will be open.

Thursday, June 8:
8:30 A.M.—Registration opens
9:00 - 1:30—Pre-conference excursion to the National Museum or Women in the Arts (Washington, D.C.)
1:00 - 2:00—Conference Convenes. Please join us for welcoming remarks and a preview of the art exhibit.

2:00 - 3:30—Featured Panel I:
INSCRIPTIONS OF SEXUALITIES
Patricia Moran, University of California, Davis, chair
Patricia Moran, University of California, Davis, "Gunpowder Plots: Sexuality and Censorship in Woolf's Later Works"
Emily Blair, University of California, Davis, "Prostituting Culture and enslaving Intellectual Liberty: Virginia Woolf's Disavowed Victorian Predecessor Margaret Oliphant"
Georgia Johnston, Saint Louis University, "Woolf and Bestiality"

3:30-3:45 BREAK

3: 45 - 5:15—SESSIONS I :
WOOLF AND CONTEMPORARY CULTURE
Diana Royer, Miami University Hamilton, chair
Jamie Carr, University of Rhoda Island, "Novel Possibilities: ReReading Sexuality and 'Madness' in Woolf's *Mrs. Dalloway*, Beyond the Film"
Sherida Yoder, Felician College, "Woolf Sightings in Anne Tyler's *Ladder of Years*"
Diana Royer, Miami University Hamilton, "Words Sprung Free: The Quoted Woolf"

A SENSE OF PLACE
Bonnie Kime Scott, University of Delaware, chair
Carol Hansen, City College of San Francisco, "A Woolfian Asheham House"
Jacqueline Wilkotz, Towson University, "Beyond Perennial Borders: Virginia Woolf's Fields and Gardens"
Bonnie Kime Scott, University of Delaware, "Exploring the Political Nature of Woolf's Early Landscapes"

BETWEEN THE ACTS
Ellen Tremper, Brooklyn College, chair
Sheila Walsh, Northeastern University, "Words and Threads: The 'Terms' of Influence and Representation in Between the Acts"
Alison Lewis, "Loss of Center: Virginia Woolf's *Between the Acts*"
Monica Stufft, Muhlenberg College, "Between the Cracks of Miss LaTrobe's Acts: The Responsibility of the Artist in Between the Acts"

GENDER CROSSINGS I

Justyna Kostkowska, Middle Tennessee State University, chair
Ellen Gerber, Muhlenberg College, "Investigating Cross-Gender Similarities in Woolf's Works"
Stephanie Zappa, Chabot College, "Ginny and Donna, or A Writing, Teaching, Mothering Life: Virginia Woolf, Donna Reed, and the Angel in the House"
Justyna Kostkowska, Middle Tennessee State University, "The Many-Sided Flower: Percival as *The Waves*' Other Androgyne"

5:30-7:00—Opening Reception
President Freeman Hrabowski, UMBC, welcoming remarks.

7:00-8:15—Plenary Panel: "New Directions in Woolf Study—Woolf and Post-Colonialism"
Jessica Berman, University of Maryland, Baltimore County, chair
Susan Stanford Friedman, University of Wisconsin, Madison, "Woolf, Cultural Parataxis, and Transnational Landscapes of Reading: Toward a Locational Modernist Studies"
Sonita Sarker, Macalester College, "Virginia Woolf and the Possibility of a Postcolonial Modernism"

8:30-10:00—Plenary Panel: Circulating Histories: The Archive, The Library, and the Reader
Mark Hussey, Pace University, chair
Ted Bishop, University of Alberta, "Woolf and the Violence of the Meta-Archive"
Anna Snaith, Anglia Polytechnic University, "'Stray Guineas': Woolf, Women Readers, and the Marsham Street Library"
Melba Cuddy-Keane, University of Toronto, "Brow-Beating, Wool Gathering, and the Brain of the Common Reader"

8:30 - 10:30 Film *Charulata* by Satyajit Ray
Friday, June 9:
7:30 A.M. — Breakfast Virginia Woolf Miscellany meeting, J. J. Wilson, Sonoma State University, chair
8:30 — 5 Registration
8:30—10:30 Film Charulata by Satyajit Ray (second screening)
8:30 - 10:00—SESSIONS II:
QUESTIONS OF CONSCIOUSNESS, SPIRITUALITY AND SUBJECTIVITY
Richard Pearce, Wheaton College, chair
Lynnette Beers, Chapman University, "'I Never Met a Bug I Didn't Like': Buddhist Teachings as Reflected in Woolf's Fiction"
Courtney Carter, Hood College, "Mrs. Dalloway and the 'New Science'"
Andrea Harris, Mansfield University, "'Death is the Extreme': Death and Writing in Woolf and Blanchot"

WOOLF AND HISTORY

Masami Usui, Doshisha University, chair
Alice Gasque, University of South Dakota, "History and 'The Journal of Mistress Joan Martyn'"
Audrey Johnson, Washington State University, "'I told you in the course of this paper that Shakespeare had a sister': Feminist Revision of Victorian Historiographical Strategies in *A Room of One's Own*"
Chris Luebbe, University of Michigan, "Theories of History in Woolf's *Between the Acts*"
Masami Usui, Doshisha University, "A Paradox of 'A House of History's Own" in *Orlando* and *A Room of One's Own*"

285

Conference Program

INTIMACY AND IRONY IN MRS. DALLOWAY

Ned Sparrow, Maryland Institute, College of Art, chair

Angela Chan, Maryland Institute, College of Art, "Intimate Privacy"

Ned Sparrow, Maryland Institute, College of Art, "First the Warning, Nominal, then the Irony, Irrevocable: Woolf's Then and Now Irony"

WOOLF AND OTHER WRITERS I: LARSEN, CARTER

Jane Fisher, Canisius College, chair

Anne MacMaster, Millsaps College, "'A Lack of Acquiescence': From Woolf's Clarissa Dalloway to Nella Larsen's Helga Crane"

Kathryn Laing, "Chasing the Wild Goose: Virginia Woolf's *Orlando* and Angela Carter's *The Passion of New Eve*"

10:00-10:30—Break

10:30-12—Sessions III:

WOOLF, WRITING, AND LANGUAGE THEORY

Emily Dalgarno, Boston University, chair

Victoria Blythe, New York University, Gallatin College, *The Waves* as a Grammatology"

Judith Allen "Virginia Woolf's Metaphorical Mode: Pushing the Boundaries of Language"

Emily Dalgarno, Boston University, "Virginia Woolf: Language and the World as Picture"

WOOLF AND PHYSICS

Holly Henry, Pennsylvannia State University, chair

Barri Gold, Muhlenberg College, "'Fear No More the Heat of the Sun': Virginia Woolf Revisits Nineteenth-Century Energy Physics"

Kristin Yngve, Muhlenberg College, "Playing the Artist and the Physicist: Woolf's Use of Color for Identity Construction in *The Waves*"

Michael Whitworth, University of Wales, Bangor, "Porous Objects: Self, Community, and the Nature of Matter"

ORIENTALISM/COLONIALISM

Steven Putzel, Pennsylvannia State University, chair

Chene Heady, Ohio State University, "'Accidents of Political Life': Satire and Edwardian Anti-Colonial Politics in *The Voyage Out*

Suzanne Lynch, Cambridge University, "*Mrs. Dalloway* and the Question of National Identity"

Steven Putzel, Pennsylvannia State University, "Woolf and British Orientalism"

WOOLF AND POLITICS

Paula Hooper Mayhew, Fairleigh Dickinson University, chair

Carolyn Tilghman Bitzenhofer, University of Notre Dame, "Obscure and Ordinary Lives: Virginia Woolf and the Women's Co-operative Guild"

Kathryn Harvey, Mount Saint Vincent University, "Harnessing the Minnows: the Importance of Politics to Virginia Woolf's Art"

Paula Hooper Mayhew, Fairleigh Dickinson University, "Contentious Feminists: H.G. Wells and Virginia Woolf on Gender"

PHILOSOPHICAL PERSPECTIVES I

Penelope Cordish, Goucher College, chair

Renée Dickinson, University of Colorado at Boulder, "Operating Ontologically: Defining and Defying Borders in *Between the Acts*"

Wendy Weber, University of North Carolina, Greensboro, "Reading Between and Beneath the

286

Acts: Woolf's Interrogation of Knowability in *Between the Acts*"
Justine Dymond, "The Phenomenological Challenge to the Inside/Outside Dichotomy in Woolf's *To the Lighthouse*"

12:00 - 1:30—Lunch
Conference attendees are invited to buy their lunch in the University Dining Hall, near the dormitories. The Pub in the Campus Center is not participating in the conference.

1:30 - 3:00—SESSIONS IV:

WOOLF, TAGORE AND RAY'S *CHARULATA*
Sangeeta Ray, University of Maryland, College Park, chair
Henry Schwarz, Georgetown University, "Cosmopolitan Modernism: Realism and Gender in Tagore and Ray"
Sangeeta Ray, University of Maryland, College Park, "Reading Charulata, Reading Tagore"
TEACHING I: *A ROOM OF ONE'S OWN*
Karen Levenback, The George Washington University, chair
Nancy Shay, Richard Montgomery High School, "'I'm Not a Feminist or Anything, But. . .': Teaching *A Room of One's* Own in High School"
Aimee Wiest, University of Maryland, Baltimore County, "Considering *A Room of One's Own* Within a Widening Context"
Karen Levenback, The George Washington University, "Teaching *A Room of One's Own* in the New Millennium: The War Continues"
Katie Marts, The George Washington University, "Opening Doors to *A Room of One's Own*"

FEMINIST & LESBIAN RE-READINGS
Anne Fernald, Purdue University, chair
Amy Vondrak, Syracuse University, "If You Saw Me Would You Buy Me? : Virginia Woolf, Commodity Out of Bounds"
Ann Martin, University of Toronto, "Sleeping Beauty in a Green Dress: *Mrs. Dalloway* and Fairy Tale Configurations of Desire"
Anne Fernald, Purdue University, "O Sister Swallow: Sapphic Fragments as English Literature in Virginia Woolf"

WOOLF AND PHOTOGRAPHY
Maggie Humm, University of East London, chair
June Foley, New York University/ The New School, "Woolf and the Photography of Julia Margaret Cameron" ,
Nicola Luckhurst, Oxford University, "Photo-Portraits: Virginia Woolf and Giselle Freund"
Maggie Humm, University of East London, "Belonging and Unbelonging: Transformations of Memory in the Photographs of Virginia Woolf"

ORLANDO
Pierre-Eric Villeneuve, chair
Jane de Gay, University of Leeds, "'. . . though the fashion of the time did something to disguise it': Staging Gender in Woolf's *Orlando*"
Urmila Seshagiri, University of Illinois, Urbana, "Imperialists and Gypsies: Cultural Boundaries in Woolf's *Orlando* and Vita Sackville-West's A Passenger to Teheran"
Pierre-Eric Villeneuve, "*Orlando* Unbound"

3:00 - 3:30–Break

3:30- 5:00—Featured Panels II:
A: VIRGINIA WOOLF AND THE UNLIKELY OTHER
Jane Lilienfeld, Lincoln University, chair
Eileen Barrett, California State University, Haywood, "*Jacob's Room* and Giovanni's Room: Homoerotic Space in Woolf and Baldwin"
Vara Neverow, Southern Connecticut State University, "Resisting Patriarchy from Virginia Woolf to Suzy McKee Charnas"
Jane Lilienfeld, Lincoln University, "*Something I've Been Meaning to Tell You*: Alice Munro as Unlikely Heir to Virginia Woolf"
Monica Ayuso, "The Unlikely Other: Borges and Woolf's Translation"

B: WOOLF AND THE MATERIAL WORLD
Jennifer Wicke, The University of Virginia, chair
Sara Blair, The University of Michigan, "Real Space, Real Time: Virginia Woolf and the Geography of Bloomsbury"
Mark Wollaeger, Vanderbilt University, "Woolf, Picture Postcards, Modernity"
Jennifer Wicke, The University of Virginia, "Frock Consciousness, Self-Fashioning: Virginia Woolf's Dialectical Material-ism"

5-7 Dinner
Conference attendees are invited to buy their dinner in the University Dining Hall, near the dormitories. The Pub in the Campus Center is not participating in the conference.

7-8:30–Plenary Panel:
A ROOM OF ONE'S OWN: **CULTURAL DIGRESSIONS**
Jessica Berman, University of Maryland, Baltimore County, chair
Michèle Barrett, Queen Mary and Westfield College, "Reason and Truth in *A Room of One's Own*"
Brenda Silver, Dartmouth College, "Virginia Woolf//Hypertext"
Susan Gubar, Indiana University, "From a Feminism of One's Own"

8:45-11:00—Performance:
A STAGED READING OF *THE WAVES*
Adapted by Marjorie Lightfoot, Arizona State University; directed by Alan Kreizenbeck, University of Maryland, Baltimore County; by permission of the Society of Authors. (Theater)

Saturday, June 10:
7:30 A.M.—Breakfast — International Virginia Woolf Society Meeting
Vara Neverow, Southern Connecticut State University, chair

8:30 — 5 Registration

8:30 - 10:00—SESSIONS VI:

WOOLF AND ROMANTICISM
David Vallins, University of Hong Kong, chair
Kathryn Miles, University of Delaware, "Recipe for Romance: Woolf's Neo-Romanticism and Night and Day
Caroline Webb, "'All was dark, all was doubt, all was confusion': Nature, Culture, and *Orlando*'s Ruskinian Stormcloud"
David Vallins, University of Hong Kong, "'Whose shape is that within the car? & why': *Mrs. Dalloway* and 'The Triumph of Life'"
PSYCHOANALYTIC PERSPECTIVES
Herbert Marder, University of Illinois, chair
288

Rishona Zimring, Lewis and Clark College, "'They bore her, thus bound—where?': Sara Pargiter, Antigone, and the Resistance to Elegy in *The Years*"

Janice Stewart, University of Windsor, "A Single Narcissus: 'The Mother of Us All' and 'the Father of Psychoanalysis'".

Caroline Harmon, "Mass and Edge: the Development of Selfhood and National Identity in The Waves"

MASCULINITIES
Georgette Fleischer, Columbia University, chair

Caroline Kley, Rutgers University, "The Entrapped Male: Virginia Woolf's Perspective"

Shaun Carey, City University of New York, "Virginia Woolf and the Sons of Feminism: *The Hours* as a Revision of *Mrs. Dalloway*"

Georgette Fleischer, Columbia University, "Resketching Masculinities in 'A Sketch of the Past': the Feminist Reception of Virginia Woolf's Unfinished Family Memoir"

TEACHING II: NON-TRADITIONAL APPROACHES
Ruth Saxton, Mills College, chair

Lisa Haines-Wright, with Erin McCluskey, Beloit College, "Out From In-Between: Woolf and the Pedagogy of Interstitial Space"

Keith Beyer Emerson, Art Institute of Chicago, "Ceda el Paso: Woolf in Identity Interrogative Dynamics of Adult ESL Education"

Ruth Saxton, Mills College/Stephanie Zappa, Chabot College, "'Just what are we supposed to get out of this book?': Students Teaching Virginia Woolf and Toni Morrison in a High School-College Collaboration"

10:00 - 10:30—Break

10:30 - 12:00—SESSIONS VII:

UNIVERSITY PRESS PUBLISHING IN THE HUMANITIES: A WORKSHOP DISCUSSION
Mark Hussey, Pace University Press, chair

Maura Burnett, The Johns Hopkins University Press; Cathie Brettschneider, University Press of Virginia; Mark Hussey, Pace University Press

PHILOSOPHICAL PERSPECTIVES II
Linda Raphael, The George Washington University, chair

Mark Rollins, University of Georgia, "'The World Itself is Without Meaning': Virginia Woolf's Sense of the Absurd in *Mrs. Dalloway*"

Colleen Donovan, University of Georgia, 'I Will Go Down With My Colours Flying': Virginia Woolf's Nietzschean Nationalism in *Between the Acts*"

WOOLF AND OTHER WRITERS II: VEXED RELATIONSHIPS -BYATT, LESSING, DIVAKARUNI
Debrah Raschke, Southeast Missouri State University, chair

Karin Westman, College of Charleston, "A.S. Byatt and 'V. Woolf': Mapping a Misreading of Modernism"

Nancy Knowles, University of Connecticut, "Dissolving Stereotypical Cultural Boundaries: Allusions to Virginia Woolf in Chitra Banerjee Divakaruni's *Sister of My Heart*"

Debrah Raschke, Southeast Missouri State University, "'It won't be fine' tomorrow: Doris Lessing's Struggle with Woolf"

LIFE MATTERS/HISTORICAL CONTEXTS
Madelyn Detloff, California State University, Los Angeles, chair

Abigail Burnham Bloom, The New School, "Laura Stephen and Virginia Stephen: A Relationship Neither Wanted"

Donald Blume, Florida State University, "'Because It Is There': George Mallory's Hidden Presence in *To the Lighthouse*"

Masami Usui, Doshishi University, "The Trauma Caused By Mother's Death in Virginia Woolf and Kyoko Mori"

Madelyn Detloff, California State University, Los Angeles, "Un-Ruly Un-Subjects: The Melancholic Stakes of Recuperating Woolf's Madness"

WOOLF AND MUSIC
Pierre-Eric Villeneuve, chair

Kella Svetich, University of California, Davis, "Playing the Musical Semiotic in *The Voyage Out*"

Vanessa Manhire, Rutgers University, "'The Lady's Gone A-Roving': Woolf and the English Folk Revival"

12:00-1:30—Lunch
Conference attendees are invited to buy their lunch in the University Dining Hall, near the dormitories. The Pub in the Campus Center is not participating in the conference.

1:30-3:00—SESSIONS VIII:
SUBJECTIVITY AND PERFORMANCE
Brian Richardson, University of Maryland, College Park, chair

Genevieve Abravanel, Duke University, "Woolf in Blackface: Identification Across *The Waves*"

Emily Ravenwood, Ohio State University, "E Pluribus, Unum: The Single Character in Woolf's *The Waves*"

Donna Decker Schuster, Marquette University, "Reconfiguring Identity in *To the Lighthouse* and *A Room of One's Own*"

JACOB'S ROOM
Marlene Briggs, Cornell University, chair

Kathleen Wall, University of Regina, "'Significant Form in *Jacob's Room*: Ekphrasis and the Elegy"

Diana Swanson, Northern Illinois University, "With Clear-Eyed Scrutiny: Gender, Authority and the Narrator as Sister in *Jacob's Room*

Marlene Briggs, Cornell University, *Jacob's Room* as Counter-Monument: The Great War, the Cenotaph, and the Haunted Postwar Politics of Remembrance"

TEACHING III: NEW CONTEXTS FOR UPPER LEVEL TEACHING
Beth Rigel Daugherty, Otterbein College, chair

Linda Raphael, The George Washington University, "Profiting from Woolf's Misconstruction and Instruction in the Classroom"

Moira Baker, Radford University, "Woolf sin fronteras: Teaching Woolf, International Women Writers and Human Rights Issues"

Beth Rigel Daugherty, Otterbein College, "Teaching Woolf/Woolf Teaching"

WOOLF AND OTHER WRITERS III: REVISIONARY CONNECTIONS—CUNNING-HAM, LE GUIN, AMIS
Natania Rosenfeld, Knox College, chair

Penelope Cordish, Goucher College, "Visions and Revisions: Woolf, Cunningham, and Inter-Textuality"

Alisha Rohde, Ohio State University, "Time Travel and Ms. Woolf: Responses to Changing Perspectives on Time"

Natania Rosenfeld, Knox College, "Rehabilitations: From 'Time Passes' to Time's Arrow"
WOOLF AND OTHER MEDIA
Leslie Hankins, Cornell College, chair
Cheryl Hindrichs, Ohio State University, "Spirals of Seashell, *The Waves*: Woolf, Dulac, and Surrealist Cinema"
Clifford Wulfman, Yale University, "Beyond Bounds: Woolf and the Poetics of Hypertext"
Leslie Hankins, , Cornell College, "HyperWoolf: HyperMedia or HyperHypes?: Thoughts on New Technologies for Adaptations of Literature"

3:00 - 3:30—Break

3:30 - 5:00—Featured Panels III:
A: WOOLF AND THE CITY
Jeanette McVicker, State University of New York, chair
Jeanette McVicker, State University of New York, "Six Essays on London Life A History of Dispersal"
Janet Winston, Virginia Commonwealth University, "'Victoria, Billowing on Her Mound': Virginia Woolf's and Lytton Strachey's 'Ambiguous Memorials' to the Queen"
Sonita Sarker, Macalester College, respondant

B: RE-VISITING *A ROOM OF ONE'S OWN*:
(please see the conference flyer for updated information on this panel)
Laura Doyle, The University of Massachusetts, Amherst, "The Body Unbound: Political Openings in Woolf's Syntax of Suspension"
C: PAINTING THE WAVES : Isota Tucker Epes and Suzanne Bellamy
Featured Art and Performance Events :
5:00 - 5:45
Suzanne Bellamy, SHAPES OF THE BRAIN: A GEOGRAPHY OF THE SENSES
Vara Neverow, Southern Connecticut State University, chair

6:00-7:00
Joyce Zymeck, A ROOM OF HER OWN: MUSIC INSPIRED BY THE WRITINGS OF VIRGINIA WOOLF
Krystyna Colburn University of Massachusetts, Boston
Tim Anderson, University of Maryland Baltimore County, cello
Vara Neverow, Southern Connecticut State University, chair

7:00-8:30—Dinner Among *The Waves* — Dinner Banquet (Costumes Optional)

8:30 Memorial to Noel Annan — Mark Hussey, Pace University

8:45 - 9:45—Woolf Society Players

Sunday, June 11:

7:30 A.M.—Breakfast — Planning Meeting — 2001 Conference, Michael Whitworth, University of Wales, Bangor, chair

8:30 - 10:00—SESSIONS IX:
MATERIAL WOOLF
TBD, chair
Elizabeth Outka, University of Virginia, "'The Shop Windows Were Full of Sparkling Chains': Consumer Desire and Woolf's *Night and Day*"

John Young, University of Michigan, "Why is Mrs. Hilbery in *Mrs. Dalloway*?"
Jennifer Cook, Northeastern University, "Propaganda for Peace: Virginia Woolf's Battle in World War II"

SOUND AND SILENCE
Christine Darrohn, Marshall University, chair
Bruce Gilman, LaSierra University, "Drop Upon Drop, Silence Falls: Reading Meaning into Woolf's Void"
Todd Avery, Indiana University, "Talking to the Other; or, Wireless Ethics: Levinas, Woolf, and the BBC"
Christine Darrohn, Marshall University, "Listening to Her Others: Woolf and Modernist Aural Alterity"

INTER-TEXTUALITY/ QUESTIONS OF RECEPTION
Sally Greene, Independent Scholar, chair
Candy Loren, University of Toronto, "Inter-textual Chain Reactions: *To the Lighthouse* in Dialogue with A Passage to India"
Catherine Galloway, University of Cambridge, "Close Reading: Virginia Woolf and Anna Banti"
Joan Ruffino, University of Wisconsin- Milwaukee, "Through the Narrative Window: A Creative Reading of Virginia Woolf's *A Room of One's Own*"

IMPERIALISM
Krystyna Colburn, University of Massachusetts, Boston, chair
Purvi Shah, Rutgers University, "Living in the 'Beyond' of Imperialism: the Search for a Substantial Self in *The Waves*"
June Chung, University of California, Los Angeles, "Civilization, Imperialism, and Virginia Woolf's Discontents in *Mrs. Dalloway*"
Krystyna Colburn, University of Massachusetts, Boston, "Empire in Miniature: Virginia Woolf and Queen Mary's Dollhouse"

10:00-10:30—Break

10:30-12:00—SESSIONS X:
WOMEN, WRITING, AND WORK
Ann Murphy, Assumption College, chair
Shannon Forbes, Marquette University, "The Transgression of Boundaries in *To the Lighthouse*: Cam's Rejection of the Angel in the House and Identity as a Modern Woman"
Jeanne McNett/Ann Murphy, Assumption College, "Challenging Boundaries: Careers and the Society of Outsiders"

QUESTIONS OF GEOGRAPHY AND TRAVEL
Diane Gillespie, Washington State University, chair
Stevens Amidon, University of Rhode Island, "*The Years* : A Cartography"
Jeanne Dubino, Plymouth State College, "Virginia Woolf's Travel Writing"
Marilyn Schwinn Smith, Five College Associate, "Woolf's Russia: Out of Bounds"
Diane Gillespie, Washington State University, "'The Rain in Spain. . .': Woolf, Cervantes, Andalusia, and *The Waves*"

TEACHING IV: AP ENGLISH/FIRST YEAR COLLEGE
Rhoda Trooboff , National Cathedral School, chair
Cathy D'Agostino, New Trier Township High School, "Learning to Read (with) Literature: Virginia Woolf in the AP English Classroom"

Ellen Walker, The Pembroke Hill School, "Teaching the Students to Stretch: *Mrs. Dalloway* and *To the Lighthouse* in the AP English Classroom"
Lois Gilmore, Bucks County Community College, "'She Speaks to Me': Virginia Woolf in the Community college Classroom"
GENDER CROSSINGS II
Karen Levenback, The George Washington University, chair
Deborah Spanfelner, Binghamton University, "What Does it Mean to Write Like a Woman?"
Kathleen Lipovski-Helal, Indiana University, "Coloring Outside the Lines: Anger in *Mrs. Dalloway* and *To the Lighthouse*"
Lisa Carstens, Virginia Wesleyan University, "The Science of Sex Change in *Orlando*"

DISCUSSION SESSION: "Posted Readings/Posited Meanings" Pierre-Eric Villeneuve and Jessica Berman, University of Maryland, Baltimore County, leaders

12:00 - 1:15—Featured Speaker:

Michael Cunningham
Georgia Johnston, Saint Louis University, chair

1:30-2:30—Closing Lunch Reception (box lunches available)

Appendix: Author & Title index to *Selected Papers* from the First through Ninth Annual Conferences on Virginia Woolf

[Note: Tables of Contents may be viewed at www.pace.edu/press]

I: *Virginia Woolf Miscellanies: Proceedings of the First Annual Conference on Virginia Woolf*, Edited by Mark Hussey and Vara Neverow-Turk, 1991.

II: *Virginia Woolf: Themes and Variations. Selected Papers from the Second Annual Conference on Virginia Woolf*, Edited by Vara Neverow-Turk and Mark Hussey, 1993.

III: *Virginia Woolf: Emerging Perspectives. Selected Papers from the Third Annual Conference on Virginia Woolf*, Edited by Mark Hussey and Vara Neverow-Turk, 1994.

IV: *Re: Reading, Re: Writing, Re: Teaching Virginia Woolf. Selected Papers from the Fourth Annual Conference on Virginia Woolf*, Edited by Eileen Barrett and Patricia Cramer, 1995.

V: *Virginia Woolf: Text and Contexts. Selected Papers from the Fifth Annual Conference on Virginia Woolf*, Edited by Beth Rigel Daugherty and Eileen Barrett, 1996.

VI: *Virginia Woolf and the Arts. Selected Papers from the Sixth Annual Conference on Virginia Woolf*, Edited by Diane F. Gillespie and Leslie K. Hankins, 1997.

VII: *Virginia Woolf and Her Influences. Selected Papers from the Seventh Annual Conference on Virginia Woolf*, Edited by Laura Davis and Jeanette McVicker, 1998.

VIII: *Virginia Woolf and Communities. Selected Papers from the Eighth Annual Conference on Virginia Woolf*, Edited by Jeanette McVicker and Laura Davis, 1999.

IX: *Virginia Woolf Turning the Centuries. Selected Papers from the Ninth Annual Conference on Virginia Woolf*, Edited by Anne L. Ardis and Bonnie Kime Scott, 2000.

Appendix

295

Appendix

Briggs, Marlene A. "Veterans and Civilians: The Mediation of Traumatic Knowledge in *Mrs. Dalloway*" VIII: 43-49

Brosnan, Leila "'Words Fail Me': Virginia Woolf and the Wireless" VI: 134-141

Brown, Terry "Being There: Woolf's London and the Politics of Location" IV: 16-21

Brownstein, Marilyn L. "Silver Spoons and Knives: Virginia Woolf and Walter Benjamin (some notes on a practical approach to cultural studies)" III: 204-209

Burford, Arianne "Communities of Silence and Music in Virginia Woolf's *Pilgrimage*" VIII: 269-275

Burke, Joan "Teaching Virginia Woolf and H. D.: 'A Line to Think Out'" IV: 285-289

Callahan, Anne "Virginia Woolf and Postmodern Feminism" I: 215-222

Caramagno, Thomas C. "Laterality and Sexuality: The Transgressive Aesthetics of *Orlando*" V: 183-188; "The Lure of Reductionism in Psychological Treatments of Woolf's Life" VI: 320-326

Carpentier, Martha C. "Why an Old Shoe? Teaching *Jacob's Room* as *l'ecriture feminine*" IV: 142-148

Carubia, Josephine M. "'The Higgledy-Piggledy' Puzzle A Fractal Analysis of the Patterns of Patterns in Virginia Woolf's Fiction" VI: 260-268; "'The Blessed Island of Good Boots': Virginia Woolf's Deployment of Fetishism in *To the Lighthouse*" VII: 282-288

Caughie, Pamela L. "Virginia Woolf and Postmodern Feminism" I: 215-222; "'Re-iterating the Differences': Virginia Woolf and (Postmodern) Theory" VII: 239-241; "Virginia Woolf in the Age of Mechanical Reproduction" IX: 34-40

Chapman, Wayne K. "Leonard and Virginia Woolf Working Together" I: 209-211; "Virginia Woolf's Contributions to Anonymous, Composite Reviews in the *Nation & Athenaeum*, 1924-1928" VII: 63-69; "Leonard Woolf, Cambridge, and the Art of the English Essay" IX: 215-222

Christian, Barbara "Layered Rhythms: Virginia Woolf and Toni Morrison" III: 164-177

Cliff, Michelle "Virginia Woolf and the Imperial Gaze: A Glance Askance" III: 91-102

Colburn, Krystyna "Women's Oral Tradition and *A Room of One's Own*" IV: 59-64; "Spires of London: Domes of Istanbul" V: 250-254

Colburn-McGuire, Penny "Interiors: Woolf and Dostoevsky" I: 121-123

Cole, Sarah "The Ambivalence of the Outsider: Virginia Woolf and Male Friendship" VI: 191-197

Collier, Patrick "Woolf, Privacy, and the Press" IX: 223-229

Connolly, Margaret "Meredith, Woolf, and the Art of Comedy" VI: 197-205

Connolly, Paul "The Life of the Mind, the Life of the Party" IV: 1-6; "Opening Questions: A Workshop in Writing to Read Virginia Woolf" IV: 251-258

Cordish, Penelope "Virginia Woolf's Mountain Top-That Persistent Vision" I: 191-198

Cornell, Portia "How Vita Sackville-West Survived the Masterpiece Theatre Massacre" III: 189-191

Courington, Chella "Virginia Woolf and Alice Walker: Family as Metaphor in the Personal Essay" III: 239-245; "From *Clarissa* to *Mrs. Dalloway*: Woolf's (Re)Vision of Richardson" IV: 95-101; "Teaching Woolf in a Multicultural Context" VII: 49-50

Cramer, Patricia "Notes from Underground: Lesbian Ritual in the Writings of Virginia Woolf" I: 177-188; "*Virginia Woolf: Lesbian Readings*: A Preview" VII: 3-5; "Response" IX: 116-126

Crown, Kathleen "Two Judith Shakespeares: Virginia Woolf, H. D., and the Androgynous Brother-Sister Mind" V: 81-86

Cuddy-Keane, Melba "Opening Historical Doors to the *Room*: An Approach to Teaching" IV: 207-215; "Passage to China: East and West and Woolf (Abstract)" VI: 11-12; "Thinking Historically About Historical Thinking" VII: 59-60; "*Mrs. Dalloway*, Film, Time, and Trauma" VII: 171-175; "'A Standard of One's Own': Virginia Woolf and the Question of Literary Value" IX: 230-236

Cumberland, Debra L. "'A Voice Answering a Voice': Elizabeth Barrett Browning, Virginia Woolf and Margaret Forster's Literary Friendship" V: 193-198

Appendix

Fernald, Anne "A Room, A Child, A Mind of One's Own: Virginia Woolf, Alice Walker and Feminist Personal Criticism" III: 245-251

Fisher, Jane "*Jacob's Room* and the Canon: Teaching Woolf During the Culture Wars" IV: 290-293

Flesher, Erika "Picturing the Truth in Fiction: Re-visionary Biography and the Illustrative Portraits for *Orlando*" VI: 39-47

Flynn, Deirdre "Virginia Woolf's Women and the Fashionable Elite: On Not Fitting In" VIII: 167-173

Fox, Crystal J. "'She Looks Quite Capable of Having Deceived': Critical Avenues and Answers in Virginia Woolf's 'Memoirs of a Novelist'" IV: 162-167

Fox, Susan Hudson "Woolf's Austen/Boston Tea Party: The Revolt Against Literary Empire in *Night and Day*" III: 259-265

Francis, Jo "The Making of *The War Within*" VI: 206-217

Freed, Lorie "Text as Microfilm and Text as Software" V: 241-244

Friedman, Susan Stanford "Uncommon Readings: Seeking the Geopolitical Woolf (Abstract)" VI: 3

Froula, Christine "War, Civilization, and the Conscience of Modernity: Views from *Jacob's Room*" V: 280-295

Fuegi, John "The Making of *The War Within*" VI: 206-217

Galstad, Alison Ames "Dame Ethel Smyth: Composing Her Life" VI: 166-174

Garcia-Rodriquez, Antonia "Virginia Woolf from a Latin American Perspective" I: 43-45

Garratt, Lindsay "The Image of the Circle in Woolf's 'Mrs. Dalloway's Party'" VII: 303-304

Garvey, Johanna X. K. "'A Voice Bubbling Up': *Mrs. Dalloway* in Dialogue with *Ulysses*" II: 299-308

Gay, Penny "Bastards from the Bush: Virginia Woolf and her Antipodean Relations" III: 289-295

Gibaldi Campell, Ann "Virginia Woolf and Hlne Cixous: Female Fantasy in Two of Woolf's Short Stories" III: 71-76

Gillespie, Diane F. "'Her kodak pointed at his head': Virginia Woolf and Photography" II: 33-40; "The Biographer and the Self in *Roger Fry*" V: 198-203; "Panel Summary: 'The Loves of the Arts': Theories of Aesthetic (R)evolution" VII: 153; "Make Art, Not War: Virginia Woolf's Between the *Arts*" VII: 154-155; "'Human nature is on you': Septimus Smith, the Camera Eye, and the Classroom" VII: 162-167; "Metaphors of Illness and Wellness: John Donne, Virginia Woolf, and Susan Sontag" IX: 127-133

Gilmore, Lois J. "Virginia Woolf, Bloomsbury, and the Primitive" VIII: 127-135

Glorie, Josephine Carubia "Mapping the Epistemic Terrain in Virginia Woof's *To the Lighthouse*" IV: 155-161

Goldman, Jane "Artist and Feminist Communities of 1910: Post-Impressionism, Suffrage Aesthetics, and Intersubjectivity in *To the Lighthouse*" VIII: 259-268

Gordon, Troy "The Place of Cross-Sex Friendship in Woolf Studies" IX: 102-111

Gough, Val "The Mystical Copula: Rewriting the Phallus in *To the Lighthouse*" III: 216-223; "Teaching Woolf as Feminist Mystic" IV: 294-298; "With Some Irony in Her Interrogation: Woolf's Ironic Mysticism" VI: 85-90; "'A Responsible Person Like Her': Woolf's Suicide Culture" IX: 183-191

Graff, Agniezka "On integrity, legal trespassers, and peeling potatoes: *A Room of One's Own* re-read in Polish" VII: 202-208

Grant, Amanda "Life Without Boundaries" I: 199-201

Gray, Julia "First Encounters: Student Responses to Woolf" VIII: 276-282

Greenberg, Judith "Woolf's Ancient Song: Traces of the Dead Echoing into the Future" IX: 140-147

Greene, Sally "Notes on a Vanishing Point" VI: 29-31; "Virginia Woolf and the Courtier's Art: The Renaissance Wit of *A Room of One's Own*" VI: 292-301; "Virginia Woolf, 'Poet Historical'" VII: 61-62; "Virginia Woolf, Renaissance Woman" IX: 11-16

Grey, Julia "Truth Defined by Absence" VII: 304-305

Ito, Yuko "The Production of the South Country in the Bloomsbury Group's Writings" VII: 257-261; "The Masked Reality in Leonard Woolf's Colonial Writings" VIII: 136-141

Jacobsen, Sally A. "Was Virginia an 'Apostle' of G. E. Moore? Woolf's Idea of Friendship in her 1918-1919 *Diary*" II: 329-337; "Using Bloomsbury Art to Teach *Mrs. Dalloway, To the Lighthouse*, and *The Waves*: A New Historical Approach" IV: 48-52

Johnston, Georgia "After the Invention of the Gramophone: Hearing the Women in Stein's *Autobiography* and Woolf's *Three Guineas*" I: 88-96; "Women's Voice: *Three Guineas* as Autobiography" II: 321-328; "Virginia Woolf's Autobiographers: Sidonie Smith, Shoshana Felman, and Shari Benstock" V: 140-144; "Raising Community" VIII: 1-5; "Introductions" VIII: 193-194

Johnston, Judith L. "'Necessary Bore' or Brilliant Novelist?: What Yourcenar Understood About Woolf's *The Waves*" I: 125-132

Jones, Danell "The Chase of the Wild Goose: The Ladies of Llangollen and *Orlando*" II: 181-189

Jones, Ellen Carol "Figural Desire in *Orlando*" III: 108-114

Kanwar, Anju "Briscoe's *alt[a]r*native: *Durga* or *Sati*? Woolf and Hinduism in *To the Lighthouse*" V: 104-109

Kato, Megumi "The Politics/Poetics of Motherhood in *To the Lighthouse*" VIII: 102-109

Keller, Julia "Inventing Virginia Woolf: Literary Biography As Art Form" VII: 11-12

Kirschner, Susan "Opening Questions: A Workshop in Writing to Read Virginia Woolf" IV: 251-258

Knowles, Nancy "A Community of Women Looking at Men: The Photographs in Virginia Woolf's *Three Guineas*" VIII: 91-96

Koenigsberger, Kurt "Excavating the Elephant and Castle: Joanna Southcott and the Voice of Prophecy in *A Room of One's Own*" VII: 98-104

Kramer, Lynn "One Retrospective Lupine View: A Terrified Student's View of Virginia Woolf's *Three Guineas*" II: 97-102

Krouse, Tonya "'I would rather be a cyborg than a goddess': Lily Briscoe, Mrs. Ramsay, and the Postmodern Sublime" VII: 294-301

Kumin, Maxine "'This curious silent unrepresented life'" VII: 144-146

Kyle, Traci Lynn "From He to She to You and Me: Grounding Fluidity, Woolf's *Orlando* to Winterson's *Written on the Body*" V: 177-183

Laing, Kathryn S. "Addressing Femininity in the Twenties: Virginia Woolf and Rebecca West on Money, Mirrors and Masquerade" VI: 66-75

Lambert, Elizabeth G. "Evolution and Imagination in *Pointz Hall* and *Between the Acts*" II: 83-89; "Proportion is in the Mind of the Beholder: *Mrs. Dalloway*'s Critique of Science" III: 278-282; "Virginia Woolf Joins Jane Wagner and Lily Tomlin in The Search for Signs of Intelligent Life in the Universe" V: 26-29; "Mrs. Dalloway Meets the Robot Maria" VI: 277-282

Landon, Lana Hartman "A Community of Correspondences: Two Women, Letters, and *The Voyage Out*" VIII: 17-22

Langham, Linda J. "Virginia's Pages: Collecting Woolf's First Editions & Letters" III: 230-238

Laurence, Patricia "The China Letters: Julian Bell, Vanessa Bell, Ling Shu Hua (Abstract)" VI: 10-11

Lazarre, Jane "Structures of Common Experience: Learning from Virginia Woolf" I: 57-61

Lee, Hermione "Responses to a Life of Virginia Woolf" VII: 13-15

Leps, Marie-Christine "From Contingency to Essence: Fictions of Identity in Novels and Films" IX: 276-283

Levenback, Karen L. "Virginia Woolf and the Great War: Civilian Immunity and Strategic Bombing" IV: 80-86

Levy, Heather "'Julia Kissed Her, Julia Possessed Her': Considering Class and Lesbian Desire in Virginia Woolf's Shorter Fiction" III: 83-90; "*The Voyage Out* of

Appendix

Wilson, Deborah "Fishing for Woolf's Submerged Lesbian Text" IV: 121-128; "Between the Arts: Woolf, Pedagogy, and the Persistence of Authority" VIII: 109-116

Wilson, J. J. "From Solitude to Society Through Reading Virginia Woolf" III: 13-18

Wilson, Jean Moorcroft "Leonard Woolf: The Pivot or Outsider of Bloomsbury?" I: 213-214; "Conceived with Kindness: the Woolf Family Perspective (Abstract)" VI: 1-2

Winterhalter, Teresa "Guns and Big Guns in *A Room of One's Own*" IV: 72-79

Wright, G. Patton "Virginia Woolf's Uncommon Reader: Allusions in *Between the Acts*" I: 230-233

Wussow, Helen "Travesties of Excellence: Julia Margaret Cameron, Lytton Strachey, Virginia Woolf, and he Photographic Image" VI: 48-56

Yokas, E. "Beyond Therapy: Ramsay's Journey Through Psychoanalysis" VI: 228-236

Yom, Sue Sun "Bio-graphy and the Quantum Leap: Waves, Particles, and Light as a Theory of Writing the Human Life" V: 145-150

Young, John "Canonicity and Commercialization in Woolf's Uniform Edition" IX: 236-243

Zappa, Stephanie "Woolf, Women, and War: From Statement in *Three Guineas* to Impression in *Jacob's Room*" V: 274-279

Zeck, Jeanne-Marie "'Shining in the Dark': Jinny's Reign as Sun Goddess" III: 126-131

Zimring, Rishona "Gissing, Woolf, and the Drama of Home" VII: 85-91

Zucker, Marilyn "A dramatic performance by members of the Virginia Woolf Society" II: 288-290; "Virginia Woolf and the French Connection: A Devotion to Language" VIII: 29-35

Zwerdling, Alex "The Common Reader, the Coterie and the Audience of One" I: 8-9

Index

Index

Index

Index

Printed in the United States
15980LVS00003B/108